A Special Standing
in the World

A Special Standing in the World

The Faculty of Law
at The University of Hong Kong, 1969–2019

Christopher Munn

HKU PRESS
香港大學出版社

Hong Kong University Press
The University of Hong Kong
Pokfulam Road
Hong Kong
https://hkupress.hku.hk

ISBN 978-988-8528-31-8 (*Hardback*)

British Library Cataloguing-in-Publication Data
A catalogue record for this book is available from the British Library.

Book design by Jennifer Flint Creative.

10 9 8 7 6 5 4 3 2 1

Printed and bound by Hang Tai Printing Co., Ltd. in Hong Kong, China

Contents

Abbreviations and Conventions

Abbreviations

ACLE	Advisory Committee on Legal Education
AIIFL	Asian Institute of International Financial Law
BA	Bachelor of Arts
BBA	Bachelor of Business Administration
BLIS	Bilingual Legal Information System
CCPL	Centre for Comparative and Public Law
CEDAW	Convention on the Elimination of all Forms of Discrimination against Women
CEE	common entrance examination
CFA	Court of Final Appeal
CLE	clinical legal education
CLIC	Community Legal Information Centre
CO	Colonial Office
CPE	Common Professional Examination
CPEC	Common Professional Examination Certificate
CPG	Central People's Government
DAB	Democratic Alliance for the Betterment and Progress of Hong Kong
DOPLE	Department of Professional Legal Education
EWHC	High Court of England and Wales
FCO	Foreign and Commonwealth Office
GDP	gross domestic product
HCAL	High Court Constitutional and Administrative Law Proceedings
HKCA	Hong Kong Court of Appeal
HKCFA	Hong Kong Court of Final Appeal
HKCFAR	The Authorised Hong Kong Court of Final Appeal Reports
HKCFI	Hong Kong Court of First Instance
HKDC	District Court of Hong Kong
HKDSE	Hong Kong Diploma of Secondary Education Examination
HKLII	Hong Kong Legal Information Institute
HKLJ	*Hong Kong Law Journal*
HKLR	Hong Kong Law Reports
HKLRD	Hong Kong Law Reports and Digest
HKRS	Hong Kong Record Series (Public Records Office Hong Kong)
HKPLR	*Hong Kong Public Law Reports*
HKU	The University of Hong Kong
HKUA	University of Hong Kong Archives
HSBC	Hongkong and Shanghai Banking Corporation
ICAC	Independent Commission Against Corruption
ICCPR	International Covenant on Civil and Political Rights

ICESCR	International Covenant on Economic, Social and Cultural Rights
JD	Juris Doctor
JP	Justice of the Peace
KC	King's Counsel
LLB	Bachelor of Laws
LLM	Master of Laws
LPC	legal practitioners course
LSE	London School of Economics
MCL	Master of Common Law
MTR	Mass Transit Railway
NGO	non-governmental organization
NPC	National People's Congress
NPJ	non-permanent judge
OBE	Order of the British Empire
PCLL	Postgraduate Certificate in Laws
PhD	Doctor of Philosophy
PRC	People's Republic of China
QC	Queen's Counsel
RAE	Research Assessment Exercise
RTHK	Radio Television Hong Kong
SAR	special administrative region
SARS	severe acute respiratory syndrome
SBS	Silver Bauhinia Star
SC	Senior Counsel
SCLET	Standing Committee on Legal Education and Training
SCMP	*South China Morning Post*
SJD	*Scientiae Juridicae Doctor*: Doctor of Legal Science
SPACE	School of Professional and Continuing Education (HKU)
UGC	University Grants Committee
UK	United Kingdom
UKPC	United Kingdom Privy Council
UN	United Nations
UPGC	University and Polytechnic Grants Committee
US	United States
VC	Vice-Chancellor
WTO	World Trade Organization

Conventions

1. All currency is in Hong Kong dollars unless otherwise indicated.

2. Except for some more recent events described in Chapter 8, this book covers events up to 30 April 2019 – fifty years, to the month, from the formal establishment of the Department of Law at HKU.

3. LLBs and other degrees and qualifications given in brackets after names refer to HKU unless otherwise stated: in most cases the main qualification only is given.

4. Date ranges in brackets after names of staff refer to their period of time at HKU.

Foreword

History helps us understand how we have become what we are today, and it gives us meaning and direction as we face the challenges of the future. We believe that the best way to celebrate the fiftieth anniversary of the founding of the Faculty of Law at the University of Hong Kong (HKU), and the admission of its first cohort of students in 1969, is for us to commission and publish a history of the Faculty's first fifty years. We are immensely grateful to Dr Christopher Munn, a distinguished historian of Hong Kong legal institutions, for taking up this great challenge and the solemn responsibility of writing this history.

In 1972, thirty-three Bachelor of Laws (LLB) students became the first HKU law graduates. The teachers, administrative staff, and students in those days could hardly have imagined that the Faculty of Law would, in 2018, produce a total of 767 students who had successfully completed one of its increasing suite of programmes: the original LLB degree, three LLB double degrees, the Juris Doctor degree, the Postgraduate Certificate in Laws, eight Master's Degrees, and a set of research degrees. Legal education at HKU has indeed prospered and matured in the last five decades, achieving its dual mission of educating generations of solicitors, barristers, judges, academics, and other members of Hong Kong's legal community – and increasingly graduates who embark on callings which are not strictly legal – and producing works of legal scholarship which have received local, regional, and international recognition.

This book is published in loving memory of all those who have taught, studied, or worked in the Faculty of Law, or in some way supported or contributed to its work but are no longer with us today in this world, and in solidarity with all the teachers, staff, students, alumni, benefactors, and friends of the Faculty who have the fortune to personally witness the celebration of its fiftieth anniversary this year. The book is dedicated to future members of the community of teaching, learning, and scholarship that the Faculty of Law will continue to be in the next fifty years, in the hope that the Hong Kong they live in and contribute to building will remain a special city where the rule of law and human rights flourish.

'Law, Justice and Humanity: 50 Years and Beyond' was chosen as the theme of the Faculty's Golden Jubilee celebrations in recognition of law in the service of justice and the best values of humanity. May a future historian, perhaps fifty years in the future, look back and marvel at the first and glorious hundred years of the HKU Faculty of Law, where the study of law was harnessed in the service of justice and humanity.

Professor Michael Hor, Dean of the Faculty of Law, HKU
Professor Albert H.Y. Chen, Chairman of the Faculty Board
April 2019

Introduction

The Faculty of Law at the University of Hong Kong (HKU) is a cornerstone of the rule of law in Hong Kong. Graduates of the Faculty make up over half of Hong Kong's legal profession, and of the Judiciary. Some hold prominent positions in government, politics, and business. A few have even made their mark in arts and culture. The Faculty was the first institution to establish Hong Kong law as a field of serious study. It also quickly became a leading centre of research into Chinese law. Its staff and alumni contributed widely to the transformation of Hong Kong law from its origins as a sluggish backwater of English law into a flourishing field of activity, where fundamental rights, freedoms and obligations are tested almost daily against the Basic Law – the centrepiece of 'one country, two systems' under which Hong Kong maintains its common law system as a special administrative region (SAR) of the People's Republic of China (PRC). The Faculty has been instrumental in establishing a legal profession trained in Hong Kong law, firmly rooted in Hong Kong, and able to function bilingually – a vital feature of Hong Kong's modern legal system.

It is therefore a surprise to some that the Faculty of Law is only fifty years old – half as old as HKU itself, decades younger than the leading law schools in other parts of China, and younger by several years than those in some of Britain's other late colonial possessions, in Africa and Malaya. It is still more remarkable that in each of the past seven years the Faculty has been ranked among the top twenty law schools in the world, commended for both the quality of its teaching and the breadth of its research. This research now extends beyond Hong Kong and Chinese topics to cover comparative legal studies and transnational issues, such as the globalization of trade and finance, the rise of information technology, and human migration. The promoters of a school of law at HKU predicted in 1965 that there was 'a real possibility that it could develop into a law school with a special standing in the world.' Today that prediction has been exceeded in ways they could hardly have imagined.

This book explores the history of the Faculty of Law at HKU from its foundation as a small Department of Law in 1969 to its fiftieth anniversary in 2019. It places the Faculty in the context of the broader history of Hong Kong and, in addition to tracing its institutional growth, pays special attention to contributions by Faculty members and alumni to Hong Kong's development over the past fifty years.

The book's first two chapters deal with the Faculty's prehistory. *Chapter One* examines the growth of Hong Kong's legal profession in the century or so before the creation of the Department of Law. At this time it was neither a prerequisite nor a custom for solicitors to take a university degree, and, although most were trained in London, a small but growing number took their articles and exams in Hong Kong. For barristers the route to practice was through attendance at an Inn of Court in London or Dublin. The chapter describes the introduction of legal topics as part of the general Arts degree at HKU in the early twentieth century. This was pursued energetically in the 1920s. However, a lack of funds and interest prevented legal studies from taking root, and by the late 1930s they had fizzled out. The chapter concludes with calls in the 1950s and 1960s for a law school at HKU. *Chapter Two* takes up these calls and examines proposals put forward in the 1960s. These rested on concerns that the colony had too few lawyers and on claims that Hong Kong law had diverged so far from its English roots that the legal training provided in England was inadequate for local needs. In seeking to make a career in law available to men and women who could not afford to go to England, the idea was also founded on a strong appeal to social justice. The chapter discusses resistance to the idea among some officials and lawyers, as well as an attempt at a stopgap measure through extramural teaching of the University of London Bachelor of Laws (LLB) at HKU during 1964–1969. This had only limited success. But it was a key step towards the establishment of the Department of Law in 1969.

The remaining six chapters explore the fifty-year history of the Department, the School, and finally the Faculty of Law at HKU. The fifty years are divided into three broad periods, for which paired chapters alternately discuss the institutional development of the Faculty and its wider impact on law, politics, and society. Fortuitously or not, the three historical periods are framed by important events and transitions for both the Faculty and Hong Kong.

Chapter Three discusses the first fifteen years of the Department of Law (1969–1978) in the Faculty of Social Sciences, its separation into a School of Law (1978–1984), and the creation of a full-fledged Faculty of Law in 1984. The LLB degree and Postgraduate Certificate in Laws (PCLL) became the main qualifications for entry into Hong Kong's legal profession. Taught initially in a makeshift building some distance from the main campus, law students developed their own distinct culture and traditions, growing in numbers from an initial intake of 40 in 1969 to about 120 in the mid-1980s. The staff, recruited mainly from the United Kingdom (UK) and Australasia, developed courses to meet Hong Kong's needs, focusing on the primary purpose of training lawyers to practise in Hong Kong. The early impact of graduates and staff is the theme of *Chapter Four*. Graduates began to enter the legal profession in the mid-1970s. Staff produced the first modern texts on Hong Kong law, publishing them as books or as articles in the *Hong Kong Law Journal*, a town–gown initiative aimed at stimulating scholarship in this new field. The colony was then 'a legal backwater', and much of the research focused on unreformed labour laws, draconian police powers, and the vigorous campaign against corruption launched in the early 1970s. Then, in 1984, after two years of negotiations, the governments of the PRC and the UK issued the Sino-British Joint Declaration on the Question of Hong Kong, a blueprint for it to maintain its way of life and common law legal system as an SAR of the PRC from 1997. This was to be a catalyst for far-reaching reforms.

Chapter Five describes how the Faculty developed its curriculum and resources to prepare students for the transition to and beyond 1997. This was a time of consolidation. Student numbers continued to increase, but at a less rapid pace. Staff were recruited, and retained, from a wider range of jurisdictions, including Mainland China and Hong Kong itself. Although the primary aim continued to be to train lawyers, the LLB was reformed to provide a more liberal education with greater attention paid to public law. New postgraduate degrees were introduced, some focusing on Chinese law – then undergoing rapid reform – and some teaching common law to scholars from Mainland China. *Chapter Six* explores how Hong Kong law became a subject of intensive research as it was reformed to reflect the idealized picture of Hong Kong set out in the Joint Declaration. Much of this reform was stimulated by the Hong Kong Bill of Rights Ordinance 1991, an official response to anxieties about the future under Chinese rule: the ordinance swept away many old colonial laws and became a bulwark of freedom before and beyond 1997. The vital role played by Faculty members in the inception, drafting, implementation, and analysis of the Bill of Rights forms a case study in how legal academics, in partnership with the community, can have a profound impact on law reform. The other key historic achievements in these years were the production of a fully bilingual statute book – one of most ambitious projects of its kind anywhere – and the promulgation of the Basic Law of the Hong Kong SAR, an enactment of the PRC to implement the Joint Declaration and provide a constitutional framework for post-1997 Hong Kong. The chapter discusses the Faculty's contributions to these projects. It also examines its role in cultivating an understanding of the rule of law by disseminating research to the wider community.

Chapters Five and Six both conclude with something approaching a crisis of confidence in the quality of legal education in the late twentieth century. This was the result partly of too rapid an expansion of legal education in the 1980s and 1990s, not only at HKU but also in a new law school at the City University of Hong Kong and at HKU's School of Professional and Continuing Education. It reflected concerns that, after years of shortages, Hong Kong now had too many lawyers. The crisis produced the first full review of legal education in Hong Kong since the 1960s. This controversial exercise recommended substantial reforms, including abolishing the PCLL. The Faculty responded with a root-and-branch reform of the PCLL and a complete remodelling of the LLB, extending it from three years to four. *Chapter Seven* explores these changes and describes how the Faculty, through its teaching and research, and its partnerships with other institutions, emerged as a leading law school not only in Hong Kong and Mainland China and the East Asia region, but also in the world. A milestone in these years was the Faculty's move in 2012 into its own building on HKU's new Centennial Campus, which has state-of-the-art teaching facilities and has become a centre for the Faculty's many activities.

The final chapter, *Chapter Eight*, examines the Faculty's engagement with law, politics and society in modern-day Hong Kong. Some of this has been controversial, dealing with encroachments on academic freedom and unfinished business under the Basic Law, notably the requirement for Hong Kong to enact its own national security laws, and the policy of progressive democratization with the ultimate aim of achieving universal suffrage. The Faculty played an influential role in these processes. Its connection with the Occupy movement, a prolonged and unsuccessful protest in late 2014 to demand genuine universal suffrage, brought it notoriety in some people's eyes. The chapter also briefly surveys a range of activities in which the Faculty has had an impact on the development of law and policy through research, advocacy, and partnership with other organizations. It ends with a brief survey of the events marking the Faculty's fiftieth anniversary year.

Fifty years is a short span. It is barely more than half a lifetime in a city that now has the world's longest average life expectancy – eighty-eight years for women (the majority of the Faculty's alumni) and eighty-two for men. Many of the Faculty's earliest graduates are still active in legal practice, public affairs, and other pursuits. Most of its early teachers are still alive. This has allowed me to interview a good cross-section of people connected with the Faculty's history – an enjoyable exercise that has yielded many helpful insights. However, finding perspective, continuity and balance for so recent a period – and one packed with such momentous events – presents special difficulties. In its twenty-second year as an SAR of the PRC, Hong Kong, like many other communities around the world, is grappling with deep social problems and seemingly intractable political division. Its legal system, though remarkably robust, faces many challenges. While no one can predict how events will unfold in the future, it is almost certain that the Faculty of Law at HKU will continue to play an influential part in Hong Kong's destiny in the years and decades to come.

Chapter 1

A Veneer of English Juristic Ideals

Lawyers and Legal Education in Hong Kong, 1841–1963

The colony of Hong Kong, according to one of its early attorneys general, was designed to be 'a little miniature representative of Great Britain, its laws, its manners, its institutions.'[1] Colonial Hong Kong imported its legal system and nearly all of its lawyers and judges from England. For most of the 156 years of British rule (1841–1997) the qualifications for practising law followed those in England. As in England, the profession had two branches: barristers, who argued cases in the courts, and solicitors, who advised clients, instructed barristers, and handled contracts, wills and other transactions requiring legal expertise. Law was taught at the University of Hong Kong (HKU) for twenty-five years, from 1915 to 1940, but only as a small and shrinking part of a general arts degree, not as training for the profession. A few solicitors served their articles and took their examinations in Hong Kong under local regulations. However, before the introduction of formal legal training in the late 1960s, most of Hong Kong's solicitors and all of its barristers trained and qualified in England. The legal profession was thus mainly the preserve of a privileged elite: men born and educated in Britain who sought a career in the colonies, and the sons and daughters of local families who could afford an expensive overseas training.

---

1. Thomas Chisholm Anstey, Attorney General 1856–1859, speaking at a public meeting in Newcastle, June 1859. Disillusioned with the colony, and having recently been suspended from office, Anstey was speaking ironically. *Newcastle Chronicle*, 25 June 1859, in The National Archives, Colonial Office: Original Correspondence Hong Kong, 1841–1951 (hereafter 'CO'), series 120/75, 228.

During the fifty years after the founding of HKU in 1911, various proposals were put forward for a school of law. None was successful, largely because of a lack of funding. By the 1960s, however, the urge to establish a school was strong enough for the university, the government and the legal profession to take the idea seriously. The demand for lawyers was increasing as the population grew and prospered; this demand was poised to increase further with a planned expansion of legal aid. Some areas of Hong Kong law had diverged so far from English law as to render much of the training provided in England irrelevant. Although legal qualifications in Hong Kong were now tied more closely than ever to those in England, places in law schools for overseas students were in short supply. In the egalitarian spirit of the age it also seemed wrong to restrict the practice of law to the wealthy few or to people from overseas, when other professions – notably medicine and engineering – had for many decades been filled by people trained in Hong Kong. Conditions were ripe for legal training to begin in Hong Kong on a formal footing. This began in 1964 with external courses for the University of London taught at HKU's Department of Extra-Mural Studies. It progressed in 1969 to the creation of a Department of Law with courses tailor-made for Hong Kong and a degree recognized for entry into the local legal profession.

This chapter explores legal training in Hong Kong up to the 1960s. It discusses the backgrounds of lawyers, and their training, in the colony's first hundred years. It then describes the reform of legal training in England, where most of Hong Kong's early lawyers obtained their qualifications. Finally, it examines the various half-hearted initiatives in legal education at HKU before World War II and the coalition of demands in the decades after the war for the introduction of comprehensive legal education suited to Hong Kong's special needs.

The Introduction of English Law

The British acquired Hong Kong Island by conquest in 1841. Early British administrators issued proclamations – the famous 'Elliott proclamations' – assuring Chinese inhabitants of free exercise of their customs and telling them that, pending Her Majesty's pleasure, they would be governed according to the laws and customs of China. Officials then considered the possibility of separate legal systems for Chinese and Westerners. However, by the time the island was formally declared a British colony in 1843 they had decided that all inhabitants would be governed under a single system – one that was applied to Kowloon and (with modifications) to the New Territories when the colony was extended in 1860 and 1898 respectively. The law of England, as it stood on 5 April 1843, was to be in full force, except where inapplicable to local circumstances or where altered by local legislation or imperial legislation applied to Hong Kong.[2]

---

2. The reception date of 5 April 1843 – the day on which the colony obtained its own legislature – was fixed in 1846. Supreme Court Ordinances, Nos. 15 of 1844, 6 of 1845, and 2 of 1846.

Within Hong Kong, the Supreme Court, established in 1844 with a Chief Justice, exercised a jurisdiction similar to that of the highest courts in England, with a route of appeal to the Judicial Committee of the Privy Council. English procedures, with certain modifications, were followed. The Supreme Court admitted lawyers to practise in the colony mainly on the basis of their training and qualifications in London, Dublin and Edinburgh. It could also admit, for three-month periods, 'fit and proper persons' who had no qualifications 'to appear and Act as Barristers, Advocates, Proctors, Attornies and Solicitors.'[3] This was a practical recognition of the dire state of early British Hong Kong – a remote, unhealthy, and crime-ridden place which many critics of imperial policy believed to have been a bad choice. 'You can go to Hong Kong for me' became a saying of contempt in nineteenth-century England. 'What barrister would leave a decent practice, to endure, even as a Judge, the climate and society of Hongkong?' asked a London newspaper in 1851.[4]

Seven London barristers turned down the offer to serve as Hong Kong's first Chief Justice, despite a generous annual salary of £3,000. The eighth choice, John Walter Hulme, son-in-law and collaborator of the renowned jurist Joseph Chitty, arrived in Hong Kong in 1844. His wretched fifteen-year term was plagued with debt, illness and quarrels, culminating in a seven-month suspension in 1848 on charges of drunkenness, of which he was subsequently exonerated. No colonial judge had had 'so hard a time of it', he claimed in his (unsuccessful) request for a knighthood in 1860.[5] Despite the crowded state of the London Bar and the opportunities offered by the colonies,[6] Hong Kong hardly possessed any barristers in its first decade other than the Attorney General, who was allowed private practice.

---

3. In England barristers acted as advocates in the higher courts. Various terms were used for the other branches of the profession: attorneys practised in the common law courts, solicitors in the Court of Chancery, and proctors in the Admiralty and Ecclesiastical Courts. The Supreme Court of Judicature Act 1873 referred only to barristers and solicitors, and, with certain exceptions, the terms 'attorney' and 'proctor' then lapsed. The professions of solicitor, attorney, and proctor – along with that of barrister – were all recognized in Hong Kong in the Supreme Court Ordinances of 1844, 1845, and 1873 and in the Legal Practitioners Ordinances, Nos. 13 of 1856 and 3 of 1871, where the term 'attorney' was defined to embrace 'solicitor'. The first Solicitors Ordinance, No. 9 of 1899, aligned formal terminology with that current in England, and with common usage in Hong Kong, by classifying all attorneys, solicitors, and proctors as 'solicitors'.

4. As late as 1885, when defendants in 'a trial of considerable magnitude' in Hong Kong sought the services of a prominent Queen's Counsel (QC) from England, 'some gentlemen declined to go out on any terms; others demanded prohibitive fees.' John A. Turner, *Kwang Tung, or Five Years in South China* (London: S.W. Partridge & Co., 1894), 99; *Weekly Dispatch*, 15 June 1851, quoted in *China Mail*, 24 August 1851; *Law Times*, 3 October 1885.

5. Hulme was an unfortunate choice. He gained a reputation for laziness and severity, particularly towards non-European defendants. His quarrels with governors – notably Sir John Davis, who engineered his suspension on trumped-up charges – arose partly from professional differences but were mainly the manifestations of personality clashes. Hulme to Fortescue, 8 March 1860, CO 129/79, 473–6; G.B. Endacott, *A Biographical Sketch-Book of Early Hong Kong* (Hong Kong: Hong Kong University Press, 2005), Chapter 9; May Holdsworth and Christopher Munn, *Dictionary of Hong Kong Biography* (Hong Kong: Hong Kong University Press, 2011), 202–3.

6. Daniel Duman, *The English and Colonial Bars in the Nineteenth Century* (London: Croom Helm, 1983), Chapter 1.

The early Supreme Court was reduced to admitting an assortment of attorneys and clerks – 'Quarter Sessions pettifoggers' prone to 'vulgar pot house oratory and looser professional principles,' according to the colony's earliest historian, William Tarrant, a former ship's steward who was himself admitted to practise with no legal training whatsoever.[7] Among these practitioners was the Irish-Australian Percy McSwyney – journalist, opium dealer, deputy registrar of the Supreme Court, coroner, and temporary attorney – who, according to Tarrant, committed 'swindling and barefaced robbery' on Chinese litigants to 'an extent difficult to be conceived.' McSwyney ended his days in a hospital for destitute seamen, where he died of dysentery in 1851.[8]

The most successful early barrister was W.T. Bridges, a rapacious character who combined official positions with a flourishing legal practice (1851–1861): this he advertised on a 'gorgeous' bilingual gilt and black signboard hung outside his chambers on Queen's Road: a Doctorate of Civil Law he had recently obtained from Oxford University was rendered in Chinese as an official rank. From these premises he also ran a money-lending business, taking balls of opium and other 'questionable goods' as security. Bridges left Hong Kong after being tainted in a string of official scandals, shortly before a powerful enquiry into civil service abuses was to hear evidence. He retired to Devon, became a country magistrate, and published *A Handy Book for Justices of the Peace* in 1877. His legacies were the Hong Kong Cricket Club, of which he was a founding member, and (some believe) the partnership that later took the name of Deacons, Hong Kong's oldest solicitors' firm.[9]

From the 1860s a more settled and respectable legal profession emerged, although shortages of lawyers were a recurrent problem. After an unhappy short-lived experiment from 1858 to 1864, engineered for their own benefit by William Bridges and Attorney General Thomas Anstey, the two branches of the legal profession rejected successive proposals for amalgamation, a policy adopted in most other colonies.[10] Barristers enjoyed a monopoly on

---

7. William Tarrant, *Hongkong: Part 1, 1839 to 1844* (Canton: Friend of China, 1861), 89. Tarrant, an employee in the Surveyor General's Department, was admitted for three months in 1846. He was deprived of his government position in 1847 after exposing corruption. In 1850 he took over the newspaper, *The Friend of China*, an organ fiercely critical of government. Later in the 1850s he was fined and imprisoned for criminal libel after accusing senior officials of corruption. Endacott, *Biographical Sketch-Book*, Chapter 19.

8. *Friend of China*, 7 May 1851; Holdsworth and Munn, *Dictionary of Hong Kong Biography*, 319–20.

9. Holdsworth and Munn, *Dictionary of Hong Kong Biography*, 48–50; Norton-Kyshe, *History of the Laws and Courts of Hongkong*, Vol. II, Chapter 34; *Deacons: Celebrating 160 Years of Legal Services* (downloaded from Deacons' website).

10. Bitterly opposed by the Hongkong Law Society, the amalgamation of 1858–1864 was part of Bridges's scheme to exclude attorneys from the Supreme Court: it was, observes Norton-Kyshe, 'neither more nor less than an Ordinance to empower barristers to act as attorneys.' It was repealed on the initiative of John Smale (Attorney General 1860–1866, Chief Justice 1866–1882), who claimed that, far from reducing costs, the system had been 'prostituted by the profession' and had triggered a flight of attorneys from the colony. Proposals for amalgamation continued to be advanced up to the late twentieth century. In a partial fusion from 1873 to 1925, barristers were permitted to hold

most forms of advocacy in the Supreme Court. But they dealt with litigants through attorneys or solicitors, who also had rights of audience in the lower courts. A third 'branch' of the profession – informal and barely regulated – could be said to exist in the powerful class of interpreters and clerks, indispensable intermediaries between English-speaking solicitors and their Chinese clients. Enriched by commissions, these men were often accused of touting for work and of generally exploiting the courts, even to the extent of forging evidence and financing speculative lawsuits.[11] Yet it was from this rising class of middlemen that many of Hong Kong's earliest home-grown lawyers emerged. Most of these lawyers, like their Western counterparts, were trained in England under a system then undergoing extensive reform.

Legal Training in England

The century and a quarter between the British colonization of Hong Kong and the establishment of the Department of Law at HKU was framed by two large inquiries into legal education in England and Wales. The first, by a House of Commons Select Committee reporting in 1846, revitalized the teaching of law by stimulating professional training at the universities and the introduction of qualifying examinations.[12] The second inquiry was by a committee appointed by the Lord Chancellor in 1967. Reporting in 1971, the Ormrod Committee (named after the judge who chaired it) reviewed legal education in England and Wales and made recommendations for its expansion, building on the elaborate mixture of university and professional training that had developed over the previous century.[13]

In its historical survey the Ormrod Committee saw this dual system, in which both the legal profession and the universities played a part, as the most striking feature of legal training in England, in contrast to the university-based systems of continental Europe.

consultations with clients and take fees without the intervention of a solicitor, though in practice the dual system was maintained. Wesley-Smith, 'Nineteenth-century Fusion of the Legal Profession in Hong Kong'; Norton-Kyshe, *The History of the Laws and Courts of Hong Kong from the Earliest Period to 1898* (Hong Kong: Noronha & Co., 1898, reprinted by Hong Kong: Vetch and Lee, 1971), Vol. I, 494.

11. Concerns about abuses by solicitors' clerks and interpreters persisted into the late twentieth century. The problem came to a head earlier in the century when an attempt by the government to deport the (alleged) leader of a network of champerters resulted in an appeal to the Privy Council that became Hong Kong's first constitutional case. Christopher Munn, 'Margins of Justice in Colonial Hong Kong: Extrajudicial Power, Solicitors' Clerks, and the Case of Li Hong Mi, 1917–1920,' *Law and Humanities* 11, no. 1, (2017): 102–120.

12. *Report from the House of Commons Select Committee on Legal Education* 1846 (hereafter the '1846 Report').

13. *Report of the Committee on Legal Education* 1971 (the 'Ormrod Report'). The discussion in this section draws mainly on the *Ormrod Report*, Chapter 1, Duman, *The English and Colonial Bars*, Harry Kirk, *Portrait of a Profession: A History of the Solicitor's Profession, 1100 to the Present Day* (London: Oyez Publishing, 1976), Chapter 3, and William Twining, *Blackstone's Tower: The English Law School* (Hamlyn Lectures; 46th Ser. London: Stevens & Sons, 1994), Chapter 2.

Since the middle ages, universities had concentrated on civil law: derived from Roman law, this was the foundation of most continental legal systems. In England the evolution of a distinctive indigenous system of common law had encouraged the growth of specialized institutions – the Inns of Court – to train and regulate the profession. The Inns of Court, close to the courts in London, concerned themselves with the common law, while the universities, like their continental counterparts, confined their teaching to civil law, to the exclusion of local law. Early efforts to establish the study of English law, notably by William Blackstone at Oxford in the mid-eighteenth century, were not sustained, although his *Commentaries on the Laws of England* became a staple legal text, and a point of reference for colonists intent on protecting their rights as 'freeborn Englishmen.' The first modern law school – established at University College, London in 1826 – produced only 135 law graduates in the whole of the nineteenth century.

By the 1840s, when English law was planted in Hong Kong, legal training in England was in a torpid state. The 1846 Select Committee found that 'no legal education worthy of the name, of a public nature, is at this moment to be had' in England or Ireland. Except for a few courses at University College, London, there was virtually no teaching of law of any kind at the universities. The Inns of Court – once centres of learning rivalling the great universities – had long since ceased to provide effective training. Although they still controlled admission to the Bar, they were little more than social clubs. Intending barristers joined an Inn of Court, where they were required to keep a certain number of terms and eat a certain number of dinners, studied law in the chambers of a senior practitioner, and performed 'exercises' – a kind of debate which by the 1840s had degenerated into a 'mockery', a 'mere farce'. There was no formal instruction or test before the call to the Bar. The student was simply thrown 'on such chance instruction or studies as might fall in his way.'[14]

The other branch of the profession – the solicitors and attorneys – was subject to greater control. Since 1731 they had been required to serve a five-year apprenticeship with a senior practitioner, or 'articles', supplemented in the early nineteenth century by lectures organized by the Law Society of England and Wales. Under the Solicitors Act 1843 the period of articles was reduced to three years for those with a degree from a reputable university: this was unlikely to be a law degree, since by the 1840s the teaching of law at the universities had practically ceased.[15] From 1836, attorneys were required to pass a final law examination supervised by judges: the Solicitors Act 1843 made this a statutory requirement, necessary, along with an oath of allegiance, for enrolment and admission by the courts. Yet, observed the 1846 Select Committee, the examination was 'altogether inadequate', and served 'merely as a guarantee against absolute incompetency.'[16] A typical question was 'What is the

---

14. *1846 Report*, xi & lvi.

15. Attornies and Solicitors Acts 1728 and 1843.

16. *1846 Report*, xiv & xvi.

difference between a verdict and a judgment?' The pass rate was over 95 per cent.[17] Seen from this perspective, the admission of 'fit and proper' persons without qualifications to practise law in early Hong Kong might not have been so extreme an expedient.

The 1846 Select Committee's report triggered reforms aimed at improving training and raising standards. The universities revived the teaching of law, beginning with the establishment of the Bachelor of Civil Law degree at Oxford in 1852, followed in the mid-1870s by the BA in Jurisprudence, and the Bachelor of Law (LLB) degree at Cambridge in 1855. By the early twentieth century there were eight law faculties in the country. Although the universities now taught common law, most treated it as one of the liberal arts rather than purely as a preparation for the profession. Although a university degree reduced the required period of articles by two years, the majority of solicitors continued to train without a degree. From 1860, solicitors' examinations were split into preliminary, intermediate, and final examinations. In 1877 control of examinations passed from the judges to the Law Society, which gradually expanded the rules for articled clerks and the provision of vocational training. The society established a School of Law for articled clerks in 1903, which in 1962 merged with the tutorial firm (the 'law crammer') Gibson and Weldon to form the College of Law. Those who passed university entrance exams were exempted from the preliminary exams. From 1922, graduates with recognized law degrees were exempted from the intermediate exams (later known as 'Part I'); articled clerks were required to take an academic year either at the School of Law or through university courses subsidized by the Law Society.[18]

The Bar – the 'senior' branch of the profession and a vocation for gentlemen – stubbornly adhered to its ancient forms of self-regulation and was slow to reform. The Inns of Court controlled admission to the Bar and prescribed educational standards and training. Most candidates already held university degrees: this shortened the time in which they had to keep terms at an Inn from five years (twenty terms) to three (twelve terms), and the number of dinners they had to eat each term from six to three. In 1852 the four Inns of Court established a Council of Legal Education to organize lectures and examinations, though most candidates continued to study privately. A Royal Commission on the Inns of Court in 1854–1855 urged the need for a proper system of examinations. Compulsory Bar final examinations were introduced in 1872, against objections from some senior barristers.[19] With modifications, this remained the main qualification for the next hundred years.

---

17. Kirk, *Portrait of a Profession*, 53.

18. The final examinations were replaced by the Common Professional Examination in 1980.

19. The opponents argued that a barrister's competence was continuously assessed by the solicitors who engaged him and by the judges before whom he appeared. Moreover, the introduction of examinations would discourage gentlemen amateurs from entering the Inns, not with the aim of practising law, but to acquire knowledge to help them manage their estates and fulfil their duties as JPs or MPs. Duman, *The English and Colonial Bars*, 79–80.

Barristers were 'called' to the Bar in ceremonies held at their Inns. A newly minted barrister was expected to serve a pupillage of one or two years with an experienced barrister, but was not required to do so until 1959. As with the articles served by prospective solicitors, the amount and quality of training through apprenticeship varied widely. Premiums were payable for entry into pupillages (200 guineas) and articles (£200). Bar students had to pay admission fees and call fees to their Inns, and incurred expenses for dinners, books, wigs and gowns, and general maintenance, since they were prohibited from most forms of paid work. Upon being called, a barrister had to find chambers and establish a practice through patronage and connections, a process which might take several years, and which in many cases never happened. Solicitors also paid premiums for their articles, and had to pay stamp duty of £100 on qualification; this was abolished in 1947, and from the 1960s premiums disappeared in England and articled clerks began to receive salaries.

Legal Training in Early Colonial Hong Kong

In Hong Kong the Supreme Court controlled the admission of both barristers and solicitors, mainly on the strength of qualifications obtained in England.[20] From 1845 the Supreme Court could also admit 'Solicitors, Attornies and Proctors' who had served as articled clerks in Hong Kong for three years (five years from 1871). This was the first recognition of local legal training. Although it extended only to solicitors, the training helped launch the careers of some of the earliest of Hong Kong's barristers to be appointed Queen's Counsel (QC), a recognition of excellence awarded by the Crown to senior barristers.[21] The first was Edward Pollard, an Australian, who was articled locally to the attorney Norton D'Esterre Parker in 1847 after having served briefly as a judge's clerk. From that year Pollard was admitted to practise as attorney as an unqualified 'fit and proper person' in a series of end-to-end three-month periods up to September 1853, when the Supreme Court decided the colony had enough qualified attorneys. He then went to England to train as a barrister and was called to the Bar by Middle Temple in 1858. He was admitted to practise as barrister in Hong Kong in 1859 and in 1865 he became the colony's first QC.[22]

---

20. Early Supreme Court Ordinances (Nos. 15 of 1844 & 6 of 1845) and the Legal Practitioners Ordinance (No. 3 of 1871) empowered the court to admit as barristers persons who had been admitted as barristers or advocates in Great Britain or Ireland, and to admit as attorneys (solicitors) persons admitted as such in courts at Westminster, Dublin, or Edinburgh or as proctors in any ecclesiastical court in England. From 1845 to 1871 the court could also admit persons who had been admitted to practise as solicitors, attorneys, or proctors in other British colonies.
21. In England, on the recommendation of the Lord Chancellor; in Hong Kong, on the recommendation of the Chief Justice, through the Governor and Secretary of State. The title was changed to 'Senior Counsel' in 1997, and appointments since then have been by the Chief Justice, after consultation with the chairman of the Hong Kong Bar Council and president of the Law Society of Hong Kong, under section 31A of the Legal Practitioners Ordinance.
22. Pollard was a cocky character. He clashed with the irascible Chief Justice Smale, who, in a celebrated case in 1867, summarily convicted him of contempt of court, fined him $200, and suspended him from practice for fourteen days.

A similar course was followed by John Joseph Francis, an Irish-born soldier in the Royal Artillery, who, after service in the Second Opium War in 1859, bought himself out of the army, settled in Hong Kong, and articled with the solicitor William Gaskell. After admission as attorney and solicitor in 1869, he gave up his practice in 1873 to study for the Bar at Gray's Inn and the University of London. He was called to the London Bar in 1876 and was admitted to practise in Hong Kong in 1877. For the next quarter-century, until his death in 1901, J.J. Francis was Hong Kong's leading barrister, representing clients ranging from Korean royalty to humble labourers. He was made a QC in 1886, the third to be appointed in Hong Kong.[23] Francis played a key part in the foundation of the Po Leung Kuk (1880) and the College of Medicine for Chinese (1887). From time to time he also acted as a magistrate and judge. As a member of the Sanitary Board he chaired a committee formed to deal with the outbreak of bubonic plague in 1894.[24]

Solicitors

Before being admitted to practise, solicitors serving their articles locally were examined on their legal knowledge. The first Legal Practitioners Ordinance (1856) provided for examinations set by a committee of the Attorney General, a barrister, the Registrar of the Supreme Court, and two attorneys appointed by the court.[25] The ordinance introduced measures to regulate articled clerks' contracts and solicitors' fees – an attempt to address exorbitant charges imposed on Chinese clients. But its main purpose was to advance the prospects of a recent arrival in the colony: Yung Wing, the first Chinese graduate of Yale University, who was serving as an interpreter in the Hong Kong Supreme Court and wished to train as a lawyer. The ordinance allowed time as a court interpreter to count towards articles. It also stated that no one would be excluded from qualifying as a solicitor 'merely by reason of Alienage or that he is by birth a Chinaman.' However, the plan fell foul of colonial prejudice and vested interests. The newly formed Hongkong Law Society petitioned against

Pollard appealed to the Privy Council, which, finding in his favour, ruled that no one could be found in contempt without first having an opportunity to be heard. Pollard left for England in 1871, was among the counsel engaged in the famous Tichborne case, and in 1874 was gazetted a bankrupt, with debts of some £15,000. Norton-Kyshe, *History of the Laws and Courts of Hong Kong*, I, xx, & II, 122–30 & 235.

23. Hong Kong's second QC, Thomas Child Hayllar (1874), practised in Hong Kong from 1868 to 1882, when he abruptly left the colony after a personal quarrel with Governor Sir John Hennessy. Before his arrival in Hong Kong, Hayllar practised law for several years in Bombay and was Government Professor of Law at Bombay University, 1866–1868. *The Law Journal*, 31 August 1868.

24. Walter Greenwood, 'John Joseph Francis, Citizen of Hong Kong, A Biographical Note,' *Journal of the Hong Kong Branch of the Royal Asiatic Society* 26 (1986): 17–45.

25. Ordinance No. 13 of 1856. The local examination system also applied to attorneys, solicitors or proctors admitted to practise in other colonies but not to those already admitted by the courts in Great Britain, who continued to be automatically eligible for admission in Hong Kong.

the provision. The Chief Justice described it as a 'very dangerous' precedent.[26] A vicious campaign was launched against Yung in the press. The British legal fraternity, said Yung, realized that if he obtained a practice 'they might as well pack up and go back to England, for as I had a complete knowledge of both English and Chinese I would eventually monopolize all Chinese legal business.' Yung decamped to Shanghai and embarked on a distinguished career in the Chinese government.[27]

A new Legal Practitioners Ordinance in 1871 restricted local articled clerkships to British subjects. Maintained until 1976, this provision imposed a restraint on the admission of Chinese, since British nationality derived from either birth in a British territory or naturalization, and most of Hong Kong's inhabitants up to the 1960s were born in Mainland China.[28] Only a handful of early solicitors took their articles locally. Some were part of a tight circle of firms, well connected with Chinese businessmen, which dominated legal business in the latter half of the nineteenth century. A few coalesced into large solicitors' firms that survive to this day.[29] Most of the locally trained solicitors came from Britain, but one was born in Hong Kong: Daniel Edmund Caldwell, admitted to practise in 1883, was the eldest son of Daniel Richard Caldwell, a notable figure in early Hong Kong, and his Chinese wife, Mary Ayow. Fluent like his father in Chinese and English and schooled in Hong Kong and England, D.E. Caldwell was Hong Kong's first fully home-grown solicitor. He was trained by his uncle, Henry Caldwell, who had also articled in Hong Kong after fleeing from Singapore with embezzled money. In 1886 D.E. Caldwell went into partnership with Charles David Wilkinson, cofounder of Wilkinson & Grist. The firm still goes by Caldwell's Chinese name (高露雲律師行), even though in 1891 he too disappeared with embezzled funds.[30]

---

26. Hulme to Mercer, 14 May 1856, CO 129/57, 43.

27. Bowring to Labouchere, 7 & 19 July 1856, CO 129/57, 37–53 & 166–80; Yung Wing, *My Life in China and America* (New York: Henry Holt, 1909), 60–2.

28. Ordinance No. 58 of 1976. A similar restriction, abolished in 1974 after Britain joined the European Economic Community, applied in the UK. After the Promissory Oaths Act 1868, which repealed various statutes and orders requiring barristers to take an oath of allegiance, the requirements for barristers were a matter for regulation by the Inns of Court: the Consolidated Regulations of the Four Inns of Court 1952, consolidating earlier regulations, declared that aliens were ineligible for admission, unless there were special reasons.

29. Among the earliest solicitors to train and qualify locally were Henry Jefferd Tarrant (admitted 1851; admitted as barrister 1863), James Brown (1855), Henry Charles Caldwell (1865), John Joseph Francis (1869), William Henry Brereton (1871), Henry Lardner Dennys (1874), Henry James Holmes (1874), Daniel Edmund Caldwell (1883), Francisco Xavier D'Almada e Castro (1897), and Frank Barrington Deacon (1898). Brereton employed Victor Deacon (1880–1882), founder of the firm Deacons. D.E. Caldwell went into partnership in 1886 with Charles David Wilkinson, cofounder of Wilkinson & Grist.

30. Daniel Richard Caldwell was a police officer, court interpreter, and Registrar General who was dismissed from government service in 1861 for having assisted pirates and other bad characters in carrying out crimes and avoiding justice. He then set himself up as a 'Chinese agent', helping Chinese in the courts and heading a semi-official secret police. His brother, Henry Charles Caldwell, was Registrar of the Court of Judicature of Singapore until his abrupt

From 1901, solicitors admitted in Hong Kong were eligible to apply to practise in Great Britain without the need to take further examinations, provided they were male and of good character, had practised for at least three years, and had British nationality. Although this limited reciprocity may have had some symbolic importance, it had little practical use.[31] A mere 25 of the 180 or so solicitors admitted to practise in the colony's first 100 years trained and qualified locally. The more usual route was qualification in Britain.[32] For this reason, the profession continued to consist mainly of Westerners, supplemented by a few London-trained Chinese. The first of these was Ho Wyson, the son of a protestant minister who had made a fortune in property. Ho trained and qualified in England, where he was also the first Chinese solicitor. Admitted to practise in Hong Kong in 1887, he was held back by 'bashful modesty' and office hours lasting only 'from 12 to 3, with an interval of one hour for tiffin.'[33] Only about thirty-five of the solicitors enrolled in the colony's first hundred years were of local origin – mostly from Chinese, Eurasian, Portuguese, and Indian families. Some, such as Tso Seen-wan and Lo Man-kam (Sir Man-kam Lo from 1948) became prominent in politics. Admitted in 1897, Tso went into partnership with the Englishman Paul Mary Hodgson in 1927, one of several cross-cultural alliances from this time. Lo founded the firm Lo & Lo in 1915 at the age of twenty-three with his brother, Lo Man-wai. Tso and Lo, both from wealthy Hong Kong families, qualified in England – in Lo's case with distinction.[34] Members of the D'Almada family, originating in Macao, laid the roots of a legal dynasty that still flourishes today. The first to join the legal profession,

---

departure in 1856, shortly after which it was discovered that he had been misappropriating funds entrusted to him as administrator of intestate estates and trustee of monies held by the court. After establishing himself in Hong Kong from 1859 onwards (where, probably through his brother's influence, he evaded a warrant for his arrest from Singapore), he eventually paid back the money. Norton-Kyshe, *History of the Laws and Courts of Hong Kong*, I, 590; Carl T. Smith, 'The Firm of Wilkinson and Grist, Solicitors' (unpublished manuscript), 13–24; Anstey to Newcastle, 8 August 1859, CO 129/76, 124–6.

31. Order in Council, 4 November 1901 under the Colonial Solicitors Act 1900. Earlier Colonial Attorneys Relief Acts 1857–1884, which contained similar, though less flexible provisions, were not extended to Hong Kong. Black to Chamberlain, 31 March 1898, CO 129/282, 187–9; Blake to Chamberlain, 8 October 1900, CO 129/301, 161–5; *Hong Kong Government Gazette*, 27 March 1902.

32. The extant Solicitors' Rolls kept by the High Court only begin in 1906: 112 solicitors were admitted in Hong Kong from then until 1940. A further sixty-seven admissions during 1844–1898 are listed in Norton-Kyshe, *History of the Laws and Courts of Hongkong*, I, Appendix IV. Three more admissions can be traced in newspapers for the missing period mid-1898–1905, bringing the total to 182. The Solicitors' Rolls indicate whether a solicitor admitted in Hong Kong was also admitted in Great Britain.

33. *Hongkong Telegraph*, 3 September 1891; Norton-Kyshe, *History of the Laws and Courts of Hong Kong*, II, 544–5.

34. The Lo brothers were sons of the wealthy Eurasian compradore Lo Cheung Shiu. They were sent to England for education under the guardianship of Ho Fook, another prominent compradore whose early career included a term as interpreter with the solicitors Dennys & Mossop in the 1880s. Lo Man-kam came first in the First Class Honours Law Society examinations in London in June 1915. M.K.: *Born 21st July 1893, Died 7th March 1959* (Hong Kong, ?1959), 9; *Law Times*, 24 July 1915.

Francisco Xavier D'Almada e Castro, articling with D.E. Caldwell and C.D. Wilkinson, was admitted to practise after passing examinations in Hong Kong in 1897.[35]

The solicitors' examinations in early Hong Kong were in written form. Following the reforms in England, the 1871 Legal Practitioners Ordinance divided local examinations into preliminaries (taken before entering into articles) and finals (taken before admission to practise). The Chief Justice had discretion to exempt persons from the preliminary examinations: from 1913, degree-holders from HKU were specifically exempted by law, as were those who had passed any examination that would lead to exemption in England; from 1918, students who had passed certain HKU matriculation examinations (for entry into the university) were also exempted.[36] The Chief Justice had powers to issue regulations for the final examinations, in the absence of which the regulations in England were to apply. The exam papers were very similar to those set in England.[37] The first local regulation appears to have been issued in 1925, when variations were made from the English exams. Admiralty law, no longer examined in England, was retained because it was in common use in Hong Kong, while divorce law was omitted because it was less in demand: in fact, it was not possible to divorce in a court in Hong Kong until 1933.[38]

Barristers

While solicitors might train and qualify in Hong Kong, there was no possibility for barristers to do so before the 1970s. Only those previously called to the English or Irish Bars, or admitted as advocates in Scotland, could practise in Hong Kong. This did not prevent a few Chinese with resources and talent from qualifying. The earliest to do so was the Singapore-born Cantonese Ng Choy (Wu Tingfang), a court interpreter in Hong Kong who used a bequest from his father-in-law to finance his training at Lincoln's Inn. He was called to the London Bar in 1877 and admitted to practise in Hong Kong in the same year. Groomed

---

35. No fewer than ten members of this extended family were solicitors in Hong Kong up to the 1960s; six of them trained and qualified locally. Another eight were admitted as barristers in the fifty years from 1927. D'Almada Remedios, 'More than a Generation of Lawyers' in Hong Kong Bar Association, *Hong Kong Bar Association 50th Anniversary* (Hong Kong: Sweet & Maxwell, 2000), 12–14; Solicitors' Rolls, 1906–1940, and Barristers' Rolls, 1844–1941.

36. By then the HKU matriculation examinations had almost entirely replaced the Oxford Local examinations (one of the grounds of exemption in England) for secondary schools in Hong Kong. Ordinances Nos. 19 of 1913 & 24 of 1921; *Hongkong Government Gazette*, 16 August 1918; Stubbs to Churchill, 14 November 1921, CO 129/469, 330–34; Cunich, *A History of the University of Hong Kong* (Hong Kong: Hong Kong University Press, 2012), I, 185–86.

37. Report by W. Meigh Goodman, 4 October 1900, CO 129/301, 163–65.

38. The standard subjects, examined in both Hong Kong and England, were property and conveyancing law, the law and principles for matters determined by the highest courts in England, bankruptcy, probate, criminal law, proceedings before justices of the peace, and private international law. As in England, the exams took place over a gruelling three-day period. The *Hong Kong Government Gazette*, 27 February 1925 & 15 October 1926.

for high office by the reforming Governor Sir John Pope Hennessy, Ng was Hong Kong's first Chinese magistrate (1880) and first Chinese member of the Legislative Council (1880–1882). He left Hong Kong in 1882, having lost prestige after Hennessy's departure and his fortune in a property bubble. A career with the Chinese government led to his appointment in 1896 as China's Minister to the United States, Peru, and Spain. He was a commissioner for the abortive late Qing legal codes 1902–1906, for which he unsuccessfully urged jury trials and adversarial procedures.[39] Ng's brother-in-law, Ho Kai (Sir Kai Ho Kai from 1912), followed in his footsteps at Lincoln's Inn and was admitted to practise in Hong Kong in 1882. He was the brother of Ho Wyson, the first Chinese solicitor. Qualified in medicine as well as law, Ho Kai taught medical jurisprudence at the College of Medicine in what was probably the first systematic teaching of any branch of the law in Hong Kong. As a Legislative Councillor 1890–1914, he was the voice mainly of the privileged classes. He practised in the courts while promoting Western-style reforms in China through writings and contacts with other reformers.[40]

A total of forty-seven barristers were admitted between 1844 and 1899. Only a few stayed for any length of time. The pace of admission quickened in the early twentieth century as court business grew in volume and complexity – in both the Hong Kong Supreme Court and its sister-court, the British Supreme Court in Shanghai; fifty-eight more barristers were admitted between 1900 and 1941.[41] Nearly half of the names were Chinese, including some who were later to serve in courts in China.[42] Among the others were a few from India, a Japanese (Rokuichiro Masujima), and Hong Kong's first female barrister, Lo Soon Kim Teo, admitted in 1932 shortly after creating a similar record in Singapore. But this picture of

39. In 1987 the Ng Choy/Francis Mooting Prize, in memory of Ng and John Joseph Francis (who had supported Ng in his application for admission to practise), was established for the best mooter in the LLB course at HKU, with funds raised by the barrister and magistrate Walter Greenwood. Luk, 'A Hong Kong Barrister in Late-Ch'ing Law Reform,' 11 *HKLJ* (1981), 339–55; Linda Pomerantz-Zhang, *Wu Tingfang: Reform and Modernization in Modern Chinese History* (Hong Kong: Hong Kong University Press, 1992); 'Ng Choy/Francis Mooting Prize' HKU Archives (HKUA): Board of the Faculty of Law – Minutes (1985).

40. G.H. Choa, *The Life and Times of Sir Kai Ho Kai: A Prominent Figure in Nineteenth-Century Hong Kong* (Hong Kong: Chinese University Press, 2000). For about ten years, from 1884, a generous competitive government scholarship was awarded to students from local schools for the study of law, medicine, or civil engineering in Britain. However, most of the recipients whose names are known went into medicine or engineering. *Hongkong Government Gazette*, 17 May 1884; Sweeting, *Education in Hong Kong Pre-1841–1941: Fact and Opinion: Materials for a History of Education in Hong Kong* (Hong Kong: Hong Kong University Press, 1990), 279 & 324.

41. The figures exclude lawyers in government service, who were exempted from enrolment under the Legal Practitioners Ordinance. Barristers' Roll, High Court, Hong Kong.

42. Notably Lu Hsing-yuan (Hing Yun Loo or Loo Hing Yuen), admitted to the Hong Kong Bar in 1916, later president of courts in Canton, Attorney General in Sun Yat-sen's Canton Government (1923–1925), and president of the Provisional Court in Shanghai (1927), and F.T. Cheng (Fatting Tinsik Cheng), admitted to the Hong Kong Bar in 1917, who served in various legal and judicial capacities in China before becoming a judge of the Court of International Justice, The Hague (1936–1945) and the last ambassador of the Republic of China to the UK (1946–1950).

diversity is deceptive. Most of the fifty-eight barely had a practice in Hong Kong: Masujima, for example, left for more important business in Tokyo halfway through the case for which he was admitted, a forgery trial in which the defendants were Japanese;[43] Lo Soon Kim Teo does not appear to have taken on any cases in Hong Kong. With a few exceptions – notably Lo Hin-shing and Leo D'Almada Jr – the Supreme Court was dominated by a handful of barristers of English origin. Among them were advocates with ability, such as Marcus Slade KC, E.H. Sharp KC, Eldon Potter KC, F.C. Jenkin KC, C.G. Alabaster KC, and Harold Sheldon KC,[44] along with others who were less in demand, such as Sir Henry Pollock KC, who was said to be 'prolix to no purpose.'[45] In 1922 the Bar was so depleted that an emergency law was enacted to permit solicitors to act as advocates.[46] Yet opportunities for men from England were dwindling, wrote the barrister Somerset Fitzroy in a new proposal for fusion in 1938: unless the solicitors' and barristers' professions were amalgamated, the only members of the Bar in future 'must be Hong Kong men – Chinese, Eurasian, Portuguese, and may be Indian' – a prospect, in his view, much to be deprecated.[47]

Judges and Magistrates

Dominated by men with barely any experience at the Bar, Hong Kong's Judiciary also left much to be desired in Fitzroy's account of the legal profession in the 1930s. The small judicial establishment consisted of the Chief Justice and, from 1862, one other judge, along with two magistrates, rising in number in the early twentieth century to five by 1939. Professional requirements were not set by law until 1939, when a qualification as a barrister and a minimum of five years' experience as barrister or solicitor were specified for judges.[48]

---

43. The 'Million Dollar Forgery Case' (1913) involving counterfeit banknotes shipped from Japan to Canton via Hong Kong. The defendants were convicted. *Hongkong Telegraph*, 3 March 1913, *China Mail*, 31 March & 1–8 April 1913.

44. Sharp practised from 1894 until his death in 1922. Slade was admitted in 1897 and retired in 1913. Potter, admitted in 1907, practised almost until his death in 1951 and was the first president of the Hong Kong Bar Association in 1948. His fellow student at Gray's Inn, F.C. Jenkin, followed him to Hong Kong in 1912. The two dominated the Supreme Court until Jenkin's suicide in 1936. Alabaster (knighted in 1942) was the son of Sir Chaloner Alabaster, an expert on Chinese law, and was Attorney General 1930–1945. Sheldon, admitted to practise in 1925, became a magistrate in Hong Kong in 1940.

45. A member of a well-known family of English lawyers, Pollock made his name in politics in Hong Kong, where he was a member of the Legislative Council 1917–1941 and the Executive Council 1926–1941. He played a key role in the foundation of HKU. The comment on his ability is from the judge Henry Gompertz: Gompertz to May, 21 September 1917, CO 129/447, 155–8.

46. Ordinance, No. 7 of 1922, enacted in March and expiring at the end of the year.

47. Fitzroy to the Secretary of State, 2 August 1938, CO 129/566/11. The London-based *Law Journal* took a more positive view: Hong Kong, it noted, had a 'fine supply' of lawyers, and the Judiciary were 'regarded and rewarded with less disrespect than in other and larger units of Empire.' *The Law Journal*, 30 January 1937, 86.

48. Ordinance No. 10 of 1939.

In practice, all of Hong Kong's permanent judges held qualifications as barristers. Whereas many other colonies had opened their judiciaries to local recruitment, the Hong Kong bench was effectively closed to local candidates. Judges were recruited initially from among barristers in England and later from among judges and law officers with service in Hong Kong or other colonies. By the early twentieth century qualifications as barristers were often obtained by serving colonial officials – mainly 'cadets' (later known as 'administrative officers') – through private study, and examinations and dinners at the Inns of Court while on leave. They were encouraged by certain exemptions, and by bonuses and improved prospects. Nine of Hong Kong's twenty-one permanent judges during 1890–1950, including three chief justices, obtained their qualifications in this way.[49]

With a few brief exceptions, early magistrates had little, if any, training in law and relied on the Attorney General for legal advice. Barristers recruited to serve as magistrates from England in the 1850s did not stay long. One of them, Henry Tudor Davies, was warned that 'he would find a very different description of legislation to that which was current in England at the date of his departure.'[50] Groomed for the position of Chief Justice, he fell out with the Governor and left after only two years to join the newly formed Chinese Imperial Maritime Customs. By the late nineteenth century the position was the preserve of cadets with rudimentary legal training in Hong Kong and a knowledge of Chinese sufficient to enable them to exercise control over their interpreters.[51] In the 1890s cadets who had passed examinations on the law of evidence, the Ordinances of Hong Kong, and magistracy procedure were given priority in magistrates' appointments.[52] Most occupied the position for a year or two as a junior posting in a government career that might lead eventually to a

49. The three chief justices were Sir James Russell (1888–92), Sir Joseph Horsford Kemp (1930–34) and Sir Leslie Gibson (1948–50), all of whom began their careers as cadets. The process is illustrated by the career of Roger Edward Lindsell MA (Cantab), who joined the Hong Kong government as a cadet in 1909, passed his final examinations in Cantonese in 1911, and served in various positions, including Postmaster General, Deputy Registrar of the Supreme Court and Magistrate. He took his Bar examinations and completed the requisite number of dinners at his Inn of Court in London during periods of long leave in 1920 and 1929. He was called to the Bar by Inner Temple in 1930. After several periods as acting judge he served as Puisne Judge in Hong Kong in 1934 until his retirement in 1940. For achieving first class in the Criminal Law and Procedure paper in the Part 1 Bar Examinations of 1920 he was awarded a bonus of £25 by the Hong Kong Government (his annual salary in 1919 was £500). Cadets were exempted from admission examinations for Inns of Court. Civil servants 'exercising judicial functions abroad' (including the colonies) were eligible for a dispensation of four of the terms to be kept at an inn. Lindsell to Under-Secretary of State for the Colonies, 31 October 1920, CO 129/466, 339–43.
50. Norton-Kyshe, *History of the Laws and Courts of Hong Kong*, I, 407.
51. Some cadets were highly proficient in Chinese: Henry Gompertz, for example, a cadet who became Puisne Judge 1909–1925, was fluent in three dialects. However, until the Official Languages Ordinance 1974 allowed proceedings in Chinese in magistrates' courts, only English could be used in court proceedings, with interpretation for witnesses and defendants where necessary.
52. Barker to Knutsford, 14 October 1891, CO 129/251, 287–93.

colonial governorship. Some continued as magistrates for most of their career. A few took the opportunity to train as barristers with the prospect of higher judicial office.

This method of producing judicial officers became so entrenched in Hong Kong in the early twentieth century that it was cause for comment. 'Is it or is it not a good thing that the judicial, magisterial and administrative posts should be filled by the same class of Civil Servants, whose qualifications are ascertained by the same tests,' asked *The Law Journal*, before answering the question with some 'doggerel of Far Eastern origin':

> They have no need to study law,
> They're always right by right divine ... [53]

Some governors certainly saw it as a good thing, and urged the creation of a special 'legal class' of cadet officers with a virtual monopoly on judicial and legal positions.[54] The Colonial Office in London rejected such ideas as 'impractical and absurd.' Instead, in the early twentieth century a unified Colonial Legal Service emerged to supply the empire with judges, magistrates, attorneys general, and law officers: the minimum qualifications set for judges in Hong Kong in 1939 reflected this arrangement, as did the policy introduced that year of replacing all cadet-magistrates with qualified barristers. Members of the Colonial Legal Service moved between judicial and legal positions within and among the colonies, culminating for a few in a chief justiceship. Many of Hong Kong's colonial judges had formerly served in non-judicial positions in Hong Kong or other colonies. For some, the chief justiceship was their first judicial appointment other than a term as magistrate.[55] No fewer than six of Hong Kong's twenty-one colonial chief justices had formerly served as attorney general in Hong Kong, despite a principle that no one should serve successively as attorney general and chief justice in the same colony.

Quite apart from questions of judicial independence, a bench composed of 'book-made lawyers' with long service in government but little if any experience of advocacy was, according to some lawyers, one of the reasons why the courts in Hong Kong were so inefficient. The solution, they urged, was the recruitment of experienced barristers direct from London.[56] Criticisms persisted after World War II, when a separate judicial branch of the Colonial

---

53. *The Law Journal*, 24 September 1938, 206.

54. Both Sir Matthew Nathan (Governor 1904–1907) and Sir Frederick Lugard (Governor 1907–1912) recommended schemes along these lines: Nathan to Lyttelton, 10 December 1904, CO 129/324, 442–4; Lugard to Harcourt, 20 April 1911, CO 129/423–61.

55. Chief Justices Hulme (1844–1859), Smale (1866–1882), Gibson (1948–1951), and Roberts (1979–1988) had no judicial experience before their appointments. Various others, notably Piggott (1905–1912), Rees-Davies (1912–1924), Kemp (1930–1934), and Hogan (1955–1970), had only brief experience as magistrates or acting judges in Hong Kong or other colonies.

56. See, for example, the conversations with barristers reported in May to Long, 8 February 1918, CO 129/447, 121–88.

Legal Service was created. Some lawyers saw this as a closed 'civil service judiciary', a form of professional 'apartheid' departing from the English practice of appointing judges from the private Bar. Why was it that in Hong Kong, 'the most important, affluent and sophisticated of our Colonies', members of the Supreme Court Bench were not appointed from the practising Bar, asked the Chairman of the Bar Association, Gerald de Basto, in 1970.[57] The first permanent appointments from the local Bar to the Judiciary did not take place until the 1970s, beginning with the District Court in 1973 and the Supreme Court in 1977.

Legal Studies at HKU, 1915–1940

Following trends in Britain, universities within the British Empire and beyond introduced legal education and founded law schools: among the earliest were those at Sydney (1855), Bombay (1855), and Melbourne (1857). Within China, law schools were established at Peking University (1905), Soochow University (1915), and Tsinghua University (1929): the Comparative Law School at Soochow, an American missionary initiative, taught Anglo-American law as part of its curriculum, making it the first law school in China to provide systematic training in the common law.[58] Even in Japan, which had adopted German-style legal codes at the turn of the century, the barrister Rokuichiro Masujima was conducting a private school of English law in Tokyo, from which he sent students to study at the Inns of Court.[59] In Hong Kong, the largest enclave of the common law in China,[60] plans for formal legal education moved more slowly, hindered by a shortage of funds and a lack of interest.

In 1908 plans were advanced for a university in Hong Kong, financed mainly by local donations led by the Parsee merchant Sir Hormusjee Mody. The emphasis was to be on professional training. Three faculties were proposed – medicine, engineering, and law.

---

57. De Basto to Sir James McPetrie of the FCO, 7 May 1970, FCO 40/298, 60–3. De Basto and Benjamin Liu were appointed district judges in 1973. They were the first barristers from the private bar in Hong Kong to be appointed to permanent judicial office without having first serving as magistrates.

58. The other elements of its tripartite curriculum were the civil law and Chinese legal systems. Alison W. Conner, 'Training China's Early Modern Lawyers: Soochow University Law School,' 8 *Journal of Chinese Law* (1994), 1–46; Robert E. Tindall, 'The Graduate School of Law, Soochow University, Republic of China,' 7 *International Lawyer* (1973), 711–15.

59. Memorandum by Lionel Curtis, CO 129/527, 37.

60. The other common law jurisdictions were the British leased territory of Weihaiwei (1898–1930), over which the Hong Kong Supreme Court had appellate jurisdiction (though it was never used), and the extraterritorial jurisdiction exercised over British subjects throughout China by the British Supreme Court for China (1865–1943). Before the creation of the Shanghai court, the Hong Kong Supreme Court had extraterritorial jurisdiction over British subjects in China 1844–1865. Several lawyers practised in both the Hong Kong and the Shanghai courts, and from 1912 the senior judge of the Shanghai court sat on appeals in Hong Kong, an arrangement that was made reciprocal in 1926. Douglas Clark, *Gunboat Justice: British and American Law Courts in China and Japan (1842–1943)* (Hong Kong: Earnshaw Books, 2015); Carol G.S. Tan, *British Rule in China: Law and Justice in Weihaiwei 1898–1930* (London: Wildy, Simmonds and Hill, 2008).

Experts were consulted on proposals and financial estimates: the legal experts were Henry Pollock, Ho Kai, and Francis Bowley, a solicitor then also filling part-time the position of Solicitor General. The three-faculty proposal proved too expensive, and the law faculty was dropped. Soon after the opening of the university in 1911, however, a small and hurriedly organized Faculty of Arts was established to teach subjects not covered by the two main faculties: the proponent of the university, Governor Sir Frederick Lugard, was opposed to the teaching of non-utilitarian subjects on the ground that they were 'apt to fire the immature imagination of imaginative races' and lead to unrest, but he had belatedly discovered that a much-sought-after royal charter would not be granted to a university with only two faculties and had reluctantly accepted proposals by Ho Kai and others that a Faculty of Arts should provide courses 'for the sons of gentry who aim at official posts.'[61] Law was to be among the miscellany of subjects taught by this third faculty.

The early Faculty of Arts was mainly funded by donations from the philanthropist Cheung Pat Sze: but for his death a month before the ceremony, in 1916, he would have been among the first recipients of an honorary Doctor of Laws degree (the only honorary degree conferred by HKU in its early decades).[62] The ambit of the Faculty of Arts was wide. Apart from English, history, economics and Chinese, it taught mathematics, commerce and even physics and chemistry. From 1915, thanks to further funding from Cheung, commercial law and international law (with an emphasis on the law of peace and the law of war) were added as options in the intermediate and final courses of a four-year undergraduate programme. Jurisprudence was added in 1917.[63] The first lecturer in law was Kingsley Brayshay, a graduate in jurisprudence from Oxford, who was also the university's honorary librarian and a champion cricketer. The external examiners included Joseph Kemp, Attorney General and architect of Hong Kong's draconian system of emergency regulations, and Thomas Baty, legal advisor to the Japanese government whose views on China's non-status in the community of nations were later to be used by Japan to justify invasion.[64] Brayshay became professor of jurisprudence in 1919 but resigned in 1920 when the position was discontinued because of a funding crisis. A commission that year into the university's finances recommended cutbacks. As a result, the professorship remained

---

61. Cunich, *A History of the University of Hong Kong*, I, 96–9, 110; Alfred H.Y. Lin, 'The Founding of the University of Hong Kong: British Imperial Ideals and Chinese Practical Common Sense' & Peter Cunich, 'Godliness and Good Learning: The British Missionary Societies and HKU' in Chan Lau Kit-chin & Peter Cunich (eds.), *An Impossible Dream: Hong Kong University from Foundation to Re-establishment, 1910–1950* (Hong Kong: Oxford University Press, 2002), 3–4 & 55–6.

62. *SCMP*, 15 December 1916.

63. HKU *Calendar*, 1914/15, 73 & 79, & 1917/18, 84.

64. Baty, a British national, lived in Japan from 1916 until his death in 1954. He continued to serve the Japanese government during World War II. He was investigated for treason after the war but was not prosecuted: instead, he was stripped of his British nationality. Peter Oblas, 'Britain's First Traitor of the Pacific War: Employment and Obsession,' *New Zealand Journal of Asian Studies* 7, No. 2 (December 2005): 109–33.

vacant and jurisprudence was placed under commercial training and taught for a while by the solicitor, Henry Macnamara.[65]

Healthier university finances in the 1920s enabled an expansion of the Faculty of Arts, including the appointment in 1924 of a new lecturer in political science and jurisprudence (from 1926, reader in law and politics), George Keeton, a Cambridge graduate and a member of Gray's Inn. Keeton returned to England in 1927 to pursue a distinguished career in teaching and writing, first at Manchester University and later at University College, London.[66] His short time at HKU was marked by a surge of interest in legal studies, which he did much to foster. He hoped to do for Chinese law 'what Sir Henry Maine did for India.'[67] His interests embraced comparative law, mixed legal systems, and the new legal codes of China, Japan, and Siam. His prolific output included a two-volume text on extraterritoriality in China (1928).[68] At HKU he laid on courses in Roman, English, Hindu, Muslim, and Chinese law, 'taught comparatively wherever possible', and embarked on an ambitious programme of research into the legal systems of East Asia.[69] He turned his lectures into an introductory textbook, *The Elementary Principles of Jurisprudence*.[70] Together with his senior students he founded the HKU Law Society and the *Hong Kong University Law Journal* (1926–1927), the first serious law periodical to be produced in Hong Kong, attracting contributions from students, graduates and faculty, and from scholars in the region. The first issue was so successful that copies travelled around the world.[71]

---

65. Brayshay had suffered from declining health. He died in England in 1922 at the age of 32. Macnamara began his practice as a solicitor in Hong Kong in 1920 and, after qualifying in England, was admitted to the Hong Kong Bar in 1932. He was appointed a magistrate in 1939. HKU *Calendar*, 1920/21, 143, & 1924, 104; *SCMP*, 31 April & 28 May 1920, & 27 May 1922; Cunich, *A History of the University of Hong Kong*, I, 224–5.

66. Obituary in 18 *Anglo-American Law Review* (1989), 1–6. For Keeton's reminiscences see 'Forty-five Years On', a foreword to 1 *HKLJ* (1971), 6–8.

67. G.W. Keeton, 'Legal Opportunities in China' (address to the HKU Law Society, 1926), *Hong Kong University Law Journal* 1 (1926–1927), 11. Henry Maine's *Ancient Law* (1861) was a seminal text on legal anthropology and one of the first Western works to examine the development of legal systems outside Europe, though it had little to say on China.

68. G.W. Keeton, *The Development of Extraterritoriality in China* (London: Longmans, 1928): this was preceded by a series of articles on the subject published in the *Law Quarterly Review*, 1926–1927.

69. G.W. Keeton, 'Forty-five Years On', 7; HKU *Calendar*, 1923, 143–7; D.M.E. Evans, *Legal Education in Hong Kong: Reports of the 1966 and 1969 Working Parties on Legal Education* (Hong Kong: Hong Kong University Press, 1974), 2–3.

70. Keeton found that his students – most of whom were Chinese – were familiar with ideas of natural law and sovereignty, having come across similar doctrines in the Chinese classics. However, the conception of law existing for the promotion of private rights was 'alien' to them. 'Duty seems relatively a more important conception than right, whilst Law as the creature of the State was a constant stumbling-block to students whose contact with it had hitherto been limited to a knowledge of ancient custom.' Keeton, *The Elementary Principles of Jurisprudence* (London: A. & C. Black, 1930), v.

71. Among the HKU contributors were Irene Ho-Tung, one of the first female undergraduates, who produced two historical articles on Chinese law and who, as Irene Cheng, later sat on the Strickland Committee on Chinese law and custom (1948–1950).

Keeton's *Law Journal*, like much of his teaching, looked beyond Hong Kong to the legal systems of China, Japan, the Dutch East Indies, French Indochina, Fascist Italy, and Weimar Germany. The articles addressed subjects ranging from customary law to new legal codes in a rapidly changing world. They were topical and scholarly. Yet, apart from notes on recent commercial cases in England, they had little to say on law in Hong Kong. The only article on a Hong Kong topic dealt, somewhat dismally, with the difficulties faced by judges in ascertaining the meaning of parts of the Qing Code, which (though it was obsolete in China) they were now attempting to apply in Chinese inheritance disputes.[72] A full training in law, Keeton remarked, was 'out of the question' at this time: 'the legal work of this University, as far as I see it, will never be such that it will directly fit our students for professional legal work.'[73]

An attempt to expand the teaching of law a few years after Keeton's departure underlined this point. In 1930, Lionel Curtis, the proponent of imperial federation and world government, put forward a scheme for a school of law at HKU. His hope was that the Inns of Court in London would be 'moved to take the same kind of interest in the establishment of a School of Law at Hongkong as is taken by City Corporations like the Cloth Workers in technical schools in the textile industries.'[74] Curtis garnered the support of Robert Feetham, a South African judge, and Rokuichiro Masujima, the Japanese barrister. Feetham was a constitutional law expert engaged by the Shanghai Municipal Council to advise on the recently announced policy of Britain and the US to gradually relinquish their extraterritorial rights. He had at first suggested Shanghai as a location for the school but became convinced that HKU was the right place, sheltered as it was in British

---

72. H.K. Woo, 'The Difficulty of Authenticated Translation of Chinese Laws in Hongkong Courts: a Case in Point', *Hong Kong University Law Journal* 2 (1926–1927), 126–30. The court was asked to decide opposing claims to the administration of an intestate estate left by a wealthy tailor by the younger brother and the 'sole surviving concubine', who was surrogate 'compassionate mother' (*tsu mo* or *shu mo*) of the two infant heirs. The two sides had submitted conflicting translations of the relevant part of the Qing Code, both of which had been approved as authentic by the court translator, who testified that either version could be correct. 'How then can I administer the law?' asked the exasperated Chief Justice, Sir Henry Gollan. Finally, Sir George Staunton's *Ta Tsing Leu Lee* of 1810 – the only English translation of the Qing Code available – was produced. This, combined with an established practice in the Probate Registry of granting letters of administration to concubines, supported the concubine's case, and the court decided in her favour: *In the estate of Chan Yan alias Chan Yung, Deceased* (1925) 20 HKLR 35. H.K. Woo (Hangkam Kwingtong Woo, LLB (Lond.) 1877–1957) was admitted to practise as a solicitor in 1913 after training in England. His nephew, Woo Pak-chuen, was the founder of the solicitors' firm PC Woo & Co. (1945) and a prominent politician in the 1960s and 1970s. P.C. Woo's daughter, Woo Tsz-tong, was admitted as a solicitor in 1958 after having served articles with her father and uncle.

73. Keeton, 'Forty-five Years On', 7 & 'Legal Opportunities in China', 2. The course in commercial law nevertheless covered a great deal of practical material, such as contract, company law, shipping law, insolvency, and arbitration, as well as a special series of lectures on Chinese commercial law.

74. Curtis to Passfield, 13 September 1930, CO 129/527, 13–14; Cunich, *A History of the University of Hong Kong*, I, 325.

territory 'from the perpetual storms' of Chinese politics.[75] Feetham saw as the school's main purpose the promotion of a proper understanding of China's new legal codes – this, he said, was 'perhaps the biggest contribution that the University could make to the salvation of China.' Masujima, on the other hand, in his devotion to English law, saw the proposed school as a training ground for Chinese 'legal missionaries' who, like the judges and barristers in India, would spread 'the blessings of justice bestowed by the existence of the Common Law Bar.' The establishment of a satisfactory legal system was one of the conditions laid down for ending the extraterritorial justice applied since the nineteenth century to foreign nationals in China.[76]

Curtis and Feetham obtained enthusiastic support from Sir Henry Gollan, the Chief Justice of Hong Kong, and William Hornell, Vice-Chancellor of HKU. Hornell drew up plans for a small school of law, initially within the Faculty of Arts but later to evolve into a full faculty. The starting cost would be £6,000–£7,000 per annum. The university could not provide the finance, Hornell stressed. 'We have not got a penny nor is there any present prospect of raising any money here for a School of Law.'[77] The project therefore turned on Curtis's proposal to raise the funds in London. He had been advised by those familiar with the notoriously conservative Inns of Court that any hope of squeezing money out of them for HKU was 'a fantastic dream.'[78] A fund-raising dinner hosted by Curtis proved them right. No money was forthcoming. The scheme sank without trace.

Colonial Office officials were in any case sceptical about the prospect of 'China, in its new found liberty, sending its youth to learn English law at Hong Kong' and about the 'effect a veneer of English juristic ideals would have upon a Chinaman.'[79] Feetham had heard objections from 'the conservative and rather timid type of intellect which probably flourishes in Hongkong' that the school would produce 'half-baked lawyers' who would create 'political trouble' in the colony.[80] Legal studies at HKU went into decline. Keeton's replacement, Robert Robertson, took the title of Professor of Economics and Political Science on his promotion in 1929. The university's Law Society merged with the Commerce Society. The journal, now called the *Journal of the Law and Commerce Society*, turned its attention to economics. Keeton's syllabus was maintained in the 1930s. But law was now taught along with economics and accountancy in what the Vice-Chancellor described as 'an astonishing hash' in a Department of Commerce criticized both for its irrelevance and

75. Minute by Gent, 12 September 1930, CO 129/527, 2–3; *SCMP*, 8 January 1930.
76. Feetham to Curtis, 17 April 1930, CO 129/527, 19–22; Masujima, 'Proposals Regarding China "Extraterritoriality" Question', CO 129/527, 23–5; 'Extraterritoriality and Administration of Justice in China: Resolutions adopted by the Conference on the Limitation of Armament at Washington December 10, 1921.'
77. Hornell to Curtis, 28 May 1930, CO 129/527, 54.
78. Curtis to Passfield, 19 September 1930, CO 129/527, 9.
79. Minute by H.B., 15 September 1930, CO 129/527, 5.
80. Feetham to Curtis, 17 April 1930, CO 129/527, 21.

for its failure to emphasize 'the value of a University as an instrument of civilization in a commercial community.'[81] In 1938 the Court of the University – the supreme governing body – passed a resolution urging the creation of a school of economics and politics, if necessary 'at the expense of the present courses in Commercial Law and Jurisprudence at any rate until such time as there is a demand for courses in Law leading to a Law Degree.'[82] A University Development Report in 1939 made no mention of law.[83] By 1941 the subject had disappeared from the HKU *Calendar*.

An education at HKU offered few advantages to students wishing to pursue a career in law. The practice followed in England since 1843 of cutting two years off articles for degree-holders training as solicitors was not adopted for HKU graduates in Hong Kong until 1948.[84] Only one pre-war HKU graduate became a solicitor in Hong Kong. This was Kan Yuet-keung (BA 1935), son of one of the founders of the Bank of East Asia, who in October 1940, after further study at the London School of Economics (LSE) and articles in England, became the last solicitor to be enrolled in Hong Kong before the Japanese invasion in December 1941. After the war he became a senior partner in Lo & Lo and was president of the Law Society of Hong Kong 1957–1958. Knighted in 1972, he held prominent positions in business and politics. He was Chairman of the Bank of East Asia 1963–1983 and a member of the Legislative Council 1961–1972 and Executive Council 1966–1980, where he was the leading voice of law-and-order conservatism. Other home-grown solicitors before the war tended to take the faster, non-university route to qualification.

The passing of a public examination at any university 'within the British dominions' exempted a student from the entrance exams for entry into an Inn of Court in London – a small concession in a training that remained firmly English-based. Several early Faculty of Arts students from HKU became barristers in Hong Kong after training in England. The first was Lo Hin-shing, one of the first five students to enter the Faculty of Arts, in 1912. 'Bright but erratic,' according to his student report, Lo took six years to obtain his BA, winning a prize for international law from the examiner, Thomas Baty. Further studies in England were financed by Lo's elder brother, who had made a fortune in property on the wealth pouring into Hong Kong after the 1911 Revolution, and who had intended for Lo to return as a solicitor to help with his business. Lo had other plans. He took an LLB at Cambridge and was called to the Bar by Inner Temple in 1923. After a brief attempt at articles with a London solicitor he spent the next three years attending lectures at LSE, observing

81. Vice-Chancellor Duncan Sloss, quoted in Cunich, *A History of the University of Hong Kong*, I, 334; *Report of the University (1937) Committee* (Hong Kong: Noronha & Co., 1937), 245; Northcote to Macdonald, 27 June 1938, *Hong Kong Sessional Papers* (1938), 210.

82. Minutes of the 51st meeting of the Court, enclosed with Northcote to Macdonald, 27 June 1938, 218.

83. HKU, *Committee on the Development of the University, Report of 4 March 1939* (Hong Kong: HKU, 1939).

84. Ordinance No. 37 of 1948, First and Second Schedules.

trials at the Old Bailey, and enjoying a glittering social life: he took dancing lessons from Rudolf Valentino and, deciding that plain Lo Hin-shing was not grand enough, had himself announced at parties as the 'Prince of Shaukiwan'. He returned to Hong Kong in 1926, now nearly forty, and built up a practice as a criminal barrister. During World War II he advised the Japanese government of occupation on English and Chinese law. After the war he was one of Hong Kong's few Chinese magistrates, widely admired for his compassion and good humour. He finally retired from the permanent bench in 1970 at the age of eighty. His daughter, Helen Lo, became Hong Kong's first female judge, in 1986.[85]

Lo Hin-shing's leisurely progress from matriculation at HKU to admission to the Hong Kong Bar lasted twelve years. The handful of other early barristers to emerge from HKU moved more quickly. Leo D'Almada e Castro Jr, the first of the D'Almadas to become a barrister, failed his third year at HKU in 1921, largely on account of a poor result in jurisprudence. His aim in life, he later recalled, was to do nothing. Yet, after being 'packed off' to Oxford by his wealthy parents, he returned in 1927 a full-fledged barrister at the age of twenty-three. He established a flourishing practice, mainly in criminal law, and lectured part-time in commercial law at HKU for a year. In 1937 he was appointed as the Portuguese community's representative on the Legislative Council. During the war he helped organize Portuguese from Hong Kong seeking refuge in Macau and joined the Hong Kong Planning Unit in London after a hazardous journey through China. In 1945–1946, after liberation, he presided over the General Military Court of the temporary British Military Administration – effectively filling the role of chief justice, trying cases ranging from robbery to high treason.[86] He was made a King's Counsel in 1947 and served on the Executive Council 1949–1959.[87]

Among the other pre-war Faculty of Arts students who were to become prominent in law and public life after the war were Sir Oswald Cheung QC, a King Edward VII scholar at HKU 1938–1941, and Patrick Yu, a government scholar 1938–1941 who received a wartime degree in 1942. Both had distinguished war records: Yu served with British Naval Intelligence and the Chinese Nationalist Army, Cheung with British Military Intelligence in China and in India. After the war, they completed their educations on government scholarships at Oxford and Lincoln's Inn and were called to the Bar in London, Yu in 1950, Cheung in 1951. In 1965 Cheung was the first Chinese in Hong Kong to be appointed a QC.

---

85. Lo Hin-shing, *Reminiscences and Observations* (Hong Kong: Cosmos Printing Press Ltd, 1975); Lo Hin-shing, interviewed on *Time to Remember*, RTHK, 23 June 1973; HKU Arts Faculty, Annual Reports of Students, HKUA: Lo Hin-shing, 1912–1918; John Griffiths, *Reminiscences and Observations of a Hong Kong Chai Lo* (Bishop Auckland: The Pentland Press Ltd, 1997), 41–3.

86. Notably, the trial of the collaborator George Wong, the first treason trial in Hong Kong after World War II, in which Lo Hin-shing was assigned as counsel for the defence.

87. HKU Faculty of Arts, Annual Reports of Students, HKUA: Leo D'Almada e Castro, 1919–1921; Citation for Leo D'Almada e Castro, 56th Congregation HKU (1961), *SCMP*, 25 January 1976.

After long public service, he retired as Senior Member of the Executive Council in 1986. Yu was Hong Kong's first Chinese crown counsel in the Attorney General's Chambers, a position he resigned in 1952 because of the discriminatory treatment of Chinese employees: he later declined offers of judgeships from three chief justices for the same reason, preferring instead to pursue a successful practice as barrister. As a member of Hong Kong's first University Grants Committee, Yu was to play a key role in the establishment of the school of law at HKU. He was also pupil-master to some of its earliest graduates.[88]

After World War II

During the Japanese occupation of Hong Kong (1941–1945) the university was dispersed. Its campus was so extensively looted and shell-damaged that it looked as if it had been bombed.[89] The staff was depleted by death or repatriation. Twenty-two graduates and undergraduates had died at the hands of the enemy. Among them were two of Hong Kong's most promising young lawyers. Lo Tung-fan (BA 1927, LLB London 1930, Gray's Inn 1930, Hong Kong Bar 1931), the son of a solicitors' interpreter, had helped form a Special Constabulary in 1941, serving as its Deputy Superintendent. During the occupation he was arrested as a British spy, imprisoned, and executed.[90] Donald Anderson (BA 1932, LLB London 1936, Gray's Inn & Hong Kong Bar 1936), from an old Eurasian family, was one of several barristers to be appointed to the Magistracy during its professionalization in 1939–1941 – the first unmistakably 'local' judicial officer since Ng Choy. A lieutenant in the Hong Kong Volunteers, he was killed in action at Wong Nai Chung Gap on 19 December 1941.[91]

The university was not fully functional again until 1949. Law was not one of the subjects to be revived. A school of law might be desirable in theory, observed the Keswick Committee on Higher Education in 1952, but circumstances did not justify one. The demand from would-be solicitors was 'very small', since it was faster to qualify with a five-year articled clerkship (the two-year discount on articles for degree-holders introduced in 1948 still required a total training of at least six years). The demand from barristers was 'negligible', since they still had to qualify in Britain. The only need was for evening courses in subjects such as company law, required by the accountancy profession: these, the committee advised, could be provided by the university's Department of Extra-Mural

---

88. Patrick Yu, 'Wartime Experiences in Hong Kong and China' Parts 1 & 2, & Oswald Cheung, 'Wartime Intelligence in China', in Clifford Matthews & Oswald Cheung (Eds.), *Dispersal and Renewal: Hong Kong University During the War Years* (Hong Kong: Hong Kong University Press, 1998), 51–9 & 312–44.
89. Cunich, *A History of the University of Hong Kong*, I, 426–8.
90. *SCMP*, 21 January 1946.
91. *SCMP*, 2 December 1936; Tony Banham, *Not the Slightest Chance: the Defence of Hong Kong, 1941* (Hong Kong: Hong Kong University Press, 2003), 131.

Studies.[92] A survey of graduate employment later in the 1950s came to a similar conclusion, despite repeated complaints by the Public Service Commission about the failure to recruit Chinese-speaking magistrates, which it attributed partly to the lack of legal training at HKU. 'Since officers are expected to apply British practice it appears reasonable to assume that training can best be obtained in the United Kingdom,' the survey concluded.[93]

The attempt to recruit Chinese-speaking magistrates was part of the short-lived '1946 outlook', a set of policies drawn up during the war for a liberated Hong Kong. Among its features – novel to Hong Kong – were representative government, social welfare, and localization of the senior public service. Progress towards these aims was interrupted by renewed civil war in China, the 1949 Communist revolution, and a massive influx of refugees into Hong Kong: the priority was now external security and internal order in a colony on the front line of the Cold War, the 'Berlin' of the Far East. Localization in Hong Kong's Judiciary and Legal Department nevertheless resulted in the recruitment of two lawyers who were to rise to high office. The first, Simon Li Fook-sean, was recruited as a crown counsel in 1953 and later served as magistrate (1957) and as Hong Kong's first Chinese judge (acting district judge 1964; puisne judge 1967). The second, the Shanghai-born future Chief Justice (1988–1996) Yang Ti Liang, joined the Magistracy in 1956 as the first Chinese to be appointed on permanent terms: Yang had enrolled in the Faculty of Arts at HKU before going to London for his legal training.[94] These were, however, exceptions in what was to remain for many years a largely unlocalized judiciary and government legal service, which were supplied mainly by recruits from Britain and Australasia and the decolonizing territories in Africa and the Pacific.

In addition to a small influx from the now-defunct British Supreme Court in Shanghai,[95] the post-war reconstruction brought military lawyers to Hong Kong. Several decided to

92. *Report of the Committee on Higher Education in Hong Kong, 1952* (Hong Kong: Government Printer, 1952) ('the Keswick Report'), 23 & 35.

93. R.F. Simpson, *Graduate Employment in Hong Kong and the Problems of University Expansion* (Hong Kong: HKU, 1959), 76.

94. Li (Lincoln's Inn, 1951) was from an old Hong Kong family whose other legal members include Andrew Li, the first Chief Justice of the Hong Kong Special Administrative Region (1997–2010) and Gladys Li SC, chairman of the Bar Association (1995–1996). Yang was from a wealthy gentry family based in Shanghai and had begun his legal training at the Comparative Law School at Soochow University: in 1949, as the People's Liberation Army was about to enter Shanghai, his parents sent him and his brothers to Hong Kong. Yang finished his training in London and was called to the Bar by Gray's Inn in 1954. After returning to Hong Kong, he practised as a barrister for eight months before joining the Judiciary as a magistrate in 1956. Yang, *An Introduction to Our Family* (Hong Kong: Ye Olde Printerie, 1979), 14.

95. Notably the barrister J.R. Jones MC, CBE, a veteran of both World Wars, who practised in Shanghai court from 1924 and was Secretary to the Shanghai Municipal Council 1928–1936. After the Japanese surrender in 1945 he helped stabilize currency systems in East Asia before moving to Hong Kong in 1947. He was legal adviser to the Hongkong and Shanghai Banking Corporation, served on several government committees, and was the first president of the re-established Hong Kong Branch of the Royal Asiatic Society.

remain, and three became prominent members the profession. Brook Bernacchi, a major in the Royal Marines who arrived in 1945 as legal advisor to the Commander of British Forces, was the first private barrister to be admitted by the reconstituted Supreme Court: his first brief was to defend three men charged with treason. As founder of the Reform Club (1949) and an elected member of the Urban Council (1952–1995), Bernacchi was a campaigner for constitutional reform and social equality at a time when political activity outside the elites was discouraged – even, at times, repressed. His comrade in the Royal Marines, Major Peter Vine, arrived in 1946, having just sat his solicitors' finals on board HMS *Sultan* in Singapore, to serve as a prosecutor in the Hong Kong War Crimes Trials. After demobilization he returned to Hong Kong in 1947, joined the firm of Deacons, and built a distinguished career as a solicitor. Another lawyer in the Hong Kong War Crimes Trials, Lieutenant-Colonel Leslie Wright, was admitted as a barrister in 1947 and practised in Hong Kong for nearly fifty years. Both Vine and Wright were to make generous donations to the Faculty of Law at HKU.

A suggestion by Peter Vine while president of the Law Society of Hong Kong 1962–1964 was the immediate stimulus to a revival of legal education at HKU. Momentum had been building for some years. The barrister Patrick Yu had been urging the establishment of a law faculty since his return from England in 1948: it was, he thought, 'amazing' that the government had not seen fit to provide such a facility for the people of Hong Kong. In an explanatory note on a new Legal Practitioners Bill in 1948, the government acknowledged that local facilities for legal training were 'very poor indeed.' At the Opening of the Assizes in 1957 the Chief Justice, Sir Michael Hogan, said that Hong Kong's 'happy synthesis' of English law and Chinese custom could be an example for other countries; the task, he added, would be greatly assisted by 'concentrated and expert study' in a faculty of law at HKU.[96] At the university's Golden Jubilee congregation in 1961, the Vice-Chancellor, Sir Lindsay Ride, made a similar point, saying it would 'eventually' be necessary to establish a law school – law now being one of the few subjects not offered by the university. At the same event, upon receiving his honorary Doctor of Laws degree, Leo D'Almada, 'our most distinguished undergraduate', stressed the need for the study of law in a world where 'too often the Rule of Law was being crushed by the Rule of Fear.'[97]

D'Almada drew attention to the hundred or more men and women now serving their articles in Hong Kong, stressing the direct benefits that law courses in Hong Kong would bring to them. The task of establishing such courses became the focus of efforts by Peter

---

96. *SCMP*, 11 January 1957.

97. Patrick Yu Shuk-yiu, *A Seventh Child and the Law* (Hong Kong: Hong Kong University Press, 1998), 131; Legal Practitioners Bill 1948, explanatory note, *Hong Kong Government Gazette*, Supplement No. 3, 2 July 1948' *SCMP*, 11 January 1957 & 18 September 1961; *University of Hong Kong Gazette*, 18 September 1961.

Vine, in discussions with government and university, and in a key speech in April 1963.[98] Vine had been elected president of the Law Society with a mandate to raise professional standards. A new Legal Practitioners Ordinance in 1964, extending the Law Society's powers of discipline over solicitors and articled clerks, was one result of these efforts.[99] The other outcome was a concerted effort, by officials, academics and lawyers, to reintroduce law at HKU. Since 1948 holders of recognized law degrees were exempted from the Part I solicitors' examinations. This 'revolutionary' change, Vine believed, would become the standard form of entry into the profession, not least because it reduced the time under articles to two years.[100] Yet, said Vine, in the absence of a law degree in Hong Kong, local students were at a disadvantage compared with their counterparts in England. One of the government's senior lawyers, the Registrar General, W.K. Thomson, put it more forcefully in a memorandum penned a few days after Vine's speech. It seemed 'little short of tragic that the doors to a great profession are virtually closed to a large number of young men and women who have not had the good fortune to be born into wealthy homes.' Apart from the question of equity, the thrust of Thomson's argument was that the dire shortage of lawyers was likely to impede the rapid modernization now in train in Hong Kong.[101] The speech by Vine and the memorandum by Thomson stimulated action by government, judiciary, university and the profession to introduce courses leading to a law degree, first at the university's Department of Extra-Mural Studies in 1964, and then, in 1969, at a dedicated Department of Law.

Thus the reintroduction of law at HKU was driven by a combination of practical need in an increasingly prosperous society, a high-minded desire for legal research in a changing world, and the even higher ideal of social justice in a colony in which inequalities between rich and poor were beginning to receive attention. These themes, and the practical issues surrounding the establishment of the Department of Law at HKU, are discussed in the next chapter.

---

98. Vine: Address to Annual Meeting of the Law Society of Hong Kong, 30 April 1963, *SCMP*, 1 May 1963.

99. Ordinance No. 16 of 1964. The ordinance, among other things, empowered the committee of the Law Society of Hong Kong, subject to the prior approval of the Chief Justice, to make rules on a wide range of activities, including conduct and discipline, and account-keeping. Various sets of rules followed, including the Solicitors Students Rules 1964 (L.N. 105 of 1964) governing enrolment, articles, and the conduct of examinations, which were defined as those set by the Law Society of England and Wales. Much amended over the years, and renamed the Trainee Solicitors Rules in 1992, these continue to be the regulatory framework for the training of solicitors.

100. Vine to Knowles, 18 February 1965, HKUA: Registry File No. 2/1/19/2, encl. 214.

101. Thomson, Registrar General, to Deputy Colonial Secretary, 4 May 1963, HKRS 457-3-19, encl. 1.

Chapter 2

Proposals and Experiments, 1963–1969

When the University of Hong Kong reopened in 1949 after the ravages of World War II it was one of only three freestanding universities in the whole of Britain's colonial empire: the other two were the Royal University of Malta, founded in 1592, and the University of Malaya, founded in 1949 in Singapore. Over the next twenty years universities were established in the West Indies, Guyana, Mauritius, the South Pacific, and over half a dozen African colonies – most of them by amalgamating existing colleges of tertiary education. Helped by Colonial Development and Welfare funds, the new universities were designed in part to equip graduates with professional skills in preparation for decolonization.[1] Many offered legal education, ranging from basic courses for court clerks to law degrees and postgraduate training. The opening of law schools in the New Commonwealth reflected a sense of the inadequacy of training through the Inns of Court: though popular with overseas students, and now offering optional papers on African, Hindu, and Muslim law, the Inns took little account of local conditions, or of the fact that nearly all colonial territories had

---

1. FCO, *Colonial Development and Welfare Acts 1929–79: A Brief Review* (1971), 24–6 & 45. Hong Kong received £1.645 million out of the total £324 million allocated from the funds 1946–1970: over a third of this went to higher education. Hong Kong was also allocated money to fund study in the UK: among those who benefited in the late 1940s were Oswald Cheung, Simon Li, and Patrick Yu, all of whom returned to Hong Kong to practise law: HKRS 41-1-1151 'Ex-Hong Kong Students Awarded Scholarship from Colonial Development and Welfare Fund in 1946' (1946).

fused legal professions, the main exception being Hong Kong.[2] A view was also gaining ground that law students intending to return to practise overseas should be supported by their own governments, and not by the English legal profession or taxpayer.[3]

Among the most advanced of the new law schools was the Faculty of Law at the University of Malaya (Singapore), which admitted its first students in 1957, had its own law journal, and gained official recognition for its law degree as an initial qualification to enter Malaya's legal profession in 1960. By 1962 the faculty had 13 full-time and 17 part-time staff and 370 students, some from as far away as Germany and the US. In 1962 it hosted the first Southeast Asian Regional Conference on Legal Education, attracting delegates from India, Pakistan, Ceylon, Burma, Thailand, Vietnam, Cambodia, Japan, the Philippines, Indonesia, Australia, and Malaya, but none from Hong Kong: the only participant with a connection was Richard Chuan Ho Lim (BA 1927), a Singapore lawyer and politician who had been at HKU during the early heyday of legal studies under George Keeton and had practised as a barrister in Hong Kong in the 1930s.[4] Singapore was 'reaping the benefit of a faculty of law working to a local qualification,' Hong Kong's Attorney General, Maurice Heenan QC, ruefully observed in 1965. The Hong Kong Bar Association was now asking for measures 'to cure the mischief' of Singapore lawyers seeking to practise as barristers in Hong Kong.[5]

It is unlikely that Singapore lawyers posed a threat to legal standards or business in Hong Kong. Nor did rivalry with Singapore play much part in the decision to resume law courses at HKU, even if Singapore was increasingly seen as a pioneer in other aspects of law, such as legal aid and marriage reform.[6] Yet there was a sense that Hong Kong was a problematic outlier among Britain's dependent territories. After the Communist victory of 1949, Mao Zedong's government decided that Hong Kong was a question to be left for some future date. For the time being Hong Kong maintained its status as a British colony with no prospect of independence and with a precarious future. Millions of migrants from China swelled the population from 600,000 in 1945 to over 3 million in 1961; the political complications prompted officials to suspend plans for representative government. United Nations sanctions against China during the Korean War (1950–1953) nearly ended Hong Kong's

---

2. Overseas students accounted for nearly three-quarters of the intake of the Inns of Court in the early 1960s. These issues, as well as legal education within Africa, are discussed in the *Report of the Committee on Legal Education for Students from Africa* (1961) and Senate of the Four Inns of Court, 'Memorandum on Education and Training for the Bar' (1968) in HKRS 877-1-11. The 1961 committee was chaired by Lord Denning and included among its members Professor L.C.B. Gower, later one of the overseas advisors on legal education in Hong Kong.

3. See, for example, the *Ormrod Report*, 71 & 90.

4. University of Singapore, Faculty of Law, *Regional Conference on Legal Education* (University of Singapore, Faculty of Law, 1962).

5. Heenan to Colonial Secretary, 8 April 1965, HKRS 457-3-19, encl. 62; HKRS 41-2-665 'The Legal Practitioners Ordinance' (1966), in particular encls. 5 & 15.

6. The idea that assistance might be given to Hong Kong students to train in law in Singapore was floated in the 1960s: see the comments by John Rear in *Undergrad*, 3 December 1968.

traditional role as an entrepôt for China. Miraculously, abundant cheap labour and refugee capital transformed the city into an industrial powerhouse, providing wealth for investment in business, housing, and education. Unable to return to China or move elsewhere, most migrants made Hong Kong their home. Increasingly, if sometimes grudgingly, the government came to see them and their children as a permanent community, with rights and aspirations. 'We are no staging-post on a great migration; we are a terminus and a goal,' said the Governor, Sir Robert Black, when announcing plans for housing, education and welfare programmes in 1961.[7]

Rapid expansion of tertiary education – including new technical institutes and a second university teaching in Chinese – featured prominently in these plans. In 1959 a seven-year expansion plan was announced for HKU, aimed at doubling the number of students by 1966. Expansion was across the disciplines, with an emphasis on science, medicine, engineering, architecture and other practical subjects. The founding aim of the university as a bridge between China and the Western world now gave way to an emphasis on a greater association with Hong Kong itself – to 'the planning and direction of the communal effort.'[8] Plans for higher education were correlated with research into the colony's demand for 'highly educated personnel.'[9] Financial assistance to students was increased, including the launch in 1969 of a $5.5 million student aid scheme, meaning that 'no student offered a university place would be unable to accept it because of a lack of means.'[10] Syllabuses were made more relevant to Hong Kong's needs. New courses were offered in subjects such as statistics, management studies, and sociology, and a new Faculty of Social Sciences was founded at HKU in 1967. A university qualification might help those who wished to emigrate during these times of uncertainty in Hong Kong and tightening immigration restrictions overseas. But, more and more, a degree was a means of acquiring recognition, employment and status *within* Hong Kong. University education, wrote Bernard Mellor, the Registrar of HKU 1948–1974, was 'one of the larger forces in the emergence of a new identity for Hong Kong.'[11]

There was, however, no place for legal education in these plans. Legal services were statistically insignificant in the broad categories of manpower planning. The assumption

---

7. *Hong Kong Hansard*, 1 March 1961. For the rapid development of education generally during the post-war years, see Sweeting, *Education in Hong Kong, 1941 to 2001*, 137–76.

8. Claude Burgess, Colonial Secretary, introducing the new University Ordinance in 1958, providing, among other things, greater autonomy for HKU. The preamble in the old ordinance, stating as one of the aims of the university 'the maintenance of good understanding with the neighbouring country of China' was left out of the new legislation. *Hong Kong Hansard*, 26 March 1958; Ordinances Nos. 10 of 1911 & 13 of 1958.

9. Notably in the work of the Special Committee on Higher Education, appointed by the Governor in 1964.

10. *SCMP*, 25 May 1969.

11. Bernard Mellor, *The University of Hong Kong: An Informal History* (Hong Kong: Hong Kong University Press, 1980), I, 119.

persisted that this specialized function was best supplied through training in the UK. The university's seven-year expansion plan made no mention of it. Although graduates from HKU in other subjects were prominent in the legal profession,[12] law was now the only major subject not taught at HKU. The effects were beginning to be felt in a dire shortage of lawyers, in both private practice and public service. The calls for action from lawyers, judges, politicians and educators could not go unheeded. Yet difficult questions arose about the kind of teaching to be offered and the form of degree to which it would lead. Would a Hong Kong law degree gain recognition for entry into the local legal profession? Would legislation be passed to ensure this? What further training would be required within Hong Kong so that candidates need no longer go to the UK? How far should Hong Kong law be incorporated into the syllabus? Would the degree carry the same exemptions from professional examinations as a degree from a UK university? How would a law school, with its costly library and highly specialized teachers, be funded and accommodated when there was no provision in the university's already ambitious seven-year expansion plan? In short, how necessary, and how urgent, was this project when there were so many other demands on public and university resources?

University administrators, government officials, and advisors from overseas wrestled with these questions in the 1960s. Hesitant about committing to a long-term plan, they at first devised a halfway solution of part-time courses at the Department of Extra-Mural Studies at HKU leading to an external LLB degree from the University of London. This did not address demands for a syllabus tailored to Hong Kong's needs. Nor did it spare prospective barristers from further training in England. The 'pilot scheme' proved to be costly and largely unproductive. Its shortcomings were obvious from the start, yet the government persisted with it even though the university and its advisors urged the early establishment of a permanent law school. The pilot project delayed the decision. Yet once that decision had been made, events moved quickly, and a Department of Law, with its own LLB degree, opened even before questions of professional recognition and reciprocity had been explored, let alone settled. Though it proved no model for the future, the extramural experiment contributed to the momentum, and supplied the expertise, for a permanent facility to be rapidly established.

This chapter explores the road leading to the opening of the Department of Law at HKU in 1969. It begins with a brief account of the broader social and political climate in Hong Kong in the 1960s and of the state of the legal profession. It highlights some of the differences between Hong Kong law and English law at the time – one of the key justifications for a local law degree, even though reforms were leading towards convergence. It then examines the extramural experiment and its role in the development of legal education in

---

12. Notably, Samuel Gittins (BA 1929), Peter C Wong (BA 1950), John Swaine (BA 1952), and Martin Lee (BA 1960).

Hong Kong before discussing the elements leading to the opening of the Department of Law at HKU. This was, as the department's founding head, Dafydd Emrys Evans, put it, a decision 'taken at the flood', when demand, resources, expertise and resolve all cohered to create an institution which, as some then predicted, would one day achieve a 'special standing in the world.'[13]

Hong Kong in the 1960s

'Hong Kong in 1970: England in 1870. In many ways the resemblance is remarkable,' observed a Foreign and Commonwealth Office (FCO) official at the end of a momentous decade. 'The industrial revolution, pushed on its way by private venture with the spur of quick profits: hypocritical attitudes towards sex and gambling; low rates of tax with extremes of wealth and poverty – all this is true of Hong Kong now as it was of England then.' Power lay in the hands of a few rich men. Despite a general rise in living standards, many families still lived in 'appalling conditions of urban squalor.'[14] Other accounts from the time drew a similar picture. An anonymous polemic, *Hong Kong: A Case to Answer*, depicted a city plagued with drug addiction and violent crime, its laws tilted in favour of a rich bourgeoisie and enforced by a corrupt police.[15] Hong Kong was the 'industrial colony', concluded a more measured survey by HKU academics. Its laissez-faire policies were stuck in the nineteenth century. It had only 'one brand of politics' – authoritarian and undemocratic. Yet rapid economic growth had provided full employment and a continuous rise in real wages, and by 1969 two-fifths of the urban population were living in low-cost public housing. Although irredeemably colonial, the government tried to understand the aspirations of the people. The 'ultimate sanction of violent protest' ensured that it sought 'to act in accord with the general will.'[16]

Hong Kong was convulsed by two episodes of violent protest in the mid-1960s. In the 1966 Star Ferry Riots, youths rampaged for three nights in Kowloon, causing $20 million worth of damage and leading to 1,465 arrests. The riots were triggered by opposition to a proposed increase in ferry fares. A commission of inquiry chaired by the Chief Justice found a pervasive sense of 'not-belonging' among the younger generation. The commission

---

13. D.M.E. Evans, 'Taken at the Flood' in Raymond Wacks (ed.), *The Future of Legal Education in Hong Kong: Papers Presented at a Conference Held by the Faculty of Law, University of Hong Kong to Commemorate Twenty Years of Law Teaching, Hong Kong, 15 and 16 December 1989*; Report by Cowen, Guest, and Pannam, 18 February 1965: HKUA: Registry File No. 2/1/19/2 Part 2, encl. 222.

14. Minute by E.O. Laird, 21 September 1970, FCO 40/264, 5.

15. Hong Kong Research Project, *Hong Kong: A Case to Answer* (Hong Kong Research Project, c. 1974), 7–19.

16. Keith Hopkins (ed.), *Hong Kong: The Industrial Colony: A Political, Social and Economic Survey* (Hong Kong: Oxford University Press, 1971), in particular 57, 207–8, 248, 272, 318. The quotations are from the chapters on the political and legal systems by John Rear, senior lecturer in law at HKU.

also heard, but refused to believe, allegations of widespread police abuses.[17] In 1967, more prolonged disturbances, sparked by labour grievances and fed by Cultural Revolution ideology, escalated into terrorism: 51 people were killed and 832 were injured by bomb explosions, police action and other causes.[18] If the 1966 riots revealed wide gaps between government and people, the 1967 ordeal brought the community together, as people opted for order and stability over revolutionary turmoil. Taken together, the two episodes were a turning point – a 'watershed' – in Hong Kong's history, focusing attention on Hong Kong's social problems and galvanizing the government into a programme of reform.

In the late 1960s and early 1970s, without conceding any formal power and while simultaneously reinforcing the law on public order, the government set in motion a series of reforms aimed at bridging the gaps between officials and people. City district offices were opened in the urban areas to tap public opinion and co-ordinate local services. The powers of unofficial members of the Executive and Legislative Councils (UMELCO) to investigate complaints were expanded. New ordinances were enacted to improve labour conditions (1968), tackle corruption (1970), and modernize the laws on marriage, divorce, family, and inheritance (1967–1972). Localization of the civil service was accelerated. A committee was established to advise on the greater use of Chinese in government, resulting in a declaration of equal status with English in the Official Languages Ordinance 1974.[19] Plans were drawn up for cheaper and more accessible courts of justice, leading to the establishment of the Labour Tribunal (1973) and Small Claims Tribunal (1976), where the use of Cantonese was encouraged and lawyers were excluded.

That many of these new policies came to fruition some years after they were conceived has magnified the 1970s in popular memory as the 'MacLehose decade', a golden era of reform and prosperity under the charismatic leadership of Hong Kong's longest-serving governor, Sir Murray MacLehose (1971–1982). The achievements of this 'government in a hurry'[20] were considerable: compulsory free schooling for all children, a near-eradication of corruption in the police and civil service, an acceleration of public housing provision, new roads and towns, the Mass Transit Railway system, country parks, cultural projects and other public goods, all promoted by a determined and responsive government – 'your government', as MacLehose now termed it. But they also masked the extent to which reforms were already in progress before the 1970s – even before the 'watershed' moment

17. *Kowloon Disturbances 1966: Report of Commission of Inquiry* (Hong Kong: Government Printer, 1967). For the political background, see Gary Ka-wai Cheung, *Hong Kong's Watershed: the 1967 Riots* (Hong Kong: Hong Kong University Press, 2009), Chapter 1, & Lethbridge, *Hard Graft in Hong Kong: Scandal, Corruption, the ICAC* (Hong Kong: Oxford University Press, 1985), Chapter 3.

18. The authoritative account is Cheung, *Hong Kong's Watershed*.

19. Ordinance No. 10 of 1974.

20. A description by MacLehose himself, quoted in Smart and Lui, 'Learning from Civil Unrest' in Bickers and Yep (Eds.), *May Days in Hong Kong*, 158.

of 1966–1967.[21] These reforms sought to address the challenges of a rapidly growing population of migrants from Mainland China and their children – people who, after the Communist revolution of 1949, increasingly saw Hong Kong as a permanent home. The other, less obvious watersheds were the points in the early 1960s when, for the first time, the ratio between the sexes was broadly equal and over half the population (then about 3.5 million) was born in Hong Kong.

One of the main fields of reform in the 1960s was education. Government-funded tertiary education was greatly expanded, with a focus on vocational training, and an increase in the number of scholarships, bursaries, grants and other forms of assistance for students who might not otherwise be able to afford a university education. Among the initiatives of these years was a plan to reintroduce the teaching of law at HKU and make it the basis for training lawyers in Hong Kong, put forward at a time when concerns were being raised about a shortage of lawyers. The plan was to bear fruit in the MacLehose decade, as graduates began to join the legal profession in increasing numbers in the 1970s. But its origins are to be found in the early 1960s.

The Legal Profession in the 1960s

A modernizing, expanding Hong Kong required more lawyers who were familiar with the city's special circumstances. In the mid-1960s Hong Kong had one lawyer for every 12,000 people – a mere sixth of the provision in England and Wales (1:2,000) and about half that in Singapore (1:7,000).[22] The shortage of lawyers was reflected in high legal costs and, some said, low professional standards.[23] Society had moved beyond the days when many private disputes could be settled by family or neighbourhood elders. Nor could lawyers now be seen as a service only for the rich. New flats were being sold at the rate of about 10,000 a year to members of a growing middle class, requiring legal services for the first transaction and for every change of ownership thereafter.[24] Even the poorest had access to professional advice with the introduction of means-and merits-tested legal aid for criminal defendants in the Supreme Court (1962) and civil cases in the Supreme and District Courts (1966). Although progress was too slow for some critics, legal aid found a ready demand in

---

21. Recent research has stressed continuities between the 1960s and 1970s. See, for example, Ray Yep and Tai-lok Lui, 'Revisiting the golden era of MacLehose''Revisiting the golden era of MacLehose and the dynamics of social reforms.' *China Information* 24 (3), 249–72.

22. 'Hong Kong's Need for Lawyers,' note by Heenan, 14 April 1965, HKRS 457-3-19, encl. 63.

23. See, for example, Pannam, Memorandum re. London LLB course, February 1965, HKUA: Registry File No. 2/1/19/2, encl. 189, 12 & 18.

24. Thomson, Registrar General, to Deputy Colonial Secretary, 4 May 1963, HKRS 457-3-19, encl. 1.

divorce proceedings, wage and workers' compensation claims, and 'running-down' cases.[25] There was a general increase in litigation: the Supreme Court's annual civil caseload saw a threefold rise over the decade. To reach the Singapore ratio – and maintain it – Hong Kong would need fifty-five new lawyers a year for the next twenty-five years, the Attorney General, Maurice Heenan, calculated in 1965.[26]

Hong Kong had 310 active lawyers in 1965: 35 barristers, 175 solicitors, and about 100 lawyers in public service, including the Judiciary. Every year, at the Opening of the Assizes, the profession convened in the Supreme Court to hear the Chief Justice's address, a wide-ranging lecture crammed with such detail that some took bets on how long it would last. The small community of barristers, clustered in crowded chambers in Central, dealt mainly with commercial disputes and criminal trials. The 1960s, recalls the barrister Henry Litton, were a relaxed time before the 'creeping pall of seriousness started to envelop the legal profession': a 'brief was then a brief: a few pieces of paper tied up with a pink ribbon,' and 'bundles of authorities' carried into court on trolleys were yet unheard of. 'There was a monthly dinner for the entire profession, in one of the clubs in Sai Ying Pun,' where 'a few members of an even older profession would join the party towards the end of proceedings.'[27]

Though few in number, barristers were serious enough about their interests to have their own body, the Hong Kong Bar Association, founded in 1948 and led in the 1960s by local men such as Leo D'Almada, Oswald Cheung, Samuel Gittins, Gerald de Basto, Charles Ching, and Henry Litton. Apart from its professional concerns (fees, discipline, accommo-dation shortages, and so on), the association was adopting 'a highly critical attitude' towards certain government policies, such as emergency regulations, corporal punishment, and telephone tapping.[28] Along with solicitors and judges, barristers were also prominent in

---

25. The introduction of legal aid lagged behind reforms in England (from the late 1940s) and Singapore (from the 1950s). Prior to legal aid, criminal defendants on capital charges in Hong Kong (and in appeals involving questions of law or at the discretion of judge) had legal representation at public expense. 'Pauper' litigants (with property worth $500 or less) could petition to sue or defend in *forma pauperis*, in which a barrister assigned by the court would represent the litigant without fee but with a share of any costs awarded if the litigant won. Legal aid was extended to the District Court in 1973 for criminal cases where the offence carried a maximum sentence of fourteen years' imprisonment or more (the District Court's maximum sentencing powers were raised from five to seven years in 1973) and to all criminal cases there in 1978. In 1984 it was introduced for committal hearings in magistrates' courts, where, since 1979, a separate system of legal advice was available through the Duty Lawyer Scheme. For the history of legal aid in Hong Kong see the account by Lo Pui-yin (PhD 2012) in Legal Aid Services Council, *Legal Aid in Hong Kong* (Hong Kong: Legal Aid Services Council, 2006), Chapter 2.

26. 'Hong Kong's Need for Lawyers,' note by Heenan, 14 April 1965, HKRS 457-3-19, encl. 63.

27. Litton, 'Recollections of a Brash Young Barrister,' Hong Kong Bar Association, *Hong Kong Bar Association 50th Anniversary*.

28. Roberts to Colonial Secretary, 4 June 1970, HKRS 41-2-955, encl. 1. The issues are discussed in the *Annual Reports* and *Statements* of the Hong Kong Bar Association from the mid-1960s.

the Hong Kong branch of JUSTICE, formed in 1965.[29] They continued to train and qualify overseas, almost invariably in London, although some prepared for their Part I examinations through correspondence courses.[30] The syllabus contained nothing on Hong Kong law. The Hong Kong Bar was nevertheless assuming a local character in composition and outlook. As well as its interest in politics, the Bar Committee was sufficiently concerned about the 'bad odour' created by barristers seeking admission from other jurisdictions – particularly those, such as Singapore, with fused professions – to ask for restrictions. As a result, in 1968 new requirements were added to the Legal Practitioners Ordinance for admission to general practice: residence in Hong Kong of at least eight months, a prohibition on practice as a solicitor in a country with a fused legal profession, and at least twelve months' pupillage, in England or Hong Kong – the first time pupillage became mandatory, reflecting a requirement introduced in England in 1959.[31]

At this time, partly in connection with the planned law school at HKU, the Chairman of the Bar Association and the Chief Justice floated the idea of an Inn of Court in Hong Kong to control the admission and discipline of barristers and concern itself with legal education and law reform. The Hong Kong government supported the idea, not least because it would replace the Bar Committee, which was concerning itself too much, and too critically, with government policies: the inclusion of the Chief Justice and the Attorney General in the governing body would ensure that the Inn confined its public utterances 'to very infrequent comments on subjects of wholly professional concern.' It might be known as 'The Queen's Inn' and have a royal charter, suggested the Attorney General, Denys Roberts. But officials in England found the idea 'pretentious' for such a small Bar and declined to support a charter. The Bar Association revived the idea in 1972, when the first HKU LLB students were about to graduate, this time suggesting that the Inn be created by local ordinance. But the response from London was still negative and the proposal was dropped.[32]

The larger branch of the profession, the solicitors, had formally incorporated the Law Society of Hong Kong in 1907, though its roots went back to the 1850s. A new Legal

29. JUSTICE was the name given to the British section of the International Commission of Jurists. Prominent among its early members were the barrister Samuel Gittins, the solicitor Ian MacCallum, and the judge Alan Huggins. Its early activities included a proposal on legal aid and a detailed critique of the 1968 Public Order Ordinance.

30. 'Report of the First Working Party on Legal Education', in Evans, *Legal Education in Hong Kong*, 50.

31. For particular cases the Supreme Court was also empowered to admit barristers from overseas who did not meet the residential requirement. Hong Kong Bar Association, *Annual Reports 1964*, 7–9, & *1966*, 6–10; Ordinance No. 25 of 1968; *Hong Kong Hansard*, 26 June 1968; HKRS 41-2-665 'The Legal Practitioners Ordinance' (1966).

32. Officials also pointed out that the Inns of Court in London no longer individually exercised disciplinary control of barristers, having passed this function to a senate. Another possible drawback, noted by sceptical officials in Hong Kong, was that it might make fusion of the profession more difficult. Fusion was favoured by the new Chief Justice, Sir Ivo Rigby (1970–1973) despite strong opposition in both branches of the profession. 'Establishment of Inn of Court in Hong Kong' FCO 40/300 (1970); HKRS 41-2-955 'Inn of Court: Proposed Establishment of an … in Hong Kong' (1970); Hong Kong Bar Association, *Annual Statement 1973/74*, 31–3.

Practitioners Ordinance 1964 gave the society disciplinary control over solicitors and their articled clerks and other employees, including clerks and interpreters, against whom accusations about excessive commissions continued to be made.[33] The profession was expanding quickly, partly because of a right of audience in the District Court (established 1953) but mainly because a property boom had spurred a growth in conveyancing, now increasingly for multi-storey, multi-owner buildings. Solicitors' firms – about fifty in all, of varying sizes – were localizing and beginning to employ women: the first of these, Patricia Loseby and Irene Ngan, were admitted in 1953 and 1956 respectively; another dozen were admitted by 1965, though they struggled against prejudice in a male-dominated world.[34] About two-thirds of the 200 solicitors enrolled between 1946 and 1965 were from Hong Kong families: half of these had trained and articled locally. Articled clerks were now numerous enough in Hong Kong to have their own association, though many did not complete their training.

At the same time, training for solicitors in Hong Kong was more closely based on the English model. Whereas earlier examinations for solicitors qualifying in Hong Kong had been adjusted to meet local needs, from 1948 the final examination was to be the one set by the Law Society of England and Wales, following an English syllabus. Candidates had the option to take it in England or Hong Kong, which became one of the overseas centres for the English solicitors' exam. To begin with, most went to England: from 1948, periods of up to a year spent on attending courses and preparing for finals in England (including travelling time) could be counted towards articles, which were now three years for degree-holders and five for most others.[35] Those who trained and qualified in Hong Kong continued to be eligible, after three years' practice, to practise in England without further examination.[36]

---

33. Proposals for an outright ban on commissions for introducing work were opposed by the Law Society, largely on the basis that clerks had formed special relationships with clients because of linguistic barriers between them and solicitors. A compromise was agreed whereby, under rules made by the Law Society, clerks already in employment were allowed to continue to take commissions, set at a ceiling of 20 per cent: some 250 clerks were still receiving them in the mid-1980s, when this policy was discontinued. Ordinance No. 15 of 1964; CO 1030/1341 'Solicitors' Practice Rules, Hong Kong' (1960–1962)' *SCMP*, 2 December 1984.

34. Although born in England, Patricia Loseby was educated in Hong Kong and articled in Hong Kong with her father, Frank Loseby (famous for his assistance to Ho Chi Minh during his detention in Hong Kong 1930–1931). She was also the niece of Charles Loseby QC (a former MP), who practised in Hong Kong 1946–1955. Irene Ngan was the daughter of the Legislative and Executive Councillor Ngan Shing-kwan, founder of the China Motor Bus Company. For the experiences of early female solicitors see Law Society of Hong Kong, *Celebrating a Centenary: The Law Society of Hong Kong 1907–2007* (Hong Kong: The Law Society, 2007), 67–8.

35. Legal Practitioners Ordinance, No. 37 of 1948; HKRS 41-1-7813 'Colonial Solicitors, Examinations for' (1953).

36. The Overseas Solicitors (Admission) Order (No. 1848 of 1964), made under the Solicitors Act 1957, essentially repeated the reciprocal provisions of orders under the Colonial Solicitors Act 1901, but eligibility was now extended to citizens of Commonwealth countries, and to females as well as males. Hong Kong was one of only eight overseas territories whose solicitors could, after three years' local practice, enrol as solicitors in the UK without further examinations. Most of the others, like Hong Kong, had split legal professions at this time. But two (Northern Rhodesia and Nyasaland) had fused professions.

Increasingly, candidates took their exams in Hong Kong, enrolling as students with the Law Society of Hong Kong as required by rules introduced in 1964.[37] Many relied on correspondence courses run by the College of Law in England and, from 1963, lectures laid on by the Department of Extra-Mural Studies at HKU in conjunction with the Law Society and Articled Clerks' Association.[38] Examinations, taking place first at the City Hall and later in the Loke Yew Hall at HKU, were held in two parts, each part concentrated into three full, successive days. English Law Society exam papers were flown in and the scripts were sent back for marking, with microfilmed copies kept as backups. The Law Society of Hong Kong administered the exams and provided invigilators. It took much determination for students to prepare for them without supervised study. Many would wait for the last minute before cramming for the exams. Some would retake them repeatedly, moving back and forth between Hong Kong and England, where the solicitors' examinations were held at different times from those in Hong Kong. One solicitor studied for twenty years before finally qualifying.

Among the solicitors who qualified without ever going to England was Elsie Leung, who embarked on her legal training in 1961. Leung's family was not part of the Hong Kong elite and had no connections with the legal profession. Although she later became one of the first to graduate with a Master of Laws from HKU (1988), she did not take a first degree, and instead took the traditional route to practice through a five-year apprenticeship. As a woman, she faced obstacles in finding a solicitor willing to take her as an articled clerk. One thought that women only wanted to acquire legal qualifications as a form of dowry. Another advised her to learn shorthand and typing in case she did not succeed in the law. Eventually the firm of P.H. Sin & Co. took her on. Her widowed mother paid a premium of $10,000, out of which she received 'pocket money' of $100 a month, rising gradually to $300. She studied and completed assignments through correspondence with the College of Law in England and trained with the senior partner, Peter Sin, a conscientious, if severe, teacher. Leung passed her Part II examination in 1967 and was admitted as a solicitor in January 1968, the sixteenth woman on Hong Kong's Solicitors' Roll.[39] She came to specialize in family law. In the 1970s she was a leading figure in the Hong Kong Federation of Women Lawyers and an advisor to several non-governmental organizations. In 1983 she led the first delegation of Hong Kong women lawyers to Beijing. She entered politics as a founding member of the Democratic Alliance for the Betterment and Progress of Hong

---

37. Students Rules 1964, made under the Legal Practitioners Ordinance.

38. 'Law Studies at the University': Senate paper, 1 April 1964, HKUA: Registry File No. 2/1/19/2, encl. 22; 'Report of the First Working Party on Legal Education' (1966), in Evans, *Legal Education in Hong Kong*, 50; Hughes to Registrar, HKU, 3 April 1964, HKRS 457-3-19; Vine: Address to Annual Meeting of the Law Society of Hong Kong, 30 April 1963, *SCMP*, 1 May 1963.

39. Elsie Leung: interview with the author, 14 November 2017.

Kong (DAB). In 1997 Leung was appointed the first Secretary for Justice of the Hong Kong Special Administrative Region.

Another solicitor who qualified entirely through self-study was Gallant Y.T. Ho, who decided at an early age that he wished to become a lawyer, partly through the influence of his father, a bookseller, who involved him in the family business while he was still at school, taking him to his meetings with solicitors and accountants. The family's finances were not sufficient to allow Ho to train in England. Instead, he acquired an economics degree (with first-class honours) from HKU in 1965. He then took Part I of the English solicitors' examinations, partly in Hong Kong and partly in London, and entered two-and-a-half years of articles with a local solicitor. Ho calculated that the $25,000 premium required for this, combined with the opportunity cost of salary forgone, was enough to buy one or two flats. In parallel, he studied for the external LLB degree with the University of London, which he did not complete, partly because of the disturbed state of Hong Kong in 1967. Ho took the Part II solicitors' examinations in Hong Kong in 1969 and, after two years as an assistant solicitor, went into partnership with a colleague in 1971. In 1977 he started his own firm, Gallant Y.T. Ho & Co., which became one of the largest in Hong Kong, a pioneer in extending legal services to the New Territories and to business ventures in Mainland China. Ho was to become a large benefactor to HKU and other educational institutions and an employer of several of HKU's early law graduates. His sister, Betty Ho, taught law at HKU from 1988 to 2002.[40]

Hong Kong Law and English Law

The English examinations, whether for solicitors or barristers, contained nothing on the law in Hong Kong. How serious an issue this was depended on the area of law in question and the time at which the question was asked. Since the 1840s Hong Kong had variously adopted new English laws, continued to apply old laws, and devised its own laws tailored to the colony's special needs. The many differences in detail had never been systematically set out. Nor, up to the 1960s, did any reliable textbook on Hong Kong law exist.[41] Hong

---

40. Gallant Y.T. Ho, interview with the author, 28 November 2017.

41. The few studies of aspects Hong Kong law then in existence were not encouraging. For example, the report of the Strickland Committee on Chinese law and custom in Hong Kong, published in 1953, warned that many of its conclusions must be considered 'as open to doubt' given the paucity of judicial authority and legislation on the subject. A survey of press laws by the barrister Vermier Chiu in 1963 concluded that the 'discrepancies between the laws of the Mother Country and those of her Colony' only served 'to lay the former open to ridicule,' and hindered the healthy development of a free press in Hong Kong. *Chinese Law and Custom in Hong Kong: Report of a Committee appointed by the Governor in October, 1948* ('The Strickland Report') (Hong Kong: Government Printer, 1953), 7; Vermier Chiu, *A Comparative Study of the Free Press in England and Control of Publications in Hong Kong* (Hong Kong: Newspaper Society of Hong Kong, 1963), 26.

Kong's early legislators had established that the 'Law of England' was to be in full force, except where it was inapplicable to local circumstances – a matter to be decided by the courts. The date of reception of English law was fixed as 5 April 1843, the day on which the colony obtained its own legislature.[42] Any laws enacted in England after that date had no force in Hong Kong unless they were expressly applied to the colony by Parliament, by the Queen through an order in council, or by the legislature in Hong Kong. The legislature, comprising the Governor and an appointed council with an official majority, was required to make laws for the 'peace, order, and good government of the colony.' Officials in London occasionally prompted governors to adopt English-based law reforms. On some issues they supplied model legislation for colonies to enact.[43] Local enactments were subject to disallowance by the Crown: the power was rarely invoked since it eroded the prestige of a governor; in any case, modern communications increasingly allowed prior consultation between the Governor and the FCO.[44]

In 1843 the law of Hong Kong was substantially the same as the law of England. By the mid-1960s, after a century of law reform and codification in England, the Hong Kong legislature had enacted over 3,000 ordinances, some adopting reforms in England, others introducing provisions peculiar to Hong Kong or taking measures from other colonies. Law reform in Hong Kong up to the late twentieth century was a patchy, tardy process, hindered by a shortage of resources and carried out in fits and starts according to the exigencies of the times or the interests of particular officials. Many aspects of Hong Kong law remained as they were despite changes in England. Much of it was 'at least a century behind the times,' complained the solicitor-legislator Woo Pak-chuen in 1965. Modern textbooks no longer dealt with acts long since repealed in England but still in force in Hong Kong, some dating back to the seventeenth century. Finding out exactly what the English law was on a given subject in 1843 was 'no mean task,' the Attorney General acknowledged.[45]

---

42. The provisions are in the Supreme Court Ordinances, Nos. 15 of 1844, 6 of 1845, and 2 of 1846, recast in No. 12 of 1873 and replaced with a new formula in the Application of English Law Ordinance, No. 2 of 1966.

43. The practice was common in the 1930s. Examples include a model ordinance establishing juvenile courts, enacted in 1932 with modifications, the Dangerous Drugs Ordinance, No. 35 of 1935, and the Sedition Ordinance, No. 13 of 1938.

44. The constitutional arrangements were set out in the Letters Patent and Royal Instructions to the Governor, first issued in 1843: the various iterations since 1843 are traced in LegCo InfoPacks LC03/2011–12 and LC04/2011–12 (Legislative Council website). Members of the Legislative Council were appointed by the Secretary of State on the advice of the Governor. Two of the unofficial members were appointed on nomination by particular sectors – one representing the justices of the peace, the other the Hong Kong General Chamber of Commerce. This arrangement was abolished in 1973, when all members were either appointed or *ex officio*. The official majority was effectively ended in 1976, when Governor MacLehose declined to fill all the official seats, while reserving the power to do so if the need arose. Steve Yui-sang Tsang (Ed.), *Government and Politics* (Hong Kong: Hong Kong University Press, 1995), Chapter 2; Miners, 'Disallowance and the Administrative Review of Hong Kong Legislation by the Colonial Office, 1844–1947,' 18 *HKLJ* (1988), 218–48.

45. *Hong Kong Hansard*, 11 March & 8 December 1965.

Hong Kong most closely followed new English legislation on criminal law, with local equivalents of the Homicide Act 1957, Dangerous Drugs Act 1965, Misrepresentation Act 1967, and Theft Act 1968, all of which drew on the English originals.[46] But the colony had so far decided not to adopt the Sexual Offences Act 1956,[47] and attempts to reform laws against abortion and homosexual acts along English lines met resistance from politicians.[48] The criminal courts largely followed English procedure but relied heavily on summary justice. Defendants had no right to elect trial by jury, which was mandatory only for a handful of serious offences. Except in capital trials, juries could, since 1851, return majority verdicts – a rare example in which Hong Kong was ahead of England, where they were only allowed in criminal trials from 1967.[49] Over the years Hong Kong had developed its own punitive legislation for combatting triads, maintaining order, and fighting corruption, sometimes against objections from London: in 1970, for example, the Governor threatened to disclaim responsibility for tackling corruption if FCO officials did not withdraw their opposition to draconian anti-bribery legislation.[50] Governors had also long resorted to emergency regulations, most recently in the 1967 disturbances, when a spate of regulations introduced

46. Homicide Ordinance, No. 16 of 1963, Dangerous Drugs Ordinance, No. 41 of 1968, Misrepresentation Ordinance, No. 47 of 1969, and Theft Ordinance, No. 21 of 1970.

47. Some elements of the 1956 act were incorporated in amendments to the Crimes Ordinance in 1978, (Ordinance No. 25 of 1978), enacted as part of an omnibus revision of the laws on sexual crimes at a time of growing concern about the prevalence of rape and other sexual offences.

48. Until 1972 abortion was illegal and punishable by a maximum life imprisonment, a penalty which continued in force after partial legalization. Since an English case of 1939 it was a defence in common law for a medical practitioner to carry out an abortion to save the life of the mother or prevent her from being reduced to a physical or mental wreck. The Abortion Act 1967 gave statutory effect to this defence. An attempt to introduce similar legislation in Hong Kong was opposed by unofficial executive councillors in 1968. It was eventually enacted for a three-year trial period in 1972, made permanent in 1976, and extended in 1981 to permit abortions within the first twenty-four weeks of a pregnancy in certain other circumstances. In 1969 an attempt was made to introduce English reforms of 1967 decriminalizing homosexual acts between consenting male adults. This provoked public opposition and was abandoned. The law was not reformed until 1991. *SCMP*, 14 & 24 March & 29 April 1969, 24 February & 6 July 1974; *Hong Kong Hansard*, 27 August 1969, 1, 15, & 29 March 1972, & 10 & 25 March 1976; Ordinances Nos. 60 of 1971, 15 of 1972, 12 of 1976, & 13 of 1981; HKRS 41-2-670 1–4 'Penal Code Criminal Consolidation Bill' (1970).

49. The Hong Kong jury originally consisted of six men. In 1858 the size was increased to seven to make it easier to return majority verdicts. Property qualifications for jury service were abolished in 1851, over a hundred years before abolition in England – a change deemed necessary at the time in Hong Kong because of the small pool of colonists available for jury service. Ordinances Nos. 4 of 1851 & 3 of 1858.

50. Officials in the FCO had objected that the provision allowed a court to convict on suspicion, rather than being satisfied beyond reasonable doubt that an actual offence had been committed. They withdrew their objections, and Section 10 of the Prevention of Bribery Ordinance came into force, making it a criminal offence for government employees to be in control of wealth in excess of their official income without a satisfactory explanation. Trench to Secretary of State for Foreign and Commonwealth Affairs, 19 February 1970, FCO 40/295, encl. (10); Douglas-Home to Trench, 14 September 1970, FCO 40/296; Ordinance No. 102 of 1970; Ray Yep, 'The crusade against corruption in Hong Kong in the 1970s: Governor MacLehose as a zealous reformer or reluctant hero.' *China Information* 27(2), 197–221.

new offences, increased the powers of the police and lower courts, and expanded existing powers of detention without trial. Throughout the first century or so of British rule the tendency of legislation – in labour matters, street management, education, the press, religion – had been to criminalize activities deemed likely to undermine social order or challenge colonial authority. Even adultery by Chinese women had been made a criminal offence so that patriarchy might be preserved.[51]

In civil law the pattern was varied.[52] In one of the largest areas of litigation, the law of contract, Hong Kong courts closely followed jurisprudence in England, a sensible course given Hong Kong's position as an entrepôt. But company law was based on the English Companies Act 1929, and not the more recent 1948 act. Bankruptcy law continued to attach a moral stigma to insolvents while other parts of the common law world were removing it. Hong Kong had its own Civil Code, modelled in part on the Indian code and last comprehensively overhauled in 1901. Since World War II the colony had developed its own complicated rent control legislation, the object of much litigation and dissatisfaction. The system of land tenure, through leaseholds from the Crown rather than freehold, placed property law on a different footing from that in England. In addition, the growth of multi-storey buildings in the 1960s encouraged the rise of tenancies in common, a form of severable co-ownership that was no longer possible in England after the Law of Property Act 1925. This act, simplifying the law on real property and conveyancing, was one of many key English statutes with no equivalent in Hong Kong. Solicitors had been petitioning for a modernization of Hong Kong's conveyancing laws since 1885: they renewed their demands in 1965, calling for parts of the English act of 1925 to be adopted.[53]

Another English enactment of 1925 – the Administration of Estates Act, providing, among other things, for more equitable treatment of widows – was also passed over. Non-Chinese domiciled in the colony who died without leaving a will had their estates dealt with under the Statute of Distribution 1670. This state of affairs was part of a general neglect of reforms in family law.[54] Intestate estates of Chinese domiciled in the colony were subject to a separate system. From the early twentieth century judges had attempted to apply Qing law and custom in inheritance disputes – and by extension to other aspects of family

---

51. Chinese Marriage Preservation Ordinance, No. 42 of 1912 (consolidating provisions enacted in 1903 and 1910), still invoked as late as the 1950s, and repealed in 1970 by the Marriage Reform Ordinance.

52. A systematic comparison can be found in the 'Submission of the Second Working Party to the Law Society (of England)' (1969), Annex III, in Evans, *Legal Education in Hong Kong*, 89–106.

53. Reforms eventually came in the Conveyancing and Property Ordinance, No. 62 1984: for its background, and the pre-1984 system, see Sarah Nield, 'Conveyancing and Property Ordinance 1984' 15 *HKLJ* (1985), 48–67.

54. For example, laws permitting married women to own property independently of their husbands were only enacted in 1906 – a generation after similar legislation in England. The Supreme Court did not gain the power to grant divorces (for Christian marriages or their civil equivalents) until 1933, some 75 years after the civil courts in England. Ordinances Nos. 5 of 1906, 35 of 1932, & 9 of 1933.

law – among Chinese inhabitants, using the law and custom current in 1843 as a reference point. The courts had built up an elaborate, if incomplete, body of case law on questions such as marriage rites and adoption practices, the status of concubines, and the circumstances in which a man might take more than one wife. This fulfilled early promises to Chinese inhabitants about protection of their customs. It also reflected a policy of encouraging wealthy merchants to settle in Hong Kong. But it preserved a patriarchal system that had been repudiated in China itself by modern marriage laws enacted in 1930 and 1950. The question of whether Hong Kong should follow these reforms had been raised as early as 1932 in a lecture given to the HKU Law and Commerce Society by the university's solicitor, William Shenton, who correctly predicted that the colony's courts would continue to distribute intestate Chinese estates under the old law.[55] It was odd, said one critic in the 1960s, that 'some of the most cultured people' in the Far East should be subjected to 'theoretical concepts of the customs of a riff-raff living in this same region of Kwangtung Province a hundred and twenty years ago.'[56]

Beginning in 1948, urged on by mass petitions organized by the Council of Women, the government commissioned a series of studies of Chinese law and custom with the aim of modernizing Hong Kong's marriage and inheritance laws – a 'melancholy progression' of committees and reports, as one official described it.[57] More generally, a Law Reform Committee, chaired by the Chief Justice, was established in 1956 to consider whether legal reforms in the UK should be introduced in Hong Kong. Although not all UK legislation was suitable, some conformity was desirable so that Hong Kong had the 'full benefit of the guidance to be obtained from the cases decided in England and the numerous text books produced there,' the committee advised.[58] The committee submitted five reports with recommendations on subjects ranging from defamation to the obligations of hotel proprietors. But it lost steam in the early 1960s and many of its recommendations, including proposals on intestate succession, remained unimplemented.[59] There was a worldwide shortage of law draftsmen, said the Attorney General, Maurice Heenan, in 1963: for as long as resources were inadequate and the priority was to maintain law and order, new legislation would always be the 'Cinderella' of his department.[60]

A reforming energy nevertheless set in under Heenan and his successor, Denys Roberts QC. Heenan expanded the Legal Department by recruiting lawyers from decolonizing

---

55. *SCMP*, 11 April 1932.

56. Haydon, 'The Choice of Chinese Customary Law in Hong Kong,' 11 *International and Comparative Law Quarterly* (1962), 231–50.

57. Secretary for Home Affairs, Ronald Holmes, *Hong Kong Hansard*, 3 June 1970. The main reports were: the Strickland Report (1953), the Ridehalgh-McDouall Report (1957), and the McDouall–Heenan Report (1965), which formed the basis of the 1970 reforms.

58. Hong Kong Law Reform Committee, *Second Report* (Hong Kong: Government Printer, 1957), 2.

59. Hong Kong Law Reform Committee, *Reports* 1957 (2), 1959, 1963, & 1964.

60. *Hong Kong Hansard*, 29 March 1963.

territories in Africa and elsewhere. One of these, Garth Thornton (who arrived in Hong Kong in 1970 and served as Solicitor General 1973–1979), was a leading expert on law draft-ing.[61] From the mid-1960s a succession of ordinances sought to modernize Hong Kong law and align it more closely with that in the UK. The Arbitration Ordinance 1963 imported provisions from an English act of 1950. An ordinance of 1965 placing time limits on legal actions drew on other recent English acts; formerly, laws dating back to 1623 had applied. The Application of English Law Ordinance 1966 recast the whole basis of Hong Kong law by specifying which pre-1843 English statutes were in force in the colony, instead of relying on a general reception: 70 were selected for application, in full or in part, after scrutiny of nearly 1,800 ancient statutes. At first, the wording of the ordinance caused confusion by apparently reviving old common law and applying more recent English acts that were never intended to be applied in Hong Kong.[62] In 1967 Hong Kong's archaic Code of Civil Procedure was replaced by Supreme Court Rules based on new English rules.

In the late 1960s a series of ordinances, drawing on English reforms, modernized Hong Kong's system of family law. The Matrimonial Causes Ordinance 1967 gave the courts greater powers over maintenance and the care of children; amendments in 1971 and 1972 made it easier to obtain a divorce, paving the way for a huge increase in divorces in the 1970s.[63] The Intestates' Estates Ordinance 1971 removed inequalities between male and female heirs. The Legitimacy and Affiliations Proceedings Ordinances 1971 provided for recognition and maintenance of children born out of wedlock. Other ordinances abolished remaining restraints on the property of married women and allowed a husband and wife to sue each other in tort.[64] The aim of these and other reforms, said the Attorney General, Denys Roberts, was to end the idea 'that a man owned his wife like a chattel.'[65] Finally, on 7 October 1971, the Marriage Reform Ordinance came into force: now, only marriages and unions of concubinage contracted under Qing law before that date were recognized by law; all new marriages had to be voluntary, monogamous, and registered. This long-awaited reform prospectively abolished one of the two large areas of Chinese law and custom. The

---

61. His *Legislative Drafting*, first published in 1970 and now in its fifth edition, continues to be one of the leading authorities on the subject for Commonwealth jurisdictions: C.G. Thornton, *Legislative Drafting* (London: Butterworths, 1970).

62. The confusion was eventually resolved by amendments in 1971 and by *Oceania Manufacturing Co. & Another v Pang Kwong-hon & Others* [1979] HKLR 445. The legal issues are traced in John Rear, 'Application of English Law (Amendment) Ordinance,' 2 *HKLJ* (1972), 115–20, Peter Wesley-Smith, *The Sources of Hong Kong Law* (Hong Kong: Hong Kong University Press, 1994), 119–129, & Oliver Jones, 'Noxious Antiquity? Life in Hong Kong without the Application of English Law Ordinance,' 39 *HKLJ* (2009), 793–834.

63. Ordinances Nos. 37 of 1971 & 33 of 1972.

64. For example, to recover damages from a spouse (indemnified by insurance) in a case of negligent driving. Ordinances Nos. 27 & 35 of 1972.

65. *Hong Kong Hansard*, 26 May 1971.

other, New Territories land law, was unaffected for the time being; it was increasingly a matter of litigation as new towns encroached on rural land.

Thus, at a time when proponents of a law school at HKU were stressing the differences between Hong Kong law and English law, a vigorous policy of aligning the two systems was in full swing. This modernizing tendency was to continue in the 1970s with new laws on financial regulation, the environment, consumer protection, and other subjects. The drive for reform was to be boosted further by the creation in 1980 of a permanent Law Reform Commission, which took account of law reforms not only in England but also in other jurisdictions.

The Extramural Experiment, 1964–1969

Despite a pattern of alignment, differences between Hong Kong and English law permeated the comments by experts invited to Hong Kong in the 1960s to advise on legal education. Examiners in London, they pointed out, were acutely conscious of the futility of setting questions that could have little relevance to local conditions, or would be answered differently if local law applied. Lawyers in Hong Kong, on the other hand, tended to minimize the differences. In fact, the lack of knowledge of local law was 'quite remarkable,' an obstacle to reform and an aspect of the generally low quality of legal work.[66] Articles or pupillage in Hong Kong could therefore not be relied on to instil local knowledge. In any case, opportunities were limited by the smallness of the profession and wide variations in standards. Many lawyers admitted that there were some to whom 'they would not like to entrust potential entrants to the profession.' Some solicitors refused to take on articled clerks outside the family for fear they would lure away clients. Those who did continued to require premiums of $10,000 or $20,000 – up to $70,000 in some cases – when articled clerks in England now received salaries. One leading solicitor told the advisors that he always urged prospective clerks to go to England, where they could obtain better, and certainly cheaper, training.[67]

Invited by the university, the overseas advisors were of crucial importance in bringing forward concrete plans for a tailor-made law degree at HKU. Some of their ideas for a model faculty of law took years – even decades – to implement. But their presence instilled a sense of urgency, and their recommendations found a receptive ear in the university and

66. Gower & Cowen, 'Report on Legal Training in Hong Kong', 5 April 1967, HKRS 457-3-19, encl. 98, 5–6; Pannam, Memorandum re. London LLB course, February 1965, HKUA: Registry File No. 2/1/19/2, encl. 189, 17.

67. Some firms justified the premium on the ground of a high dropout rate among articled clerks, for whom expensive office space had to be made available. Gower & Cowen, 'Report on Legal Training in Hong Kong', 5 April 1967, HKRS 457-3-19, encl. 98, 14–15; Pannam, Memorandum re. London LLB course, February 1965, 19. Vine to Knowles, 18 February 1965, HKUA: Registry File No. 2/1/19/2 Part 2, encl. 214.

legal profession. Among these advisors were Zelman Cowen, Dean of Law at Melbourne University, and his colleagues Clifford Pannam[68] and Mary Hiscock;[69] L.C.B. ('Jim') Gower, a leading advocate for reforming legal training in England and a founding member of the Law Commission of England and Wales;[70] and Anthony Guest, a fellow of University College, Oxford.[71] Cowen's interest in legal education in Hong Kong dated back to a visit to HKU in 1956; he made four further visits, in 1961 and 1965–1966.[72] An even older connection, George Keeton, professor of jurisprudence at HKU in the 1920s, now head of law at University College London, was also appointed an advisor, though his planned return visit to Hong Kong did not materialize. The keenest advocates of a law school within Hong Kong were three successive Vice-Chancellors of HKU, Sir Lindsay Ride (1949–1964), William Knowles (1964–1965), and Kenneth Robinson (1965–1972); Chief Justice Sir Michael Hogan (1955–1970); and Attorneys General Maurice Heenan (1961–1966) and Denys Roberts (1966–1973). The Bar Association and Law Society also gave support.

The main obstacle was financial. A law school – or any form of law teaching – fell outside the university's seven-year development plan (1959–1966). This ambitious programme was aimed at doubling the number of undergraduates to over 1,800 by 1966 with a near doubling of government subvention to almost $10 million per annum, as well as substantial new building.[73] Government officials understood the need for legal education but believed that priority should be given to training for 'strategically important occupations' such as doctors and technologists, the need for which was 'almost self-evidently greater.'[74] Their solution to the growing calls for Hong Kong-based legal education was to delay a decision on a law school until later in the decade and, in the meantime, to expand law courses at the university's Extra-Mural Department. The idea was inspired by the Registrar General's plea, in his influential memorandum of May 1963, 'for the sort of part-time law courses he

---

68. Cowen was Governor General of Australia 1977–1982. Dr Clifford Pannam QC practises at the Victoria Bar, and is a world expert on the horse and the law. The Melbourne connection was through the HKU Vice-Chancellor Sir Lindsay Ride, who had been a student there in the early 1920s.

69. Mary Hiscock, now emeritus professor of law at Bond University, was the first full-time female member of the Faculty of Law at the University of Melbourne (1963). She was, among other things, a pioneer in the comparative study of Asian law and legal systems.

70. His article, 'English Legal Training: A Critical Survey' 13 *Modern Law Review* (1950), 137–205, contained a scathing account of the complacent, wasteful, and backward state of legal education at the time. An expert on company law and legal education, Gower was founding Dean and professor of law at the University of Lagos 1962–1965: his fierce resistance to government interference led to his dismissal. He was Vice-Chancellor of Southampton University 1971–1979.

71. Guest (who happened to be visiting Singapore when invited to HKU) was an expert on contract law and the law of credit. He was professor of English law at King's College London 1966–1995.

72. Cowen to Rhodes, in Faculty of Law, University of Hong Kong, *Thirty Years: The HKU Law School 1969–1999* (Hong Kong: Faculty of Law, HKU, 1999), 2.

73. *SCMP*, 20 September 1959.

74. Minutes by AS(GC) & PACS (G), 22 & 24 February 1965, HKRS 457-3-19.

had himself pursued in Glasgow as a youth.'[75] The result was a half-measure, incapable of supplying the needs of the legal profession or of instilling an element of Hong Kong law in legal training. Despite being seen as a cheap option, it turned out to be hugely expensive. At best, it provided a trickle of law graduates pending a more permanent arrangement. Nevertheless, in bringing expertise to Hong Kong it paved the way for the introduction of a more effective and durable system of legal education.

Established in 1957, the Extra-Mural Department of HKU was part of a worldwide movement to expand adult education. The wide variety of courses laid on by the department found a ready demand, particularly among young adults.[76] Increasingly, its focus was on providing professional training to support Hong Kong's economic development. It therefore seemed appropriate to place legal education under its wing – indeed, the Keswick Committee on Higher Education in 1952 had recommended as much, albeit on a smaller scale than was now envisaged. The department already offered courses for Part I of the solicitors' examinations and other aspects of law. Its energetic head, Ieuan Hughes, had a degree in law; in 1964 he became a founder committee member of the Association of Law Teachers and Schools in South East Asia, an organization in which the Law Faculty at the University of Singapore, now held up as a model of its kind, was taking a leading role.[77]

The extramural pilot scheme consisted of a full law curriculum, taught to part-time students, and leading to an external LLB degree from the University of London. The degree would exempt prospective solicitors from their Part I exams and cut articles from five to two years, obviating any need to go to England, since they could already take their finals in Hong Kong. Prospective barristers would still need to qualify in England, but the LLB would exempt them from the Part I exams (or most of them) and reduce their time spent in England by at least a year.[78] Hasty negotiations between HKU and the University of London resulted in approval for teaching to commence in October 1964 for a part-time degree programme lasting three years: the usual length of part-time degrees was five years, but the Hong Kong programme was treated as a full-time one. The syllabus was to be the same as that taught in London: a proposal for developing an optional course in Hong Kong law did not come to fruition, though some teachers took the trouble to point out differences between English and Hong Kong law as they themselves acquired an understanding of local law.[79] Admissions were subject to approval by the University of London, whose

---

75. Mellor, *The University of Hong Kong: An Informal History*, I, 141.

76. For its history see Lawrence M.W. Chiu & Peter Cunich, *HKU SPACE and Its Alumni: The First Fifty Years* (Hong Kong: Hong Kong University Press, 2008), in particular 112–17, which deals with the external LLB degree.

77. The faculty organized two regional conferences in Singapore, in 1962 and 1964. Hong Kong sent delegates to the second. Harry E. Groves, 'Southeast Asian Regional Conference on Legal Education,' 15 *Journal of Legal Education* (1962–1963), 429–33; HKU, *Vice-Chancellor's Report*, 1964–1965, 60.

78. Minute by PACS(G), 3 July 1964, HKRS 457-3-19.

79. John Rear, interview with the author, 2 December 2017.

staff would also mark examinations. The pilot project was to be for five years: a decision would be taken in 1967 on whether a full department of law, with its own degree, should be established at HKU, admitting the first students in 1969.[80]

The government provided funding of $1.4 million for the first three years, rising to just over $2 million for the full five years. With much difficulty and expense, premises were leased on the eighth floor of a new building at 92–94 Queen's Road Central (later known as the Chiao Shang Building) opposite Central Market, which housed on its lower floors the China Merchandise Emporium, selling goods made in Communist China: the 'town centre', as it was known, was temporarily moved to other buildings during the 1967 disturbances.[81] A central location was considered essential for part-time students, who would need to attend classes after work.[82] Students were to be given access to the Legal Department's library in the Central Government Offices. Applications for enrolment in the course were invited in August 1964: 194 applied, most of them civil servants, including a large number of police officers, and more than a quarter with university degrees; 30 were accepted for classes commencing in October.[83] The response promised a 'flying start,' remarked the University Registrar, Bernard Mellor.[84] Proponents of a permanent law school took it as overwhelming evidence of pent-up demand.

Finding teachers was a more serious challenge. In the hurry to get courses off the ground in 1964, teaching began with four part-time lecturers drawn from the local legal profession. In December Clifford Pannam, senior lecturer in law at the University of Melbourne, arrived for a three-month visit to organize tutorials, by himself and additional part-time staff, and to evaluate the quality of teaching and the prospects of the scheme. His assessment was mixed. The lecturer on contract was a skilled teacher. The lecturer on constitutional law, though confused by students' questions, showed promise. But the Roman law lecturer admitted he was only 'one short step ahead of his class' and believed that *four-hour* one-on-one cramming sessions were the best way of getting students through their exams. The lecturer on the legal system was 'a problem' whose off-the-cuff approach had Pannam squirming. 'He can't answer questions. He contradicts himself. He gets confused.' He was

80. Senate Paper 86/364 'Law Studies at the University', 1 April 1964, HKUA2/1/19/2 ('Law Courses 1962–66, Vol. I Part II'), encl. 22; AS(GA) to PACS(G), 17 May 1965, HKRS 457-3-19.

81. Parts of the centre were moved to the International Building in Central and parts to the main HKU campus. The move, in July 1967, had to be done by government staff with police support because private contractors refused to undertake the task. Evans, 'Taken at the Flood', 30; memo by Harrison, Government Secretariat, 22 July, HKUA, Law Department (1967–1968) VC's Numbered Files (1960s–1970s) Box 2 Folder 5 VC 233/66, encl. 50.

82. The premises only became available in March 1965: in the early months lectures were held in the Legislative Council Chamber on Lower Albert Road and tutorials were conducted in the Labour Department's premises in Rediffusion House, Wan Chai. Pannam, Memorandum re. London LLB course, February 1965, 11.

83. 'Applicants Registered for LLB', HKUA 2/1/19/2 ('Law Courses 1962–66, Vol. I Part II'), encl. 107.

84. Mellor to Keeton, 3 September 1964, HKUA 2/1/19/2 ('Law Courses 1962–66, Vol. I Part II'), encl. 104.

a 'complete failure in a very important subject.'[85] Pannam and other advisors believed that
the nature of the pilot project, combined with the cost of living and 'the political sword
of Damocles' over Hong Kong's future, offered little incentive to experienced teachers
from overseas. Despite this scepticism, the Extra-Mural Department managed to recruit
three full-time staff in 1966–1967. Among them, Dafydd Evans and John Rear were to be
founder-members of the Department of Law; the third, Vincent Shepherd, returned to
England in 1969, having left his mark on Hong Kong as a TV personality and commenta-
tor, known (as the blurb for his column in the *China Mail* put it) 'for his opinions on just
about everything.'[86]

Pannam believed that the very existence of the pilot project created a risk that 'people
in high places' would mistakenly see it as a first step towards satisfying Hong Kong's needs
for local legal education. In fact, it was 'little more than an attempt to establish a colonial
coaching college, a sort of oriental Gibson and Weldon,' a 'cram course' designed 'to enable
students to acquire a London LLB in three years.' Aimed at people in full-time employment, the demand for it bore no relation to the demand for places in a university faculty.[87]
Although Pannam made no predictions about the outcome, the results were disappointing,
even when set against the high overall failure rate for external law students at the University
of London, which was 40–50 per cent in some years. The high dropout rate caused anxiety
among teachers. Over half of the students withdrew by the end of year one through
failure or loss of interest. Out of the eighty-eight students in the five-year pilot scheme,
1964–1969, only fifteen obtained degrees.[88] Since students were expected to complete the
part-time programme in three years, when other external LLB students took five years, this
was hardly surprising. Yet it confirmed early concerns among legislators about the cost-
effectiveness of the scheme. The undertaking was 'not one for the faint-hearted,' observed
Dafydd Evans.[89] Those who persevered were 'mature' students with various day jobs: they
consisted of 'government servants, legal clerks, a banker, and a number in private business,'
Evans recalls, 'but none was anything like a typical law undergraduate.'[90]

Among the fifteen who graduated, several were to play important roles in law and other
fields. Sir Joseph Hotung, a businessman, philanthropist and connoisseur of the arts, sat on

85. Pannam, Memorandum re. London LLB course, February 1965, 3 & 7–10.

86. *SCMP*, 1 May 1968.

87. Pannam, Memorandum re. London LLB course, February 1965, 13.

88. Chiu and Cunich, *HKU SPACE and Its Alumni: The First Fifty Years*, 116; John Rear, interview with the author, 2
December 2017; Phillips to Colonial Secretary, 19 July 1966, HKUA, Registry File No. 2/1/19/1, encl. 30; 'University
of Hong Kong: Law Studies' (agenda item for Finance Committee), 10 August 1966, HKRS 457-3-19, encl. 90; *Vice-
Chancellor's Report*, 1964–1965, 60.

89. Concerns about the high cost per student were raised in the Finance Committee of the Legislative Council.
Some students deferred taking their degree examinations beyond the end of the pilot project in 1969, so the number
of fifteen may not be final. Minute by AFS(R), 10 July 1964, HKRS 457-3-19.

90. Evans, 'Taken at the Flood', 13 & 15.

various government bodies, including the Judicial Officers' Recommendation Committee, and was appointed the first chairman of the Hong Kong Arts Development Council in 1994. Dennis Minns became managing director of the Hongkong and Shanghai Bank's Trustees' Division and was closely involved with several of Hong Kong's largest charitable funds. Paulette Tsoi, a French citizen married to a Hong Kong businessman, was the first Frenchwoman to be admitted to practise as a solicitor in Hong Kong, in 1971. Five of the graduates were police officers. Among them was Superintendent Michael Ko Chun, who had joined the police force as a corporal in 1950 and who, after retiring from the force in the 1980s, became a lawyer. The Department of Extra-Mural Studies continued to lay on courses for the University of London external LLB, although until a reorganization in 1983 the courses were not as comprehensive as they had been under the pilot scheme.[91]

From Kiddy Car to Grand Prix: The Accelerating Momentum for a Law School

In February 1965, barely six months into the extramural project, the overseas advisors Zelman Cowen and Anthony Guest joined Clifford Pannam in Hong Kong to assess progress and advise HKU on the further development of law studies as an internal discipline. They were asked to focus on the extramural scheme – the adequacy of staffing and facilities, admission policies, courses for the second and third years, the prospects of an optional paper on Hong Kong law, and so on. At this stage, questions about the future, including the possibility of '*internal* law studies' as a 'permanent feature of the University' in 1969 or beyond, were merely hypothetical, to be dealt with later by separate policy reviews. Their visit, recalls Dafydd Evans, was 'probably the single most important factor' in getting the extramural experiment 'up and running.'[92] Yet their report passed quickly over the extramural scheme, dealing with most of the questions relating to it in a scant one-page appendix. Instead, the thrust of the report was a powerful justification for the immediate establishment of a faculty of law, to start teaching in 1967.

The 1965 report set out the 'many cogent reasons for now proceeding with a more realistic and comprehensive programme of legal studies.' These were by now familiar in legal circles: the shortage of lawyers, the strong demand for legal education, the 'irrelevance of a legal education leading to a London LLB' when so much of Hong Kong law differed from English law. Local systems of legal education now existed in most former colonies, the report pointed out. Yet it was a mistake to view them merely as a product of independence: Hong Kong's continuing status as a dependent territory had no great bearing on the issue. Not only would a law faculty provide a relevant education, but it would also contribute to 'the formulation, systematization, and reform of the local law,' as staff produced

---

91. Chiu and Cunich, *HKU SPACE and Its Alumni: The First Fifty Years*, 116–17.
92. Evans, 'Taken at the Flood', 14.

much-needed texts on Hong Kong law. The faculty would contribute to the wider com-munity of social studies and offer a sound liberal education even for those who chose not to enter the legal profession. It would also attract a higher quality of teachers than those willing to apply for positions in extramural courses. There was a real possibility that it 'could develop into a law school with a special standing in the world.'[93]

For these reasons the report recommended that the university should resolve on the immediate establishment of a law faculty and at once advertise for a dean and a senior lecturer to prepare curriculums, advise on the design of a building and the formation of a library, and establish relations with the profession. The magnitude of these tasks was so great that it would not be practical to offer courses for a tailor-made Hong Kong LLB until 1967. In the meantime, the extramural courses leading to the London LLB should continue, reinforced with additional full-time staff and part-time practitioner-teachers. There should be no gap in offering law courses, and the new faculty might continue to offer part-time evening courses to satisfy the obvious demand. But planning for the new faculty should have first claim on the time of the dean and the senior lecturer.

The advisors recommended a four-year, full-time course of studies for a Hong Kong LLB – longer than that required for the London external LLB because of the need for a preparatory year to train students in logic and critical analysis and to provide courses in subjects such as history, politics and economics. The non-legal component was desirable so that the course provided a truly liberal education rather than mere technical training: this could even extend in some cases to joint degree courses in arts and law. The faculty should have an intake of 50 students – a figure the advisors regarded as the minimum economic size. It was essential for it to be accommodated on campus, preferably in its own building, with a large library at its heart and a courtroom for moots. External examiners should be appointed to maintain academic standards, and strong relations should be forged with the legal profession, the Judiciary and the government to ensure that the degree provided a foundation for professional training. It was not necessary to await professional recognition of the Hong Kong LLB before moving to establish a faculty. That could be worked out later. The immediate establishment of the faculty, however, was 'a matter of urgency.'

The university found the advisors' report so compelling that within a few weeks it obtained Senate and Council approval of its recommendations, on the understanding that the project would not have to compete with other expansion plans and that the internal LLB degree would start in a department of law rather than a full-blown faculty. Most of the funding – estimated at over $11 million for capital outlay and expenditure in the first four years – would have to come from an additional government grant. The Bar Association,

---

93. Report by Cowen, Guest, and Pannam: HKUA: Registry File No. 2/1/19/2 Part 2, encl. 222 & HKRS 457-3-19, encl. 60.

the Law Society, and the Attorney General gave their strong support.[94] The government, however, dug in its heels. Officials believed that the advisors had prejudged the planned longer-term policy review when the extramural scheme had barely got off the ground. They were not surprised that the proposal had sailed through the university's Council, apparently without discussion, when it did not have to compete with other plans. They were taken aback by the 'excessive' financial implications and continued to hold the view that the need for 'doctors, dentists, technologists, etc.' had a stronger claim. The proposal, 'pressed forward with gay abandon', seemed to be 'an attempt to graduate straight from the kiddy car to Grand Prix racing.' Despite support from the Attorney General, the government declined to commit funds. The shortage of lawyers was not so great a concern as to warrant 'an absolute priority to this field of studies,' the acting Colonial Secretary informed the Vice-Chancellor in May 1965.[95]

The rebuff did not dampen support for the idea of a law school. On the contrary, the momentum grew rapidly. Attention now shifted to the supply of barristers. In his address at the Opening of the Assizes in January 1966 the Chief Justice, Sir Michael Hogan, publicly joined the campaign. He pointed to the strain on the courts and legal profession caused by a one-third increase in caseload in 1965. He had 'considerable anxiety' about whether the profession in its present numbers would be able to carry the burden of a planned expansion of legal aid. He asked 'how much longer we can accept a system whereby those who seek to be admitted as barristers in this territory must go to England to obtain their primary qualification.' The answer, he said, was to 'press more strongly for the opening of the long awaited Faculty of Law in the University of Hong Kong and link that faculty with admission to the Bar.'[96]

Later that year Hogan appointed a working party (the 'First Working Party') under the Senior Puisne Judge, Sir Ivo Rigby, with representatives from the professions, the universities, and the Attorney General. Its tasks were to consider, *first*, the practicalities of training in Hong Kong, if possible through collaboration with the universities, to enable a candidate to qualify for the Bar without the need to go overseas; and, *secondly*, whether existing arrangements for solicitors to obtain their qualifications without going overseas were satisfactory. The First Working Party's proceedings were not entirely smooth. One contentious issue was the number of students to be admitted to a local university law course, the professional bodies being worried about 'dilution of their earnings if there were to be a "flood" of new recruits freed from the financial and cultural problems' of having to qualify in the

---

94. HKU Council paper 79/365 'Law Studies', 12 April 1965, Council Resolution, 22 April 1965, & Knowles to Colonial Secretary, 11 May 1965, HKUA 2/1/19/2 ('Law Courses 1962–66, Vol. I') encls. 231, 267, & 276.

95. Minutes by AS(GA), 17 May 1965, DFS, 21 May 1965, & Ag.CS, 22 May 1965, & Hamilton to Knowles, 27 May 1965, HKRS 457-3-19, encl. 69.

96. *SCMP*, 14 January 1966.

UK.[97] Initially, both the Bar and the solicitors' representatives also clung to the idea that graduates with a law degree from HKU should still be required to take the final examinations set by the English Bar or the Law Society of England and Wales as qualifications to practise in Hong Kong, arguing that this would maintain standards, ensure reciprocity, and retain the close association between Hong Kong and English law at a time when disparities between the two systems were lessening. The university and the Attorney General objected that this would frustrate the aim of introducing training in local law and would still require prospective barristers to go to England. They also pointed to the widespread dissatisfaction with the existing state of legal education in England.[98]

The Bar Association eventually withdrew its proposal that HKU law graduates should take the English Bar final examinations after a noncommittal response from judges overseeing legal education in England. Partly through the intervention of Gower and Cowen during their visit to Hong Kong in early 1967, the Law Society was persuaded to withdraw a minority report insisting that graduates intending to become solicitors should have to take the English Part II exams: this concession was subject to provisos that there would continue to be reciprocity for Hong Kong solicitors to practise in England, that a 'Law Council' would be created to control conditions for admission and the content of postgraduate training, and that the postgraduate course for solicitors would be not less than two and a half years – provisos which, though vaguely reflected in the final report, were not met in full, partly because of opposition by the university to external control over its teaching.[99] Reporting in June 1967, the First Working Party unanimously recommended the establishment of a three-year LLB honours degree in a Department of Law at HKU, incorporating a strong component of Hong Kong law. For intending barristers and solicitors, a further professional examination and a period of articles or pupillage would be sufficient for admission without the need to go overseas. This route to practice should be in *addition to*, not instead of, the existing routes through overseas qualifications. Finally, the First Working Party recommended the creation of a statutory board on legal education, along the lines demanded by the Law Society, comprising representatives of the Judiciary, the Attorney General, HKU, and both branches of the legal profession.[100]

---

97. Rear, 'Rear Window' in Faculty of Law, University of Hong Kong, *Thirty Years*, 9.

98. The debate is traced in 'Law Dept – Working Party on Local Qualifications of Lawyers (1966–1968)' HKUA, VC 233/1/66/7/8.

99. The postgraduate course, when eventually established, was for one year only. The First Working Party's report contained a modified version of the Law Society's views on a 'Law Council', and the university went along with this in the interests of reaching agreement. However, under amendments to the Legal Practitioners Ordinance in 1972, this was established only as the Advisory Committee on Legal Education, with advisory functions only. T.S. Lo to Rigby, 13 April 1967, Robinson to Rigby, 24 April 1967, and Robinson to Gower, 22 May 1967, 'Law Dept – Working Party on Local Qualifications of Lawyers (1966–68)' HKUA, VC 233/1/66/7/8, encls. 40 & 48.

100. 'Report of the First Working Party on Legal Education' in Evans, *Legal Education in Hong Kong*, 50.

In parallel, the overseas advisors addressed these questions in a second report – this time by Zelman Cowen and Lawrence Gower – submitted to the Vice-Chancellor in April 1967. They were now able to speak of an 'overwhelming' case, 'accepted by everybody,' for a local law degree. They amplified arguments in the 1965 report. The extramural scheme was patently unsatisfactory. The attempt to cover the whole degree course by evening work in three years had proved beyond the capabilities of most students: it was 'difficult to understand' why the University of London was prepared to treat a palpably part-time course as a full-time one.[101] The English Bar and solicitors' examinations were increasingly coming under criticism as tests of competence for practice in England: it would be 'lamentable' if they continued to be the test of professional competence in Hong Kong. Practically everywhere in the common law world the trend was towards institutional training. In Hong Kong the only body capable of undertaking this was HKU. The advisors recommended that the basic qualifications for legal practice in Hong Kong should be an LLB from HKU (or another approved university[102]), a post-degree professional course and an examination conducted by the university in conjunction with the professional bodies, and a further period of pupillage, articles, or restricted right to practise.

These recommendations converged with those by the Chief Justice's First Working Party. The advisors sketched out the curriculum and staffing requirements for an LLB honours degree course, reluctantly accepting that three years, rather than four, was more realistic if the aim was to increase the supply of lawyers. The suggested curriculum included not only the standard legal subjects – taught primarily with Hong Kong law as the basis – but also English literature, sociology, economics, and other non-law courses, intended partly to encourage a critical approach. For graduates wishing to become lawyers, the advisors recommended an additional, compulsory nine-month course, dealing with practical issues, and taught mainly through 'learning by doing' in moots, mock trials, a legal aid clinic, and other hands-on exercises. This would be followed by a period of restricted, supervised practice as pupil or articled clerk, on completion of which the barrister or solicitor would be able to practise independently.[103] The advisors stressed the importance of a strong law

---

101. Report by Cowen and Gower, 5 April 1967, HKRS 457-3-19, encl. 98.

102. The report noted that the Chinese University of Hong Kong had no plans for teaching law, except in courses on business administration, and suggested that, since its language of instruction was Chinese, it might be difficult for it to teach a comprehensive programme of English law. On the other hand, it would be well equipped to teach and research Chinese law and custom.

103. At the time, the usual practice was for barristers to serve pupillage after call to the Bar (mandatory pupillage had not yet been added to the Legal Practitioners Ordinance). Solicitors, in contrast, had to complete their articles *before* being admitted to practise. The advisors recommended this be changed so that solicitors could be admitted to a restricted practice of law before embarking on articles: this, they said, would help avoid the treatment of articled clerks as 'sweated labour' and encourage payment of a salary rather than the taking of a premium. The recommendation was not pursued, and when pupillage became mandatory in Hong Kong in 1968, barristers were required to complete their pupillage before being admitted to an unrestricted practice of law.

library: 'to the lawyer the library is what the laboratory is to a scientist.' They also recommended the establishment of a law journal to enhance the prestige of the law school and
provide a quick means of publishing writing on local law.

Taken at the Flood: The Decision on the Department of Law at HKU

The reports by the overseas advisors and the Chief Justice's First Working Party armed the
university with strong justifications for establishing a law school and securing funding. The
path was assisted by the creation in 1965 of the University Grants Committee (UGC), a
government-appointed body tasked with advising on the funding of universities throughout Hong Kong in the light of community needs. With the opening of the Chinese
University of Hong Kong in 1963, the colony now had two universities with a total student
population of over 4,000, expected to rise to 6,000 in the early 1970s. Modelled on a body
in the UK, the UGC was intended to provide impartial and expert advice on an increasingly complex area of public spending. Its first chairman was Michael Herries, the taipan
of Jardine, Matheson & Co. Later chairmen (when the committee was for a time known
as the University and Polytechnic Grants Committee or UPGC) included two future chief
justices (Yang Ti Liang 1981–1984 and Andrew Li QC 1989–1993) and the barrister and legislator John Swaine QC 1984–1988. Six of its first nine members were overseas academics,
most based in the UK. The two others were the industrialist Ann Tse-kai and the barrister
Patrick Yu, who used his voice on the committee to drive home the case for a law school.

One of the UGC's first acts was a 'visitation' to HKU in early 1966, during which Vice-
Chancellor Robinson raised the proposed Department of Law. The UGC took the view that
a local law degree would be feasible only if graduates, in particular intending barristers, had
an opportunity to proceed to practise as a lawyer without going overseas.[104] The reports by
the Chief Justice's First Working Party and the overseas advisors in 1967 outlined a scheme
for achieving this, and, though the details still had to be devised, the university indicated
that it was prepared to organize the postgraduate pre-admission courses recommended in
the reports. Discussions between HKU and the UGC crystalized into a request for funds of
$7.2 million for the preparations, capital outlay, and recurrent expenses of the Department
of Law 1968–1974.

As these proposals were being drawn up, a final obstacle arose in the form of opposition
from unofficial members of the Governor's Executive Council, who considered the First
Working Party's proposals to be 'too lavish' when they were put to the council in early 1968:
in particular, they believed that a four-year full-time programme (a three-year LLB and a

---

104. UGC, Report October 1965 to June 1968, 14 & 24; Herries to Robinson, 19 May 1966, Robinson to Herries, 5 July
1966, & Robinson to Gower, 20 March 1967, HKUA, Registry File No. 2/1/19/2 'Academic Affairs (Courses/Law)'
(1966); Robinson to Mellor, 7 July 1966, Registry File No. 2/1/19/3 'Working Party on Law Courses' (1966–1972).

one-year postgraduate course) 'could not readily be justified in Hong Kong.'[105] A decision was deferred while meetings took place between Attorney General Denys Roberts and the three other lawyer-members of the council – Kwan Cho-yiu, Kan Yuet-keung, and Woo Pak-chuen. They came up with pared-down plans that were quite different from those agreed by the First Working Party. Their discussions centred on a 'Modified University Plan' consisting of two years of general law plus a year of 'solicitor or barrister subjects', with the award of an LLB at the end of the third year – a compression of the undergraduate degree and the postgraduate course into three years rather than four.[106]

These vague and ill-conceived plans were received with dismay by the university. Dafydd Evans, now deeply immersed in the planning of the proposed law school, observed that the 'Modified University Plan' would require 'reducing the *status* of law as an academic force' and lead to 'a sterile feeding of fact without argument' on the lines of the old Gibson & Weldon system. It would attract only second-rate staff and would produce a degree that failed to measure up to academic standards. The plan was out of touch with experience elsewhere in the world and the 'three Honourable gentlemen' seemed to be unaware how much more complex the law had become in their professional lifetimes. 'I am afraid that I have little patience with certain local practitioners who have had the benefit of reading jurisprudence at Oxford or Cambridge and are now bent on the creation of a second-rate University in Hong Kong for those not sufficiently privileged to go abroad for their education.' The university 'ought to have a Law School and it would be of great long-term benefit to Hong Kong, but it should not have one at any cost,' Evans advised.[107]

A revised submission to the Governor's Executive Council reflected the university's concerns, stressed the three-year nature of the proposed LLB and the possibility of including some 'professional' subjects in the third year, and left open the exact length and format of the pre-admission course (which, it was then assumed, would be part-time). The unofficial members of the Executive Council relented, and the council accepted the First Working Party's report.[108] In April 1968 the UGC informed the university that approval in principle had been given to the First Working Party's proposals. In July the government

---

105. Executive Council memoranda XCR(68)8 & XCR(68)71 & Executive Council minutes, 9 January 1968.

106. The other two proposals were (1) a 'Law School Plan' along the same lines as the 'Modified University Plan' but with the award of a professional qualification rather than an LLB; and (2) a course of extramural lectures totalling eighteen months, preparing students for the English solicitors' and bar examinations (on the assumption that the English Council of Legal Education would permit the bar finals to be taken in Hong Kong, without the usual requirement of dinners at the Inns of Court). Robinson to Evans, 12 February 1968, HKUA: Law Department (1967–1968) VC's Numbered Files (1960s–1970s) Box 2 Folder 7 VC 233/67, encl. 75.

107. Kwan, Kan, and Woo had taken their law degrees at the University of London. Evans was also disappointed with Roberts's apparent unwillingness or lack of political influence 'to talk the Unofficial Members of ExCo down to the ground.' Evans to Robinson, 13 February 1968, HKUA: Law Department (1967–1968) VC's Numbered Files (1960s–1970s) Box 2 Folder 7 VC 233/67, encl. 76.

108. Executive Council memorandum XCR(68)71 & Executive Council minutes, 12 March 1968.

gave final approval for a Department of Law within the Faculty of Social Sciences at HKU: although many had assumed that, as in other universities, there would be a freestanding faculty of law, HKU had resolved that no faculty should consist of fewer than three departments, as would be the case with law.[109] Courses for a three-year LLB honours degree would begin in September 1969 with an intake of forty students.[110] The plan was announced by the Attorney General, Denys Roberts, in the Legislative Council on 22 May, in reply to a question by Woo Pak-chuen.[111]

The challenge now was to implement the plan with a lead-time of little more than a year. The new degree course required staff, syllabuses, and accommodation. Looking further ahead, preparations had to be made to ensure that the degree was recognized for admission to practise in Hong Kong. It was here that the extramural scheme played a vital part. Since 1966, law courses there had been taught mainly by full-time staff, led by Dafydd Evans. Then in his late twenties, Evans had been seconded from the London School of Economics (LSE) through the efforts of his fellow Welshman Iuean Hughes.[112] In addition to his teaching duties, Evans set about co-ordinating the longer-term development of legal education. Behind the scenes he had argued the case for a system based on local qualifications and had extensively redrafted the original draft report of the Chief Justice's First Working Party. When the prospect of a department of law became clearer, he immersed himself in the practical planning.

In 1967 Evans and his two colleagues John Rear and Vincent Shepherd joined the board of the newly established Faculty of Social Sciences, where the planned Department of Law was eventually to be located. Quite unexpectedly, Evans was elected the first Dean of the Faculty and tutor for admissions 1967–1968, positions that fell completely outside the role for which he had been recruited: Evans was no doubt a neutral arbiter at a time when various subjects were jostling for resources in a rapidly developing faculty; the evening timetable of the extramural courses also left him with time during the day. His work as Dean involved him in subjects ranging from psychology to statistics, but not, for the time being, law. The experience, Evans recalls in his memoir 'Taken at the Flood', was invaluable when he turned to the task of 'building from the ground floor up' the new Department of Law.[113]

The technical aspects of the new department – administrative, financial, and curricular – were by now easy to deal with, Evans recalls. Other 'major problems' were not so straight-forward. 'Staff, premises, and library could not be conjured up out of thin air.' There was a

---

109. Following a recommendation in the Jennings-Logan Report (1953).

110. Herries to Robinson, 26 April 1968 HKUA, Registry File No. 2/1/19/4 'Academic Affairs (Courses/Law)' (1968); UGC, Report October 1965 to June 1968, 14 & 24; Evans, *Legal Education in Hong Kong*, 9–10.

111. *Hong Kong Hansard*, 22 May 1968; Evans, *Legal Education in Hong Kong*, 5–9.

112. Evans, 'Taken at the Flood', 14.

113. Evans, 'Taken at the Flood', 16.

universal shortage of law teachers. The Extra-Mural Department's town centre was 'manifestly inadequate' yet there was no room for the planned Department of Law on campus. What passed for a law library was 'patently understocked.' Having earlier dragged its feet, the government now insisted that the new department should start teaching in September 1969. 'At the best of times, to attempt to meet such a deadline would have been laughed out of court but the government was quite determined that the initial intake should not be delayed by one year (as I proposed in vain),' Evans recalls. The difficulties were compounded by the fact that Evans's secondment ended in autumn 1968, when he returned to his position at LSE. At this time LSE was a hotbed of New Left student protests and 'not a particularly happy place.' Evans gladly applied for the Chair of Law and headship of the department at HKU when it was advertised internationally later in the year. He had not been the first choice: in 1967, on the advice of L.C.B. Gower, who thought Evans too lacking in seniority, Vice-Chancellor Robinson had approached Gerald Dworkin, then at Monash University, but Dworkin had declined; Gower had then tried to promote another candidate from Monash, H.B. Connell.[114] Evans's appointment as professor and head of the planned Department of Law was announced in February 1969. He made a brief visit to HKU during the Easter vacation 'to keep things moving': the Department of Law was formally established on 1 April 1969 to coincide with this. He returned to Hong Kong in July, entering a 'planning cocoon' that lasted barely three months.[115]

A law librarian, Malcolm Quinn, who had formerly worked in East Africa, began work in June 1969 on assembling books and journals, drawing on a government grant of $600,000. Administrative staff – C.S. Shum, Henley Chan, and David Ng Ping-keung – transferred from the extramural scheme. Three lecturers joined the department over the following months. Bernard Downey, a former lecturer at LSE and the Council of Legal Education, joined in late 1969. Alan Smith, who had lectured at the University of East Africa, arrived in January 1970. John Rear had already moved over from the extramural project. After three years of letter-writing and public speaking on various causes, he was by now well known as a critic of government policy: his opposition to detention without trial in the aftermath of the troubles of 1967 had made him persona non grata in some circles, although

114. Ieuan Hughes, the Director of Extra-Mural Studies at HKU, had also suggested Clifford Pannam, who had helped with the extramural LLB course. In 1974, Dworkin, now at the University of Southampton, was later appointed one of the external examiners of the HKU LLB. Four candidates, including Evans, were considered for the position. Robinson to Dworkin, 19 May 1967, Dworkin to Robinson 13 June 1967 & Hughes to Robinson, 3 June 1967, HKUA: Law Department (1966–1967) VC's Numbered Files (1960s–1970s) Box 2 Folder 5 VC 233/66, encls. 30, 34, & 41; Robinson to Gower & Gower to Robinson, 15 & 24 July 1968, HKUA, Law Department (1966–1967) VC's Numbered Files (1960s–1970s) Box 2 Folder 7 VC 233/67, encls. 99 & 99A.
115. Evans, 'Taken at the Flood', 18–20; Mellor to Evans, 2 April 1969, HKUA, Registry File No. 2/1/19/4 'Academic Affairs (Courses/Law)' (1968); Evans, 'Law in the Quadrennium 1974–1978', 25 September 1972, HKUA: Board of the Faculty of Social Sciences – Minutes (1972).

the Governor had assured the FCO that, while he was 'idealistic and naïve in his political attitudes,' he was 'not a communist.'[116] Rear felt that he was simply 'saying things that in a normal political climate in a developed democracy would be accepted as part of everyday discourse,' and that there was something unhealthy in a society that reacted so sharply to criticism.[117] He was an exponent of the law to the public as legal correspondent of the *South China Morning Post*, a contributor to the *Far Eastern Economic Review*, and a broadcaster: in 1969 the text of his series of radio talks, 'This is the Law', was published in English and Chinese as a layperson's guide to Hong Kong law.

On 22 May 1969, one year after the planned Department of Law was announced, the university invited applications for admission to the three-year degree course, starting in September.[118] Degree regulations for the new LLB were urgently approved. The syllabus for the first-year courses was finalized. The department was to be housed on a floor in what became the Knowles Building, a new thirteen-storey teaching and administration block at the heart of campus. But the building was not ready until 1973. In the meantime, the department was allocated a 'government surplus hand-me-down'[119] – part of the former Police Married Quarters at the junction of Caine Road and Seymour Road, a three-storey block of flats built in 1922. The library was on the creaking top floor, its bookshelves placed as close as possible to the load-bearing walls. The middle floor housed offices and classrooms which, though spacious, were somewhat awkwardly laid out. There was one lecture room and one photocopier. The ground floor was not used. The building was noisy, the acoustics were poor. It was two miles away from campus: separated from other students, 'we really felt like the "heroes trapped in Shau Kei Wan,"' wrote Christopher Chan, one of the first students, referring to an old Hong Kong saying.[120] Yet its very inconvenience 'gave it a character in keeping with our pioneering spirit,' recalls Evans.[121] On 29 September 1969 the new Department of Law opened its doors to students.

116. In 1968 one senior crown counsel asked Attorney General Denys Roberts to ban Rear from the library in the Legal Department. Roberts not only rejected the suggestion but invited Rear and his wife to a dinner party at his house, at which, Rear recalls, 'a senior army officer and his lady ceremoniously abandoned our table when they discovered who I was.' Rear, 'Rear Window', 10; Trench to FCO, 12 November 1968, FCO 40/145, encl. 16.

117. John Rear, interview with the author, 2 December 2017.

118. 'Opening of the Department of Law in the University of Hong Kong' (press release), 22 May 1969, HKUA, Faculty of Social Sciences Board Minutes; *SCMP*, 24 May 1969.

119. Evans, 'A Wandering Minstrel Sings' in Faculty of Law, University of Hong Kong, *Building for Tomorrow on Yesterday's Strengths* (2004).

120. '英雄被困筲箕灣，不知何日到中環' ['A hero trapped in Shau Kei Wan, don't know when I will reach Central'] – a reference to the notoriously inadequate transport links between Shau Kei Wan, in the Eastern District of Hong Kong Island, and the Central business district: trams were so infrequent that, rather than wait for the next one, the 'heroes' would climb on the external running boards, holding on to the window frames. Christopher Chan (LLB 1972), '我所知道的法律系' ['What I know about the Department of Law'].

121. Evans, 'Taken at the Flood', 20; Randolph O'Hara, 'The Library of the University of Hong Kong, 1911–1973' (Thesis submitted for Fellowship of the Library Association. Ann Arbor, Michigan: University Microfilms International, 1984), 203–9.

Chapter 3

A Landmark Adventure

From Department to School to Faculty, 1969–1984

The forty students who embarked on the first Bachelor of Laws (LLB) courses at HKU in September 1969 were 'a brave bunch,' said the head of the new Department of Law, Dafydd Evans.[1] They had no guarantee the degree would be accepted as a qualification for practising law in Hong Kong, or indeed anywhere else. Nor had they much idea of what further training they would need to be able to practise. These matters were still under discussion between the university, the profession, and the government; they were not to be finally agreed until 1972. Even the details of the LLB were not yet decided: the syllabus for the first year had been approved (too late, however, to be included in the 1969–1970 HKU *Calendar*), but the contents of the other two years were merely headings, 'subject to alteration': most of the planned courses proved to be too ambitious for the available resources. Although law was part of the Faculty of Social Sciences, and the call for students stressed that admission was not confined to intending practitioners, it was clear the LLB offered little to those who might wish to take law as part of a liberal education.[2] 'We are all groping on a very uncertain and rugged path,' said one student.[3]

It was hardly surprising, then, that interest in the new degree was lukewarm. Of the 110 applicants to HKU in 1969 who included law in their choices, only 36 put it down as a

---

1. Evans, 'Taken at the Flood', 20–21.
2. Syllabus for the Degree of Bachelor of Laws, 12 May 1969 & Press Release, 22 May 1969, HKUA: Board of the Faculty of Social Sciences – Minutes (1969).
3. Ruby Fung (LLB 1974) in *Law Media*, July 1971.

first choice. Evans attributed this to uncertainty about the weight that professional associations would give the degree, the practice among solicitors of demanding unreasonably high premiums from their articled clerks, lack of publicity, and ignorance among schoolteachers about the legal profession. Despite the shortage of lawyers in Hong Kong, the 'advantage of having a law degree from Hong Kong University was not clear to students,' Evans told the newspapers, one of which then ran the headline 'New school of law has empty places.'[4] This was premature. The department soon announced that all forty places had been filled, a feat achieved by relaxing entry standards. 'Some of them would never have been admitted today with the "A" level and other examination records they had,' wrote Evans twenty years later, 'but we interviewed everyone and found something that seemed to us special in all of those we admitted.'[5] This proved to be a wise decision. At the time, 'A' level results were an unreliable guide to undergraduate performance in law, as in other subjects.[6] Academically and professionally, the first intake – twenty-three men and seventeen women – was a resounding success. Thirty-five of the forty graduated with an LLB and twenty-three went on to pass the Postgraduate Certificate in Laws (PCLL), the one-year course established in 1972 as a requirement for entry into articles or pupillage.[7] Several of these early graduates went on to pursue outstanding careers.

'Once they were in,' recalls Evans, this pioneer cohort 'became part of the great venture.' Without their enthusiasm, and that of the next few intakes, 'the department might have withered in an early frost.'[8] This chapter examines the first fifteen years of full-time legal education at HKU, from the founding of the Department of Law in 1969 to the School of Law in 1978 and the establishment of the Faculty of Law in 1984. The chapter focuses on the rapid expansion in student numbers and early attempts to balance the needs of the legal profession with the desire among teachers to develop courses that went beyond vocational training. It also explores some of the experiences of students and teachers in these formative years.

---

4. 'Report on Admissions 1969', HKUA: Board of the Faculty of Social Sciences – Minutes; *Undergrad*, 1 September 1969; *Hongkong Standard*, 5 September 1969.

5. Evans, 'Taken at the Flood', 21.

6. A report in 1970 concluded that there was 'no significant correlation' between 'A' level results and university examination results among students in the Faculty of Social Sciences. Other reports in the early 1970s produced similar conclusions. By the end of the decade, however, teachers were generally satisfied that 'A' levels were good predictors of suitability. Reports on Admissions, 30 December 1970 & 1 December 1971, 'Correlation between Advanced Level Examination Results and Performance at the LLB First Examination', July 1973, & Memos by Wesley-Smith, 24 July 1980, Andrew Hicks, 13 February 1981, & Albert Chen, 7 March 1981, HKUA: Board of the Faculty of Social Sciences – Minutes (1970–1973) & Board of Studies of the School of Law – Minutes (1980 & 1981).

7. These figures include students in the first intake who, for various reasons, deferred their LLB or PCLL examinations by one or more years.

8. Evans, 'Taken at the Flood', 21.

The HKU Bachelor of Laws Degree

In the summer of 1969 Dafydd Evans and John Rear, guided by Bernard Mellor, the University Registrar, worked urgently on the content of the new LLB degree. The fact that law was to be taught in the Faculty of Social Sciences offered scope for collaborative courses with existing or planned subjects such as criminology or urban studies, along the lines of innovative programmes taught in some other universities: the Hong Kong Bar Association, no less, had urged that legal education should reveal the wider role of law in promoting social change, protecting individual rights, and meeting demands for social justice.[9] On the other hand, in order to meet Hong Kong's pressing demand for lawyers – the raison d'être for creating the degree – the university had to consider the needs of the profession, as well as the weight to be given to Hong Kong law. What emerged was a degree structure geared almost entirely to professional needs, and one closely resembling the University of London LLB – the same degree taught until recently at the Department of Extra-Mural Studies, and one familiar to the many Hong Kong lawyers who had trained in London or at universities with similar degrees.

These similarities were 'entirely intentional.' The 'law of Hong Kong is basically English law,' prospective students were advised in a degree description that stressed the universality of the common law. Evans took the view that the degree had to be one that the profession in Hong Kong could identify with. The overseas experts and the Chief Justice's working party of 1966 had advised that the teaching and examinations for the Hong Kong LLB should be of a comparable standard to that provided in British universities so that reciprocal arrangements between Hong Kong and England for solicitors could continue. The Law Society of Hong Kong made it clear that its recognition of the Hong Kong LLB and of any scheme for further training was conditional on the retention of reciprocity. The Law Society of England and Wales agreed that retention would be possible if the right conditions were met. Moreover, the London degree was also the model with which Evans himself, having taught at LSE, was most familiar. 'We simply did not have the time to devise an innovative degree the acceptance of which might have had to be delayed until it could be assessed in action,' recalled Evans. Putting together the HKU syllabus therefore relied on an ample supply of 'string and sealing wax and scissors and paste.'[10] While doing this, Evans also

---

9. Hong Kong Bar Association, *Annual Report 1969–70*, 18–19.

10. Evans, 'Taken at the Flood', 19–20 & 23–4; Faculty of Social Sciences, 'Handbook for Undergraduate Applicants' 1971 & 1972; 'Report of the First Working Party on Legal Education' (1966), 55–7. The university had earlier examined syllabuses from Ceylon and Singapore, which were also similar to the syllabus eventually adopted for HKU: 'Law Dept – Working Party on Local Qualifications of Lawyers (1966–68)' HKUA, VC 233/1/66/7/8, encls. 1 & 8.

designed the academic dress for the new LLB degree – a deep blue hood with old gold silk edge lining, to be worn with the standard dark gown.[11]

The first two years of the LLB consisted of a common syllabus for all undergraduates on the main branches of law: legal system and legal method, public law, contract (I) and property (I), plus a moot programme in the first year; evidence and procedure, tort, property (II) and criminal law (I) in the second year, plus a 6,000-word dissertation. Standard teaching consisted of two lectures and one tutorial a week for each course taken. Attendance was obligatory, even (in Evans's view at least) for lectures. Registers were kept and students received notes from Evans himself if they failed to attend: one first-year student was not allowed to sit examinations because of persistent absence.[12] The plan had been to offer third-year students a choice of fifteen subjects, from which they were to select four, in addition to a course in either jurisprudence or comparative law. The fifteen subjects were to include further courses in criminal and public law together with specialities such as industrial property, international trade, and landlord and tenant – even a pioneering course on the legal system of the People's Republic of China. Students were to choose according to whether they planned to qualify as a barrister or solicitor.[13]

In the event, the first batch of third-year students were given only six courses: jurisprudence (compulsory), conflict of laws, family and domestic law, trusts and estates, mercantile law, and business associations; they were also required to do a law-drafting exercise. Staff shortages, combined with the demanding work of designing new courses, had made the original plan too ambitious.[14] Some of the subjects in the original third-year list were also held over for the planned postgraduate training. Others were offered but not taught because student interest was insufficient. Among the new courses taught in the 1970s were international law and labour law (1972), industrial and intellectual property (1975), and evidence and procedure (1976).

To begin with, the standard English authorities were prescribed as texts – Wade and Phillips's *Constitutional Law*, Jackson's *Machinery of Justice in England*, and Cheshire's

---

11. Evans, 'Department of Law: Academic Dress', April 1970, HKUA: Board of the Faculty of Social Sciences – Minutes (1970) – approved by Senate, June 1970.

12. Under university regulations, attendance at lectures was not compulsory, but Evans held that, since the LLB and PCLL required students to 'follow instruction', attendance had to be watched carefully. Evans, 'Notice to All Students: Attendance at the University and Completion of Curricula', 21 February 1973, Evans to Kvan, 19 March 1974, & 'Attendance and Absence at Lectures and Tutorials' 8 November 1979, HKUA: Board of the Faculty of Social Sciences – Minutes (1973, 1974, & 1979).

13. Students were to have picked from groups of courses, rather than being given a completely free choice. The list of fifteen was reduced to ten in 1971, when students were also informed that not all of the subjects would be offered in any one year. Syllabus for the Degree of Bachelor of Laws, 12 May 1969, HKUA: Board of the Faculty of Social Sciences – Minutes (1969); Evans to the Dean of the Faculty of Social Sciences, 16 November 1971, HKUA: Board of the Faculty of Social Sciences – Minutes (1971); *Hong Kong Hansard*, 22 May 1968.

14. Evans, 'Law in the Quadrennium 1974–1978', 25 September 1972, HKUA: Board of the Faculty of Social Sciences and Law – Minutes (1972).

Modern Law of Real Property, for example. Although up-to-date commentaries began to appear in the 1970s, there were, at the time, few reliable texts on Hong Kong law;[15] in any case, the Supreme Court adhered closely to English judgments in many areas of law. Yet, while early course outlines might have been nearly identical to those offered by English universities, staff made some effort to incorporate Hong Kong law and Hong Kong conditions into their lectures and teaching materials. The 'moots' – a form of mock appeal hearing – also included topical issues: one moot in 1978 caught the public eye because it involved an application for judicial review of the Governor's recent controversial amnesty for corruption offences.[16] Many of the dissertations were on Hong Kong topics and contained original research into issues ranging from the legal status of Chinese herbalists to deportation and police powers, along with the Hong Kong experience in matters such as workers' compensation, accomplice evidence, and credit cards. The best dissertations were published by the HKU Law Association in its journal *Justitia*.

Although participation in moots, dissertations, and other assignments counted towards the degree, the LLB was primarily an exam-oriented degree. LLB students were examined at the end of each of their three years, usually in May, with the First Examination held at the end of the first year, and the Final Examination Parts I and II at the end of the second and third year respectively. Retakes were possible for those who failed. In exceptional cases, a student who failed in one paper might be deemed to have satisfied the examiners if he or she had performed well in other papers or in the moots and dissertation. But no one could proceed to the second or third year without having passed the First Examination.[17] In consequence, several students had to retake a year, a few withdrew, and some were 'discontinued' (as expulsion was delicately termed). Over one-third (sixteen) of the 1972–1973 first-year students failed their First Examination or withdrew before it took place: six were discontinued and two transferred to other subjects, another six were allowed to repeat the first year, but only two eventually graduated. Another sixteen students were discontinued in 1975 for failing their first-or second-year exams.[18] Although the dust then settled, the discontinuation rate in law continued to be high – evidence of the difficulty of the subject and of the department's determination to maintain standards.

---

15. The only specifically Hong Kong text prescribed in early syllabuses was G.B. Endacott, *Government and People in Hong Kong 1842–1962*, a historical survey of constitutional development.

16. The partial amnesty, issued to defuse a rapidly spreading police mutiny was for corruption offences committed before 1 January 1977, other than the most heinous cases or cases in which suspects had already been served with warrants. The moot was organized by John Miller (lecturer 1976–1980) and was held in the Supreme Court. It took the form of an application by a member of the public for an order of *mandamus* against the Commissioner of Police over a corruption case covered by the amnesty. *SCMP*, 21 January 1978.

17. The LLB degree regulations, amended from time to time, are in the annual HKU *Calendar*.

18. LLB enrolment lists, HKUA: Board of the Faculty of Social Sciences – Minutes (1972–1975); Degree Congregations in the *University of Hong Kong Gazette*.

Control of examinations, under a board chaired by the Dean of the Faculty, was rigorous. Students were assigned numbers so that examiners were unaware of their identities, a practice not universal at HKU at the time. Most First Examination papers and all Final Examinations were marked by two internal examiners – usually the staff who had taught the courses and set the exams. At least ten scripts for each paper, including all failed scripts, were sent to external examiners. These were experienced academics, usually based in England, starting with Aubrey Diamond, Professor of Law at Queen Mary College, London.[19] External examiners were a university requirement and common practice in the UK, though not in some other places. They were not, Evans explained, a reflection of the 'colonial' status of HKU but an opportunity to 'make ourselves and our standards known in an established and respectable manner,' a source of advice, and a way of gaining acceptance of the LLB degree for the purpose of reciprocity and postgraduate studies at other universities.[20] Honours were divided into the usual three classes, with a division in the second into upper and lower, and a pass for those who failed to obtain honours. First-class honours were rare: only six were awarded in the first fifteen years of the LLB.

Despite the outward emphasis on the English foundations of Hong Kong law and the paucity of texts on Hong Kong, staff made efforts to present the law as it was applied in Hong Kong and, as far as the curriculum allowed, 'to treat the law as one aspect of a very much wider group of social, economic and political phenomena.'[21] Early examination papers give some idea of the extent to which teachers sought to mould courses to fit the Hong Kong context and encourage critical thinking. Some subjects in particular required wide departures from the English texts. Thus, family law papers included questions on traditional Chinese marriage and concubinage, as well as the impact of the Marriage Reform Ordinance 1970. Papers on property law carried questions about customary systems of landholding (such as *tso* and *tong*, forms of common ownership in the New Territories recognized in Hong Kong law) as well as local conveyancing practices, landlord and tenant law, and issues arising from multi-owner buildings. Apart from setting out cases on the rights of employers and employees, papers on labour law invited students to consider the efficacy of Hong Kong's evolving employment law and the restrictions still in force on strikes and unions.

Most thought-provoking of all were the papers on public law and legal systems. Although these always included questions on English institutions and general principles – the role of

---

19. Diamond's appointment as sole external examiner lasted from 1969 to 1973. From 1974, reflecting the widening scope of courses, several external examiners, based in England or elsewhere in the Commonwealth, served at any given time.

20. Evans, 'Taken at the Flood', 22–3.

21. Department of Law description in Faculty of Social Sciences, 'Handbook for Undergraduate Applicants' 1971 & 1972.

'judge-made law', the relationship between law and morality, and so on – they were also among the most Hong Kong-specific of all the papers. The questions invited critical analysis of topical issues, such as the remedies for abuse of authority by the Governor and his officials, the extent of police powers, the control of obscene publications, or the possibility of fusion in the legal profession. Students were offered gobbets on law from Laozi, Xunzi, and other Chinese philosophers. A question in 1974 set out a thinly disguised version of the Diaoyutai dispute, which had recently been the focus of student demonstrations.[22] Other questions invited students to discuss the legal aspects of extraordinary scenarios, such as a unilateral declaration of independence by the Governor of Hong Kong or a war between Britain and the People's Republic of China.

Early public law papers usually carried a question on the tendency of the courts in Hong Kong to follow English judgments even where they were not binding, reflecting, as one question suggested, 'a colonial inferiority complex unworthy of Her Majesty's judges.'[23] The few Hong Kong cases referred to in the examinations tended to emphasize the conservatism of the Hong Kong courts; some did not show them in a particularly positive light.[24] In the papers on contract, tort, criminal, and mercantile law, the emphasis was on

22. The uninhabited Diaoyu Islands, northeast of Taiwan, are claimed by both Japan and China. The discovery of possible oil reserves and the reversion of the islands from American to Japanese control gave rise to mass protests in Hong Kong in the early 1970s, some of which resulted in clashes with police and prosecutions under the Public Order Ordinance.

23. LLB First Examination: Elements of Public Law and Legal Systems II, 1974, question 9(a): see also Peter Wesley-Smith's editorial on this subject in 14 *HKLJ* 1984, 137–41. A reference point in several other papers was the statement by Huggins J in *R v Chan Wai-keung* [1965] HKLR 815, that 'Once a principle of the Common Law has been clearly propounded by the House of Lords there can be no doubt that that decision establishes the law of Hong Kong...'

24. A favourite was *Gensburger v Gensburger* [1968] HKLR 403, an appeal against damages for 'criminal conversation' in an action brought by a husband for compensation for adultery by his wife. Actions for criminal conversation had been abolished in England by the Matrimonial Causes Act 1857. The Supreme Court (mistakenly) assumed that they had not subsequently been abolished in Hong Kong, but had remained part of the English law received by the colony on 5 April 1843. However, the recent Application of English Law Ordinance 1966 listed the pre-1843 English acts applicable to Hong Kong and stated, in addition, that the common law was in force in Hong Kong, but without specifying a date of reception. The court therefore ruled that, in the absence of a reception date, it was no longer necessary to look to the laws of England as they existed on 5 April 1843, because the new ordinance had 'brought the reference to the Common Law up to date': since there was no longer any action for criminal conversation in England, it naturally followed that there was no such action in Hong Kong. The general effect of the judgment was that the law in Hong Kong was automatically altered by English Acts of Parliament, even where (as in most cases) they were not intended to apply to the colony. The result, declared John Rear in the *HKLJ*, was calculated 'to bring Hong Kong's law into total confusion'; the judgment was all the more confusing for having overlooked a 1908 Supreme Court decision that the action of criminal conversation had, after all, been abolished by legislation in Hong Kong as early as 1858. The Application of English Law Ordinance was promptly amended to clarify that Hong Kong law was not affected by English enactments not expressly applied to the colony. However, the inclusion in the amendment of the words 'at any time', though intended to apply to post-1843 enactments, encouraged some lawyers to argue that the ordinance had now also repealed all pre-1843 English statutes not listed in the ordinance as applying to Hong Kong. The puzzle was eventually resolved by the *Oceania* case of 1979, which effectively reinstated the old formula

English judgments, reflecting the close adherence of Hong Kong law to English principles and procedures. Yet the hypothetical cases on which students were asked to advise drew on situations familiar in Hong Kong: the criminal liability of conspirators in a race-fixing case, for example, or the legal position of *pak pai* (unlicensed taxi) drivers, or the impact of Typhoon Elsie (1975) on a construction contract. The parties had Hong Kong names, and the fictional companies had an authentic Hong Kong ring – the Wonderful Garment Co., the Hairy Wig Factory, the Archipelago Hotel – in a parallel world of reckless business-men, quarrelsome siblings, and hapless tourists. Some questions had an even more 'local' flavour: the defence available to a (fictitious) lecturer arrested after showing students a sexually explicit film to illustrate the law relating to objectionable publications; the liability in tort, if any, of the university in the case of a bright student who hangs himself when his application for admission is mistakenly rejected; or the criminal liability, if any, of a lazy second-year law student who surreptitiously borrows another student's notes.[25]

The Postgraduate Certificate in Laws

As the first batch of LLB students revised for their final examinations, the university, the government, and the profession discussed what further training was necessary for a holder of an HKU LLB degree to practise law in Hong Kong. In June 1969 the Chief Justice, Sir Michael Hogan, and the Vice-Chancellor of HKU, Kenneth Robinson, appointed a working party (the 'Second Working Party') to make proposals for professional examina-tions in Hong Kong and recommend changes to the Legal Practitioners Ordinance. It was chaired by Alan Huggins, a Supreme Court judge, and included the Attorney General and Registrar General and representatives of the Bar Association, the Law Society, and the two universities. Dafydd Evans and John Rear represented HKU. After his arrival in Hong Kong later in the year, a third law teacher, Bernard Downey, also attended meetings, bringing his experience as lecturer and examiner for the Council of Legal Education, the body formed by the Inns of Court to supervise the training of barristers.[26] The Second Working Party reported in 1971 and its recommendations were implemented in 1972. These were, essentially, that the LLB degree, plus further training at HKU leading to a postgraduate certificate, followed by articles or pupillage, should form the qualifications for admission to practise, in addition to the existing method based on training in England.

The Second Working Party produced its recommendations almost simultaneously with those of the Ormrod Committee, appointed in 1967 to advise on legal education

---

for the reception of English law. Rear, 'Application of English Law (Amendment) Ordinance', 2 *HKLJ* (1972), 115–20; Wesley-Smith, *The Sources of Hong Kong Law*, 119–29.

25. Extant examination papers have been collected on the Hong Kong University Library Digital Initiatives website. From the late 1970s the papers become somewhat less fantastical in style.

26. 'Report of the Second Working Party on Legal Education' in Evans, *Legal Education in Hong Kong*, 31–132.

in England and presenting its voluminous report in early 1971.[27] Some thought that the Second Working Party should await the Ormrod Committee's report, but the chairman, Alan Huggins, ruled this out as unrealistic. It would have left the LLB students at HKU in limbo, and there was no guarantee anyway that the Ormrod recommendations would be implemented. In the event, the main conclusions of the working party were consistent with the spirit and content of the *Ormrod Report*.[28] The *Ormrod Report* urged better integration of academic and professional training, with a university law degree forming per se part of the recognized qualification for practice, rather than merely exempting candidates from some of the professional examinations. A majority of the Ormrod Committee also favoured further institutional training beyond the degree at universities, rather than through the existing separate schemes organized by the legal profession: among the advantages were the quality and range of teaching available at a university and the provision of a common educational scheme for both branches of the profession. The Ormrod Committee therefore recommended a three-stage training process consisting of (1) the academic stage; (2) the professional stage, comprising (a) institutional training and (b) in-training (pupillage or articles); and (3) continuing education or training.[29]

In Hong Kong, the Second Working Party recommended a scheme that effectively anticipated stages (1) and (2) of the *Ormrod Report*. After examining the curriculum, the working party endorsed the LLB degree at HKU as the foundation for training lawyers for practice in Hong Kong. It recommended that the existing method of admission through British qualifications should continue, although it expected that in due course the local qualification would largely replace this. It also noted that HKU expected its LLB degree to be recognized by other universities, and for exemption from parts of the qualifying examinations in England. It then recommended a further period of practical training: two years' pupillage for barristers, and two and a half years' articles for solicitors. During this time, intending practitioners would be required to attend part-time courses in five or six subjects specified by the professional bodies which they had not already taken for the LLB. On satisfactory completion of the courses, they would be awarded a postgraduate certificate, which would be accepted by the two professional bodies as proof of competence. The Second Working Party considered whether the additional courses should be taught at the Department of Extra-Mural Studies at HKU or even at a new institution, to be established along the lines of the College of Law and Inns of Court School of Law in England. It concluded that teaching them at the Department of Law at HKU would be the best way of maintaining standards and avoiding duplication of resources.[30]

27. *Report of the Committee on Legal Education* (the '*Ormrod Report*'), presented to Parliament in March 1971.

28. Minutes of the Working Party on Legal Education, 2 May 1970, HKRS 671-2-262.

29. *Ormrod Report*, 34, 41–2, 45–6, 56–67.

30. 'Report of the Second Working Party on Legal Education' in Evans, *Legal Education in Hong Kong*.

There was much overlap in the subjects – some compulsory, some optional – specified by the two professional bodies. Most subjects were already offered, or planned, under the LLB degree, though it was expected that some would be more practical or advanced in nature. The Law Society was most concerned that subjects such as conveyancing and probate should address real problems arising in Hong Kong. At the same time it insisted on reciprocity between Hong Kong and English qualifications as a precondition for endorsing the Second Working Party's recommendations. The Bar Association expected that examinations for the postgraduate certificate would be of a level at least as high as that of the Bar final examination in England. It opposed the idea of part-time pupillage, taking the view that students should not start pupillage until after they had completed all formal courses and examinations.[31] This prompted a departure in practice from the Second Working Party's proposal that the postgraduate training would be part-time and spread over the period of pupillage or articles. Instead, the training was to be concentrated in a single year, followed either by a year's pupillage for barristers or one and a half years' articles for solicitors.[32] The resulting three-stage route to practice – a law degree from HKU, a professional course at HKU, and a period of apprenticeship – was, in fact, identical to that outlined by the university's overseas experts, Zelman Cowen and L.C.B. Gower, in their 1967 report.[33]

Amendments to the Legal Practitioners Ordinance and associated rules to allow recognition of the HKU LLB and the planned new postgraduate certificate were announced in the Legislative Council in May 1972, only a few weeks before the first batch of LLB students took their final examinations.[34] The old route to admission continued to be open

31. The Bar was not united on this question. Much to the consternation of Evans (who was not consulted), in early 1973, shortly after the Chief Justice had issued new Barristers (Qualification) Rules embodying the Second Working Party's recommendations, an amendment to the rules was moved in the Legislative Council by the barrister-member Oswald Cheung to give HKU LLB graduates the option of starting pupillage before completing the PCLL. The aim, said Cheung, was to allow LLB graduates to put their long summer vacation between LLB and PCLL to good use. This option was removed when revisions were made to the Legal Practitioners Ordinance in 1976. Gittins to Secretary to the Working Party on Legal Education, 7 May 1970, HKRS 671-2-262; Evans, 'Taken at the Flood', 24; Barristers (Qualification) Rules 1973 & Resolution of the Legislative Council, *Hong Kong Government Gazette*, Legal Supplement No. 2, 19 January & 16 February 1973, LN 9/73 & 28/73; Hong Kong Hansard, 14 February 1973; Evans to Rigby, 22 February 1973, HKRS 671-2-262.

32. The decision to concentrate the course in a single full-time year had a bearing on fees. The UGC had proposed setting fees on a cost-recovery basis, perhaps in the region of $3,000 or more, rather than the standard fee of $1,100. Its argument was that, as proposed by the Second Working Party, this was a 'professional in-service course' to be taken by students, some of whom would already be in employment, and all of whom 'could reasonably regard themselves as on the verge of a relatively lucrative professional career.' This prompted lengthy explanations from HKU of the social value of lawyers, the need to attract students from poorer backgrounds, and the actual income that freshly minted lawyers might expect. In the end, the fee was set at $1,500. Correspondence between HKU and the UGC in HKUA: Registry File No. 2/1/19/3, encls. 25–30.

33. Gower & Cowen, 'Report on Legal Training in Hong Kong', 5 April 1967, HKRS 457-3-19, 7 & 11–13.

34. Ordinance No. 32 of 1972; Students (Amendment) Rules 1972 & Barristers (Qualification) Rules 1973, *Hong Kong Government Gazette*, Legal Supplement No. 2, 15 September 1972 & 19 January 1973, LN 177/72 & LN 9/73.

for lawyers qualifying in the UK or taking the English solicitors' examinations in Hong Kong. Solicitors admitted under the new system were eligible for enrolment in England as if they had qualified under the old system. Thanks to intensive advocacy by the Second Working Party, the HKU LLB was also accepted for exemption from Part I of the English Law Society's final examinations in the same way that UK degrees were exempted. The reciprocity demanded by the Law Society of Hong Kong for solicitors qualifying in the colony was therefore retained.

As with the LLB three years earlier, the one-year postgraduate course was put together in a hurry. It had to begin in September 1972 so that the first LLB graduates could, if they intended to practise law, move quickly to the professional training stage. There were constraints on the course's form and content. It had to be distinguished from the LLB degree both in content and teaching style. The First Working Party had made it clear that students should not be re-examined on subjects they had taken for the LLB. The university was anxious that the postgraduate course should not be seen as an unofficial 'fourth year' of the LLB, which would risk eroding the integrity of the LLB and would conflict with the official decision that the LLB should be a three-year course. The government urged that the postgraduate course should be 'training of a practical nature.'[35] The professional bodies wanted it to be relevant to Hong Kong's needs, and had specified what subjects should be offered and which of them should be compulsory. Evans and his colleagues, however, were concerned that the course, taught in a university, should be more than just a scheme for meeting professional requirements. They therefore at first resisted demands for it to include courses on workaday subjects, such as accounts.[36] The professional bodies said they did not want the examinations to 'add any letters after a student's name.' The university, however, decided that if it had to issue certificates, then the course must have a name. Thus the 'Postgraduate Certificate in Laws', or 'PCLL', came into being.[37]

Another constraint was resources. The PCLL was to be an intensively taught practical course. The Second Working Group had recommended two additional staff to teach the PCLL. In 1972 the Department of Law had nine staff, one short of the approved establishment of ten. All were heavily engaged in preparing new courses and producing materials on Hong Kong law in the absence of textbooks.[38] The necessary additional staff for the PCLL were not to be appointed until 1973. In the meantime, the department had to put together

35. Herries to Robinson, 27 March 1972, HKUA: 'Law Department: Working Party on Local Qualifications of Lawyers (1971–73)', VC's Numbered Files (1960s–1970s) Box 2, Folder 4, VC 233/1/71, encl. 15.

36. Accounts and financial management were later covered by the course on 'The Lawyer and his Practice', introduced in 1980.

37. The choice of abbreviation was a matter of some delicacy: 'PCL' was rejected largely to avoid confusion with the 'BCL', or Bachelor of Civil Law at Oxford. Evans, 'Taken at the Flood', 23–4 & 31.

38. Evans, 'Law in the Quadrennium 1974–1978', 25 September 1972, HKUA: Board of the Faculty of Social Sciences and Law – Minutes (1972), 5.

the regulations and syllabus. The immediate outcome was the laying on of four new courses for the PCLL – practice and procedure, landlord and tenant, conveyancing, and taxation – and a requirement for students to take some of the third-year LLB options they had not previously taken. This was, Evans admitted, 'partly didactic and, initially at least, only partly practical in the sense of training exercises.' It was 'the best we could do with the material available at the time.' The creation of an effective training course to 'prepare the graduate for that last phase of training in articles or pupillage was to take some time and considerable hard work and experimentation.'[39]

Much of that work was done by Peter Willoughby, who joined the department in September 1973 as senior lecturer in charge of the PCLL course and remained at HKU until his retirement from the Chair of Professional Legal Education in 1986. Willoughby had trained as a solicitor and had lectured at Gibson and Weldon's tutorial firm 1960–1962 and its successor, the College of Law 1966–1972. During the intervening four years, in 1962–1966, he had joined Professor L.C.B. Gower and his team in Nigeria. There, Willoughby had helped found the Nigerian Law School and had taught a one-year vocational course to train law graduates for the Nigerian Bar.[40] Gower and Zelman Cowen had in mind this Nigerian model and similar initiatives in Australia when, in 1967, they recommended a one-year professional pre-admission course for Hong Kong. Gower also helped recruit Willoughby for HKU on the strength of his experience in Nigeria and England.

In his memoir on the evolution of the course, Willoughby drew attention to the PCLL's African antecedent.[41] There were, however, important differences. The Nigerian course was designed initially to introduce students trained in England to Nigeria's law and its fused profession. The PCLL was intended for LLB graduates of HKU, who already had a grounding in local law. The Nigerian course was conducted under the auspices of a Council of Legal Education and was closely tied to bar examinations prescribed by the profession. The PCLL, though designed to meet the needs of the profession, was a university course, a bridge between 'the purely academic stage of legal education and the purely practical stage' of articles or pupillage. In fact, it followed exactly the Ormrod recommendation of a vocational year in an institutional setting, and it was a point of pride for Evans that HKU should be the first university to implement this part of the *Ormrod Report*.[42] HKU went even further by introducing a common examination for both branches of the profession – an objective which, amid the wrangling between different interests, the Ormrod Committee had been unable to agree on.[43]

---

39. Evans, 'Taken at the Flood', 25.
40. Alan Milner, 'Legal Education and Training in Nigeria', 17 *Journal of Legal Education* (1964–1965), 285–306.
41. Willoughby, 'The Postgraduate Certificate in Laws: Some Reminiscences', in *Thirty Years*, 42.
42. Peter Wesley-Smith: interview with the author, 23 October 2017; Ormrod Report, Chapter 5.
43. For a discussion of the politics surrounding Ormrod, see Twining, *Blackstone's Tower*, 33–8.

Even so, bringing practical training into a university did not fit easily with traditional ideas of scholarship. Willoughby was determined to provide 'an intellectually challenging continuum between the LLB and PCLL, rather than an abrupt move to an arid practical training course.' Evans similarly refused to allow the PCLL to become 'simply a cram course.' Attempts to teach practice in Australian universities had proved to be 'neither "academic" nor truly practical,' said Willoughby. Moreover, staff teaching the PCLL saw themselves as academics with a duty to research as well as to teach. 'As one somewhat outspoken Australian colleague once put it, "I do not want the words 'practical training course instructor' to appear on my CV!"'[44]

Like the LLB, and unlike the separate systems of qualification in England, the PCLL was a common programme for both barristers and solicitors. The courses designed specifically for the PCLL had a practical bent. Some lecturers went 'down town' to talk to practitioners and judges about suitable materials, particularly for courses, such as Landlord and Tenant, that had a heavy Hong Kong law element. Students were asked to put together and negotiate contracts and, recalls their lecturer Lester Dally, 'had lots of fun trying this (what seemed to be then) very new approach.'[45] An 'intellectual rigour' was nevertheless maintained even in the most applied subjects. As an example, Willoughby describes how students taking revenue law learned for the first time how to construe statute law. Some courses were recast, renamed, and augmented over the years: for example, a new course on the lawyer and his practice was introduced in 1980.[46] Yet the early curriculum, heavy on tax, property, and land law, reflecting the interests of teachers and the needs of the profession, did not develop much. The organization of the PCLL was split from the LLB in 1975, with separate courses and examinations, but still with teachers covering both LLB and PCLL courses. Willoughby became the department's first Director of Legal Education and gradually built up a staff specializing in the PCLL, despite a lack of resources. Teaching was intensive and the workload heavy. 'I have at present four assignments to mark consisting of drafts of complex agreements. (50 students times 4 equals 200 agreements to pick through word by word.) They weigh over 7 pounds and stand about 9 inches deep,' wrote one lecturer in 1979. Without more staff, he added, 'the PCLL course remains in crisis and its teachers are under considerable pressure.'[47]

---

44. Willoughby, 'The Postgraduate Certificate in Laws: Some Reminiscences', 42; Evans, 'Law in the Triennium, 1981–1984', 14 February 1979, HKUA: Board of the Studies of the School of Law – Minutes (1979), 4.

45. Dally, 'Pride and Privilege' in *Thirty Years*, 60.

46. It was renamed 'the lawyer's practice' in 1983, when over half the PCLL intake consisted of women, to 'remove the appearance of male chauvinism.' Memorandum by Sandor, 13 September 1983, HKUA: Board of the Studies of the School of Law – Minutes (1983).

47. Quoted in Evans, 'Law in the Triennium, 1981–1984', 14 February 1979, HKUA: Board of the Studies of the School of Law – Minutes (1979), 4.

Although it remained primarily an exam-based degree, the early PCLL contained some element of 'clinical' or 'situational' teaching. For part of his course on commercial law and practice Roderick O'Brien joined with Ian Campbell from the Department of Architecture, who had a scale model of a multi-storey building. Campbell described how it was built while O'Brien explained the various contracts, payment instalments, and certifications as construction progressed.[48] The course on practice and procedure included visits to courts and a week-long advocacy training element, including exercises presided over by a senior judge.[49] From 1973, under the supervision of Bernard Downey from HKU and the solicitor Bryan Tisdall, PCLL students joined a legal aid scheme managed by the Hong Kong Council of Social Services. Working in pairs, they acted as case clerks at sessions held in city district offices, taking statements and preparing materials for lawyers either in private practice or in the Department of Law serving on a voluntary basis. Although the main aim was to provide free services to poorer people who were not eligible for government legal aid, the scheme did not apply means testing, so that in some cases clients attended to check up on advice they had already received from well-known solicitors in Central. Clients were rarely turned away: one exception was a man who arrived in a limousine and asked for advice about a $10 million mortgage case.[50] As student numbers increased it became more difficult to give everyone an opportunity to take part. In 1979 the Law Society, with funding from the government, introduced its own free Legal Advice and Assistance Scheme, along with the Duty Lawyer Scheme for vulnerable defendants in magistrates' courts.[51] Teaching staff and HKU law graduates continued to participate in the free legal advice scheme, but students largely ceased to be directly involved with clients until the introduction of the Clinical Legal Education course under the LLB programme in 2010.

---

48. Roderick O'Brien, interview with the author, 4 July 2018.

49. In one exercise, the students 'tended to open proceedings before the Master in Chambers as if it were a State trial. When they were told that this needed to be done in a much more summary fashion they then opened proceedings before a Judge in accordance with that advice.' The observation was by David Napley, President of the Law Society of England and Wales and author of *The Technique of Persuasion* (1970), who was invited to observe and report on the course. He found it to be admirable in most respects. Napley, Report on Advocacy Training, September 1976, HKUA: Board of the Faculty of Social Sciences – Minutes (1976).

50. Willoughby, 'Myself a Mandarin: Clinical Legal Education' in *Thirty Years*; Bramwell, 'Legal Aid and Advice: Interim Report', 1 February 1979, HKUA: Board of the Studies of the School of Law – Minutes (1979); *SCMP*, 11 January 1977.

51. Under the Duty Lawyer Scheme lawyers represented defendants for a flat fee in certain offences, such as loitering or unlawful possession (where usually the only witnesses were policemen), and in extradition proceedings and for juveniles charged with offences where conviction might affect their later lives. It was, said the organizers, a recognition of 'ample evidence that things have gone wrong and that there have been miscarriages of justice.' The scope was gradually extended over the years. The scheme benefited thousands of defendants and led to a marked increase in acquittal rates. *Law Society Legal Advice and Assistance Scheme: Report of the Management & Administration Committee* (1979), 8.

The University and the Profession

The First and the Second Working Parties recommended that an advisory committee should be formed to advise on the education, professional training, and qualifications for barristers and solicitors.[52] Following amendments to the Legal Practitioners Ordinance in 1972, the Advisory Committee on Legal Education was established to advise the Chief Justice and the Vice-Chancellor of HKU. The former chairman of the First Working Party, Sir Ivo Rigby, now Chief Justice, appointed Alan Huggins, chairman of the Second Working Party, to head the new committee. The committee consisted of representatives from the Law Society, Bar Committee, and HKU, and a judge nominated by the Chief Justice, who would also be the chairman. Control of the committee by the Judiciary reflected the role of the Chief Justice as the ultimate rule-making authority for solicitors and barristers.[53] In a sphere with jealously guarded interests – the professions with their privileges and traditions, the university's insistence on its right to decide the content of teaching – this was also a formula that had delivered results through the two working parties.

The Advisory Committee on Legal Education was the forum for discussing whether the curriculums for the LLB and PCLL were a sufficient educational basis for graduates intending to enter the legal profession. Evans, who was a member of the committee, was prickly about this function; in fact, he was unhappy with the whole idea that an outside committee should give advice to the university. When the Law Society's representative, Peter Vine, suggested there might be subjects more useful to an intending solicitor than compulsory jurisprudence under the LLB, Evans retorted that 'it was not in any way incumbent upon him or the university to justify any part of a degree course which had already been established.' He was particularly incensed by Vine's claim to 'act as a watchdog for the public to ensure that the investment of public money which this Department represents was not wasted' and that he had been asked by a member of the University and Polytechnic Grants Committee (UPGC) (Oswald Cheung) to keep an eye on the department to this end.[54] The jurisprudence paper – covering topics such as legal theory and the relationship between law and morality – was retained as a compulsory subject, with the support of the Bar Association. Another issue in the early years was the insistence by the Law Society that two LLB 'core subjects', family law and business associations, should be compulsory for all

52. Reports of the First & Second Working Parties on Legal Education in Evans, *Legal Education in Hong Kong*, 55–6 & 46–7.

53. Rules made by the Law Society since it had acquired rule-making powers in 1964 required the Chief Justice's approval; amendments to the Legal Practitioners Ordinance in 1972 conferred on the Chief Justice new rule-making powers for barristers. All such rules were subject to negative vetting by the Legislative Council.

54. Evans to Robinson, 8 May 1972, Evans to Huang, 3 March 1973, & Minutes of Legal Education Advisory Committee, 16 March 1973, HKUA: 'Law Department: Working Party on Local Qualifications of Lawyers (1971–73)', VC's Numbered Files (1960s–1970s) Box 2, Folder 4, VC 233/1/71, encls. 16, 32, & 34.

intending solicitors. From 1981 the Law Society dropped its insistence on family law, though it continued to insist on keeping business associations, a subject 'essential to the work of the average solicitor practising in Hong Kong.' Despite these differences, the profession generally accepted the university's autonomy in designing courses.[55] Differing views about the objectives and content of the PCLL were, however, to re-emerge in the late 1990s.

The advisory committee was one of many points of contact between the department and the profession. Senior lawyers served as external examiners for the PCLL. From 1979 some were appointed as honorary lecturers: by 1984 the list had grown to twenty-eight and included judges, administrators, and lawyers, several of whom took a very active role in advocacy training, conveyancing and other courses for the PCLL.[56] From 1978, when the department became an autonomous School of Law, two members of the profession sat on its Board of Studies. In 1980 Bernard Downey left HKU to become a district judge but continued to sit as an external member of the board until 1994. Some other teachers moved into legal practice in Hong Kong and maintained contact with HKU. Judges presided over student moots, some of which were held in the Supreme Court. Lawyers, judges and other prominent citizens founded prizes and scholarships and sponsored the publication of *Justitia*.[57] One of the most enduring joint projects was the *Hong Kong Law Journal*, founded in 1971 by the barristers Henry Litton and Gerald de Basto and edited by law teachers at HKU, starting with John Rear: its impact is discussed in Chapter 4. From 1974 the *Journal* published a series of Law Lectures for Practitioners, an annual programme founded by Peter Willoughby and the President of the Law Society, Peter C. Wong, and co-sponsored by the Law Society and HKU. The first in the series included two lectures by Willoughby, two by Bernard Passingham (an expert on matrimonial law from England), one by the barrister Denis Chang, and another by the solicitor and former HKU law lecturer Alan Smith. The event attracted 120 lawyers, academics, students, and articled clerks. Later lectures, held in the Hilton Hotel, had standing room only.[58]

A highlight of these early years was the visit by the Master of the Rolls, Lord Denning, in April 1977. Then in his seventy-ninth year, Denning was a towering figure in jurisprudence,

---

55. Vine to Evans, 17 January 1979, HKUA: Board of the Studies of the School of Law – Minutes (1979).

56. For an assessment of their contributions, see in particular Willoughby, 'Appointment of Honorary Lecturers', 20 May 1985, HKUA: Board of the Faculty of Law – Minutes (1985).

57. These included, in the 1970s and early 1980s, the Simon K.Y. Lee Medal in Law, the Brian McElney Medal in Law, the Baker & McKenzie Prize for Business Associations and Postgraduate Prize, the Y.M. Wong Memorial Prize, the Rowdget W. Young Medal in Law, the Maxwell Law Prize for the most promising PCLL student intending to become a barrister, the Woo Po Shing Medal in Law and Overseas Summer School Travelling Scholarship, the Stikeman Elliott Prize in International Trade Law, and the Downey Book Prizes. In 1981 the Mr Justice Pickering Memorial Loan Fund was established to provide interest-free loans to final-year LLB and PCLL students. The fund was named after Wilfred Pickering, a Court of Appeal judge who died in 1980 after twenty-five years in the Hong Kong Judiciary. It drew on generous donations from barristers and solicitors.

58. *SCMP*, 23 March 1974; Judith Sihombing: interview with the author, 10 November 2017.

famous for his role in reviving judicial review, his lucid judgments, and his practical, if mor-
alistic, approach to social questions. He gave two talks in the Law Lectures for Practitioners
series. His remarks on the death penalty in Hong Kong seemed to please both sides in this
hotly debated subject. On 16 April he paid a day-long visit to the Department of Law to
preside over a moot by PCLL students on a panel with Yang Ti Liang and the solicitor
Mabel Lui (LLB 1974). The case drew on a real tax appeal, entered by the department's
own Professor Peter Willoughby (whose 'hobby of appealing tax cases' was to culminate
in 1997 in a victory in the House of Lords).[59] The panel found for the taxpayer, represented
by Lilian Mak and Michael Hui (both LLB 1976): it was, said Denning, a rare case where
persuasive advocacy made him change his initial view formed on a reading of the papers.

The moot was followed by a buffet lunch, a talk by Denning, and a reception, where he
mingled with students. The students, wrote the lecturer Andrew Hicks, were 'astounded
that someone so brilliant, so important, so powerful could be so modest, unpompous,
unstuffy, warm and accessible to them.' Alexa Cheung (LLB 1976), who had argued for
the losing side (a 'hopeless one, but we tried our best'), was about to go to London for
her Master of Laws (LLM). On learning this, Denning invited her to visit him, which she
did.[60] 'I was captivated by his whole persona,' she recalled in a speech at an LLB graduation
ceremony in 2013, 'I told myself that I will practise law, which I did until 1997.'[61] Six years
later, in September 1983, HKU took mooting to the international level when it co-hosted
the first Commonwealth Law Mooting Competition, held in Hong Kong along with the
Commonwealth Law Conference.[62]

Law Students How Are You?

Nearly 1,000 undergraduates embarked on the LLB course during the 15 years from 1969
to 1984. Of these, approximately 84 per cent graduated and 63 per cent went on to take
the PCLL. Most law students were school-leavers of Hong Kong origin, with a higher proportion of women than the university average[63] and with more women than men in most

---

59. The 1997 case involved tax on bonds purchased in Hong Kong on or after his retirement and transferred to
the UK prior to his return there. Willoughby successfully argued that income from the bonds should not be taxed
because he was not ordinarily resident in Britain when they were purchased and because they were bought as part of
a retirement plan with the intention to defer tax, not avoid it. *Commissioners of Inland Revenue v Willoughby* [1997]
4 All ER 65.

60. Hicks, 'Lord Denning's Visit' in *Thirty Years*, 58–9; *Law Media*, June 1977 & January 1979.

61. HKU Faculty of Law, *Newsletter*, Spring 2013.

62. Nine teams took part. In the first round Hong Kong was beaten by the Australian team, which went on to win
the competition. Allcock, 'Commonwealth Mooting Competition', 28 September 1983, HKUA: Board of the Studies
of the School of Law – Minutes (1983).

63. The male/female ratio among law graduates in the early 1970s was 1.4:1, compared with the general university
ratio of 2.4:1 in 1974. Robert Ribeiro, 'The Hong Kong Law Student', *Journal of Malaysian and Comparative Law*
(1976), 241–9.

years from the late 1970s, a trend attributed by some to the tendency of schools to stream girls into arts and languages and boys into science and mathematics, and to a generally better performance by women at interviews.[64] Although most entrants were young school-leavers, there were several 'mature' students, including an annual batch of government and police scholars and, for a few years from 1980, part-time students in full-time employment attending an 'extended course'. After the dearth of applicants for the first intake in 1969, the numbers of HKU applicants putting law as their first or second choice rose dramatically – to 229 in 1970, 395 in 1975, and to a peak of 878 in 1981, before dipping to 728 in 1983. Admissions committees had a plentiful, even overwhelming, choice of candidates, so that making the right choices for the limited number of places – forty in the early years, rising to fifty-five in the mid-1970s and eighty in the early 1980s – was a formidable challenge. The task was not helped by occasional lobbying from outside on behalf of some applicants and an assumption by the government that the scholars it put forward would be automatically accepted.[65]

The admissions committees took their work seriously. Among all subjects at HKU, law was one that bore least direct relationship to subjects taught at school. Although 'A' level results were the prime criterion, early admissions committees put emphasis on interviews (as many as 262 in 1979), a use-of-English examination, and, in some years, tests to assess writing ability, logic, and aptitude. As a result, the Department of Law developed an admissions procedure independently from the rest of the Faculty of Social Sciences, which placed less reliance on interviews and tests. Some, like Anna Wu (LLB 1974), were attracted to law because of the weight given to interviews. But the use of interviews was greatly reduced in the early 1980s amid concerns they were having a 'depressing effect on the market' for law degrees.[66] The stress on careful selection nevertheless continued. 'We are looking for the eighty people who will best succeed in the study of law,' wrote Peter Wesley-Smith, the admissions tutor in 1980–1982. Another aim was 'to choose a class which, by virtue of its balanced composition, provides stimulus and differing backgrounds and experience.' Fluency in English was indispensable; knowledge of Chinese was not. Motivation, demonstrated by sincere reasons for studying law and some knowledge of the legal system, was also essential. Unmotivated students, no matter what their academic scores, were 'a bad risk.' So were applicants under family pressure to take law who would otherwise study something else, or those whose only interest was to make a fortune in law. In fact, it was unnecessary for applicants to want to become lawyers at all. Knowledge of current affairs

64. Sinden, 'A Commentary on the Admission Tutor's Report', 2 October 1981, HKUA: Board of the Studies of the School of Law – Minutes (1981); Peter Wesley-Smith: interview with the author, 23 October 2017.

65. Gimson, Admission Tutor's Report on Admissions Procedure, 5 September 1978 & Sussex, Report on Admissions 1979, HKUA: Board of the Studies of the School of Law – Minutes (1978 & 1979).

66. 'Profile: Anna H.Y. Wu', *The Law Society of Hong Kong Gazette*, October 1987; Admissions Reports for 1981, 1982, & 1983, HKUA: Board of the Studies of the School of Law – Minutes (1981, 1982, & 1983).

and social awareness were desirable. But 'we should not insist on vivacity, loquacious-ness, self-confidence or other qualities which might seem to be relevant to lawyering.' And personal appearance was 'quite irrelevant'.[67]

Because of the emphasis placed on competence in English, a large proportion of students came from English-medium 'Anglo-Chinese' schools, which included some of Hong Kong's most prestigious institutions. Not all, however, were from wealthy families. One early student, Patrick Chan (LLB 1974), took turns with his brothers to go to university so that one of them could work to support the family after the death of their father: Chan took a job at the Royal Observatory before joining the Department of Law.[68] Another student, Kwan Man Kwong (LLB 1975), grew up in cubicle accommodation in Sham Shui Po, helping in his father's small spice business and attending a government evening school. He learned English from the BBC World Service and the *South China Morning Post*, and was accepted by Ying Wa College at the age of 19.[69] Among all undergraduates, law students had the lowest application rates for university financial assistance.[70] They tended to be highly goal-oriented in their plans to enter the legal profession. This was hardly surprising given the specialized nature of the subject. Kwan Man Kwong and most of his classmates never thought of another career: 'people who read law became lawyers, people who studied medicine became doctors, people who read engineering became engineers.'[71]

Kwan, who enjoyed criminal law most, came to specialize in litigation as a solicitor. But a tendency among other graduates to work in conveyancing and other highly profitable activities, combined with the curriculum's emphasis on 'commercial and generally affluent activity,' raised concerns that the university was, as Robert Ribeiro put it, minting only 'one brand of "lawyer"' to serve 'the affluent elites.'[72] They 'seem to be far too pre-occupied at such an early age with financial, corporate and commercial type areas: in other words with making money,' said another teacher, Lester Dally, in 1982. He urged students to take a greater interest in 'soft' subjects like jurisprudence, which 'many would prefer to avoid' had it not been compulsory.[73]

A related concern, raised by several lecturers, was the passive approach to learning – the tendency among HKU students, as the lecturer Rodney Griffith put it, 'to accept wholesale what has been said' and the lack of 'an attitude of challenge.' A few teachers, like Lester Dally, put this down to the difficulty of studying law in a second language.[74] Others, however,

67. Wesley-Smith, memo on Admissions Criteria, 24 July 1980, HKUA: Board of the Studies of the School of Law – Minutes (1980).

68. Patrick Chan, interview with the author, 1 June 2016.

69. Kwan Man Kwong, interview with the author, 18 October 2017.

70. Ribeiro, 'The Hong Kong Law Student', 242.

71. Kwan Man Kwong, interview with the author, 18 October 2017.

72. Ribeiro, 'The Hong Kong Law Student', 245–7.

73. *Law Media*, May 1982.

74. *Law Media*, January 1979 & May 1982.

commented on the generally high standard of English – particularly *written* English – and attributed it instead to a traditional reliance on rote learning or simply to the desire to know the right answer to an exam question – a natural urge, noted one teacher, Roda Mushkat, in students the world over.[75] It was difficult to devise an examination system that could test critical thinking, recalls Peter Wesley-Smith: consequently, 'those who put their noses down and concentrated on the narrow curriculum were the ones who did well.'[76] Even so, as Raymond Wacks describes it, it was quite a jolt to come from teaching final-year LLB students in South Africa ('hard men' just out of compulsory military service and 'not remotely respectful') to his first class in Hong Kong in 1984. 'As I entered the room there was complete silence. The assembled students regarded me with a combination of terror and bewilderment. The males wore suits and ties. All looked grave, serious, young. I sported jeans and a sweater. The atmosphere was tense. I introduced myself. Every head was bowed, staring at empty pads of paper.' An invitation to students to introduce themselves 'produced palpable misery.' A provocative question – 'Human beings don't need law, do they?' – met a wall of silence. 'Classes in Durban were, by comparison, a pushover,' Wacks concluded.[77]

Whatever their comments on learning methods, lecturers were in little doubt about the quality and determination of their early students. Law students spent more time on their studies than did any other category of student – 50 per cent more than the average social sciences student.[78] Kwan Man Kwong spent over twelve hours a day, five days a week, from 9 a.m. to 10 p.m., in the library or at lectures, with breaks only for meals, on top of a seventy-five-minute commute, by ferry and on foot, to and from his home in Sham Shui Po. Such long hours were not unusual. 'Lively, hard-working, and eager to learn, they realized they were privileged to have the opportunity offered them and did their utmost to take advantage of it,' recalled John Rear of the first cohorts. 'There was a very special atmosphere: the feeling that we, staff and students, were embarked on a landmark adventure together.' They were really keen to study, recalls Roderick O'Brien of his students, and, far from being passive learners, were enthusiastic about participating in discussions. 'They displayed a measure of individualism and projected an air of urban sophistication,' said Roda Mushkat of her early students. They were something special, 'the crème de la crème.'[79]

75. Roda Mushkat: interview with the author, 5 September 2017.

76. Peter Wesley-Smith: interview with the author, 23 October 2017.

77. Wacks, 'My First Week in the Faculty' in *Thirty Years*, 74.

78. In a survey in 1974, law students spent an average 49.2 hours a week on 'serious reading' (which included teaching contact hours and private study). Architecture students came next, with 41.6 hours, followed by Arts (36.1 hours), Medicine (33.5 hours), Social Sciences (32.6 hours), Science (32.3 hours), and Engineering (29.5 hours). Ribeiro, 'The Hong Kong Law Student', 242 & 245–7.

79. Rear, 'Rear Window' in *Thirty Years*, 15; John Rear, interview with the author, 2 December 2017; Roderick O'Brien, interview with the author, 4 July 2018; Mushkat, 'Then and Now', *Building for Tomorrow on Yesterday's Strengths*, 22; Roda Mushkat, interview with the author, 5 September 2017.

There were, of course, exceptions. Some could not keep up with the work. Others found that law was not for them and changed their plans. The attrition rate at the end of the first year – nearly a quarter in 1973 and 1974, a third in 1975, and continuing at a high level into the 1980s – was among the highest in HKU. Retakes of some examinations were arranged in most years: one student spent six years repeating courses before finally failing. But the general policy was to discontinue students with little or no aptitude for the law or to allow them to switch to other subjects. Some students had to support themselves and their families with jobs in addition to their full-time studies. From time to time the demands of outside work became a matter of concern among teachers; the pressures forced a few students to defer their studies or pull out altogether. Not all graduates entered the legal profession. A few went into business or government. One early graduate, Tang Shu-wing (LLB 1982) became a stage director of international repute. Others continued their studies elsewhere before returning to Hong Kong either to practise or to pursue academic careers. Notable among these were Albert Chen (LLB 1980) and Johannes Chan (LLB 1981), both of whom, after further study overseas, returned to teach at HKU.

One of the most atypical, least 'goal-oriented' of early law undergraduates was also one of the top students. Ronny Tong (LLB 1972) came from a poor family in which his mother, a nurse, was the sole breadwinner. A bright schoolboy, he was admitted to Queen's College but did poorly in his 'A' levels after falling ill during examinations. His grades fell below the minimum standard for admission to university. His English was not very good, so he took job as a bank teller, earning extra money playing guitar with a rock band in bars in Wan Chai and Tsim Sha Tsui. An old classmate urged him to try for the new Department of Law at HKU, since few had applied in the uncertainty surrounding the status of the degree. Tong obtained an interview, where, after some adverse comments on his school record, the conversation turned to jazz, and Evans and Tong found they had interests in common. As a result of the relaxed attitude towards 'A' level results taken by the department, Tong was accepted. He continued to play in bands to pay his way through university, an occupation that left him so short of sleep that he collapsed on the floor after dozing off in the first lecture he attended. Tong was an outstanding student, the first LLB to obtain first-class honours and the top performer in the 1974 English Bar exam, which he took after a scholarship for a Bachelor of Civil Law at Oxford. A classmate, Cheng Shee-sun (LLB 1972), won a scholarship to study at Cambridge. These accolades, coming so early in the department's history, were widely seen as a mark of the quality of the new LLB degree. Both returned to Hong Kong, Cheng to found a firm of solicitors with his former classmate Christopher Chan (LLB 1972), Tong to practise as a barrister and later to serve on the Legislative and Executive Councils.[80]

---

80. 'Face to Face with Ronny Tong SC', *Hong Kong Lawyer*, July 2015; Faculty of Law, University of Hong Kong, *Res Ipsa Loquitur: The Fact Speaks for Itself*. Hong Kong: Faculty of Law, the University of Hong Kong, 2012, 38; *SCMP*, 15 May 1972.

Whatever their backgrounds, early law students came to be seen, and to see themselves, as a special group with its own esprit de corps. 'We have always been treated (to a certain extent) as outsiders,' wrote Michael Hui, chairman of the HKU Law Association, in its magazine *Law Media* in 1975. 'Recently, I had a talk with a Science student about this and he told me (good-humouredly) that the sight of a group of law students having tea in the canteen was so formidable that it scared him off.'[81] 'Our boys are said to be well-dressed gentlemen and our girls are described as "eye-catching and attractive ladies and notice-able users of make-up,"' said another soul-searching article in a 1978 issue of *Law Media* devoted to what other students thought of them. But the make-up hid 'those tired lines and our pale complexion which result from constant hard work and insufficient sleep.' And while law students were 'among the most polite students in the University,' this was a 'cold politeness', for they were really 'aloof, snobbish and self-assertive.' Most people found it hard to penetrate the 'legal terms and jargons' with which they peppered conversations in an effort to assert their superiority.[82] Contact with other students was in any case limited since most law students were 'misanthropic hermits' who spent all their time in the library. 'University life to these book-worms means nothing more than the second floor of 154–158 Caine Road,' said the magazine *Undergrad* in a piece in 1971 headed 'Law students how are you?' Some complained that the magistrates recruited from overseas were out of touch, it said. 'We would like to be assured that the generation of lawyers produced by our own University is not equally, if not more, out of touch.'[83]

Undergrad was the organ of the Hong Kong University Students' Union. Like student bodies elsewhere, the union entered a period of activism in the late 1960s and early 1970s. Apart from securing rights such as student representation on the Senate and faculty boards, its members took part in social movements outside the university. Prominent among its office-bearers were students in the Faculty of Social Sciences, of which the Department of Law was technically a part. It was perhaps natural that law students – studious, self-disciplined, and somewhat conservative – would be seen as a distinct group. At first, housed in their separate premises a mile away from the main campus, they were barely seen at all. Even when they moved to campus in 1973, to the fifth floor of the new Knowles Building, law students maintained a separate identity. They followed their own curriculum, disconnected from the increasingly integrated system for the rest of the faculty. They had their own library and their own Law Association, formed against opposition from the Student Union and Social Sciences Society, and amid divisions among law students themselves.[84]

---

81. *Law Media*, December 1975.
82. *Law Media*, January 1978.
83. *Undergrad*, 1 June 1971.
84. HKU Law Association, *1970 Annual Magazine*, 1; *Undergrad*, 1 November 1971, 6; *Law Media*, July 1970, 1–6, & December 1975, 2.

Plate 1 The first forty students in the LLB programme at HKU, photographed outside the Caine Road building in 1970. The four staff – Bernard Downey, Dafydd Evans and John Rear (teachers), and Malcolm Quinn (the first Law Librarian) – are in the centre of the front row.

Plate 2 Students hard at work in the Library of the Caine Road building.

Plate 3 Dafydd Evans, Head of the Department of Law 1969–1978, Dean of the School of Law 1978–1984, Dean of the Faculty of Law 1984–1987, with law students in the 1970s.

Plate 4 Peter Rhodes, Dean of the Faculty of Law 1987–1993.

Plate 5 Peter Wesley-Smith, Dean of the Faculty of Law 1993–1996.

Plate 6 Albert Chen, Head of the Department of Law 1993–1996, Dean of the Faculty of Law 1996–2002.

Plate 7 Johannes Chan, Head of the Department of Law 1999–2002, Dean of the Faculty of Law 2002–2014.

Plate 8 Michael Hor, Dean of the Faculty of Law 2014–2019.

Plate 9 John Rear, the first editor of the *Hong Kong Law Journal* 1971–1973 and a lecturer and senior lecturer in the Department of Law 1969–1973, and before that in the Department of Extra-Mural Studies 1967–1969.

Plate 10 Henry Litton QC, founding editor-in-chief of the *Hong Kong Law Journal* 1971–1992, Justice of Appeal 1992–1997, Permanent Judge of the Court of Final Appeal 1997–2000 and Non-Permanent Judge 2000–2015, now an Honorary Professor in the Faculty of Law. (Picture courtesy of *South China Morning Post*)

Plate 11 Bernard Downey, senior lecturer 1970–1980, district judge 1980–1994, discussing cases with students.

Plate 12 Bob Allcock, first Head of the Department of Law 1984–1986, Solicitor General of the Hong Kong SAR 2000–2007, now an Honorary University Fellow.

Plate 13 Professor Peter Willoughby, Director of Professional Legal Education 1974–1978, first head of the Department of Professional Legal Education 1978–1986. (Picture courtesy of *South China Morning Post*)

Plate 14 Professor Roda Mushkat, a member of the Faculty since 1979, Head of the Department of Law 2003–2005, now an Honorary Professor.

Plate 15 Professor Ted Tyler, Head of the Department of Professional Legal Education 1986–1991, now an Honorary Professor.

Plate 16 Professor Christopher Sherrin, Head of the Department of Professional Legal Education 1993–1997, now an Emeritus Professor.

Plate 17 Professor Raymond Wacks, Head of the Department of Law 1986–1993, now an Emeritus Professor.

Plate 18 Professor Yash Ghai, first Sir Y. K. Pao Professor of Public Law 1989–2005, now an Emeritus Professor.

Plate 19 Alexa Lam, lecturer 1977–1980, teaching a class in the late 1970s. After a distinguished career in the Securities and Futures Commission, Lam rejoined the Faculty, first as Professor of Legal Practice 2015–2018, and then Cheng Yu Tung Visiting Professor 2018–2021.

Plate 20 Peter Rhodes, Dean (standing), with Ted Tyler (third from left), Michael Wilkinson (far right) and barristers from England, introducing a session in a summer school in advocacy training *c.* 1988.

Plate 21 Betty Ho, a much-loved teacher in the Faculty 1988–2002.

The Law Association had its own magazine, *Law Media* (an 'extremely sensational' organ, according to one lecturer),[85] written mainly in English while other student magazines were turning to Chinese. It had its own sports teams, and its calendar of social events: an orientation camp for new students in September, a barn dance at Christmas, and barbecues, picnics and tea parties throughout the year. Students, like their teachers, developed relations with the profession, with occasional moots and football matches against the Articled Clerks' Association and a formal summer ball attended by the Chief Justice, the Attorney General, and other luminaries. Contacts between students and teachers, though formal, were closer than in many other parts of the university.

Despite the general reputation for aloofness, several early law students took part in wider university activities. Kenneth Kwok (LLB 1972) was prominent in Students' Union politics and a frequent contributor to *Undergrad*. The future politician Albert Ho (LLB 1974) was heavily involved in the student movements of the early 1970s, such as the Diaoyu Islands campaign: his real interests were sociology and philosophy, and he was offered a place in the Department of Law on the strength of his knowledge of current affairs.[86] Albert Chen, a future Dean of the Faculty of Law, was on the editorial teams of *Undergrad* as well as *Law Media* and *Justitia*. Other law students joined university sports teams. Although law students were said to have little time for sports, their teams often did well against other faculty teams. The debating team 'won so many times that they finally had to scrap the whole thing.'[87] The Law Choir won the Union Festival competition six years running, from 1977 to 1982: two of its members, Linda Li and Winnie Tam (both LLB 1983), were so talented they were invited to take the solo parts in a 1981 performance of Haydn's *Theresa Mass* in the City Hall.[88] A law anthem, 'The Spirit of the Law', with words by Mimmie Chan (LLB 1980) and Mathew Ho (LLB 1980), was first sung at the 1979 Union Festival.[89] Later that year, 'a very spectacular and ingenious' show about the life of law students was a highlight of 'Union Orientation Nite' in September 1979.[90]

In a further effort to improve understanding between law students and other HKU students, in January 1980 the Law Association held a special 'Law Week' consisting of an exhibition, booths offering legal advice, a talk by the barrister Patrick Yu (an honorary lecturer) on professional ethics, and a forum on 'Law – a means to control people's rights', which included on its panel the Chairman of the Magistrates' Association, Anthony Wane (another honorary lecturer). A 'Law Nite' featured student and staff performances,

85. Lester Dally, interviewed in *Law Media*, May 1982.
86. 何俊仁，謙卑的奮鬥 [(Albert) Ho Chun Yan, *My Humble Struggle*] (Hong Kong University Press, 2010), 11.
87. *Law Media*, December 1975, 2.
88. The conductor was the law lecturer Leonard Pegg, another talented musician. *Law Media*, September 1981.
89. *Law Media*, July 1979, 9, & October 1979, 4.
90. *Law Media*, October 1979.

including a drama entitled 'The Demonic Revenge' ('魔債').[91] In October that year the Law Association joined with the Urban Council to present a four-day law exhibition at the City Hall, the first of several aimed at the general public. A mock trial with students playing all the parts was filmed and then shown during the exhibition and in extracts on TV. The mock trial – on an indictment for rape – had been held in the temporary Supreme Court on Battery Path with special permission from the Chief Justice.[92] The exhibition, much of it in Chinese, prompted some to call for the translation of all of Hong Kong's laws into Chinese.[93]

Not everyone joined in these activities. Some members of the Law Week organizing committee even concluded that the whole event was a failure. Only about half of law students were even members of the Law Association.[94] Like any other community, the department had its factions, cliques, and occasional controversies: in the late 1970s, for example, the practice of testing new students through 'struggle sessions' at orientation sparked a long debate about the alleged high-handed treatment of freshmen by senior students.[95] In the early 1980s the Law Association's annual general meeting was said to be an occasion for 'open confrontation' between office-bearers and those with grudges against them: one such meeting, in 1984, went on from 6 p.m. to 3 a.m.[96]

The year of intake was the basis for deep friendships, many of which endured in later life. A few led to marriage. All students attended the same courses in their first and second years. Most enrolled in the same courses in their third year, and again in the PCLL year – 'Year IV' as it was generally known. The fifty-five-strong intake of 1979 might have been 'one of the last few small closely-knit classes,' recalls Marlene Ng (LLB 1982): the next year the intake increased to over eighty. For her, law school was a time of discovery and independence, of 'bouncing ideas around classmates, deciphering law lectures, copying notes, and skipping tutorials; it was a time to revel in the grapevine gossip that ran amok in the Law Library; and it was a time for dating, lazing about, hall functions, balls, and the choir.' By year three, 'the solidarity of the class was an unquestioned fact' as everyone 'hunkered down for the final exams,' forming study groups, dissecting questions over tea, and swapping notes.[97] A classmate, Lester Huang (LLB 1982), recalls a 'Friends of Photocopying Club' formed to share the tasks of note-taking and looking up cases in Elizabeth Sussex's fast-paced Family Law lectures: the end-product was a comprehensive typed set of notes, distributed to each

---

91. *Law Media*, January & April 1980.

92. The Supreme Court Building in Statue Square (now the Court of Final Appeal) had been evacuated two years earlier when construction of the MTR nearby had caused cracks to appear in the building.

93. *SCMP*, 3 & 8 October 1980.

94. Partly because the association's events and services were open to non-members. *Law Media*, January 1978.

95. See *Law Media*, January, April, July & October 1979, & January & April 1980

96. *Law Media*, December 1984.

97. Marlene Ng (and others), 'The Year of 1982 and PCLL of 1983', in *Thirty Years*, 64–5.

member and eventually comprising three large bound volumes. 'I am pretty confident that everyone in our group relied on those materials alone in preparing for our examinations.'[98]

The centre of activity was the crowded Law Library, located, from 1973, on the fifth floor of the Knowles Building. Many spent over twelve hours a day there, reading 'piles and piles of "small print" law reports' and 'heaps of duplicated materials.' Some complained about the poor ventilation in winter, the chilly air-conditioning in summer, the selfishness of those who hogged or hid crucial texts, the general insufficiency of holdings, and the noisy chatter. Yet for most it was a site of comradeship, a forum for discussion, even a place of joy, according to one account in *Law Media*, which also asked for tolerance of 'our human weakness', for who could 'remain speechless and motionless for over twelve hours?'[99] The Law Library was a 'bee-hive community', an unofficial common room, a subject for poems and cartoons – 'our "Wonderland"', as one rant against noise and inconsiderateness put it, perhaps sarcastically.[100] 'Because we study together in the Law Library, our friends are usually law students as well,' said the law students' representative on the Senate, Peter Man (LLB 1980). 'We tend to detach ourselves from the rest of the student community and form an independent and apparently self-sufficient world of our own in the Law Library,' said *Law Media* in 1979. With a few exceptions, 'we make little contribution to university life in the main campus, not to say the student movement in Hong Kong. We justify our passivity by pointing to the high dropout rate and the heavy workload. We shut our eyes to the happenings around us in the University and society in general, and instead dream about the financially promising, socially reputable and professionally rewarding careers awaiting us.'[101]

This somewhat cynical view was part of a constant self-questioning at a time when other students were leading campaigns against corruption and for the use of Chinese as an official language, taking an interest in affairs in Mainland China, and involving themselves in the rights and welfare of squatters and other marginal groups.[102] The huge amount of reading required of law students and the pressure of examinations contributed to a sense of detachment from the student mainstream. Competition was intense: 'everybody puts pressure on everybody,' said Alexa Cheung. Although staff denied rumours of an annual quota of failures, the high discontinuation rate added to the pressure. 'Look to your left, look to your right, next year one of you will not be here,' Evans would tell students on their

---

98. Lester Huang, in discussion with Michael Wilkinson, HKU Faculty of Law, *Newsletter*, Spring 2008.

99. 'Chrisso', 'Joy in Our Law Library', *Law Media*, April 1979.

100. Editorial, *Law Media*, April 1980, 1; 'What is Our Library', *Law Media*, May 1982.

101. *Law Media*, July & October 1979, 1.

102. A general neglect of these subjects by *Law Media* prompted one member of its editorial board, Johannes Chan, to produce its first article in Chinese (中文，願妳安息 ['Chinese, may you rest in peace!']) lamenting law students' lack of interest in the Chinese language movement then sweeping across the campus. *Law Media*, January 1979.

first day.[103] Yet, observed the 1979 *Law Media* editorial, a record of passing one examination after another, and the struggle to be in the top few per cent of the generation – a sense that 'we only are destined to be masters of tomorrow's world' – fostered complacency as well as insecurity. The very nature of the LLB degree also encouraged law students to see themselves 'as lawyers-to-be rather than as ordinary university students.' They studied nothing but 'black letter law' to the exclusion of closely related subjects such as criminology or political science. Even purely legal topics with less practical relevance – such as comparative law or the law of China – were seldom or never offered. 'Let us not be content with being mere legal technicians,' but instead struggle for 'intellectual enlightenment' and 'social awareness', the editorial concluded.[104]

This was surely too harsh an assessment. The contents of *Justitia*, the early student law journal 1972–1986, show the extent to which students brought their legal education to bear on issues of social and political concern. Articles based on student dissertations covered highly topical subjects such as restrictions on public assembly (Patrick Chan, in the 1972/1973 issue and Johannes Chan, 1981/1982), the legal position of squatters (Wally Yeung, 1973/1974), and the stigma of triad society membership (Ngan On Tak, 1975), while detailed empirical studies dealt with subjects such as industrial accidents (1979/1980), the impact of more liberal divorce legislation covering over 1,000 divorce petitions, analysed, for the first time, by computer (1981/1982), and the performance of the new Small Claims Tribunal (1976/1977). In 1971 a committee under the Hong Kong Federation of Students, composed mainly of law students and chaired by Stephanie Cheung (LLB 1972), undertook detailed research into the use of Chinese in the law and in the courts. Its report was singled out for commendation by the government committee on the subject, which concurred with its recommendation that Cantonese should be used more widely in magistrates' courts and tribunals.[105]

Keen to show an awareness of 'our responsibility towards society',[106] law students also participated in direct outreach programmes. Through the clinical legal education scheme PCLL students gave direct assistance to some of the poorest members of society. In 1976 the HKU Law Association – on a suggestion by the Justice of Appeal, Yang Ti Liang, a patron of the association – started its own Legal Education Project aimed at raising understanding

---

103. *Law Media*, January 1978 & January 1979; Audrey Eu, 'Constantly Thinking of Food' & Warren Chan, 'Hard Work' in *Thirty Years*, 21 & 56.

104. *Law Media*, October 1979, 1.

105. The recommendation, which resulted in a provision in the Official Languages Ordinance (No. 10 of 1974) allowing proceedings in magistrates' courts and certain other lower courts to be conducted in either English or Chinese, at the discretion of the court, had little immediate impact since most magistrates at the time did not speak Chinese. *Third Report of the Chinese Language Committee: Court Proceedings and the Language of the Law*, June 1971 (Hong Kong: Government Printer, 1971).

6; *SCMP*, 29 & 30 January 1971.

106. Leo S.C. Yeung in *Law Media*, July 1979, 7.

of the law in the community, which, according to one of its chairmen, Leo S.C. Yeung (LLB 1980), had a 'traditional Chinese phobia for anything legal.' The main activities were lectures and court visits for secondary schools during the summer vacation. Within the first three years alone nearly 5,000 school students had taken part in the programme.[107]

Teaching in a Legal Backwater

The teaching staff increased from four on the opening of the Department of Law in 1969 to over thirty on the creation of the Faculty of Law in 1984. During these fifteen years some sixty full-time teachers taught law at various times, two as professors (Evans and Willoughby), the rest as lecturers or senior lecturers.[108] Some stayed for a year or two before moving on. A few spent most of their careers at HKU.[109] The average span was about seven years. The longest was thirty-two: Michael Wilkinson joined in 1983 and retired in 2015 at the age of seventy, after which he continued to teach up to his death in 2019. Sixteen of the early staff were women. The first among these were Susan Kneebone (1975–1978), Judith Gimson (formerly Judith Evans) (1977–1978), and Alexa Cheung (later Alexa Lam) (1977–1980), who was also the first graduate of the Department of Law to join the staff. Roda Mushkat (1979–2005) was from Israel, via Canada, Britain, and New Zealand, having followed her economist-husband as an 'obedient wife', and having acquired an impressive array of qualifications on the way.[110] Judith Sihombing (1983–2001) had taught law in Malaysia and Australia. All but five[111] of the early staff were from places outside Hong Kong – mostly Britain, Australia, and New Zealand, with a few from North America. Some saw themselves more as lawyers than as academics, and sooner or later moved into practice. A few were recruited from the overseas staff of Commonwealth universities, notably the new African law schools. One of these, Michael Wilkinson, had spent thirteen years in Africa, first in Uganda and then, after being expelled as an alleged British spy, in Malawi. His farewell party with his students in Malawi, where the Banda regime tended to see lawyers as troublemakers, 'had to be held in an open field to avoid any possibility of hidden microphones or cameras.'[112]

---

107. *Law Media*, April 1978 & July 1979.

108. The designations 'lecturer' and 'senior lecturer' were replaced, respectively, by 'assistant professor' and 'associate professor' in 1996.

109. Over half of the staff serving during these fifteen years have left recollections of their time at HKU in interviews with the student magazine *Law Media* or brief memoirs in various anniversary souvenirs published by the Faculty, notably *Thirty Years* (1999) and *Building for Tomorrow on Yesterday's Strength* (2004).

110. Roda Mushkat: interview with the author, 5 September 2017.

111. The early staff of Hong Kong origin were Ronny Wong (1971–72), Robert Ribeiro (1972–79), Alexa Cheung (1977–80), and Agnes Yung (1983–85). Peter Rhodes (1979–1996) was born in Hong Kong and educated in Hong Kong up to the age of 10, when he was sent to boarding school in New Zealand.

112. Michael Wilkinson, interview in *Hong Kong Lawyer*, July 2018; Wilkinson, 'Twenty-one Happy Years at HKU' in Faculty of Law, HKU, *Building for Tomorrow on Yesterday's Strength*, 24.

The staff, recalls Roda Mushkat, included 'a fair number of colourful and larger-than-life characters.'[113] One of them, Barry Lovegrove (1973–1983), founded a pub in Wan Chai, The Old China Hand. Another, Bob Allcock (1973–1986), formed a rock band with Lovegrove, Peter Wesley-Smith (1973–1999), and Ray Faulkner (1971–1978). Under the name 'Junk', the band joined the 'Clean Hong Kong Campaign,' playing in housing estates from the back of a lorry and, 'since the quality of our music was variable,' padding out their limited repertoire with magic tricks, kung fu routines, and the occasional staged brawl.[114] Just as the antics of 'Junk' contrasted with the more decorous performances of the Law Choir, so, in this age of safari suits and floral shirts, the teachers tended to dress more casually than their students. 'My working costume,' recalled Richard Field (1971–1973), 'was shorts, a casual shirt, and a pair of flip-flops. My hair was also much too long. What my smartly dressed students thought they were far too well-mannered to say.'[115] HKU, noted Raymond Wacks (1984–2001), was the only university where the teachers were 'cooler than the students.' Most were barely older than their students. Joining the department at the age of twenty-three 'with the ink on my degree certificate hardly dry,' Robert Ribeiro (1972–1979) was 'constantly being mistaken for a first year student' and was 'treated by the more senior students with the disdain appropriate for someone of such lowly status.'[116]

Mushkat recalls an intimate, club-like feeling among the dozen or so full-time staff in the 1970s. 'We ate together both in the school and outside. We participated in social events together. Personally we were very aware of each other.' The atmosphere was an 'intriguing mixture of serious academic endeavour and relentless social engagement.'[117] Almost all wrote for the *Hong Kong Law Journal* or gave talks in the Law Lectures for Practitioners series, many supplying the first analyses of large areas of Hong Kong law, such as wills and succession (Dafydd Evans), family law (Leonard Pegg, Elizabeth Philips), criminal law (Bernard Downey, Peter Morrow, Penelope Jewkes), labour law (Robert Ribeiro), landlord and tenant (Peter Willoughby, Roderick O'Brien), contract law (Ray Faulkner, Richard Field), constitutional law (Peter Wesley-Smith), accident compensation (John Miller), and refugee law (Roda Mushkat). The *Journal*, observed Peter Wesley-Smith in a survey of legal texts in 1979, was 'by far the single most important source of secondary legal literature in Hong Kong.'[118] Some collected their articles or turned their lectures into textbooks, such as Peter Willoughby's *Hong Kong Revenue Law* (1981), Hartley Bramwell's *Conveyancing in*

---

113. Roda Mushkat: interview with the author, 5 September 2017.

114. Reminiscence by Lovegrove & Allcock, 'Junk Bonds', in *Thirty Years*, 43 & 49–50.

115. Field, 'Open Door', in *Thirty Years*, 46.

116. Robert Ribeiro, 'A Lecturer Among Our First Home-grown Barristers' in Hong Kong Bar Association, *50th Anniversary*, 42.

117. Roda Mushkat: interview with the author, 5 September 2017.

118. 'This type of legal writing is likely to continue, for it (1) is necessary and useful, (2) is not especially difficult to produce, and (3) fills up the curriculum vitae.' Wesley-Smith, *Legal Literature in Hong Kong* (Hong Kong: Centre of

Hong Kong (1981), and Leonard Pegg's *Family Law in Hong Kong*, which also drew on his 1974 HKU Master of Arts dissertation. The most lasting text from these years was *Chinese Labour Under British Rule* (1975)[119] by John Rear and the sociologist Joe England, described by Wesley-Smith in 1979 as 'probably the best sustained piece of work on Hong Kong law that has yet emerged.'[120]

Among the recurring themes in this early academic output were the outdatedness of much Hong Kong law and the slavish adherence to English models and English decisions. Going to Hong Kong was 'like stepping back in time,' recalled Michael Pendleton, who joined the School of Law in 1981: 'the student deference to teachers; the community's ignorance of lawyer jokes, even esteem for lawyers; and a legal and political system unable to demonstrate legitimacy.'[121] Hong Kong was 'a legal backwater,' said John Rear in an interview shortly before his departure in 1973. For this very reason, research into Hong Kong law was 'interesting and enjoyable (because it is a virgin field practically anything one does is useful) but not very rewarding from an academic career point of view.' His other reasons for leaving were the claustrophobic atmosphere – intellectually and physically – of Hong Kong and a feeling that, with the privileged lives enjoyed by expatriates, it was not a good place for bringing up his teenage daughters. 'I did not feel wholly comfortable with the idea of being part of the colonial class governing, apparently old-style, a colony at a time when the winds of change were blowing hard through the Commonwealth,' Rear recalls. He returned to England to pursue a distinguished career culminating in the pro-vice-chancellorship of the University of Northumbria. He maintained contacts with HKU as an external examiner but in 1982 gave up teaching law altogether, marking the decision with a ceremonial burning of all his lectures and other notes.[122]

Some staff left to continue their own legal education. Robert Ribeiro, for example, took a year off in 1978 to finish his training for the Bar in London, where he studied alongside some of his former students. On his return he left the university and went into private practice in Hong Kong before joining the Judiciary in 1999. Several others went into private practice in Hong Kong: among these were Ronnie Wong (1971–1972), Hartley Bramwell (1977–1982) Judith Gimson, Alexa Lam, Malcolm Merry (1981–1989), Colin Cohen (1983–1988), Agnes Yung (1984–1985), Ted Tyler (1985–1991), Anselmo Reyes (1986–1988), and Jack Young (1988–1990). Ray Faulkner and William Stone (1971–1978) set up chambers

---

Asian Studies, HKU, 1979), 22 & 25. Appendix 2 of this work contains a comprehensive list of articles and books on Hong Kong law up to 1979.

119. Revised and reissued as Joe England and John Rear, *Industrial Relations and law in Hong Kong* (Hong Kong: Oxford University Press, 1981).

120. Wesley-Smith, *Legal Literature in Hong Kong*, 35.

121. Michael Pendleton, 'Full Circle' in *Thirty Years*, 76.

122. *Undergrad*, 16 June 1973; Rear, 'Rear Window' in *Thirty Years*, 16; John Rear, interview with the author, 2 December 2017.

together; Stone was later a High Court judge in the Hong Kong SAR 1997–2011, with responsibility for running the commercial court. Bernard Downey was appointed to the Hong Kong bench as a district judge 1980–1994. Richard Field moved to McGill University then back to England, where, after twenty-two years' practice at the Bar, he was appointed a High Court judge 2002–2014; he returned to Hong Kong in 2014 as a visiting professor in the Faculty of Law and later served as a deputy judge in the High Court in Hong Kong. Bob Allcock joined the Legal Department and was Solicitor General of the Hong Kong SAR, 2000–2007. Alan Smith (1970–1973) went into banking and became chief executive of the investment bank Jardine Fleming in 1983. Roderick O'Brien (1974–1977) returned home to pursue a vocation as a priest in Adelaide; having developed a lifelong interest in Chinese law he also went on to teach at various universities in China. Barry Lovegrove bought a farm in New Zealand on the proceeds of the sale of his pub and savings from his salary at the 'highest paying university in the Commonwealth'; he later went into practice with one of his former students, and was a district judge in New Zealand 1995–2005.[123]

Despite generous pay and lavish accommodation, the turnover in staff was considerable. The department had great difficulty in recruiting and retaining adequate staff at a time of worldwide shortage of law teachers. This restricted the expansion of courses, limited growth in student admissions, and required staff to take on a heavy burden of work, including subjects with which they were unfamiliar. Robert Ribeiro recalls 'trying desperately to keep a week ahead of my students,' some of whom nevertheless recall him as one of the most organized and lucid of lecturers.[124] Some other teachers, such as Barry Lovegrove, had a more 'laid-back style' so that students were 'still labouring through the niceties of "Consideration" and "Contractual Terms"' during the last few weeks of his one-year course on contract.[125] In a story that has passed into faculty lore, one newly arrived teacher was giving his first lecture to a class of final-year students. 'There came a point when Albert Chen, one of the students, could take no more and stood up to inform the teacher that the content of his lecture was in all essential points inaccurate. He then (standing) delivered an extemporary lecture on evidence while the teacher (sitting) took notes.'[126]

From Department to School to Faculty

In 1972 the head of the Department of Law, Dafydd Evans, set out his vision for the future. A recognized system of local qualification for practising law had been secured, he noted.

---

123. *Council Brief* (Wellington Branch NZ Law Society), March 2013, 3–4.

124. Kwan Man Kwong, interview with the author, 18 October 2017; Albert Chen, interview with the author, 12 March 2018.

125. Marlene Ng (and others), 'The Year of 1982 and PCLL of 1983', in *Thirty Years*, 64.

126. Story told by Johannes Chan in Faculty of Law, HKU, *Res Ipsa Loquitur*, 62.

The department would improve this system to ensure it continued to meet the primary purpose for which legal education at HKU was established – the production of lawyers for Hong Kong. Beyond that, the main concern was to 'establish a firm base for the teaching of Law as an academic discipline in Hong Kong and as an intellectual centre for research both into Hong Kong law and into the law of the region as a whole.' This, said Evans, would require expanding the range of subjects taught for the LLB, developing graduate studies in law (in particular research into the law of modern China), and offering law courses to other students in the Faculty of Social Sciences, of which the department was a part. The aim, in brief, was to enable the department 'to survive as a *University* Law School' and to ensure its 'acceptance as a Law School of international standing.'[127]

Evans proposed an increase in student intake from forty to fifty-five per annum, partly to meet the demand for legal services in Hong Kong, but also to justify increases in staff needed to expand functions and recognize that law was 'a subject worthy of study for many who will never contemplate entry into the profession.' The department had built up fruitful relations with the profession and had earned its confidence. But there was 'one situation which we, as a University Law School, should avoid at all costs: we should not allow either our academic teaching or the students' choice of subjects to be dominated by professional requirements.' To teach only subjects required for professional qualification would consign the department to the status of some of the minor American law schools or those run by the Inns of Court and the Law Society of England and Wales. This, said Evans, would be detrimental to the department and the university, since it would fail to attract teachers of sufficient calibre. It would make students hoping to do graduate work elsewhere less acceptable to other universities because of their narrower intellectual scope. In the long run, it would be damaging to Hong Kong, which 'would not get the lawyers of the quality it needs.'[128]

Growth in Numbers

The LLB intake grew from the initial forty to fifty-five in 1974 and eighty in 1980. This was mainly the result of pressure from government, which worried about shortages of lawyers. Through the UGC and its successor the UPGC, the government designated law as a 'blister area' in which student numbers were to expand beyond projected general growth.[129] The

---

127. Evans, 'Law in the Quadrennium 1974–1978', 25 September 1972, HKUA: Board of the Faculty of Social Sciences and Law – Minutes (1972).

128. Evans, 'Law in the Quadrennium 1974–1978', 25 September 1972, HKUA: Board of the Faculty of Social Sciences and Law – Minutes (1972).

129. Executive Council Memorandum XCC(79)14 and Minutes, 20 December 1979, Executive Council Minutes and Papers.

Advisory Committee on Legal Education took a less urgent view: it was sceptical about claims of shortages and found it difficult to assess future demand, particularly in the absence of long-term policies to expand legal aid. It was concerned about the effects on legal services of a too rapid growth. In a strange echo of pre-war attitudes, it also warned of 'the dangers of social disruption which may be brought about by too many unemployed lawyers, especially in a sensitive community like Hong Kong.'[130] For its part, the School of Law wanted to give priority to consolidating the curriculum. It continued to find it difficult to recruit staff. It was also concerned that too great an increase in student numbers might pre-empt growth in other parts of the university.[131] After doubling intake in only a decade, the school 'might reasonably look forward to a period of consolidation' so as 'to permit more attention to be paid to the development of its academic role,' wrote Evans in 1983.[132] Yet he agreed that community needs must take priority. In 1982 the government, through the UPGC, asked HKU to increase the intake from 80 to 150 'in stages and as circumstances permit' in a planned expansion outside the agreed university-wide growth, to be made possible by additional funds. The university responded by increasing intake to 120 in 1984, and to 150 in 1987.

The PCLL intake grew at a similar rate, from 20 in 1972, 50 in 1978, 88 in 1984, and 140 in 1987. It had originally been intended only for LLB graduates of HKU: early regulations required Senate approval for non-HKU applicants, a power later delegated to the School of Law. From the mid-1970s, however, the PCLL increasingly attracted applications from law graduates, mostly of Hong Kong origin, with degrees from universities overseas. In 1979, when non-HKU graduates formed over a quarter of applicants, a qualifying examination was introduced to ensure that the degrees of those admitted were comparable to an LLB from HKU, and in 1983 a quota was applied (nineteen out of eighty places).[133] In 1981, after several enquiries from graduates with American degrees, the university consulted the Bar Association and Law Society, both of which were generally opposed to admitting practitioners who had gained their basic training in the US, though they agreed that the question of admission to the PCLL was ultimately a matter for the university.[134]

---

130. First Report to His Excellency the Governor of the Advisory Committee on Legal Education (1979), Annex B to Executive Council Memorandum XCR(79)245, 4 December 1979, Executive Council Minutes and Papers.

131. Evans, 'Law in the Triennium, 1981–1984', 14 February 1979, HKUA: Board of the Studies of the School of Law – Minutes (1979), 1.

132. 'Interim Year 1984–1985 and Triennium 1985–1988: Development Proposals of the School of Law', 8 June 1983, HKUA: Board of the Studies of the School of Law – Minutes (1983).

133. The qualifying exam was discontinued in the late 1980s. PCLL Admissions Reports 1979–1980 & 1983–1984, HKU Archives: Board of the Studies of the School of Law – Minutes (1979 & 1980).

134. Minutes of meeting, 11 February & 11 March 1981, HKU Archives: Board of the Studies of the School of Law – Minutes (1981).

By the early 1980s students were also applying to join the LLB in the second or third year after a year or two with overseas institutions, some as external students studying privately in Hong Kong for the University of London LLB. Several were admitted, but concerns arose in 1983 that HKU LLBs were sometimes being awarded on the strength of only a year's study at HKU: thereafter, applications for direct admission to the third year were no longer entertained.[135] Another special category consisted of 'extended course' students: non-university graduates (known as 'five-year men' because they were required to take five years' articles) or non-law graduates in full-time employment who had enrolled as students with the Law Society of Hong Kong to take the English solicitors' exams in Hong Kong under arrangements introduced in the late 1940s. In 1978, following recommendations in the *Ormrod Report*, the English Law Society announced a new system of training: the Common Professional Examination (CPE) would replace the Part I examinations formerly taken by non-law graduates, to be followed, for all prospective solicitors, by a new final course of thirty-six weeks, a new final exam, and two years' articles. As a result of these changes, from 1982 English solicitors' examinations were no longer held in Hong Kong. To prevent a rush of poorly prepared students hoping to qualify in Hong Kong by 1982, in February 1979 the roll of students kept by the Law Society of Hong Kong – then consisting of nearly 600 names – was closed except to those with a PCLL from HKU or a law degree from another recognized university.[136]

The changes, known as the 'pipeline problem', closed one of the three routes to admission as a solicitor in Hong Kong and deepened concerns about the supply of lawyers. Although the old route of going to the UK to qualify remained open, pressure on the third route – law qualifications from HKU followed by articles or pupillage – intensified. Not only did the need to increase intake become more urgent, but the first stirrings were heard in favour of other forms of legal education in Hong Kong, whether at another tertiary institution or under the Law Society, reflecting a view that it 'might not be entirely desirable' for HKU to have a 'monopoly of training and examining the final part of a law student's training.'[137] More urgently, the law school at HKU was expected to pick up the slack for students in full-time jobs who might otherwise have taken the English solicitors' examinations in Hong Kong.

Some of these students were admitted on a part-time 'extension course' spread over six years, with a cap of fifteen admissions a year. The scheme attracted 'vast numbers of applications from all sorts of unsuitable people,' partly because the school decided not to restrict

135. Minutes of meetings, 12 & 28 October 1983 & memo from Rhodes and Sihombing, 26 October 1983, HKU Archives: Board of the Studies of the School of Law – Minutes (1983).

136. *Hong Kong Hansard*, 14 March, 25 April & 12 December 1979; Ordinance No. 20 of 1979; *SCMP*, 24 February 1979.

137. Peter C. Wong, reflecting the views of some unofficial legislators, *Hong Kong Hansard*, 25 April 1979.

it to those in law-related jobs.[138] Over 300 applied but only 27 were admitted over the five years 1980–1984. The Admissions Committee was surprised by the quality of some applicants, particularly after disparaging comments had been made in the Legislative Council about the ability of this kind of aspirant lawyer.[139] But it soon became clear that 'scarcely any "five year men" types were applying.'[140] Dropout rates were high, and the solicitors' profession derived little benefit. In any case, a revitalization of the external London LLB programme at the Department of Extra-Mural Studies in 1983 now offered an alternative part-time route, though, like the earlier scheme, its success rate was initially low.[141] In 1984 the School of Law decided not to admit further students to the extension course, having concluded it was 'not only superfluous but also too extravagant in terms of resources.'[142]

Adjustments were also taking place in the training of barristers in England in the light of the *Ormrod Report*. In 1974 the Council of Legal Education announced it would phase out its Part I examinations so that in future the profession would be open only to degree-holders. Courses for the Part II examinations would be replaced by a one-year vocational course in which only thirty or forty places a year would be reserved for graduate overseas students, with priority for those with government sponsorship. This restricted the old route to practice for students from Hong Kong, who now, if they wished to be called to the English Bar, had either to obtain an English university degree or to compete for the limited number of places on the one-year vocational course.[143] The new policy was counterbalanced by a decision by the Senate of the Inns of Court in 1981 that barristers qualifying in Hong Kong of not less than three years' standing at the Hong Kong Bar would be eligible to be called to the Bar in England and Wales, subject to a brief further period of pupillage. This concession, achieved through the efforts of the Attorney General, John Griffiths QC, marked an end to the 'one-way traffic of English barristers coming here,' said the Chairman of the Hong Kong Bar Association, Martin Lee QC. But it also came at a time when a new British Nationality Act 'double-locked the door' on the colonies and when English barristers were coming to Hong Kong in ever-larger numbers.[144]

138. Evans to Board of Studies, August 1983, HKU Archives: Board of the Studies of the School of Law – Minutes (1983).

139. Report on Admissions 1981, HKU Archives: Board of the Studies of the School of Law – Minutes (1981); comments by Peter C. Wong, *Hong Kong Hansard*, 25 April 1979.

140. Memo by Wesley-Smith, 19 August 1983, HKU Archives: Board of the Studies of the School of Law – Minutes (1983).

141. Chiu & Cunich, *HKU SPACE and Its Alumni: The First Fifty Years*, 116–17.

142. 'LLB Extended Course', 2 May 1984, HKU Archives: Board of the Studies of the School of Law – Minutes (1984).

143. Hong Kong Bar Association, *Annual Statement 1974–75*, 11–12.

144. The 'double-lock' comment was made by the former Governor of Hong Kong, Lord MacLehose, in the House of Lords in 1982. The act created a new category of 'British Dependent Citizen' for British subjects born or naturalized in Hong Kong or other colonies, replacing 'Citizen of the United Kingdom and Colonies.' Restrictions

Curriculum Development and Research

English reciprocity for barristers qualifying in Hong Kong was a seal of approval for the training offered by HKU. However, intensifying pressures on HKU to produce more lawyers inhibited plans to develop the more academic side of the law school's work and raised concerns about how far, and how quickly, it could expand intake without impairing the quality of teaching. Even from a vocational point of view, the existing LLB was narrowly based. It was an 'emasculated' degree, according to one lecturer, making it necessary for the intending practitioner to take a PCLL in what should have been the fourth year of the LLB.[145] Proposals were floated in 1979–1980 for a four-year unit-based LLB, with a broader range of options and evaluation based on continuous assessment as well as examinations.[146] Owing to limited resources they were only partly implemented, and the LLB remained a three-year, exam-oriented programme tied mainly to the needs of the profession. This met the preferences of most students, who tended to 'still favour a few particular courses' even when new third-year options were introduced in the late 1970s.[147] It also reflected a pattern of entrenching courses developed in the early years according to the interests of staff.[148] The early 1980s nevertheless saw the beginnings of a broadening of the curriculum. All students continued to take compulsory courses in the first two years. But they had an increasingly varied choice in the third year, including half-year courses on banking law, planning and environmental law, civil liberties, comparative law, and criminology.

Evans's early vision that the Department of Law would become a centre of graduate studies, particularly in modern Chinese law, was also slow to take effect.[149] Discussions about a proposed course-based LLM, with an emphasis on Chinese law, began in the late 1970s, but the programme was not initiated until 1986.[150] Meanwhile, a small number of graduate students embarked on thesis-based research and two of these completed their degrees. The first to complete his research was Peter Wesley-Smith, a graduate in law and history from the University of Adelaide, who had arrived in Hong Kong on a

on settlement in the UK had been in existence since the Commonwealth Immigrants Act 1962. Hong Kong Bar Association, *Annual Statement 1981–82*, 6 & 13–14; *SCMP*, 23 August 1981.

145. Memo by Peter Morrow, 23 March 1982, HKU Archives: Board of the Studies of the School of Law – Minutes (1982).

146. Report of the Working Party on the LLB Curriculum, 5 December 1979, HKU Archives: Board of the Studies of the School of Law – Minutes (1979).

147. Evans, interview in *Law Media*, April 1978.

148. Peter Wesley-Smith, interview with the author, 23 October 2017.

149. Evans, 'Law in the Quadrennium 1974–1978', 25 September 1972, HKU Archives: Board of the Faculty of Social Sciences and Law – Minutes (1972).

150. 'Proposals of the School of Law for the Triennium 1981–1984', HKU Archives: Board of the Studies of the School of Law – Minutes (1979); 'Interim Year 1984–1985 and Triennium 1985–1988: Development Proposals of the School of Law', 8 June 1983, HKU Archives: Board of the Studies of the School of Law – Minutes (1983).

Commonwealth Scholarship in September 1970, partly to delay compulsory service in the Australian army and probable deployment in Vietnam, to which he was personally and politically opposed.[151] Although his interest was in history, the Department of History at HKU declined to take him. But Dafydd Evans welcomed him into the Department of Law, 'keen to get a foreign PhD student' at a time when the department was hardly more than a year old.[152] Evans's own interests were as much historical as legal: his inaugural lecture as Professor of Law, delivered in October 1970, dealt with the role of Chinese customary law in colonial Hong Kong, and he produced a string of articles in the 1970s on topics ranging from early Chinese wills to the precise location of Hong Kong's first Government House.[153]

Initially admitted as an LLM candidate with a field of study vaguely defined as 'Law, British Administration and Social Change in Hong Kong', Wesley-Smith narrowed in on the ninety-nine-year British lease of the New Territories from China in 1898, on the suggestion of Wang Gungwu, a historian at the Australian National University who was later Vice-Chancellor of HKU 1986–1995. The project required considerable archival research in London and in 1971 Wesley-Smith transferred his candidature to a PhD degree. Evans, busy with other things, was a 'hands-off supervisor.' Len Young and Alan Birch of the Department of History gave informal advice. But Wesley-Smith was largely left to his own devices. He completed the thesis in 1976 and published it as *Unequal Treaty 1898–1997: China, Great Britain and Hong Kong's New Territories* in 1980. It could not have been better timed. In the early 1980s the impending expiry of the New Territories lease set in motion negotiations about Hong Kong's future leading to the return of the colony to Chinese rule. Much reprinted, and reissued in a revised edition in 1998, the book was referred to by British negotiators. The Chinese government had it translated and distributed to its negotiators.[154] With this work, and through a series of articles on topics ranging from outspoken judges to anti-Chinese legislation, Wesley-Smith established Hong Kong legal history as a field of serious research.[155] He joined the teaching staff in the Department of Law in 1973, was appointed a professor in 1987, and served as Dean of the Faculty 1993–1996.

A course on the law of the People's Republic of China (PRC) appeared in syllabuses from the early 1970s but was not taught until 1982. In the meantime, some students had

---

151. Peter Wesley-Smith, interview with the author, 23 October 2017.

152. Reminiscences by Wesley-Smith, HKU Faculty of Law, *Newsletter*, January 2017; Peter Wesley-Smith, interview with the author, 23 October 2017.

153. The text of his inaugural lecture was published as 'Common Law in a Chinese Setting – The Kernel or the Nut', 1 *HKLJ* (1971), 9–32. Evans's other historical articles are in the *HKLJ*, the *Journal of the Royal Asiatic Society Hong Kong Branch*, and the *SCMP*.

154. Reminiscences by Wesley-Smith, HKU Faculty of Law, *Newsletter*, January 2017.

155. Though not, for the time being, as a course at HKU. From 1982 an optional half-year course in legal history for third-year students appeared on the LLB syllabus, but legal history was not actually taught until the early twenty-first century.

examined aspects of Chinese law in their dissertations, and questions on China trade had been covered in the PCLL course on commercial law. Roderick O'Brien, who taught this course in the mid-1970s, obtained from some of his students redacted copies of contracts for trade between Hong Kong and the PRC. He also relied on a slim volume by Mark Mobius and Gerhard Simmel, one of the few English-language publications on the subject.[156] Materials for a full course on PRC law would surely have been difficult to obtain during the Cultural Revolution (1966–1976), when law schools were closed down, lawyers were persecuted, and 'the very idea of positive law was discredited and held in contempt.'[157] From 1978, however, China's legal system entered a period of rapid revival. A new constitution was adopted in 1982. New laws and regulations were enacted. The court system was strengthened, law schools were reopened, and the legal profession was reinstated.[158] Economic reforms promoted by Deng Xiaoping included the opening of special economic zones, which were designed to operate primarily on market principles, with incentives for foreign investment and separate regulations on tax, labour, land use, dispute resolution, and other activities. The first special economic zone, established in 1980 at Shenzhen, just across the border from Hong Kong, rapidly transformed a quiet farming district into an industrial metropolis. Hong Kong became a source and channel of investment. Increasingly, the law of the PRC became a topic of more than academic interest.

The LLB course on the legal system of the PRC was first taught by Karl Herbst after his arrival in 1982. Herbst, an American formerly at the University of Pittsburgh, was an expert in Chinese and international trade law. The syllabus laid stress on efforts to codify laws and new legislation on investment in China. In 1984 the course was exempted from a rule that courses with fewer than ten students showing interest would not be considered worthwhile.[159] Together with Evans and Michael Pendleton, who joined the School of Law in 1981 and developed an expertise in the emerging field of Chinese intellectual property law, Herbst also formed a PRC Legal Studies Committee to consider proposals for developing the field. These included a proposal for a law research and services unit, focusing partly on Hong Kong law but also covering Chinese law, visits from Chinese lawyers and

---

156. Roderick O'Brien, interview with the author, 4 July 2018; Mobius & Simmel, *Trading with China* (1973)

157. Chen, 'The Developing Legal System in China', 13 *HKLJ* (1983), 292.

158. Chen, 'The Developing Legal System in China', 13 *HKLJ* (1983). In 1975 Robert Ribeiro, Peter Wesley-Smith, and Roderick O'Brien paid a visit to parts of Guangdong Province. Everyone in the legal profession there was described as a 'law worker', said Wesley-Smith. There was no distinction between judges, lawyers, and magistrates. In 1979, when Wesley-Smith visited Shanghai with 14 lawyers from Hong Kong, private lawyers were again practising in China, and charging fees for their services. Many ideas once condemned as bourgeois were now being accepted. *SCMP*, 30 August 1979; Roderick O'Brien, interview with the author, 4 July 2018.

159. Eight students had shown an interest in the course that year. 'Third Year Optional Course 1984–85', HKUA: Board of the Studies of the School of Law – Minutes (1984).

scholars, and a planned link with the Faculty of Law at Peking University.[160] These ideas were to come to fruition later in the 1980s as more teachers with expertise in Chinese law joined HKU.

The Break with the Faculty of Social Sciences

Locating the Department of Law within the Faculty of Social Sciences in 1969 was a temporary solution to an artificial restriction – the university's self-imposed policy, deriving from the Jennings-Logan Report of 1953, that no faculty should consist of fewer than three departments. It was never an easy fit, although some made the best of it by pointing out the benefits of teaching law in a larger social-science framework and the possibilities for inter-disciplinary courses. Plans to provide special law courses for other disciplines in the faculty embraced business law for management studies, family law for social work, and courses for urban studies. Most were held back by staff shortages and the need to cater for increased intakes of law students. A law course for social work students did eventually emerge in the late 1970s, after much delay. Some piecemeal instruction in law was provided in a few other subjects, including some, such as engineering and architecture, outside the faculty.[161] Pressure on the department to enrich its own teaching and promote postgraduate studies relegated 'contributory teaching' for other departments to the lowest priority.

Law therefore developed along its own path, with a separate curriculum, an independent admissions system, a specialized library and – as we have seen – a distinct student culture. There was some research collaboration with staff outside the Department of Law: this is described in Chapter 4. Relations with other departments were cordial, but it was clear, recalled Evans, 'we were not getting a fair share of the cake when we had to compete merely as one Department out of a number in a Faculty.' The change in the faculty's name in 1972 to the 'Faculty of Social Sciences and Law' – against objections from some – only highlighted 'our relative separateness.'[162] Already the department was describing itself as operating as a 'mini-faculty', though without the administrative support a faculty would normally enjoy.[163]

Evans, then HKU's youngest professor, was appointed one of the university's two pro-vice-chancellors in 1971–1977 in addition to his position as head of the Department of

---

160. 'Interim Year 1984–1985 and Triennium 1985–1988: Development Proposals of the School of Law', 8 June 1983, HKUA: Board of the Studies of the School of Law – Minutes (1983).

161. Department of Law: Triennial Plan 1978–1981, 20 October 1976, HKUA: Board of the Faculty of Social Sciences and Law – Minutes (1976).

162. Extracts from a memorandum by Evans, 14 December 1981, HKUA: Board of the Studies of the School of Law – Minutes (1982); Evans, 'Taken at the Flood', 26–7.

163. Proposals for the Quadrennium 1974–1978, 33, HKUA: Board of the Faculty of Social Sciences and Law – Minutes (1972).

Law.[164] This placed him at the centre of university planning, though he kept his two roles strictly apart. Together with heads of other 'outlier' departments, Evans persuaded the university that, in the light of their professional importance, they should be given a high degree of autonomy as schools.[165] The opportunity came when another external review – the 'Logan Rowe-Evans Report' (1974) – recommended changes to HKU's governance. While it advised no increase in the number of faculties, the report suggested that 'something more must be done for the Departments of Architecture, Law and Education,' such as the creation of boards of studies 'with wide delegated powers.' The university's Development and General Purposes Committee, of which Evans was a member, pursued the idea. It accepted that the interests of these departments were 'not always easily reconcilable with those of their Faculties' and proposed the creation of three self-contained schools, with appointed heads and boards that might include practitioners – an idea, drawing on American and Australian practice, suggested by Dafydd Evans as long ago as 1966.[166]

This recommendation was finally implemented on 1 July 1978, under new university statutes enacted in 1976 and following approval by the HKU Council in April 1978.[167] The Department of Law became a School of Law with its own dean appointed by the Vice-Chancellor, and a Board of Studies responsible for the organization of teaching. The most significant change was that the school was now fully independent of the Faculty of Social Sciences and Law because, said Evans in a message to students, the original plan that law should be studied in its social context had not achieved the desired result. The change would allow greater representation by law students on the Senate and the Board of Studies. Otherwise there would be 'no drastic changes' for students. The main change for staff was greater control over admissions, curriculum, and examinations through the Board of Studies and its network of subsidiary committees – no fewer than nineteen in 1981, ranging

---

164. He was also the university's Public Orator 1970–1971, tasked with composing and delivering ceremonial citations for honorary graduates (he was a good speaker, recalls one of his students, but it was difficult to get the substance of his lectures). He was prominent in Hong Kong's Welsh Male Voice Choir and the St David's Society, where he successfully argued against a motion that its president must be of Welsh birth or parentage, saying the idea 'smacked of racism' and it was enough for if a candidate 'felt Welsh.' Kwan Man Kwong, interview with the author, 18 October 2017; *SCMP*, 22 May 1979.

165. Evans, 'Taken at the Flood', 27.

166. At the time the Department of Education was in the Arts Faculty, and Architecture in Engineering. D.W. Logan and A. Rowe-Evans, *Report on the Academic Governance of the University of Hong Kong* (Hong Kong: HKU, 1974); Development and General Purposes Committee: Report on the Academic Governance of the University, 8 May 1975, HKUA: Board of the Faculty of Social Sciences and Law – Minutes (1975); Evans to Robinson, 6 December 1966, 'Law Dept – Working Party on Local Qualifications of Lawyers (1966–68)' HKUA, VC 233/1/66/7/8, encl. 24.

167. The School of Education was formed first, on 1 September 1976; the Schools of Law and Education followed on 1 July 1978. Alleyne: 'Faculties and Schools: Their Constitutions and Structures', 18 February 1982, HKUA: Board of the Studies of the School of Law – Minutes (1982); Statutes XXVIIA & XXVIIB, made by the Chancellor on the recommendation of the Court under section 13 of the HKU Ordinance.

from accommodation planning to scholarships and awards. The Board of Studies consisted of all permanent teaching staff, two elected student representatives, and external members from the profession, starting with the barrister Henry Litton and the solicitor Peter Vine.

The Faculty of Law

The School of Law continued in existence for six years. Although it had a high degree of autonomy in its internal affairs, which enabled teachers to focus on curriculum development and other tasks, the status was not entirely satisfactory. Evans, as Dean, was disappointed that the school had no say in resource allocation since deans of schools did not have automatic membership of the University Council or of the all-important Development and General Purposes Committee.[168] It was also a matter of presentation. 'Universities in virtually every civilized country in the world have *Faculties* of Law and I can see no good reason why this University should not also have a Faculty of Law,' wrote Evans.[169] The push for change, however, came mainly from the younger staff, who wished to be able to elect their dean: this was the rule for faculties but not for the new schools, whose deans were appointed by the Vice-Chancellor. 'In an academic institution the elective principle should, it seems to me, be maintained so far as possible,' wrote Peter Wesley-Smith, the school's expert on constitutional law.[170] There was, he recalls, 'not complete unanimity in praise of our founding head,' and a sense that the time had come for a change of leader. Some remember the move as a 'revolution' and recall 'the rather conspiratorial staff meeting' heralding the changes, 'to which the then professors were not invited.'[171]

As with the change to school status in 1978, the opportunity came with organizational reforms elsewhere in the university. In 1982, when a new Faculty of Dentistry was formed, the Vice-Chancellor invited the three schools – Education, Law, and Architecture – to indicate whether they too wished to become faculties. The Board of Studies of the School of Law almost immediately resolved that it was in favour of the school's becoming a faculty 'as soon as possible' and established a working party, chaired by the Dean, to collate written comments from members. These comments, from eight staff and two student representatives, were overwhelmingly in favour of a move to faculty status: many of them emphasized

168. From 1979 a seat was reserved for one of the three deans of schools, to be elected annually by the Senate; by agreement among themselves, the three deans sat by rotation. Extracts from a memorandum by Evans, 14 December 1981, HKUA: Board of the Studies of the School of Law – Minutes (1982).

169. Quoted by Wesley-Smith, in 'Future constitutional status of the school', 9 March 1982, HKUA: Board of the Studies of the School of Law – Minutes (1982).

170. Wesley-Smith, 'Future constitutional status of the school', 9 March 1982, HKUA: Board of the Studies of the School of Law – Minutes (1982).

171. Peter Wesley-Smith, interview with the author, 23 October 2017; Roda Mushkat, interview with the author, 5 September 2017; Pendleton, 'Full Circle' in *Thirty Years*, 76.

the importance of an elected dean; most favoured the division of the faculty into two departments, one to teach the LLB, the other the PCLL; some suggested the appointment of a sub-dean to assist with administration. There the matter rested until, in early 1984, the Council and the Senate approved the creation of the three new faculties. On 1 July 1984 the Faculty of Law was formally established with a Department of Law and a Department of Professional Legal Education. Evans was elected Dean for a three-year term – probably as part of a deal to ensure his support for the move to faculty status.[172] Robyn Martin and Peter Wesley-Smith were elected to serve on the Senate by the non-professorial teachers of the faculty.[173]

The transition to faculty status was announced with little fanfare. A new Law Anthem appeared, with words by Julianne Doe (LLB 1984) and music by Winnie Tam, in which students and graduates, 'as custodians of justice', promised to 'bring honour and glory' to the 'Law Faculty.'[174] In his foreword to the mammoth 1982–1984 issue of *Justitia*, Evans declared that 'on 1 July 1984, law teaching came of age in the University of Hong Kong' and that 'we can safely say that we have reached maturity.' Fifteen years after the establishment of the Department of Law, the Faculty now had a student population of nearly 350. It had produced 565 LLB graduates and 512 PCLLs. By the mid-1980s over half of the annual intake of the Hong Kong Bar and about a third of the intake of solicitors had an LLB or a PCLL, or both, from HKU.[175] The *Hong Kong Law Journal*, together with its various offshoots, had established itself as an authoritative voice of the legal community in a time of political controversy and accelerating legal reform. From the mid-1980s the first HKU law graduates were appointed as magistrates and judges. The next chapter explores the broader impact of the Faculty and its graduates on Hong Kong in the 1970s and 1980s.

172. Peter Wesley-Smith, interview with the author, 23 October 2017.

173. Alleyne, 'Faculties and Schools: Their Constitutions and Structures', 18 February 1982, 'Report of the School of Law Working Party on the Constitution and Structure of Schools', 8 April 1982, & Minutes of Meetings of the Board of Studies, 10 March 1982 & 14 March 1984, HKUA: Board of the Studies of the School of Law – Minutes (1982 & 1984).

174. The words and music are on the Faculty website.

175. The figures and estimates are in Edward Chan, 'A Graduate's View of 20 Years of Legal Education by the Faculty of Law' in Wacks (ed.), *The Future of Legal Education and the Legal Profession in Hong Kong: Papers Presented at a Conference Held by the Faculty of Law, University of Hong Kong to Commemorate Twenty Years of Law Teaching, Hong Kong, 15 and 16 December 1989* (Hong Kong: Faculty of Law, HKU, 1989, 33 & 35–7.

Chapter 4

Town and Gown, 1969–1984

On 5 October 1974 the first locally qualified barrister was admitted to practise in the Supreme Court of Hong Kong. The twenty-five-year-old Kenneth Kwok had received his LLB at HKU in 1972 and his PCLL in 1973. He had taken a year's pupillage with the barrister Patrick Yu, who also moved his application for admission before the court. The occasion was such an auspicious one that the Chief Justice, Sir Geoffrey Briggs (a judge not much given to ceremony), convened a Full Court of three judges and made a short speech congratulating Kwok on his achievement. 'We hope he is but only the first one to come from the University of Hong Kong and to be trained throughout in the territory of Hong Kong,' he said. Interviewed by reporters after the ceremony, Kwok said he had first taken up the study of law out of interest and had only later realized he was suitable for a career as a lawyer. Asked if he had any hobbies, he said, 'Actually there are not many leisure hours left with studying law.'

Kwok revealed that no fewer than thirty of his classmates were now serving their articles in solicitors' firms. A dozen of these – seven women and five men – were to be enrolled as solicitors in Hong Kong the following year, beginning with Daisy Yeung on 7 June 1975. When another classmate, Rosanna Wong, who was enrolled in September that year, refused to pay the customary premium for articles and demanded a salary, her employer, a senior member of the profession, 'could not believe his ears,' but took her on anyway.[1] In a booming economy, when legal services were in demand for property

1. Memoir by Rosanna Wong in *Thirty Years*, 4.

transactions, initial public offerings, and business ventures in Mainland China, firms were quick to engage law graduates from HKU. One enterprising solicitor, Gallant Y.T. Ho, interviewed practically every member of the PCLL classes graduating in the late 1970s and early 1980s. One of his recruits, Amanda Liu (LLB 1980), later became the managing partner of the firm he founded.[2]

Only one of Kwok's classmates was also serving pupillage for the Bar in 1974: this was Mok Yeuk Chi, admitted in December that year. Others were to follow. Mok also did his pupillage with Patrick Yu, who had been influential in the establishment of the LLB at HKU. Yu's crowded chambers at No. 9 Ice House Street were to welcome several other early graduates as pupils or practitioners, including Herman Poon and Mary Kao (both LLB 1972), Patrick Chan (LLB 1974), David Yam (LLB 1975), and Susan Kwan (LLB 1977).[3] Those who had sown the seeds for the Department of Law in the 1960s, should take pride in the 'rich harvest' that was now being reaped, said Yu on moving the admission of Kenneth Kwok in 1974.

This chapter explores the early impact of the law school at HKU on the legal profession during the 1970s and 1980s, and the school's contributions to debates about law in Hong Kong. It begins by examining how far the supply of early law graduates from HKU was able to meet a growing demand for lawyers. It then discusses the founding of the *Hong Kong Law Journal*, the most important joint venture between the university and legal profession of these years: taking as examples two of the most controversial issues of the 1970s, the Fight Violent Crime Campaign and the campaign against corruption, the discussion examines how teachers of law at HKU and their colleagues in the profession developed the journal as the first sustained vehicle for analysing and influencing the development of law in Hong Kong. The chapter concludes with new catalysts for the reform of law in Hong Kong: the creation of the Law Reform Commission in 1980, in which members of the law school were to play a part, and the signing of the Sino-British Joint Declaration on the future of Hong Kong in 1984, which was to have a far-reaching impact on the development and teaching of law during Hong Kong's transition from colonial rule to its new status as a special administrative region (SAR) of the PRC.

The Supply of Lawyers

In 1978, when the Department of Law became the School of Law, twenty-five graduates were in practice at the Hong Kong Bar and some 150 graduates had either become solicitors or begun serving articles – about three-quarters of all HKU law graduates so far.[4] Over

---

2. Gallant Y.T. Ho, interview with the author, 28 November 2017.
3. Yu, *A Seventh Child and the Law*, 131–3.
4. Letter from Evans and Willoughby, *SCMP*, 16 December 1978.

the next decade HKU law graduates made up roughly a third of new barristers and solicitors admitted to practise in Hong Kong. A few entered the public service: in 1976 Maria Ip (LLB 1973), one of the first HKU graduates to join the Legal Department's training scheme, became the first Hong Kong woman to be appointed an assistant crown counsel.[5] This infusion of young local talent – particularly female talent – made a strong impact on the legal profession, and many of these early recruits rose to prominence in law, politics, and public service in later decades. The first fifteen years of law graduates with an HKU LLB or PCLL or both (1972–1987) eventually yielded over 150 barristers and about 600 solicitors.[6] Among them were twenty-three future High Court judges, half a dozen elected Legislative Councillors, three non-official Executive Councillors, and thirty Queen's Counsel (QCs) (from 1997, called Senior Counsel). The first HKU law graduates to be appointed as district judges, in 1987, were Patrick Chan, David Yam, Wally Yeung, and Jerome Chan.[7] The first QCs, appointed in 1989, were Edward Chan and Andrew Liao (both LLB 1972), and Robert Kotewall (LLB 1974).

In the short run, however, there was disappointment with the quantity, if not the quality, of HKU's output. An air of pessimism surrounded the prospects of early law graduates, particularly those planning to join the Bar. Even before the first LLB graduates had completed their PCLL, the chairman of the Bar Association, Henry Litton QC, a strong supporter of the Department of Law, wrote of the difficulties for HKU law graduates seeking to make a career at the Bar. Not only was accommodation in Central prohibitively expensive, but a barrister qualifying through HKU had no right to practise law anywhere except in Hong Kong. 'In no other profession is a Hong Kong University degree so restrictive,' he wrote. In contrast, a solicitor from HKU was entitled, after five years' practice, to become a member of the English Law Society, a status with worldwide recognition. 'The world is his oyster. As a barrister the oyster – or rather the Pearl of the Orient – is forever his world.'[8] A similar point was made by Martin Lee, the chairman of the Bar Association in 1981, when opposing a plan to allow lawyers with Australian and New Zealand qualifications to practise in Hong Kong. Endorsing these remarks, one law student, John Yan (LLB 1982) added that among other disincentives to entering the Bar were the feeling that a career as a solicitor was 'very much more financially secure,' the sense that a barrister must have a much better grasp of the law, and the need for fluency in English – something which 'many of us law students

---

5. *SCMP*, 28 September 1976.

6. The numbers of graduates are 712 LLBs (1972–1986) and 817 PCLLs (1973–1987). Most HKU LLBs went on to take the PCLL. The larger number of PCLLs reflects the growing number of graduates from other universities taking the PCLL. The figures on entry into the profession are mainly from Chan, 'A Graduate's View of 20 Years of Legal Education by the Faculty of Law.'

7. Wally Yeung and Jerome Chan had served as magistrates since 1985.

8. Hong Kong Bar Association, *Annual Statement 1972/73*, 5–6.

lack […] (or at least think we do).' Only three or four out of the fifty or so PCLL graduates each year chose to become barristers, said Yan.[9]

The question of reciprocity for barristers was partly addressed by the recognition, from 1981, of Hong Kong qualifications for admission to the English Bar, although restrictions on immigration into the UK would have prevented many from taking advantage of this. In any case, opportunities were still greater in Hong Kong. To help ease the cost of establishing a practice, the Hong Kong Bar Association made loans available to new barristers qualifying in Hong Kong, notably from the Archie Zimmern Memorial Fund created in 1985.[10] Still, it was a common view that the law school at HKU should be producing more lawyers than it actually was. In a survey in 1989, Edward Chan QC (LLB 1972) was surprised that HKU law graduates accounted for only about a third of annual admissions of barristers and solicitors. 'I would have expected a higher proportion of lawyers in Hong Kong to have obtained their training at the University,' he concluded, contrasting the figure with the 58 per cent of all registered medical practitioners in 1989 who had been trained at either HKU or the Chinese University of Hong Kong. Chan acknowledged that the Faculty of Medicine had been in existence for much longer (Dafydd Evans, erstwhile Dean of the Faculty of Law, had recently written its centenary history).[11] But the real reason, he suggested, was that, despite rapid expansion, legal education at HKU had still not caught up with the spiralling demand for lawyers: 'consequently about two-thirds of the newly admitted lawyers have been trained abroad.'[12]

The number of solicitors in Hong Kong increased from under 200 in 1969 to over 600 in 1979 and over 2,000 in 1989. Barristers in private practice increased from 44 in 1969 to 138 in 1979 and nearly 400 in 1989. Lawyers in the public service, including the Judiciary, increased from about 150 in 1969 to nearly 500 in 1989. The total size of Hong Kong's legal profession therefore grew sevenfold in the space of twenty years, from under 400 in 1969 to about 2,800 in 1989. Factors other than just a 42 per cent increase in population or a 130 per cent growth in real gross domestic product (GDP) per capita spurred this rising demand for legal services. The caseload of the Supreme and District Courts, where the services of lawyers were most required, had increased threefold. Trials had become longer and more complex. A permanent Court of Appeal and several new tribunals were created in the 1970s,

---

9. *SCMP*, 6 & 17 January 1981. The disincentives did not deter John Yan himself, who went on to take a PCLL at HKU, was admitted to practise as barrister in Hong Kong in 1984, and became a Senior Counsel in 2003.

10. The Archie Zimmern Fund commemorates the first member of the private Bar in Hong Kong to be appointed direct to the High Court: from an old Hong Kong family, Zimmern served as a High Court judge 1977–1981 and as a justice of appeal 1981–1982; he died in 1985.

11. Evans, *Constancy of Purpose: An Account of the Foundation and History of the Hong Kong College of Medicine and the Faculty of Medicine of the University of Hong Kong 1887–1987* (Hong Kong: Hong Kong University Press, 1987)

12. Chan, 'A Graduate's View of 20 Years of Legal Education by the Faculty of Law', 33–4.

and courts at all levels saw a large expansion in the 1980s.[13] Cases supported by legal aid increased fifteen times between 1969 and 1989. In addition to its greatly increased workload in prosecutions, litigation, and law drafting, the Legal Department was now tasked with managing the legal aspects of the impending restoration of Chinese sovereignty over Hong Kong. In the realm of private practice, the number of mortgages, assignments, and tenancy agreements increased twelvefold during 1969–1989. Registrations of new companies grew at the same rate. Divorces increased by twenty-five times. Since the late 1970s Hong Kong had also become a headquarters and source of investment for industrial expansion in the Pearl River Delta: China-related legal services were now becoming a lucrative source of business for solicitors in Hong Kong.

The rapid increase in lawyers exceeded the calculations in 1965 that Hong Kong would need fifty-five new lawyers a year for the next twenty-five years. It underlined the difficulties faced by the Advisory Committee on Legal Education in assessing future demand, a task made even more uncertain by reports in the 1980s that many lawyers were planning to leave Hong Kong in advance of 1997. Despite increases in intake, HKU could not produce law graduates sufficient to meet even half the demand. The shortfall was met partly by Hong Kong graduates from universities elsewhere in the world but mainly by recruitment from overseas. On the day that Kenneth Kwok was admitted as Hong Kong's first locally trained barrister, seven solicitors, all from the UK, were also admitted. In the 1980s about half of all new solicitors were recruited in this way – a larger proportion than in the 1970s. Admissions to the Bar followed a similar pattern. These years also saw the arrival of large numbers of London QCs, flying in for specific cases ranging from the corruption trials of the 1970s to the lengthy commercial crimes trials of the late 1980s. By the 1980s London QCs were appearing in Hong Kong at the rate of nearly a hundred a year. At one time as many as thirty-four were staying in the same hotel in Central. Despite the expense of accommodation and travel, it was reportedly cheaper to bring in London QCs than to engage local QCs.[14]

The Hong Kong Bar Association did not object in principle to the admission of London QCs with specialist skills on a case-by-case basis, at least until Hong Kong attained its own adequate complement of QCs: from the late 1970s, however, it sought to limit their numbers through the issue of guidelines and the mounting of occasional challenges in the courts. Since the mid-1960s the Bar had also demanded restrictions on the admission of

13. In 1976 the Supreme Court was reconstituted to comprise the High Court and the Court of Appeal, with a permanent complement of justices of appeal: previously appeals had been heard by a 'Full Court', a court of two or three judges convened as and when required. The new tribunals were the Labour Tribunal (1973), the Lands Tribunal (1974), and the Small Claims Tribunal (1976): lawyers were, however, not permitted to appear in the Labour Tribunal or the Small Claims Tribunal. In 1969 the Judiciary consisted of about 50 judges, magistrates, and other judicial officers; by 1989 the number had risen to about 150.

14. *SCMP*, 20–25 June 1978 & 7 April 1983.

junior barristers from overseas for general practice, arguing that an uncontrolled influx would undermine the aim of building a strong and independent local bar. The Hong Kong Bar would 'not allow itself to be treated as a mere annex or appendage of the English Bar,' said the chairman of the Bar Association, Denis Chang QC, in 1986.[15] Restrictions began in 1968 with a requirement of a minimum of eight consecutive months' residence in Hong Kong for a UK-qualified barrister immediately prior to an application for general admission. Following a review in 1989, an applicant was also required to have at least three years' experience in the UK, to be a Hong Kong permanent resident, or to have been ordinarily resident in Hong Kong for at least seven years; a twelve-month residence requirement was also added for UK-qualified solicitors applying for unlimited practice.[16] At a time of localization elsewhere in the public service, the Judiciary was recruiting more judges from overseas than ever before, some with considerable experience at the London Bar.

Partly in response to lobbying, the government widened the scope for admission to cover certain groups of lawyers from overseas. For example, in 1981 it extended eligibility for the Bar to Commonwealth and Irish citizens with seven years' residence in Hong Kong and a PCLL from HKU. This followed a campaign by the New Zealander Valerie Penlington (PCLL 1979), the wife of a government lawyer and future judge, who, while studying for her PCLL, had ruffled feathers at HKU with her public comments on the lack of legal talent in Hong Kong. She became the first Commonwealth barrister to be admitted under the 1981 provision.[17] In 1988 the government announced a plan to allow foreign law firms to hire Hong Kong-qualified solicitors. A response to a petition from seven American law firms accompanied by threats of trade sanctions, the plan overrode advice from a committee reviewing the Legal Practitioners Ordinance chaired by the Chief Justice. It was fiercely debated within the professional bodies. A forum organized by the HKU Law Association, attended by over 200 people, included 'lively and enthusiastic questioning' from the floor. Students attending it were overwhelmingly against the plan.[18] In what Simon Ip, president of the Law Society, described as a confrontation of 'unprecedented proportions,' professional bodies were even more strongly opposed, arguing that the plan would allow the

---

15. Speech at Opening of the Legal Year 1986, Hong Kong Bar Association, *Annual Statement 1985–86*, 15.

16. Ordinances Nos. 25 of 1968 & 46 of 1989.

17. An interview given by her to the *SCMP* on the legal profession prompted an indignant letter from Evans and Willoughby stressing the contributions of HKU's law school, disputing her claim that more lawyers meant cheaper lawyers, and – in response to her comment that Hong Kong students were relying on English textbooks – pointing out that the *HKLJ* now contained over 2,000 pages on Hong Kong law. To address the shortage of legal texts, Penlington had written a book, *Law in Hong Kong*, published by the *SCMP*. Described by the *SCMP* as 'the definitive Hong Kong law book,' it was criticized in a review by Peter Wesley-Smith in the *HKLJ* for its errors and its outrageous price ($150). *SCMP*, 18 & 21 October & 10 & 16 December 1978, 1 January 1979 & 5 April 1981; 9 *HKLJ* (1979), 110–12.

18. *Hong Kong Law Society Gazette*, December 1988 & January 1989.

practice of Hong Kong law to come under the control of unqualified persons. The government was forced to withdraw it.[19] In 1989 a scheme was introduced to allow lawyers in government service with qualifications in certain overseas jurisdictions to enter private practice without obtaining a PCLL, subject to an annual quota of ten. Following a similar recommendation by the Chief Justice's committee, full-time teachers of the HKU PCLL from the same jurisdictions were also eligible for admission as solicitors without the need for further qualifications.[20]

Since the early years of the Department of Law, teachers had been allowed outside practice under the terms of their contract with HKU subject to certain conditions, including the sharing of a proportion of earnings with the university. Only a handful of early staff had the necessary qualifications to practise as barristers or solicitors, and few took advantage of the arrangement. One of the most active was Bernard Downey, an English-qualified barrister, who represented defendants in several criminal trials in the late 1970s, usually through legal aid, including murder, blackmail, dangerous drugs, and corruption cases. In early 1980 he represented the MacLennan family in the coroner's inquest into the case of the police inspector John MacLennan, who was discovered dead from gun wounds in his locked flat shortly before he was to be questioned about allegations of homosexual acts (which were still illegal in Hong Kong at the time and the target of vigorous police action). Ill-advised public criticisms by the Attorney General of the jury's open verdict, despite comments by the coroner that suicide would be the most appropriate verdict, caused a storm of controversy, forcing the Governor to appoint a commission of inquiry under the High Court judge Yang Ti Liang.[21] Downey, who was appointed a district judge in March 1980, was not involved in this inquiry.

It was 'in the best interests of students if their lecturers have actual experience of practice in Hong Kong,' said the Attorney General when proposing the special provision for PCLL teachers in 1989.[22] Yet, observes Peter Wesley-Smith, 'managing the competing demands of legal practice and academia is an extraordinarily difficult thing to do,' and for most it was 'to the detriment of both their legal practice and their teaching.'[23] In July 1990 Jill Spruce, who had joined the School of Law as a senior lecturer in 1983, was fired after an acrimonious

---

19. In 1994 a scheme, based largely on proposals by the Law Society, was enacted for the registration and regulation of foreign law firms by the Law Society. Ip, speech at the Opening of the Legal Year, 9 January 1989, *Hong Kong Law Society Gazette*, February 1989. For a summary of the issues see Law Society of Hong Kong, *Celebrating a Centenary*, 112–15.

20. Ordinance No. 46 of 1989. The designated jurisdictions, largely reflecting the origins of lawyers in the Legal Department, were Australia, Canada (except Quebec), New Zealand, Ireland, Zimbabwe, and Singapore.

21. For an authoritative account of this episode see Nigel Collett, *A Death in Hong Kong: the MacLennan Case of 1980 and the Suppression of a Scandal* (Hong Kong: City University of Hong Kong Press, 2018).

22. *Hong Kong Hansard*, 15 February 1989.

23. Peter Wesley-Smith, interview with the author, 23 October 2017.

dispute about outside practice. An English-qualified barrister and an expert on evidence, Spruce had taken her position at HKU on assurances she would also be allowed to practise, an arrangement specified in her employment contract. In 1984, following complaints from law students that outside practice by some staff was disrupting teaching, the School of Law introduced restrictions: an upper limit of 20 per cent of time spent on outside practice was imposed and reporting requirements were increased. Over the next few years, however, Spruce's practice at the Bar grew considerably and she was slow to submit reports. The issue came to a head in 1988. In a ten-day trial in April she secured the acquittal of an immigration officer accused of manslaughter, having earlier represented him in a coroner's inquest. In another high-profile case in October she appeared for Hopewell Construction in a dispute with the MTR Corporation. The hearing lasted sixteen consecutive days, during which she found substitute teachers and shifted some lectures and classes to Saturdays, or cancelled them, claiming ill health.[24]

On learning of this, the head of the Department of Law, Raymond Wacks, withdrew permission for Spruce to engage in outside practice and referred the matter to the Vice-Chancellor, who initiated an inquiry. Meanwhile, Spruce continued to practise in the courts. After disciplinary proceedings, on 26 July 1990 the Council of HKU resolved to terminate her appointment on the grounds of neglect of duties, lying to her head of department, and continuing to engage in outside practice without permission. Spruce applied for a judicial review, alleging procedural flaws in the internal inquiry and a breach of the rules of natural justice. The High Court dismissed her application. The Court of Appeal, however, held that the university had made an error of law in applying regulations that did not form part of her contract: it ordered the university to pay her costs but refused to order her reinstatement or award damages, citing a 'breakdown of trust' between her and her head of department. Spruce took her case to the Judicial Committee of the Privy Council, which, in 1993, not only dismissed her appeal but also overruled the Court of Appeal's finding on the error of law. It allowed a cross-appeal by the university and ordered Spruce to pay the university's costs. HKU had spent about $6 million on legal fees, of which $3 million was recoverable. In 1994 it started bankruptcy proceedings against Spruce, rejected an offer of $500,000 from an anonymous group of lawyers to halt proceedings, and even considered hiring a detective to track her down: she was believed to be in Australia. The university eventually gave up its quest.[25] In 1995 the Faculty of Law established a committee to report on outside practice by teachers and handle disagreements.

---

24. *SCMP*, 12, 27 & 30 May, 10 & 13 June, 7 July, 7 August, 25 September, 10 October & 11 November 1987 & 8–22 April 1988; *Mass Transit Railway Corporation v Hopewell Construction Company Ltd* [1988] HKCFI 294.
25. *Re University of Hong Kong* [1991] HKCFI 131; *Jill Spruce v The University of Hong Kong* [1991] HKCA 283 & 284 & Privy Council Appeal No. 27 of 1992; *SCMP*, 7 January, 24 April, 1, 5, 6, & 10 June 1994.

The *Hong Kong Law Journal*

The Spruce affair was 'a terrible tragedy', said Neil Kaplan, a High Court judge and an old friend of Jill Spruce: the two had studied together at King's College, London and had recently co-authored a book on arbitration.[26] Spruce's former colleague at HKU, William Clarke, came to the 'profoundly disturbing conclusion' that the Court of Appeal's refusal to reinstate Spruce, a tenured senior lecturer, was 'a fundamental blow to the protection of academic freedom in Hong Kong.'[27] His remarks appeared in Volume 21 No. 3 (October 1991) of the *Hong Kong Law Journal*, an issue which also included comments on the first judgment to apply the new Hong Kong Bill of Rights Ordinance (delivered by Judge Bernard Downey) and an analysis of urgent amendments to the Letters Patent validating retrospectively the appointments of Hong Kong's magistrates in order to address doubts first raised in an article in the *Journal* in 1989.[28] The overseas experts who had advised on setting up a law school at HKU in the 1960s had urged the founding of a law journal to enhance the prestige of the school and as a quick means of producing legal literature on Hong Kong. By the early 1990s the *Hong Kong Law Journal*, now entering its third decade, had established itself as an authoritative, often polemical, voice on law and current affairs.

The *Hong Kong Law Journal* was founded in 1971 by two Hong Kong barristers, Henry Litton (shortly after his appointment as Hong Kong's youngest QC) and Gerald de Basto

---

26. Neil Kaplan, Jill Spruce & Michael J. Moser, *Hong Kong and China Arbitration: Cases and Materials* (Singapore: Butterworths, 1994).

27. Clarke, 'Academic Tenure and the Protection of Academic Freedom: *Jill Spruce v The University of Hong Kong*', 21 *HKLJ* (1991), 374.

28. In a ruling in April that year, Neil Kaplan had held that a magistrate had not been validly appointed. The ruling potentially affected all magistrates appointed since 1974, or all but one of Hong Kong's sixty-one magistrates. Doubts about the appointments had been raised by a political science lecturer at HKU, David Clark (a solicitor by training), which had been cited in proceedings. Clark had argued that magistrates' appointments made by the Chief Justice under delegated authority from the Governor were invalid because neither the Letters Patent nor the Magistrates Ordinance authorized the Governor to delegate this power. The issue was raised when counsel for the business-man Deacon Chiu and his son, on trial for conspiracy to defraud, challenged their committal proceedings on the ground that the presiding magistrate had not been validly appointed. Kaplan held that the Governor had the power to delegate appointments but that his delegation of this power had been insufficient because it had failed to make reference to the Letters Patent. The invalidity dated not to 1984 (as Clark, relying on *Government Gazette* notices, had supposed) but to 1974, when the delegation had been made; it affected all but one of Hong Kong's serving magistrates. Kaplan's ruling was overturned by the Court of Appeal in May and the Letters Patent were urgently amended shortly afterwards. In the meantime, proceedings in some courts were interrupted by challenges based on Kaplan's ruling. The Legal Department declared that anyone freed on technicalities would be rearrested. The Governor urgently signed new warrants of appointment, and a mass swearing-in of magistrates took place in the Supreme Court. Clark, 'Are All Appointments of Magistrates Since January 1984 Invalid?' 19 *HKLJ* (1989), 330–44; *In re Chiu Tat-cheong, David & Chiu Te-ken, Deacon* [1992] 2 HKLR 57; *Attorney General v Chiu Tat-Cheong, David and Chiu Te-ken, Deacon* [1992] 2 HKLR 84; *SCMP*, 23, 24, & 26 April & 16 May 1991; *Hong Kong Standard*, 26 April 1991.

QC, who provided funding and became its first editors-in-chief. The first editor, John Rear, a senior lecturer in law at HKU with six years' prior experience as an editor at Sweet & Maxwell, had ample experience of launching and editing journals; his wife, Marjorie, took on the early administration, working from Henry Litton's chambers in the Prince's Building.[29] The first editorial committee comprised Bernard Downey, Alan Smith, and Dafydd Evans – serving respectively as case editor, statute editor, and review and publications editor – along with the magistrate Frank Addison, the barrister Denis Chang, the judge Alan Huggins, the Attorney General Denys Roberts, the solicitor Brian Tisdall, and the legal advisor to the Hongkong Bank, Eric Udal. The *Journal* had correspondents at universities in Australia, Japan, Korea, Malaysia, and Singapore, reflecting an early aim to publish articles on the laws and legal systems of Asia. This interest in comparative law was also brought out in references to the earlier *Hong Kong University Law Journal* (1926–1927), whose editor, George Keeton, wrote a foreword, 'Forty-Five Years On', for the new *Hong Kong Law Journal*. Although Keeton and others contributed articles on other legal systems, the early *Hong Kong Law Journal* focused mainly on its other aim of providing 'a forum for the review, analysis and discussion of the law of Hong Kong and the practices of its courts.'[30] Later on, it also included large sections on China's legal system.

After John Rear's departure, the editorship of the *Hong Kong Law Journal* passed to other law teachers at HKU in a succession of joint editorships, starting with Bernard Downey and Peter Wesley-Smith (1973–1977) and including, in various permutations from 1978 to 1993, Downey, Wesley-Smith, Bob Allcock, William Clarke, Michael Olesnicky, Albert Chen, Judith Sihombing, Shane Nossal, and Michael Wilkinson. In 1994 a new design and editorial structure were introduced, with Peter Wesley-Smith (then Dean of the Law Faculty) as editor-in-chief and Raymond Wacks (1994–1997), then Albert Chen (1998) as editor. Rick Glofcheski took over as editor-in-chief in 1999 and Chen continued as associate editor, positions they still hold, with the support of a strong editorial team. The *Journal* quickly produced a stream of articles on Hong Kong law suitable as teaching texts, a notable achievement given tight publishing deadlines and the small size of the Department of Law. From 1974 the *Journal* also published the Law Lectures for Practitioners series. Over the years the *Journal* became the leading English-language journal on law in Hong Kong and China, with commentaries, analyses and peer-reviewed articles from scholars around the world. It was 'impossible to imagine the Faculty of Law at HKU without the *Hong Kong Law Journal*,' observed one of its longest-serving editors, Peter Wesley-Smith.[31]

---

29. Rear had edited *Current Law* and had been involved in the launch of *Medicine, Science and the Law*, the journal of the British Academy of Forensic Sciences. Rear, interview with the author, 2 December 2017.

30. Editorial by John Rear, 1 *HKLJ* (1971), 1–5.

31. For an account of the *Journal's* early years see Wesley-Smith, 'Thirty-Seven-And-A-Third Years On: an Editor's Memoir,' 40 *HKLJ* (2010), 249–52.

The *Hong Kong Law Journal* was closely intertwined with the practice of law in the city. If its analyses were often ignored by policymakers, it at least got the measure of Hong Kong law and shone a bright light into some of the darker recesses. Its founder, Henry Litton, described it modestly as 'a vehicle for exposing oddities – a good way of relieving bees in bonnets.' Litton was a generous benefactor to the *Journal*. Over the years he also contributed several articles and editorials on subjects ranging from lost share certificates to the legal treatment of Chinese money-loan associations. He was himself the subject of an editorial by John Rear in 1972 when he miraculously survived the collapse of a block of flats in one of several landslides caused by heavy rain: the editorial commented on the legal position of those affected by such disasters before moving on to discuss 'magisterial ineptitude' and claims that judges were out of touch with the 'real world,' a recurrent theme.[32] In 1988 Litton was the author of a scathing editorial on the notorious Carrian trial, in which defendants charged in one of the world's most complex commercial frauds were inexplicably acquitted on the direction of the judge after sixty-five weeks of proceedings. Litton concluded that the handling of the case had 'left many people wondering about the fitness of the judge to continue serving as a Justice of Appeal.' The judge, Denis Barker, resigned soon after the editorial was published.[33]

Litton transferred his interest in the *Journal* in 1992 to the other shareholders after becoming a justice of appeal, the first member of the private Bar in Hong Kong to be appointed direct to the Court of Appeal; de Basto had long since given up his connection on his appointment as a district judge in 1973. Denis Chang was briefly editor-in-chief until in late 1993, under an agreement with the Hong Kong Law Journal Ltd, the Faculty formally took over the management and editing of the *Journal*; he remained as chairman of a new editorial board until 2001, when publication of the *Journal* was taken over by Sweet & Maxwell. The town–gown collaboration continued. Practitioners of law wrote some of the contents, particularly in the early years. The *Journal* also offered material of direct practical use to the profession, such as commentaries on new legislation and recent judgments, and analyses of sentences and personal injury awards, even if, to Wesley-Smith's regret, judges seemed reluctant to acknowledge the *Journal's* analysis.[34] The more academic articles

---

32. Editorial by John Rear, 2 *HKLJ* (1972), 249–60.

33. Barker, who had been under attack by the press for many months, had reportedly twice offered his resignation before the Litton editorial appeared. The widely publicized editorial, coming from so respected a source, nevertheless played a critical role in the decision, as did the retirement and departure of the Chief Justice, Sir Denys Roberts, who, despite his strong criticisms in the Court of Appeal of Barker's ruling, had resisted taking action. Editorial, 18 *HKLJ* 1 (1988), 5–10; *SCMP*, 12 & 15 March 1988. For an account of the Carrian case see Ian Robinson, *The Joker's Downfall: the True Story of Carrian: Murder, Mystery & Mayhem* (Hong Kong: Gold Willow Ltd, 2014).

34. Wesley-Smith, 'Thirty-Seven-And-A-Third Years On: an Editor's Memoir', 251–2. The earliest judicial reference to the *Journal* appears to have been a critical one: in an appeal concerning a Chinese money-loan association in 1972, the judge, Alan Huggins, disagreed with the analysis in articles by Henry Litton and Denis Chang on the legal status

covered broader aspects of the law, including criminology and legal history: among early contributions were outstanding pieces by the prolific HKU sociologist Henry Lethbridge on corruption, homosexuality, prostitution, rape, and blackmail in the Hong Kong context.

From the outset the *Journal* was a vehicle for criticizing a variety of ills ranging from the slow pace of law reform to the control of policymaking by 'a narrow elite whose wealth and life-style isolates it from those whom it rules.'[35] This reflected the outspoken approach of the *Journal's* founders, Litton and de Basto, leading figures in the increasingly active Hong Kong Bar Association, and of its first editor, John Rear, who had had been prominent in political campaigns since his arrival in 1966. The *Journal* thus became part of the discourse of a burgeoning civil society in late colonial Hong Kong, which comprised a few independent-minded journalists, social activists like the formidable Elsie Elliott, organizations such as the Reform Club, the Civic Association, and the local branch of JUSTICE, and emerging new organizations, precursors of the political parties that were to form in the 1980s. The *Journal*, recalled Rear, established a tradition of 'combining careful analysis with forthright criticism when it seems justified.'

Debating Crime, Public Order, and Corruption

The first three-part volume of the *Hong Kong Law Journal* (1971) illustrates its broad scope, with articles and commentaries on a range of legal topics, many prompted by recent Hong Kong cases or new legislation. Perhaps the largest and most controversial field of discussion in the *Journal's* first decade was criminal law. Public debate in the 1970s – in the councils of government, the newspapers, the teahouses, and the streets – focused on three urgent, overlapping topics: (1) the alarming increase in crime, particularly violent crime, and the methods adopted to deal with it; (2) concerns that the wide powers available to police in the Police Force Ordinance, Public Order Ordinance, and other legislation were open to abuse; and (3) the vigorous campaign against corruption and its implications for police morale and the rule of law.

A series of articles in Part Two of Volume I (1971) set the tone. A piece by Bernard Downey pointed to the growing number of confessions to police officers and the tendency

---

of such associations, holding that the association in question was an unlawful society within the meaning of the Societies Ordinance and that the court should not be a party to the enforcement of its rules. *Yim Wai Tsang v Lee Yuk Har* [1972] HKCA 222; Litton & Tsang, 'Chinese Money-loan Associations' I & II, 1 *HKLJ* 194–205 & 262–73. Most of the twenty or so references to the *Journal* in judgments on the Hong Kong Legal Information Institute's database during the *Journal's* first decade were to its regular reports on personal injury awards – a feature warmly commended by Cons J in *Yip Kam-wan v Li Leung* [1981] HKCA 155.

35. Stephen Davies, 'One Brand of Politics Rekindled', 7 *HKLJ* (1977), 44–81. The title is a reference to John Rear's chapter 'One Brand of Politics' in Hopkins (ed.), *Hong Kong: The Industrial Colony*, which had made similar observations.

of defendants to retract them at trial, saying they had been obtained by inducements or threats of violence, or by actual violence. In the absence of clear guidance from the courts on their admissibility, 'overzealous or unprincipled police officers will continue to wring confessions from unwilling suspects, and accused persons will feel that little is to be gained or lost by retracting confessions, whether or not they are voluntary,' wrote Downey.[36] The courts were now taking an increasingly sceptical view of 'so-called "voluntary confessions"', which now accounted for an 'overwhelming preponderance' of criminal cases in the Supreme Court.[37] The issue in so many trials (as Litton remarked in a later editorial) became 'not whether the accused is innocent or guilty as charged but whether the statement made by the accused to the police was voluntary.'[38] Various studies, including two Law Reform Commission reports, tried to grapple with the problem: it was eventually alleviated by the introduction of video recording of interviews. Another article in the same 1971 issue, by John Rear, dealt with powers of arrest. Hong Kong's police were authorized to stop, search, and arrest without warrant anyone they reasonably suspected of being guilty of any offence. These powers were far wider than in England, where police could arrest without warrant only in more serious cases. The topic was to be revisited by experts at HKU in the years to follow, with studies by Johannes Chan (LLB 1981) and Peter Morrow in the late 1980s, by which time police powers, scattered over seventy different statutory provisions, had been expanded.[39]

Some of these powers were to be found in the Public Order Ordinance. This draconian law was enacted without public consultation or debate in council towards the end of 1967, a year which had seen some of the worst rioting in Hong Kong's history. The new ordinance consolidated pre-existing laws and incorporated some of the emergency regulations promulgated that year; it also drew on legislation from some of Britain's former African colonies.[40] Among other provisions, it gave the police broad powers of search and powers to control meetings and processions, almost all of which required licences if they consisted of ten or more persons. Its sweeping definitions of unlawful assembly and riot omitted the common law principle of common purpose: for example, an unlawful assembly became a riot even if only one of its members committed a breach of the peace. A backlash against the legislation, including petitions from the Reform Club and JUSTICE, forced the government to modify some of the more extreme provisions: amendments in 1970 placed

---

36. Downey, 'Confessions to Police Officers,' 1 *HKLJ*, 131–41.

37. Rigby J in *Wong Ho-ming and others v The Queen* [1970] HKCA 95.

38. Editorial, 11 *HKLJ* (1981), 147–50.

39. Rear, 'The Power of Arrest in Hong Kong,' 1 *HKLJ* (1971), 142–93; Johannes Chan, 'Arrest and Seizure in Hong Kong,' *Law Lectures for Practitioners* 1988, 63–104; Peter Morrow, 'Police Powers and Individual Liberty' in Raymond Wacks (Ed.), *Civil Liberties in Hong Kong* (New York, Oxford University Press, 1988).

40. Ordinance No. 64 of 1967. FCO 40/116 & 117 'Hong Kong: Legal Affairs: Public Order: Legislation' (1967).

restrictions on police powers of search, narrowed the definitions of meetings and processions, and included defences based on reasonable excuse.[41]

However, the ordinance continued to be contentious – a relic of 'dying 20th Century Colonialism,' as Patrick Chan described it in his LLB dissertation.[42] A notorious case in 1979 showed that its provisions extended even to people wishing to exercise a customary right of petition. Some eighty people – mostly women and children – living on unsafe boats in the Yau Ma Tei Typhoon Shelter had boarded coaches in Kowloon with the aim of petitioning the Governor for early rehousing. They had not applied for a licence for their 'gathering', and police intercepted them as their coaches emerged from the cross-harbour tunnel on Hong Kong Island. When they declined to disperse they were arrested. The adults among them – sixty-seven in all – were taken before a magistrate and convicted of unlawful assembly: most received absolute discharges but eleven – a priest, a doctor, and some social workers and students – were bound over in the sum of $300 for eighteen months. They appealed against their convictions to the Supreme Court. Their counsel, Henry Litton and Patrick Chan (now a barrister), pointed out that if the ordinance was to be used in this way then hundreds of people were taking part in unlawful assemblies every day. The judge, Derek Cons, nevertheless ruled that the gathering, no matter how peaceful and orderly, was unlawful: the desire to present a petition was not a reasonable excuse.[43] Outrage over this case prompted a further review of the Public Order Ordinance. Amendments in 1980 further narrowed definitions to exclude a large range of social, recreational, cultural and educational events, as well as meetings of fewer than thirty persons; licensing of public meetings was also replaced with a system of advance notification to the police, who could still prohibit them or impose conditions; processions still required licences.[44]

These measures still failed to satisfy critics. Not only was there no right to public assembly in Hong Kong, wrote Johannes Chan in his LLB dissertation shortly after the 1980 amendments, but the requirement for prior approval, whether by notification or by licence, gave the authorities 'absolute power to refuse permission for such meetings or processions on any grounds they wish.' If the law was 'so uncertain or is so framed that people may be liable to prosecution one way or the other, will they respect the law? If they are punished for doing something which people in other countries consider as their fundamental human right, will they obey the law?'[45]

---

41. Ordinance No. 31 of 1970.

42. Patrick Chan, 'Public Assembly – Rights and Liabilities,' *Justitia* (1972–1973), 15–24.

43. *Chow Shui & Others v The Queen* [1979] HKLR 275.

44. Ordinance No. 67 of 1980.

45. Johannes Chan, 'The Public Order (Amendment) Ordinance 1980,' *Justitia* (1981–1982), 15–22. At the time some other Western European countries and Australia did require advance notice of processions: for an analysis and comparisons, see Roda Mushkat, 'Balancing Freedom of Expression and Public order in Hong Kong,' 11 *HKLJ* (1981), 62–75.

The majority of people prosecuted under the Public Order Ordinance were young people ranging from student-protestors to youths involved in gang activities or caught by its offensive weapon provisions. One of the other debates of the 1970s was how the authorities in Hong Kong should tackle rapidly rising crime, much of it violent and involving teenagers: should punishments be made harsher and more deterrent, as many leading voices urged, or were the solutions to violent crime to be found in better education, housing, and employment opportunities? In an article in the 1971 volume of the *Hong Kong Law Journal*, the text of a recent address to the HKU Law Association, the Chief Justice, Sir Ivo Rigby, one of the progenitors of the law school, set out his own somewhat idiosyncratic views on sentencing.[46] Rigby believed strongly that first offenders, particularly young offenders, should not be sentenced to imprisonment unless there were no other suitable options. This view followed trends in punishment in England and elsewhere. Rigby urged alternative forms of sentencing, such as training centres and detention centres for young offenders, probation, suspended sentences, and community service orders, some of which were already available, or becoming available, in Hong Kong.[47] Reflecting these trends, in 1967 the Legislative Council had passed a provision prohibiting a court from sentencing offenders aged between sixteen and twenty-one to imprisonment unless there was no other appropriate punishment – a measure that some of its members later came to regret.[48]

The greater the variety of sentences other than imprisonment the better, Rigby told his audience at HKU. What separated him from progressive opinion was his support for corporal punishment, including (he suggested to the assembled students and lecturers 'with some timidity') shaving and painting young offenders' heads.[49] That idea was not pursued, but Rigby's advocacy prompted a revival of caning, which had been abolished as a judicial punishment in England in 1948 and had almost fallen into disuse in Hong Kong, though it remained on the statute books.[50] In June 1970 Rigby had issued a practice note encouraging the imposition of corporal punishment by the courts: in the eighteen months that followed some 200 sentences were imposed, compared with only 1 in the previous two years. In 1971, and again in 1974 and 1975, the Legislative Council expanded

---

46. Ivo Rigby, 'Sentencing Offenders.' 1 *HKLJ* (1971), 123–30.

47. Training centres based on the English borstal system had been introduced in the 1950s. Detention centres, a particular interest of Rigby's, were introduced in 1972 to deliver a 'short, sharp shock' to young offenders. Probation, available for offenders under sixteen since 1932, was extended to young adults in 1947 and to all adults from 1956. The suspended sentence was introduced in 1971, though on a more restricted basis than the system introduced in England four years earlier. Community service orders, introduced in England in 1972, were not introduced in Hong Kong until 1984, following recommendations by the Law Reform Commission.

48. The change was based on provisions in the English Criminal Justice Act 1967. A similar provision in the Juvenile Offenders Ordinance 1932 already applied to offenders under 16. Ordinance No. 66 of 1967.

49. Rigby, 'Sentencing Offenders', 1 *HKLJ* (1971), 123.

50. Committees in Hong Kong, reporting in 1952, 1965, and 1966 had recommended abolition.

the list of offences for which adult male offenders could be caned.[51] The revival of caning found support among legislators and resonated with public opinion. The Bar Association criticized it as a retrograde step. The *Hong Kong Law Journal* welcomed the insights into the judicial mind in Rigby's speech but expressed concern about his views on corporal punishment.[52]

The revival of caning came during years of rapidly rising crime and declining detection rates by an understaffed, underpaid, and widely corrupt police force. Reported cases of serious crime more than doubled between 1970 and 1976, from 29,000 to 62,000 per annum. Robberies increased from under 3,500 in 1970 to over 8,000 in 1972, and 13,000 in 1974, while detection rates plunged from over 70 per cent to under 20 per cent during the same period. Newspaper editorials and senior police officers blamed the courts for excessive leniency and called for tougher legislation. A series of measures by the government culminated in Governor MacLehose's Fight Violent Crime Campaign of 1973, aimed at strengthening the police force, mobilizing the community, and goading the courts into imposing stiffer sentences. In addition to the caning measures, these years saw a new provision allowing the Attorney General to apply for reviews of sentences (1972);[53] an increase in the maximum sentencing powers of the District Court from five to seven years' imprisonment (1973);[54] a mandatory minimum six months' custodial sentence for possessing an offensive weapon in a public place, along with increased powers of stop and search by the police (1972 & 1973);[55] and the introduction of detention centres for young offenders (1972).[56]

With the possible exception of detention centres, these were contentious measures. The review of sentences at the request of the prosecution, though a feature of many other jurisdictions, was not yet part of the English system. Some objected that it introduced a

---

51. Since a consolidation of the law on corporal punishment in 1954, male adult offenders could be caned for stealing from a woman or child, piracy, indecent assault of girls under sixteen, forcible detention, child stealing, grievous bodily harm, shooting with intent to maim or resist apprehension, suffocation or strangulation, illegal possession of arms, aggravated robbery, and prison offences triable in the courts. The maximum number of strokes was eighteen for robbery and arms offences and twelve for others. In 1971 assault with intent to rob, aggravated burglary, affray, and possession of an offensive weapon were added to the list. Various drugs offences were added in 1974, and in 1975 escape from prison was added. Boys under sixteen could be caned for any offence, and, following a decision by the Supreme Court in 1966, they were caned in the same way as adults – by two prison officers while tied to a 'flogging horse' – and not as previously by the prosecuting police inspector on court premises, more 'in the way of school discipline than of ordinary criminal justice,' as one old ordinance put it. Women and girls could not be caned. Caning as a judicial punishment was finally abolished in 1990. The total number of caning sentences carried out between 1970 and 1990 was 726.
52. Hong Kong Bar Association, *Annual Statement 1969–70*, 21; Editorial by John Rear, 1 *HKLJ* (1971), 118–22
53. Ordinances Nos. 18 of 1972 & 20 of 1979.
54. Ordinance No. 43 of 1973.
55. The option of a sentence of caning, in place of imprisonment, was added for this offence in 1973: some magistrates used the option as a way of avoiding the mandatory prison sentence. Ordinances No. 75 of 1972 & 45 of 1973.
56. Ordinance No. 12 of 1972.

form of double jeopardy and was a threat to judicial independence. The *Hong Kong Law Journal* was less concerned, though it felt that it undermined a convention whereby the prosecuting counsel did not address the court on such matters.[57] Critics said that the increase in the jurisdiction of the District Court (where cases were decided by a single judge) restricted trial by jury, and that mandatory minimum sentences – a new departure at the time – amounted to 'a declaration by the Government of lack of confidence in the courts.'[58] Judges and magistrates voiced opposition. The obligation to confirm a mandatory six-month prison sentence on boys as young as fourteen 'revolts the civilized mind', said one judge.[59] One magistrate refused to impose the sentence, saying it conflicted with his oath 'to do right to all manner of people.'[60] In a frank interview with *The Star* newspaper on his retirement in May 1973, Chief Justice Rigby expressed grave doubts about the fight-crime measures (including some which he had privately supported). 'I am glad I shall not be here to reap the bitter harvest when young persons serving long sentences are released,' he said.[61]

Rigby's *Star* interview became the leading article in a manifesto entitled *Fighting Crime* produced by a special committee of the Hong Kong Bar Association. This drew together practising barristers and academics from HKU, including experts on social work and psychology as well as law. Its guiding light was John Rear, whose series on 'Fighting Crime' in the *South China Morning Post* formed the backbone of the pamphlet, a survey of problems in Hong Kong's criminal justice system with recommendations for addressing them. The pamphlet included statements by the committee criticizing the government's planned fight-crime measures and a letter to JUSTICE (London) from the chairman of JUSTICE (Hong Kong), Henry Litton, asking it to use its influence in Parliament to urge the Hong Kong government to reconsider them.[62] A group of other barristers, led by Miles Jackson-Lipkin, took their concerns to the legal correspondent of *The Times*, Marcel Berlins, whose article in early 1974 on the 'appalling state' of justice in Hong Kong caused anxiety among officials

---

57. Editorial by Rear, 2 *HKLJ* (1972) 130–2. A similar provision was enacted in England in 1988. The Supreme Court, when laying down the principles that should be followed in such an application, expressed some sympathy with those who saw it as introducing a form of double jeopardy: *Attorney General v Wong Chi-fai, Wong Wai-ming, Chan Kwok-wah & Cheung Chi-man* [1972] HKCA 16.

58. The measure came before mandatory minimum sentences (other than for murder and certain driving offences) became common in other jurisdictions. The main exception was Northern Ireland, where, during the Troubles in 1970, mandatory minimum prison sentences were introduced temporarily for various offences. Hong Kong Bar Association, *Annual Statement 1972–73*, 54.

59. *Au Wing-wai and Others v The Queen* [1973] HKCA 84; *SCMP*, 31 October 1973.

60. *SCMP*, 12 January, & 10, 12, & 15 February 1973.

61. *The Star*, 25 May 1973.

62. Hong Kong Bar Association, *Fighting Crime: Comments on the Fight Violent Crime Campaign Compiled by The Special Committee on Crime and Punishment of the Hong Kong Bar Association* (1973).

in London. It also prompted a detailed response from Sir Ivo Rigby in the *Commonwealth Judicial Journal*, much of it agreeing with the criticisms.[63]

These campaigns had little, if any, immediate impact on the government's legislative plans, which were enacted with only minor modifications. The more draconian measures were repealed later in the century. The increased sentencing powers of the District Court and the provision for reviewing sentences have remained part of Hong Kong's system. The 1970s saw a gradual increase in the severity of sentences as the courts, in Litton's words, gave vent to 'society's collective sense of outrage.'[64] The campaigns did, however, stimulate the first serious research into the causes and treatment of crime in Hong Kong. Rear and others had criticized the assumption that harsh, deterrent sentences were the solution to rising crime and had called for policymaking 'from a basis of knowledge rather than ignorance.'[65] With this in mind the Bar Association's special committee instituted a Crime and Punishment Research Programme, drawing on the expertise of psychologists, sociologists, and lawyers under the auspices of the Centre of Asian Studies at HKU. The programme had mixed results: plans for empirical studies of corporal punishment (by the magistrate John Rhind) and sentencing generally (by John Rear and William Stone of the Department of Law) did not go beyond the proposal stage; but research by Mildred McCoy and Erik Kvan of the Department of Psychology into attitudes of young persons caught up in the criminal justice system resulted in a substantial book.[66] The initiative encouraged sociologists and lawyers from HKU – such as Harold Traver, Henry Lethbridge, Mary Kao, Bernard Downey, Ray Faulkner, and Richard Field – to delve more deeply into the workings of Hong Kong's criminal justice system. The results of their research were published in the *Hong Kong Law Journal* in the 1970s alongside commentaries on the more immediate impact of the fight-crime measures.

The dramatic curtain-raiser in Governor MacLehose's Fight Violent Crime Campaign was his decision not to commute the death sentence imposed on Tsoi Kwok-cheong, a twenty-nine-year-old man convicted of murder during a robbery in a shop in the New Territories. The death penalty was in force in Hong Kong until its abolition in 1993. However, since the abolition of capital punishment in Britain in 1966, governors of Hong

---

63. *The Times*, 9 January 1974; FCO 40/564 'Administration of Justice in Hong Kong' (1974); Ivo Rigby, 'Some Observations in Retrospect,' 1 *Commonwealth Judicial Journal*, No. 4 (December 1974), 16–19.

64. *SCMP*, 10 August 1975.

65. Hong Kong Bar Association, *Fighting Crime*, 23.

66. Mildred McCoy and Eric Kvan, *Attitudes towards Punishment: A Repertory Grid Study of Young Offenders in Hong Kong* (Hong Kong: Centre of Asian Studies, HKU, 1979). Other research from this initiative resulted in J.J. Rhind, *Proposals for a Statistical Study of Corporal Punishment in Hong Kong: A Draft Research Proposal* (Hong Kong: Centre of Asian Studies, HKU, c.1973), & William Stone & John Rear, *A Study of Sentencing Levels and Sentencing Policies, Current and Past, in the Courts in Hong Kong : A Draft Research Proposal* (Hong Kong: Centre of Asian Studies, HKU, c.1972).

Kong, using prerogative powers, had commuted all death sentences to terms of imprisonment. In April 1973, on the advice of his Executive Council, MacLehose decided to allow the law to take its course for Tsoi. There was nothing exceptional about this case, except perhaps the fact that the victim was an off-duty auxiliary policeman, roused from his sleep by the commotion. But MacLehose and his advisers had for some time been considering the possibility of reviving hangings. 'Something extra is required to shock young criminals,' MacLehose had written a few months earlier. 'We can think of nothing else that would have a similar effect.'[67] The decision created embarrassment for the Heath government in London at a time when Parliament was debating whether capital punishment should be restored for certain offences in the UK. It also ignited a furious debate in Hong Kong.

A torrent of editorials, petitions, and signature campaigns urged the revival of the death penalty. A minority of prominent residents – lawyers, journalists, and academics, including all four of the colony's QCs and most of its law lecturers – petitioned the Secretary of State for a reprieve. Supporters and opponents of the death penalty took to the newspapers. Among the contributions were letters to the *South China Morning Post* from Robert Ribeiro and John Rear. Ribeiro described in macabre detail the science of hanging and attacked the 'singularly crude retributionist sentiments' on the other side of the debate. Rear condemned this 'unjust and cynical' act and suggested that the executive councillors who had advised against a reprieve be asked to carry out the hanging themselves – in Statue Square 'at midday, in public, where the example can be seen for what it is – and at the same time you can prove your sincerity and your appetite for the task.'[68]

Tsoi's death sentence was commuted to life imprisonment by the Queen on 15 May 1973 on the advice of the Secretary of State in an intervention that was the first of its kind for Hong Kong – one that was 'against the express advice of the Governor in Council and the wishes of the overwhelming majority of the population,' MacLehose later declared.[69] For the rest of the decade, as politicians and newspapers continued to clamour for the death sentence, officials in London kept a close eye on capital trials in Hong Kong to ensure that such a crisis did not occur again. Denys Roberts, now Chief Secretary, sought to appease public opinion by declaring in 1975 that in future all death sentences would be commuted to life imprisonment, and that life would mean life – a declaration which the *Journal* described as 'an unofficial repeal of the law' prescribing capital punishment for murder.[70]

Just three weeks after the commutation of Tsoi Kwok-cheong's death sentence an incident occurred that was to mark the beginning of another of the great campaigns of

---

67. 'Problem of Crime in Hong Kong', 5 November 1972, & MacLehose to Roberts, 8 November 1972, in HKRS 260-1-22.

68. *SCMP*, 27 & 30 April & 6 May 1973.

69. *Hong Kong Hansard*, 17 October 1973.

70. Editorial (by Henry Litton), 6 *HKLJ* (1976), 2–5.

the 1970s – the drive to eradicate corruption. On 8 June 1973 Chief Superintendent Peter Godber, second-in-command of Kowloon District, fled Hong Kong a few days after being informed that a prosecution against him was being considered under section 10 of the Prevention of Bribery Ordinance 1970 – a new and controversial provision making it an offence for a crown servant to be in control of assets disproportionate to his official emoluments without giving a satisfactory explanation. Godber was alleged to have accumulated over $4 million in bribes, six times his total salary since joining the police force in 1952. He took refuge in England, where, since no offence equivalent to section 10 existed, he was able, at least for the time being, to resist attempts to extradite him to Hong Kong.

Godber's flight prompted Governor MacLehose to appoint a commission of inquiry by the judge Sir Alistair Blair-Kerr, whose reports pointed to pervasive corruption within the public service and a general lack of determination by the police in tackling it. Blair-Kerr recommended amendments to the Prevention of Bribery Ordinance to increase penalties, introduce greater powers to investigate suspects, and remove loopholes: one such loophole, which had enabled Godber to make his escape, was the requirement that the Attorney General officially inform a suspect in advance that a prosecution under section 10 was under consideration to give him an opportunity to make representations. Although Blair-Kerr did not explicitly recommend it, his main report provided arguments for taking the investigation of corruption out of the hands of the police. This resulted in the establishment in early 1974 of the Independent Commission Against Corruption (ICAC) with considerable powers.[71]

After a long extradition battle in the London courts, Godber was eventually brought back to Hong Kong in early 1975. The Hong Kong authorities had abandoned the section 10 charges against him and had instead secured evidence from two other corrupt policemen – Cheng Hon-kuen and Ernest 'Taffy' Hunt – sufficient to extradite him on a charge of actual bribery, an offence which also existed in England. Charges were dropped against Cheng, who agreed to testify that he had paid Godber $25,000 for helping him secure a posting to Wan Chai District, where vice establishments offered a lush field of corruption. Hunt, who in 1973 had been the first person to be convicted of a section 10 offence, was given a guarantee that no new proceedings would be brought against him or his wife. After a seven-day trial by Yang Ti Liang in the District Court, Godber was convicted of bribery and sentenced to four years' imprisonment.[72]

---

71. *First & Second Reports of the Commission of Inquiry Under Sir Alastair Blair-Kerr* (Hong Kong: Government Printer, 1973).

72. *The Queen v Peter Fitzroy Godber* [1975] HKDC 30. Godber's appeal, mainly on the ground that the generous immunities granted to Cheng and Hunt were illegal, was dismissed by the Full Court: *Peter Fitzroy Godber v The Queen* [1975] HKLR 326.

Godber's ability to evade justice for so long inflamed opinion in Hong Kong. Students organized a 'Bring Back Godber' campaign with posters and mass rallies, for which some were prosecuted under the Public Order Ordinance. As attempts to extradite Godber came up against one obstacle after another, politicians questioned a colonial relationship that allowed a scandalously corrupt British public servant to return to his own country, apparently with impunity. A community that had in the past tolerated bribes and extortion as part of the cost of living now turned against corruption. The ICAC received tens of thousands of reports in its first five years, resulting in some 1,000 prosecutions. The second half of the 1970s saw a succession of spectacular trials which revealed extensive organized corruption within the police force, the civil service, and the private sector. The campaign brought to an end the networks of syndicated corruption organized around police stations and government departments. The 'bloodletting' (as MacLehose termed it[73]) spread panic among some sections of the police. Some of the largest profiteers – including former staff sergeants who had made tens of millions through organized corruption syndicates – fled to Taiwan, Canada, and other places. Others committed suicide.

By October 1977 some 2,000 policemen (over 10 per cent of the force) were under investigation, many in connection with the 'Yau Ma Tei Fruit Market' syndicate, in which police and other officials took up to $10,000 a day for turning a blind eye to stalls selling illegal drugs. On 28 October a mass protest by police officers at Police Headquarters escalated into a march on ICAC Headquarters in Central, where staff and property were physically attacked. As discontent spread and the threat of a mass mutiny increased, MacLehose took radical action. On 5 November he announced what was to become known as the 'partial amnesty', an undertaking that in future the ICAC would not normally take action on corruption offences committed before 1 January 1977. This was followed by the summary dismissal of 118 police officers and 1 customs inspector, most of whom had allegedly been involved in the 'Yau Ma Tei Fruit Market' syndicate, under an obscure colonial regulation (Regulation 55) previously used for dealing with cases of espionage. The measure, said officials, was a quick solution to a problem that might have taken years to resolve through the courts.[74]

The *Hong Kong Law Journal* expressed sympathy with the puzzlement of the ordinary man in Hong Kong – 'the man on the Shaukiwan omnibus' – about the ease with which Godber escaped and the difficulties in extraditing him. As the Hong Kong authorities struggled with this problem, the *Journal* suggested a return to the system prevailing before the Fugitive Offenders Act 1967, under which fugitives fleeing from one part of the colonial empire to another could be returned under a simple warrant, whether or not the offence existed in both places. This anticipated a recommendation in Blair-Kerr's second report,

73. *SCMP*, 14 January 1975.
74. *SCMP*, 8 April & 15 June 1978.

which even suggested that the change should be retrospective so that Godber could be returned to Hong Kong without the need for extradition proceedings.[75] The *Journal* was concerned about the manner in which Godber's extradition was secured: it agreed with the comments made by Judge Yang in Godber's trial about the 'exceptionally wide and generous' amnesties given as apparent inducements to the prosecution witnesses Cheng and Hunt, though it concluded that, thanks largely to Yang's 'patent integrity', Godber had received 'as fair a trial as was possible in the circumstances.'[76]

While accepting that extraordinary measures were needed, the *Journal* was concerned that individual liberties should not be 'too drastically infringed' by the new measures against corruption.[77] It was dismayed by some of the ideas in Blair-Kerr's reports, such as his remarks on the ability of 'clever defence lawyers' to defeat the ends of justice under existing anti-corruption laws.[78] An article by the journalist Leo Goodstadt and the barrister Andrew Li (both later honorary lecturers in the School of Law) attacked Blair-Kerr's contention that it was 'utterly illogical' to presume that a person was innocent merely because he had been found not guilty, and his recommendation that regulations should be changed so that civil servants could be disciplined and dismissed even if they had been acquitted in corruption trials.[79] In an article published in 1976, Bernard Downey explored the history of anti-corruption laws, focusing on the operation of section 10 of the Prevention of Bribery Ordinance in recent trials and the wide powers of investigation granted to the ICAC. Concerned about the speed with which some of Blair-Kerr's ideas were enacted and the lack of effective supervision of the ICAC, Downey repeated a suggestion made by the *Journal* in 1973 for an ombudsman to oversee its activities.[80] In another article that year, Henry Lethbridge likened the ICAC to the censors of Imperial China and pointed to a new 'quasi-Chinese' style of government under MacLehose, driven by moral campaigns and neighbourhood action.[81]

Scrutiny of the anti-corruption campaign by lecturers at HKU continued in the *Journal* and other publications. The 'partial amnesty' announced by MacLehose in 1977 prompted an article by Peter Wesley-Smith in the *Far Eastern Economic Review* questioning whether a colonial governor had the power to suspend the statutory duties of the Commissioner of the ICAC through an administrative measure – a power which, Wesley-Smith noted in

---

75. MacLehose argued strongly for Blair-Kerr's proposal but the British government refused to pursue it. Editorial by John Rear, 3 *HKLJ* (1973), 249–52; Blair-Kerr, *Second Report*, 41–2; Yep, 'The crusade against corruption', 206–7.
76. Editorial by Bernard Downey, 5 *HKLJ* (1975), 129–33.
77. Editorial by Peter Wesley-Smith, 6 *HKLJ* (1976), 145–7.
78. Editorial by John Rear, 3 *HKLJ* (1973), 252–3.
79. Leo F. Goodstadt & Andrew Li, 'The Iron Rice Bowl—Hong Kong Law Regarding the Crown's Relationship with its Servants', 4 *HKLJ* (1974), 22.
80. Bernard Downey, 'Combatting Corruption: The Hong Kong Solution,' 6 *HKLJ* (1976), 27–66.
81. Henry Lethbridge, 'Corruption, White Collar Crime and the ICAC,' 6 *HKLJ* (1976), 150–78.

a later comment in the *Journal*, had been denied even to the sovereign since at least the seventeenth century. The government swiftly amended the ordinance to give legislative force to the 'amnesty.' In an analysis of the treatment of cases allegedly falling within the so-called 'amnesty', Wesley-Smith later noted with some satisfaction the courts did not view it as an amnesty at all in relation to section 10 offences committed before 1977.[82] The summary dismissal of the 119 crown servants following the uncovering of the 'Yau Ma Tei Fruit Market' syndicate under an obscure and little-used colonial regulation prompted a scathing editorial entitled 'the fragile rice bowl': this mass dismissal, one of the largest in colonial history, implied that a civil servant was dismissible at will, on the mere suspicion of having committed an offence, a state of affairs which went against recent jurisprudence and shook 'the confidence of every Crown servant.'[83]

It did not escape Wesley-Smith's attention that the swift amendments to the ICAC Ordinance in 1977 were prompted, not by anything in the *Hong Kong Law Journal*, but by his short article in the *Far Eastern Economic Review*, a publication 'with pictures' which lawyers in the Government's Legal Department were 'perhaps more likely to read' than scholarly literature. In his inaugural lecture as Professor of Law in 1989, Wesley-Smith took as his topic 'The Vanities of an Academic Lawyer.'[84] The main theme in this light-hearted talk was how little impact the Faculty of Law and its publications had made on the development of law and policy in Hong Kong. Certainly, subscriptions to the *Hong Kong Law Journal* were discouragingly low and on the decline (still only 250 by the end of the century), and its 'somewhat parlous' finances, 'firmly in the red', were relieved only by occasional donations and profits from the popular Law Lectures for Practitioners.[85] According to Wesley-Smith, many practitioners cited it without bothering to buy a copy. He once suggested that all members of the legal profession should be required to subscribe, an idea that was not pursued.[86]

From the late 1980s the *Hong Kong Law Journal* had a series of rivals in the form of glossy monthly magazines, full of pictures and funded by advertisements, distributed to all members of the legal profession free of charge. These began with the *Law Society of Hong Kong Gazette*, first issued in May 1987, which, after a rift between the society and the publisher, was succeeded in October 1989 by the *New Gazette*, produced by another publisher and edited by the barrister Gregory Barton, as the society's official organ until 1996. The Law Society's former publisher carried on with a new rival publication, *The*

---

82. *Far Eastern Economic Review*, 30 December 1977; Notes of Cases: *Cheung Sou-yat v R*, 11 HKLJ (1981), 76–9; Ordinance No. 9 of 1978.
83. Editorial by Henry Litton, 8 *HKLJ* (1978), 137–42.
84. *University of Hong Kong Gazette* (Supplement), 11 December 1989.
85. 'Hong Kong Law Journal: Report (1998), HKUA: Board of the Faculty of Law – Minutes (1998).
86. Peter Wesley-Smith, interview with author, 27 October 2017.

Lawyer. Competition between the two magazines was intense. There were allegations that *The Lawyer* was including unsolicited adverts and artwork from the old Gazette and counter-allegations that the *New Gazette* had failed to register under the Registration of Local Newspapers Ordinance.[87] *The Lawyer* lost out on advertising revenue and ceased publication after a year. The *New Gazette* contained articles on substantive legal issues interspersed with news, interviews, cartoons, and gossip, mixed in with glossy adverts for fine wines and fast cars. Because issues came out monthly, it contained more up-to-date commentaries on cases and changes in the law. Members of the Law Faculty contributed many of the more substantial articles, and the *New Gazette* included a regular feature entitled 'At the Faculty', containing monthly news on its activities. In 1993 *Hong Kong Lawyer: The Official Journal of the Law Society of Hong Kong*, began to appear, and in 1995 the *New Gazette* ceased publication.

The Law Reform Commission

The first editorial of the *Hong Kong Law Journal* noted the 'unprecedented era of reform' ushered in by the establishment of the English and Scottish Law Reform Commissions in 1965. 'In Hong Kong the picture is very different,' the editorial observed. Apart from isolated reports on topics such as Chinese marriages or taxation, 'there has been little original thinking on law and its administration in Hong Kong.' A Law Reform Standing Committee under the chairmanship of the Chief Justice had once existed, but its prime concern was not law reform but how far new English legislation should be copied in Hong Kong, and its last report – barely three pages – had been issued in 1964.[88] A Law Reform Drafting Unit had existed in the Attorney General's Chambers since 1965 but its scope was limited and it was seen as too narrowly based and inward looking. During the 1970s an informal law committee, composed of private and government lawyers, had met from time to time under the High Court judge Yang Ti Liang to discuss law reform. The Law Society also had its own active law reform committee, chaired by the solicitor Ian MacCallum. For some – including Professor Peter Willoughby – these initiatives were already enough. People who felt strongly about outdated laws could write to the newspapers or the government, he said. He had himself just submitted suggestions to the Registrar General for amending the law on patents. Hong Kong could not afford a permanent law commission along English lines, he

---

87. *SCMP*, 12 July, 5 & 9 October & 13 December 1989 & 22 October 1990.
88. The committee was formally dissolved in 1976. Hong Kong: Law Reform Committee, *Reports* (1957–1964); Stuart M.I. Stoker, 'Hong Kong's Law Reform Commission' in Michael Tilbury, Simon N.M. Young and Ludwig Ng (Eds.), *Reforming Law Reform: Perspectives from Hong Kong and Beyond* (Hong Kong: Hong Kong University Press), 54–5.

told the *South China Morning Post*, recalling a remark by a nineteenth-century judge: 'For God's sake let's have no more reforms, things are bad enough as they are.'[89]

Others, however, were critical of the antiquated state of Hong Kong's legal system. Hong Kong was ninety-four years behind in mortgage and conveyancing laws and fifty-two years behind in laws relating to trusts and joint tenancies, observed one barrister, Miles Jackson-Lipkin QC, in 1977. Industrial, road safety, and consumer protection laws were years out of date. There was still no system for compensation for people injured or killed by uninsured cars of the kind that had been in existence in Britain for over thirty years.[90] Legal institutions and practices had 'developed here haphazardly, with scarcely any real consideration of their appropriateness,' said the *Hong Kong Law Journal* in 1977. 'Much less has there been any full-fledged re-examination of basic assumptions.' A few months later, in an editorial by its new joint-editor, Bob Allcock, the *Journal* called for a law reform body in Hong Kong similar to those in Britain 'to consider the ever increasing body of reforms overseas and to initiate legislation specifically designed for Hong Kong.' There was 'everything to be gained, and nothing to be lost' by establishing such a body, wrote Allcock.[91]

This call was answered in 1980 with the establishment of the Law Reform Commission of Hong Kong, an initiative of Sir Denys Roberts, now the Chief Justice, and the new Attorney General, John Griffiths, who, unlike most of his predecessors, was recruited direct from the London Bar. The commission was to be chaired by the Attorney General, with the Chief Justice as an ex officio member. Both the Attorney General and the Chief Justice would jointly refer topics for study by the commission. Other permanent members of the commission included the Law Draftsman, judges, legislators, lawyers, and other prominent members of the community, as well as Peter Willoughby and Bob Allcock from the School of Law at HKU. Other law teachers participated in its subcommittees. The *Hong Kong Law Journal* gave the commission a lukewarm welcome. It was no more than an advisory committee which could be abolished at the stroke of a pen, said an editorial by Allcock. It was part-time, it lacked independence and legislative underpinning, it could not initiate its own research, and it was not required to publish its reports. 'The present Chief Justice and Attorney General may be keen advocates of reform but there is no guarantee that their successors will be,' said the editorial.[92]

Understandable though it may have been in the light of the demise of the earlier Law Reform Committee, this pessimism was misplaced. Since its establishment the commission has produced over sixty reports, half of which have been implemented in full, with only a handful rejected outright by the government, although the slowing pace of reform

---

89. *SCMP*, 12 November 1977.
90. Editorial by John Rear, 1 *HKLJ* (1971), 4–5; *SCMP*, 12 November 1977.
91. Editorials by Peter Wesley-Smith and Bob Allcock, 7 & 8 *HKLJ* (1977 & 1978), 291–2 & 1–4.
92. Editorial, 10 *HKLJ* (1980), 129–33.

has been the subject of criticism in recent years. The commission was most active, and the government most receptive, during its first dozen years or so, when its subcommittees considered issues ranging from arbitration (its first report, 1981) and insurance laws (1986) to damages for personal injury (1985) and divorce (1992). Its reports were detailed and scholarly, drawing not just on English examples but on practices throughout the common law world and beyond: its report on data privacy (1994), for example, examined no fewer than twenty-seven jurisdictions. In addition to studying technical issues, the commission provided a mechanism for dealing dispassionately with difficult social questions, such as the laws on loitering (1990), widely seen as oppressive. One of its first topics was whether the laws on homosexual conduct should be changed – a question referred in 1980 to a subcommittee chaired by the judge Yang Ti Liang, who was also the commissioner enquiring into the death of John MacLennan while he was being investigated for homosexual offences. Its recommendation to decriminalize homosexual acts between consenting adults in private was finally implemented in 1991.

The Sino-British Joint Declaration on the Question of Hong Kong, 1984

The Law Reform Commission exerted a modernizing, liberalizing influence on the development of law in Hong Kong in the last two decades of the twentieth century. A still more far-reaching impact came with the Joint Declaration on the future of Hong Kong signed by the governments of the PRC and the UK in 1984 and ratified in 1985. The Joint Declaration set out broadly the framework of government, the system of law, and the civil liberties to be maintained in Hong Kong after it became a special administrative region (SAR) of the PRC on 1 July 1997.[93]

Britain's ninety-nine-year lease on the New Territories was due to expire on 30 June 1997. Through the housing programmes of Governor MacLehose, this predominantly agricultural region, forming 92 per cent of Hong Kong's land area, had been transformed into a network of new towns accommodating over half of Hong Kong's total population. The leased area contained the airport, the container port, the power stations, the largest reservoirs, and most of Hong Kong's factories. In the late 1970s the dwindling period of the lease began to affect mortgages and investment decisions. In 1979, on an official visit to Beijing, MacLehose raised the matter with the Chinese leader, Deng Xiaoping, hoping that, with China's tacit agreement, a discreet amendment to the 1898 New Territories Order in Council might allow British administration to continue beyond 1997. Deng rejected this idea, holding to the long-established view that the whole colony of Hong Kong was a part of Chinese territory and that the British occupation was a problem left over from

93. *Joint Declaration of the Government of the United Kingdom and the Government of the People's Republic of China on the Question of Hong Kong* (1984).

the 'unequal treaties' imposed on China: it would be settled in an appropriate way when conditions were ripe. In 1982 talks began between Chinese and British officials, including the new Governor of Hong Kong, Sir Edward Youde, in consultation with the Executive Council in Hong Kong. The resulting Joint Declaration provided for an end to British rule in 1997, the resumption of the exercise of sovereignty by China, and the guarantee of a high degree of autonomy for Hong Kong under 'one country, two systems.'

The Joint Declaration promised continuity of a way of life that had thrived under British rule. It envisaged that Hong Kong would continue to be a free-market capitalist society, with its own finances, currency and border controls, and with private property and individual freedoms protected by law. The existing legal system, based on common law, was to continue largely unchanged, and Hong Kong was to have independent judicial power, including the power of final judgment – a measure of judicial autonomy not seen under British rule. Hong Kong's special status was to be guaranteed by a Basic Law enacted by the National People's Congress elaborating the principles in the Joint Declaration. The Basic Law prescribes the relationship between the Hong Kong SAR and Central People's Government, provides for a government made up of Hong Kong people, maintains largely unchanged the legal and other systems previously in force, lists the rights and duties of Hong Kong residents, and sets out the arrangements for an independent judiciary and a court of final appeal with the power to draw on the services of judges from other common law jurisdictions. Drafted with the involvement of Hong Kong people and promulgated in 1990, the Basic Law took effect in 1997 as the constitution of the Hong Kong SAR.[94]

The theme of the Joint Declaration was continuity between British and Chinese rule. However, despite the progressive outlook of late-twentieth-century governors, much work needed to be done to transform an authoritarian colonial system without democratic institutions into the somewhat idealized vision set out in the Joint Declaration and Basic Law, with its constitutionally guaranteed rights and freedoms, and government by local people. The programme of decolonization and disconnection from British sovereignty was complicated by intense anxieties among Hong Kong people about the prospect of returning to Chinese rule. China had only recently emerged from a period of international isolation and internal turmoil. Many people had found refuge in Hong Kong from the poverty, cruelty, and chaos of the Cultural Revolution (1966–1976) and the Great Leap Forward (1958–1962). When the HKU Law Association held a general meeting on whether to accept the Joint Declaration there was a sense of helplessness: 'some thought the best thing to do was to make money and leave,' recalls one of the participants, Johannes Chan.[95]

Not trusting the guarantees in the Joint Declaration, many with wealth and skills made plans to emigrate to Canada, Australia, the US, and other places, or at least to secure

94. *The Basic Law of the Hong Kong Special Administrative Region of the People's Republic of China* (1990).
95. Johannes Chan, interview with the author, 20 June 2018.

passports as insurance. After the violent suppression of student protests in Beijing in 1989, queues at consulates lengthened and fears for the future deepened. The British and Hong Kong governments responded with confidence-boosting measures: a new airport; accelerated political reform; full British passports for 50,000 key families; a doubling of the planned provision of first-year, first-degree places, from 7,000 in 1990 to 15,000 in 1995; and a Bill of Rights that was to sweep away old oppressive laws and promote a cultural consensus centring on the rule of law and constitutionally protected freedoms.[96] These developments were to have a profound impact on the legal system and the legal profession in Hong Kong and, not least, on the development of legal education.

---

96. Sir David Wilson, Governor, Policy Address 1989, *Hong Kong Hansard*, 11 October 1989.

Plate 22 Philip Smart, Harold Hsiao-Wo Lee Professor in Corporate Law 2007–2008, speaking to prospective law students at the LLB Admission Forum, 16 June 2001.

Plate 23 Wilson Chow, Head of the Department of Professional and Legal Education 2005–2011 and 2014 to the present, teaching a class in the K. K. Leung Building.

Plate 24 Professor Rick Glofcheski, Head of the Department of Law 1996–1999, Editor-in-Chief of the *Hong Kong Law Journal* 1999 to the present, leading a flipped classroom session in tort law in the Loke Yew Hall.

Plate 25 Albert Chen, then a first-year LLB student, introduces himself at a Mass Orientation session for new students in 1977.

Plate 26 Life in the Law Library: a cartoon from the HKU Law Association's *Law Media* magazine, April 1980.

Plate 27 The Lui Che Woo Law Library in the K. K. Leung Building.

Plate 28 The new Lui Che Woo Law Library.

Plate 29 Lord Denning, Master of the Rolls (right), and Yang Ti Liang, then a High Court judge (left) preside over a moot in the Department of Law, April 1977.

Plate 30 Puja Kapai, now an associate professor in the Faculty, then an undergraduate, argues before a panel chaired by Robert Ribeiro, a judge of the Court of Final Appeal, formerly a teacher in the Faculty, at the Grand Final of the Faculty Mooting Competition, 9 June 2000. The problem for the moot centred on international child abduction and the application of the Hague Convention.

Plate 31 Winners of the Hong Kong regional round of the Jessup Mooting Competition, 2018. From left to right: Astina Au (coach), Jason Ko, Natalie So, Brian Lee, Michelle Sum and Sakinah Sat. The team was subsequently ranked 11th out of 121 in the final rounds in Washington DC, and Natalie So was first out of the Top 100 Oralists.

Plate 32 Nihal Jayawickrama, a member of the Faculty 1985–1997, speaks at a conference on the implementation of the International Covenant on Civil and Political Rights in 1995. Next to him is his colleague, Andrew Byrnes, a Faculty member 1989–2001.

Plate 33 From left to right: Anna Wu, Carole Petersen, Kelley Loper and Vandana Rajwani celebrate the tenth anniversary of the LLM in Human Rights in 2009.

Plate 34 The mass demonstration on 1 July 2003 against proposed National Security Legislation. (Picture courtesy of *Sing Tao*)

Plate 35 The tent city at Harcourt Road during the Occupy movement, November 2014. (Picture courtesy of Professor Cheung Chan-fai, Chinese University of Hong Kong)

Chapter 5

A Liberal Education in the Law

Consolidation, 1984–1999

In the autumn of 1989 the Faculty of Law celebrated its twentieth anniversary. It marked this occasion with a dinner dance, two conferences – on Constitutions in a Modern Setting and Legal Education – and three books, *The Future of Legal Education and The Legal Profession in Hong Kong*, *The Law in Hong Kong 1969–1989*, and *The Future of the Law in Hong Kong*, with contributions from twenty Faculty members.[1] Among the guests at the celebrations was the Lord Chancellor of Great Britain, Lord Mackay of Clashfern. The anniversary year saw the establishment of the Sir Y.K. Pao Chair in Public Law, the founding of the HKU Law Alumni Association, and the launch of a fundraising campaign. It coincided with the graduation of HKU's 1,000th LLB student and the appointment of the first Queen's Counsel with law degrees from HKU – Edward Chan and Andrew Liao (both LLB 1972) and Robert Kotewall (LLB 1974).[2] In the same year Dafydd Evans, the founding head of the Faculty, was awarded the Order of the British Empire for his services to legal education.

The twentieth anniversary came during 'an extremely important period in Hong Kong's history,' in which the key legal foundations for Hong Kong's future were being laid, recalls Peter Rhodes, Dean of the Faculty of Law 1987–1993. It was 'an exciting time' for legal studies, as the Faculty adapted curricula to a changing legal landscape and offered new

---

1. Raymond Wacks (Ed.), *The Future of Legal Education and The Legal Profession in Hong Kong*, *The Law in Hong Kong 1969–1989* (Hong Kong: Oxford University Press, 1989), & *The Future of the Law in Hong Kong* (Hong Kong: Oxford University Press, 1989).

2. All three had taken the English route, rather than the Hong Kong PCLL, to practise at the Hong Kong Bar, having qualified in London after receiving their LLBs from HKU.

courses that looked beyond Hong Kong.[3] In the years leading up to the anniversary the Faculty began a full-scale review of the LLB degree and introduced a Master of Laws (LLM) degree. Towards the end of 1988 it exchanged its cramped quarters in the Knowles Building for spacious new premises on five floors of the new K.K. Leung Building. Two floors were devoted to the Law Library: its collection of 25,000 volumes more than doubled over the next decade, enriched by online databases. The new premises were opened by the Chief Justice, Sir Ti Liang Yang, on 28 October 1989 as part of the anniversary celebrations.

These years also saw the opening of a second law school, founded in 1987 at the City Polytechnic of Hong Kong (City University of Hong Kong, from 1994), which took in its first sixty students in 1988 and produced its first LLB graduates in 1991. A solution to the perceived shortage of lawyers, the decision by the University and Polytechnic Grants Committee (UPGC) to fund a new law school reflected a view that the Faculty of Law at HKU had reached its optimum size and could not continue to grow indefinitely. 'We have been expanding since we were established and have never had a chance to consolidate,' said Peter Wesley-Smith in 1989. 'Every year we've had to accommodate more students and more staff, with all the disruption caused by remodelling premises, temporary offices, inadequate library provision, and overcrowded facilities generally. At last we now have satisfactory premises and an end to the havoc caused by constant expansion. Why should we expand again?'[4] This view, reflecting consensus in the Faculty, was respected by the UPGC. The main burden of expansion in the 1990s fell on City University and HKU's Department of Extra-Mural Studies, which was restructured in 1992 and renamed the School of Professional and Continuing Education (SPACE).

Full-time student enrolment in the Faculty for all courses increased from 385 in 1984 to over 650 in 1990; it then rose more gradually to over 700 in the late 1990s. The annual LLB intake stabilized at around 150 in the 1990s before falling to 130 in 2000. The annual PCLL intake grew from 140 in the late 1980s to over 200 in the mid-1990s, before being gradually reduced to 155 by 2000; another 100 or more students enrolled in the HKU SPACE PCLL programme were taught by Faculty members. Student numbers were maintained through the introduction of joint degrees with other faculties and an increase in postgraduate students, many of them part-time. Broad stability in student numbers gave the Faculty breathing space to review curricula and introduce new degree programmes. An increasingly diverse and stable complement of staff helped advance this process and established the Faculty as a reputable centre of research.

Research and teaching matured during what became known as the 'transition period' (1984–1997), as Hong Kong loosened and then cut its constitutional ties with the United

---

3. Rhodes, 'Faculty of Law Reminiscence of 1987–1993' in Faculty of Law, HKU, *Building for Tomorrow on Yesterday's Strength*, 12; Message from the Dean, Faculty of Law, HKU, *Prospectus 1989/90*, 3.

4. Wesley-Smith to Rhodes, 1 November 1989, HKUA: Board of the Faculty of Law – Minutes (1989).

Kingdom (UK) in preparation for its new status as a special administrative region (SAR) of the People's Republic of China (PRC). Leading Hong Kong lawyers and politicians took part in drafting the Basic Law of the Hong Kong SAR, enacted under the Chinese Constitution by the National People's Congress and taking effect on 1 July 1997. The Basic Law provided for continuity of a separate legal system and conferred independent judicial power on Hong Kong. Chinese constitutional law thus became relevant to Hong Kong's future and a topic of interest to legal scholars. By declaring Chinese to be Hong Kong's official language from 1997 (while also allowing the use of English), the Basic Law stimulated an ambitious project to translate the whole of Hong Kong statute law into Chinese and to increase use of Chinese in court proceedings. The Hong Kong Bill of Rights Ordinance (1991) incorporated the International Covenant on Civil and Political Rights in domestic law: since there was at the time no direct equivalent in England, scholars, lawyers, and the courts began to look to jurisprudence from other parts of the world as they sought to understand it.

These fundamental changes to the legal system aroused a new interest in public and comparative law in all its aspects. The Hong Kong transition – a constitutional experiment without parallel – became the focus of international attention. The Basic Law 'makes us a part of the legal and constitutional system of the PRC,' said Yash Ghai in his inaugural lecture from the Sir Y.K. Pao Chair in Public Law in 1991. 'We must strengthen our efforts to learn and teach the PRC legal system. We must explore the various ways in which the Basic Law will enmesh the two legal systems and what must be the satisfactory solutions to the various legal challenges implicit in that.'[5] The need now, observed Christopher Sherrin in his inaugural lecture as Professor of Professional Legal Education in 1995, was 'not simply to educate lawyers for the hitherto cosy little jurisdiction of Hong Kong but to provide for the forthcoming status of special administrative region and the relationship with the PRC.'[6] Changes in curricula reflected and anticipated this transformation. A stream of conferences and publications analysed the implications of constitutional change, the first judgments under the Bill of Rights, and the impact of bilingual laws. Many of these activities were organized by the Faculty's first specialized research body, the Centre for Comparative and Public Law, founded in 1995. The centre attracted experts from around the world and soon became one of HKU's 'areas of excellence.'

Interest in public law was also stimulated by the growth of judicial review, a process by which the courts, upon application by an aggrieved party, ensure the lawfulness, reasonableness, and procedural propriety of decisions made by administrative bodies acting in a public capacity and by lower courts and tribunals. Influenced by the greater readiness of judges in England to intervene in relations between citizen and state, this procedure – 'the

---

5. *University of Hong Kong Gazette (Supplement)*, 6 May 1991.

6. Sherrin, 'Practice Makes Perfect', reproduced in 13 *Journal of Professional Legal Education* (1995), 131–45.

new equity', as Peter Wesley-Smith described it[7] – took root in late twentieth-century Hong Kong; it acquired a new efficacy when used to test legislation and executive acts against the Bill of Rights from 1991 and the Basic Law from 1997. Other developments, not directly connected with 1997 or with trends in English law, had an impact on law and legal education. Increasingly, the Law Reform Commission looked to other countries than the United Kingdom for solutions to legal questions, drawing in part on the research and experience of Faculty teachers and graduates.

As Hong Kong played a key role in the new industrialization of China and its re-emergence as an export economy, not only undergraduates but also experienced lawyers required training in China's rapidly developing legal system. In parallel, the shift within Hong Kong from manufacturing to re-exports, finance, and services, as well as the globalization of trade and finance, stimulated demand for training and research in topics such as international law, shipping law, and arbitration. These demands were answered in part by the new LLM degree, introduced in 1986 and focusing at first on international trade law and the law of the PRC, and by the establishment of the Asian Institute of International Financial Law within the Faculty in 1999. Links with Mainland China were fostered by institutional collaborations, visits and exchanges, and by a growing number of students and teachers from different regions and provinces of China. In 1997 the Master of Common Law (MCL) programme was introduced for graduates in law from non-common law jurisdictions, in particular those from universities in Mainland China.

'Who, in 1969, could have foreseen the extraordinary developments that lay ahead?' asked Raymond Wacks, Head of the Department of Law, in his introduction to one of the anniversary books of 1989. Looking to the next twenty years, however, he noted that 'dystopian visions' were becoming increasingly common. 'Some despair that, in the face of an obdurate government in Beijing, the prospects for the common law are grim. The Rule of Law will, in the minds of some, survive only as a memory after 1997.'[8] This pessimistic vision was not borne out by events. On the contrary, attachment to the rule of law became a prominent feature of civic identity in Hong Kong. Yet the transition to 1997 brought anxieties and disruptions. Many people doubted the guarantees made in the Joint Declaration by a fading colonial power only too ready to cast off its responsibilities for the people of Hong Kong and by a communist state that had only recently emerged from the chaos of the Cultural Revolution.

During the Faculty's twentieth anniversary year student-led protests gathered momentum in Tiananmen Square in Beijing. They were at first tolerated by the authorities and then, on 4 June 1989, violently suppressed. These events profoundly affected

---

7. Wesley-Smith, 'Licensing and Judicial Review', *Law Lectures for Practitioners* (1982), 31.
8. Wacks (ed.), *The Law in Hong Kong 1969–1989*, 1 & *The Future of Legal Education and The Legal Profession in Hong Kong*, 1.

confidence in Hong Kong's future and led to a deterioration in relations between Britain and China at a crucial stage in Hong Kong's transition. For HKU, the June 4th incident occurred after teaching had ended, near the end of examinations. But students, including many in the Faculty of Law, had actively supported their counterparts in China through-out the protests in April and May. 'They really believed China was opening up politically,' recalls Alison Conner, who was teaching a course on Chinese law at the time. 'Their hopes were dashed bitterly. It was devastating for them.'[9] The university declined to defer exami-nations. But the twenty-seven law students who failed their exams were allowed to retake them on the basis that their performance may have suffered as a result of the events.[10] Many staff attended a mass rally on 7 June organized by the HKU Staff Committee on Current Chinese Affairs.[11]

Three Faculty members – Rick Glofcheski, Nihal Jayawickrama and Andrew Byrnes – formed a research group to collect evidence of human rights violations in the June 4th incident. Together with various non-governmental organizations (NGOs), they took their report to Geneva, where they helped one of the student leaders, Li Lu, prepare his statement to the United Nations Sub-Commission on Prevention of Discrimination and Protection of Minorities: Li and other dissidents had been helped to leave Mainland China by Operation Yellowbird, a clandestine exercise based in Hong Kong. In August 1989 the sub-commission adopted a resolution expressing concern and appealing for clemency by the Chinese government. This unprecedented censure of a permanent member of the Security Council, in the face of strenuous opposition from Chinese officials, owed much to the timely and detailed reports from the NGOs.[12]

Tiananmen spurred some of the more idealistic law students to greater efforts to con-tribute to 'the human rights revolution' in China and Hong Kong.[13] But it may also have been a factor in the decline in the numbers of applicants for the LLB programme as fears deepened about the continuance of the rule of law beyond 1997.[14] It prompted many

---

9. Alison Conner, interview with the author, 17 July 2017.

10. Faculty Review Committee: Annual Reports for 1988–1989 & 1989–1990, HKUA: Board of the Faculty of Law – Minutes (1989 & 1990).

11. *Hong Kong Law Society Gazette*, July 1989.

12. Rick Glofcheski, interview with the author, 8 October 2018; Ann Kent, *China, The United Nations, and Human Rights: The Limits of Compliance* (Philadelphia: University of Pennsylvania Press, 1999), 56–60.

13. Comments by students in various years in 1991 quoted in Hong Hing-cheung, 'A phenomenographic investiga-tion of student experiences of learning in the context of the Law Faculty at the University of Hong Kong' (HKU PhD thesis, 1997) 181–2.

14. The number of HKU applicants putting down law as their first choice dropped from 826 in 1989 to 514 in 1990, 437 in 1991, and 392 in 1992. Another reason was the opening of the second law school at City Polytechnic in 1987. Rhodes to Smyth, 11 May 1992, & Minutes of the Admissions Committee (LLB), 14 May 1991, HKUA: Board of the Faculty of Law – Minutes (1991 & 1992); Report by the Faculty of Law, HKU to the Australian Law Teachers' Association (1992), 158.

lawyers to consider emigration: a survey of solicitors, barristers, government lawyers, and articled clerks in November 1989 found that 63 per cent of the 1,687 respondents planned to leave Hong Kong before 1997.[15] In the event, the numbers leaving were not so great. Lawyers had no advantages under the points-based immigration schemes used by Canada and Australia, the main destinations for Hong Kong migrants, and the barriers to entry into the legal profession were high in most jurisdictions.[16] A special British passport scheme, introduced in 1990 to encourage key professionals and others to remain in Hong Kong, reserved 3,700 places for legal professionals.[17] But the possibility of an exodus of lawyers and other professionals made the task of planning for the future even more uncertain. In the late 1980s the government was still convinced that Hong Kong had a dire shortage of lawyers. A decade later, in the late 1990s, when over 450 graduates per annum were completing the PCLL at either HKU or City University, some in the profession now believed that Hong Kong had too many lawyers, and that the general quality of entrants to the profession was declining. These concerns prompted the first full review of legal education in Hong Kong since the 1960s.

Teaching Staff: Growing Diversity and Expertise

The Faculty's permanent teaching staff grew from about thirty in 1984 to around fifty in the 1990s. The Faculty also relied on a network of part-time honorary lecturers, particularly for the PCLL, and on course consultants, external examiners, and other advisors. With the attainment of faculty status in 1984, deans were now elected for three-year terms by the permanent academic staff. The first Faculty Dean, Dafydd Evans, Head of Department since 1969 and Dean of the School of Law since 1978, was elected unopposed in 1984. Evans put himself forward again in 1987 but another candidate, Peter Rhodes, successfully contested

---

15. *New Gazette*, February 1990.
16. The main exceptions were England and Singapore. From 1981, Hong Kong qualifications were recognized for admission to the English Bar. Solicitors admitted in Hong Kong had, since 1901, been eligible to practise in England and Wales subject to certain conditions; in 1991 they became eligible for automatic admission following the removal of the requirement of three years' prior practice in Hong Kong. From 1984 to 1994 Singapore gave recognition to Hong Kong legal qualifications. During that decade a total of 452 Hong Kong lawyers were admitted, although not all actually practised in Singapore. Qualified Lawyers Transfer Regulations 1990 (UK); Legal Profession (Amendment) Act, No. 17 of 1984 (Singapore); *New Gazette*, August 1991 & March 1995; *SCMP*, 19 February 1995.
17. Under this scheme, full British citizenship was granted to 50,000 eligible persons and their families according to occupations and other criteria, without the need to reside in the UK. The aim was to encourage key professionals and public servants to remain in Hong Kong while assuring them of a place of refuge if things went wrong. Following lobbying by the professional bodies amid reports that lawyers would be excluded from the scheme, 3,700 places were eventually reserved for legal professionals and associate professionals. British Nationality (Hong Kong) Act 1990; British Nationality (Hong Kong) Bill 1990 and Explanatory Note (Hong Kong: Government Printer, 1990); *SCMP*, 29 November 1989; Bar Association, *Annual Statement* 1990–1991, 5–6.

the election. Rhodes was born and raised in Hong Kong and educated in New Zealand and Canada, where he taught at the Universities of Manitoba and Saskatchewan before joining HKU in 1979. An expert on oil and gas law, he took an LLM in international trade law during a year off from HKU in 1982–1983. Colleagues had urged Rhodes to stand for the deanship so that, after nearly twenty years with Evans at the helm, the Faculty could have fresh leadership and the prospect of reform.[18] Evans left HKU in 1990 to manage the training of solicitors in a London firm. Further contested elections took place in 1990, when Peter Rhodes was elected to a second term, and in 1993, when Peter Wesley-Smith, a teacher in the Faculty since 1973 and Professor of Constitutional Law since 1987, succeeded Rhodes as Dean.[19] Wesley-Smith was succeeded by Albert Chen, who was elected for two terms, 1996–2002. A graduate of HKU (LLB 1980, PCLL 1981), Chen had taken an LLM at Harvard University in 1982, specializing in comparative law, and had served articles with a Hong Kong firm before joining the Faculty as a lecturer in 1984. A prolific author, he rapidly established himself as a leading expert on Chinese law and the interface between the Mainland and Hong Kong legal systems.

The Dean was responsible for the management of the Faculty and its external relations, including contacts with the profession and participation in the Law Reform Commission and the Advisory Committee on Legal Education (ACLE). He chaired the Faculty Board and sat on various university bodies, including the Council, the Senate, and the General Purposes Committee. Peter Rhodes set standards for a more open, collegial system of decision-making, which his successors followed. The Dean was assisted by one or more sub-deans (known as associate deans from the mid-1990s), some with special responsibilities, and by an efficient administrative staff headed by a Faculty Secretary. The Faculty consisted of two departments: the Department of Law, the largest, taught the LLB and most LLM courses; the Department of Professional Legal Education (DOPLE) taught the PCLL. Staff from the two departments joined together for bimonthly Faculty Board meetings and a network of faculty committees. Heads of each department, appointed by the Vice-Chancellor, were responsible for the allocation of teaching duties and day-to-day administration.

In the late 1980s and 1990s the teaching staff became more diverse. Positions were usually advertised internationally, and, thanks to the growing attraction of Hong Kong as a place to work, good salaries, and bright prospects, the Faculty was able to recruit experienced staff from around the world: one exercise in 1991 drew some 120 serious applications.[20] Although some staff moved on, many committed to the Faculty for long periods, in several cases for

---

18. Peter Rhodes, interview with the author, 22 February 2018.
19. Peter Wesley-Smith, interview with the author, 23 October 2017.
20. Dean's Presentation to the UPGC – Academic Review Visit, 6 January 1992, HKUA: Board of the Faculty of Law – Minutes (1992).

their whole careers: about a third of those teaching in the 1990s are still teaching in the Faculty today. Most of the staff recruited in the late 1980s and 1990s had teaching, research, or practical experience before joining HKU, bringing with them experience from over twenty jurisdictions around the world: Botswana, Canada, the Cayman Islands, China, Gambia, Hong Kong, Ireland, Israel, Lesotho, Malawi, Malaysia, Scotland, Singapore, Sri Lanka, South Africa, Sweden, Tanzania, Uganda, and the US, as well as the old recruiting grounds of Australia, England, and New Zealand. Despite the attractions of private practice and the persistence of less favourable terms for local university employees,[21] the Faculty was also able to secure outstanding staff from within Hong Kong – a long-hoped-for achievement and one that was now essential in training lawyers for a bilingual system. Between 1984 and 2000 the Faculty recruited twenty teachers from Hong Kong, fifteen with LLBs from HKU; twelve are still teaching today. Another six from Mainland China, all with doctoral degrees from American or Canadian universities, also joined the Faculty. In combination with visiting professors and researchers, many of them experts in their fields, this diversity brought to the Faculty a wealth of knowledge and contacts at a time when Hong Kong's transition was receiving attention from around the world.

Longer and deeper connections with Hong Kong, combined with improved research facilities and greater opportunities to publish, enabled teachers to acquire expertise in Hong Kong law. Some also developed courses and texts on emerging areas of law with an international dimension, for example, Gary Heilbronn on aviation law, Peter Rhodes on international trade and financial law, Roda Mushkat on international environmental law, Katherine Lynch on arbitration and dispute resolution, and Bart Rwezaura on children and the law.

Several new appointments brought expertise in the rapidly growing field of Chinese law. Among these were some of the first Americans to have taught law in Mainland China since the normalization of Sino-US relations in the 1970s. Alison Conner had been a student of Jerome Cohen (a regular visitor to HKU) at Harvard, then the main centre of Chinese legal studies outside China. She researched Chinese legal history in Taiwan and taught law as a Fulbright senior lecturer at Nanjing University (1983–1984).[22] After a year of teaching at the National University of Singapore, she joined HKU in 1986 and played a leading part in expanding teaching of Chinese law. 'Hong Kong, for a sinophile, was the place to be,' Conner recalls. 'It was a place where you could think about China, read about China and talk about China,' even if materials were not easy to obtain. Another American, Donald J. Lewis, Fulbright Professor at Nankai University, Tianjin 1984–1985 and an expert on Chinese international trade and shipping law, joined HKU in the same year. Expertise in

---

21. Until the mid-1990s expatriate staff enjoyed subsidized university quarters, longer leave provision, and other benefits that were not extended to local staff.

22. Alison Conner, interview with author, 17 July 2017.

Chinese law was further enriched by visiting scholars from China, many eminent in their field, and the recruitment of teachers of Mainland Chinese origin, beginning in 1993 with Peter Feng (employment and intellectual property law) and continuing with Liu Nanping (jurisprudence, company law, and contract law), Yu Guanghua (civil and commercial law) and Zhang Xianchu (commercial law and judicial studies).

The most striking expansion of expertise was in public law – defined by Yash Ghai as the law applying to 'the interaction between the state and the community' and embracing constitutional law, administrative law, and human rights.[23] Already, with Ghai's appointment in 1989 as the first Sir Y.K. Pao Professor of Public Law and the recent elevation of Wesley-Smith to a Chair in Constitutional Law, observers were speaking of a 'plague of public lawyers' and a 'serious outbreak of constitutionitis' at HKU.[24] By then the Faculty had half a dozen other teachers with a strong interest in public law: William Clarke (who had introduced the course on civil liberties in 1987), Albert Chen (constitutional and administrative law), Johannes Chan (human rights and civil liberties), Nihal Jayawickrama (international human rights law), Andrew Byrnes (human rights), Roda Mushkat (international public law), and Raymond Wacks (public law, including privacy), as well as teachers whose experience elsewhere encouraged an interest in comparative law. In the 1990s they were joined by others with an interest in public law: Benny Tai, Fu Hualing, Yahong Li, and Carole Petersen. This concentration of expertise provided essential research and training at a time when public law was assuming more and more importance in Hong Kong's legal culture. It also established the Faculty as a centre of comparative public law in East Asia.

The 1980s saw an increase in female Faculty members, helped by the removal of some discriminatory practices: in 1975, for example, the differential pay scales at HKU, under which women were paid less than men for the same work, were ended. By 1989 women made up about a third of the Faculty's permanent teaching staff. The ratio of 2:1 male to female teaching staff has been broadly maintained to this day, ahead of university-wide ratios of about 5:1 in the mid-1990s, when the question of gender inequality first received serious attention, and 2.7:1 in 2019, when, thirty years later, it continues to be a topic of concern.[25] In 1989 the position of women in the Faculty became a matter of open debate when Robyn Martin, a lecturer in tort law since 1981, resigned to take up a position at the University of Bristol. Her resignation letter was published in the HKU Academic Staff Association newsletter. She was the fourth female teacher to resign from the Faculty 'in dissatisfaction with the respect given to female teachers,' she wrote. This dissatisfaction was not about numbers but about the poor prospects of women at HKU – a worldwide problem, she

23. Yash Ghai, interviewed in the *New Gazette*, March 1990.
24. *New Gazette*, March 1990.
25. The university-wide figures are from 'Full-time Academic Staff (Prof. to A.L.) (1995) in HKUA Carolyn Muir Papers, Box 4, Folder 4 and HKU website 'Quick Stats'.

acknowledged. There was a general perception that women had to wait much longer than men for promotion and needed more publications to be considered for a senior post. These claims were challenged by Peter Wesley-Smith, sub-dean in the Department of Law, in a response also published in the Academic Staff Association newsletter. He acknowledged that only 15 per cent of women had been promoted to senior lectureships, compared with 40 per cent of men. But this was because they did not remain in position as long as men. This argument was in turn dismissed by a senior lecturer in the Faculty, William Clarke, who suggested that women resigned early '*because* of the very discrimination propounded by Robyn Martin.' The correspondence on this subject was among the evidence considered by a university subgroup appointed a few years later to study the status of women at HKU. The subgroup concluded that women academic staff had 'no realistic prospect of promotion at this University' and recommended, among other things, greater attention to the gender composition of appointment and promotion panels.[26]

By the mid-1990s about a quarter of teachers were fluent in Cantonese or Putonghua (or both) and in written Chinese – an advance on the 1970s and early 1980s, when hardly any staff had much knowledge of Chinese. Their presence helped Hong Kong prepare for one of the great projects of the transition: the translation of statute law into Chinese. Several other Faculty members brought experience from countries with bilingual legal systems: some were from Canada, which had bilingualism at the federal level; Nihal Jayawickrama had been a senior official in Sri Lanka, where the system operated in Sinhala, Tamil, and English; Bart Rwezaura had been a close observer of the development of Kiswahili as a language of the law in Tanzania; Judith Sihombing had taught in Malay and English at the University of Malaya and had sat on an *istilah* (terminology) committee to translate legislation into Malay.[27] An ad hoc group in 1985–1986 chaired by Johannes Chan proposed courses in Chinese. The first course on Chinese language and the law was taught in 1987. As a mark of its significance, the first lecture was delivered by the Attorney General, Michael Thomas QC.[28] Other lectures, given in Cantonese by Johannes Chan, Albert Chen, and others, surveyed the main areas of Hong Kong law and examined legal documents used

---

26. Martin raised other concerns about the lack of recognition given to teaching skills by promotion boards and the 'top-heavy' bias towards public law in the Department of Law, to the disadvantage of private law teachers. Robyn Martin to M.G. Spooner, 23 February 1989, Peter Wesley-Smith to M.G. Spooner, 2 May 1989, W.S. Clarke to Professor Shih, 3 July 1989, & 'The Current Status of Women in the University of Hong Kong: A Report to the Working Group on Equal Opportunity', 8 December 1995, in HKUA Carolyn Muir Papers, Box 4, Folder 4. I am grateful to Peter Cunich for drawing my attention to this correspondence.

27. Judith Sihombing, interview with the author, 10 November 2017; B. Rwezaura, 'Constraining Factors to the Adoption of Kiswahili as a Language of the Law in Tanzania', 37 *Journal of African Law* (1993), 30–45. For a survey of legal language policies in various common law jurisdictions in the mid-1980s see Albert Chen, '1997: The Language of the Law in Hong Kong', 15 *HKLJ* (1985), 19–47.

28. *Law Society of Hong Kong Gazette*, November 1987.

in Mainland China. Later on, Betty Ho and Alice Lee invited students to scrutinize new bilingual legislation.[29] Further courses in Chinese were introduced in the 1990s. English continued to be the medium of instruction for the Faculty's other courses.

Interest in bilingual legal systems was stimulated by an influential article in the *Hong Kong Law Journal* by Albert Chen in 1985, which set out the challenges for Hong Kong. Fundamental among these was the production of 'lawyers and judges who can perform their legal tasks in the Chinese language' and who were 'capable of providing legal services in Chinese to Chinese-speaking people.'[30] The following year a government working party recommended a scheme of bilingual laws to prepare Hong Kong for 1997, when, under the terms of the Joint Declaration, Chinese was to be the official language, although, in addition, English could also be used in government and the courts. This altered the relationship between English and Chinese prescribed by the Official Languages Ordinance 1974, which gave equal status to the two languages but allowed only the lower courts and tribunal to conduct proceedings in Chinese and required legislation to be enacted in English. In 1987 the ordinance was amended to require all new ordinances from 1989 to be enacted in both English and Chinese. A parallel amendment to the Interpretation and General Clauses Ordinance prescribed that both English and Chinese texts were equally authentic and presumed to have the same meaning. In April 1989 the first new bilingual ordinance – the 111-page Securities and Futures Commission Ordinance – was enacted, and, after initially slow progress, by 1997 all 600 or so of Hong Kong's ordinances and over 1,000 pieces of subsidiary legislation had been translated into Chinese and authenticated. This Herculean task, probably the most ambitious of its kind in modern times, was compared by one observer to the translation of the 1,335 volumes of Buddhist scriptures from Sanskrit into Chinese in the Tang Dynasty.[31]

Teachers and graduates of the Faculty of Law made essential contributions to Hong Kong's Bilingual Laws Programme: almost every Chinese-speaking colleague was involved at some stage, recalls Alice Lee (LLB 1990). Albert Chen and Johannes Chan participated in early 'dummy runs', in which legislation was translated and submitted to the Legislative Council, and served on a Committee on the Use of Chinese in Court, chaired by Yang Ti Liang. They were also involved in the Law Society's committee on the use of Chinese among the legal profession. Various Faculty members, including Albert Chen, Alice Lee, Benny Tai, and Lusina Ho, sat on the government's Bilingual Laws Advisory Committee, formed in 1988 to vet translations and advise on their sequencing. The committee made recommendations on Chinese translations for English legal terms that had acquired subtle meanings through centuries of case law. For example, for the word 'possession', which has

---

29. Albert Chen, interview with the author, 12 March 2018.
30. Chen, '1997: The Language of the Law in Hong Kong', 16.
31. Henry Lee, cited in *Hong Kong Hansard*, 23 July 1986.

various meanings in law according to context, the neologism '管有' was used.[32] Several early law graduates played leading roles in the process. Eric Au (LLB 1979), Deputy Law Draftsman and head of the Legal Department's law translation team until his untimely death at the age of thirty-nine in 1992, was one of the pioneers of bilingual legislation. In 1994 the High Court judge Patrick Chan (LLB 1974) chaired a steering committee to monitor and supervise the use of Chinese in the courts. His colleague and former class-mate Wally Yeung (LLB 1974) heard the first High Court case in Cantonese, in 1995, and produced the first High Court judgment in Chinese.[33] Among other early graduates who, as judges, promoted the use of Chinese were Jerome Chan (LLB 1974) and David Yam (LLB 1975).

The expanding discipline of law in Hong Kong encouraged debate on bilingualism and other subjects, not least at the new law school at the City Polytechnic, whose first head, Derek Roebuck, set about organizing a digest of the common law in Chinese.[34] The Faculty's relations with the new law school were cordial and sometimes competitive. Despite differ-ences in style and emphasis, the two schools had similar objectives and served the same legal profession. There was some movement of staff between the two institutions, mainly from the City Polytechnic to HKU.[35] Derek Roebuck sat on the board of the Faculty at HKU 1987–1996, and curricula were to some extent co-ordinated: there were even plans for 'crossover courses.' Shortly after the opening of the second law school, the growing community of legal academics formed the Law Teachers Association of Hong Kong, with Dafydd Evans as president and Michael Wilkinson as secretary. Its first directory, issued in 1989, listed more than 70 law teachers. Most were employed in the law schools at HKU and the City Polytechnic, but several were teaching law as a component of other programmes in other institutions.[36]

---

32. Alice Lee, interview with the author, 13 April 2018.

33. *Sun Er-jo v Lo Ching and others* [1995] HKCFI 597.

34. The project, organized by Derek Roebuck and Zhao Bingzhi, resulted in three publications in the 1990s in English and simplified Chinese by the Peking University Press: *A Digest of Hong Kong Contract Law, A Digest of Hong Kong Criminal Law*, and *Criminal Procedure of Hong Kong*. The process is explained in Derek Roebuck, 'The Chinese Digest of Common Law', *Institute of Advanced Legal Studies Bulletin*, Issue 6, Autumn Term 1990–1991, 17–21, & 'China and the Year Books', *Law Lectures for Practitioners* (1989).

35. Among the early teachers who moved from City Polytechnic/University to HKU were Benny Tai, Anne Cheung, Yu Guanghua, Fu Hualing, Zhang Xianchu, and (via HKU SPACE) Carole Petersen.

36. Among these programmes were the Higher Certificate in Legal Executive Studies at the Hong Kong Polytechnic University, a Chinese Law Programme and law-related courses in the Department of Government and Public Administration at the Chinese University of Hong Kong, and commercial law courses at the Hong Kong Polytechnic, the Hong Kong Baptist College, the Hang Seng School of Commerce, and Shue Yan College. *Law Society of Hong Kong Gazette*, February 1988; Law Teachers Association of Hong Kong, *Directory of Law Teachers* (Hong Kong, 1989).

Hong Kong now had its own specialists on legal education. The designer and first head of the PCLL programme at the City Polytechnic was Professor Neil Gold, a world expert on skills-based legal education. At HKU another proponent of skills-based education, Stephen Nathanson, used his experience in designing professional courses in Canada and England to develop problem-based learning in his commercial law and practice course for the PCLL at HKU.[37] Yash Ghai had been a member of the International Legal Center's Committee on Legal Education in the Developing Countries, which in 1975 had produced a critical report on the subject.[38] He was president of the Commonwealth Legal Education Association in the early 1990s. Others – such as Jill Cottrell, Christine Booth, Janice Brabyn, and Gary Heilbronn – took a keen interest in the tools for teaching law, including video recordings and computers, which were introduced in the Faculty in the late 1980s. A stream of visiting professors brought new teaching methods: for example, in 1987 the introductory week for the PCLL class focused on practical skills with the help of Gary Goodpaster, an expert on negotiation from the University of California, and another skills specialist, Keith Jobson from the University of Victoria, British Columbia.[39] The Faculty hosted conferences on legal education in 1989, 1992, and 1995.

At the 1989 conference a leading authority on legal education, William Twining of University College London, spoke about trends over the past fifteen years. Among these were an increase in the scale of legal education; a diversification of the content of under-graduate law degrees to include greater socio-legal topics, interdisciplinary courses, and joint degrees; new subjects prompted by changing patterns of legal practice, such as consumer law and environmental law, and an increased emphasis on public law and inter-disciplinary fields such as criminology and law and economics; a trend towards four-year undergraduate degrees; and an expansion of research. These trends, Twining predicted, would continue over the next fifteen years. There would also be greater emphasis on the teaching of practical skills, a wider use of computers, and an expansion of continuing legal education.[40] At the time of Twining's visit, these trends were already evident in changes in progress at the Faculty of Law, notably in the comprehensive review of the LLB curriculum in 1985–1990 and the introduction of the mainly part-time LLM degree in 1986.

---

37. The approach, originating in the teaching of medicine, was based on the principle that knowledge is more effec-tively acquired in realistic problem-solving contexts. It involved practical exercises and examinations based less on the regurgitation of knowledge than on applying skills to drafting actual legal documents. Nathanson, 'Problem-Solving in Professional Legal Education' & 'Interview with Stephen Nathanson' 7 & 11 *Journal of Professional Legal Education* (1989 & 1993), 121–39 & 137–43.

38. International Legal Center, New York, *Legal Education in a Changing World: Report of the Committee on Legal Education in the Developing Countries* (1975).

39. *Law Society of Hong Kong Gazette*, October 1987.

40. Twining, 'Developments in Legal Education in the Commonwealth: Beyond The Primary School Model' in Wacks (Ed.), *The Future of Legal Education and The Legal Profession in Hong Kong*, 39–59.

Reform of the Bachelor of Laws, 1985–1990

The review of the aims, structure, content of the LLB was begun in 1985 by a working party of faculty members. Its elected chairman, Peter Wesley-Smith, was a proponent of broadening the study of law so that, in addition to providing professional training, it could offer 'a good general, Liberal education, and a cheap one' both to prospective lawyers and to students who had other plans.[41] Other staff, in varying degrees, shared this view. The LLB still followed the narrow structure put together by Evans and Rear in 1969. Despite revision of some syllabuses and the introduction of a few new courses, it was generally agreed that the curriculum was ripe for revision. The working party reported in November 1988 after holding thirty-one meetings and consulting widely with students, the professional bodies, and other groups, including the eighteen District Boards – bodies set up in 1982 as a step towards representative government.[42] The Faculty Board and its Curriculum Committee discussed the report at length. Most of its proposed reforms were implemented in 1990.

The 'Wesley-Smith Report' (as it became known) was the first review of the LLB since the 'Miller Report' of 1979, named after John Miller, the chairman of the working party that produced it.[43] Both reviews came after institutional changes: the creation of the School of Law in 1978 and of the Faculty of Law in 1984. The 1985 review followed swiftly on the Sino-British Joint Declaration of 1984 and was aimed partly at preparing for the changes in 1997. The Miller Report had recommended replacing the three-year LLB with a four-year LLB, while maintaining the PCLL year; implementing a unit-based curriculum after the compulsory first and second-year courses, with a wider range of options; and producing assessments that were not based entirely on final examinations. The aims were to expand the horizons of students beyond preparation for legal practice and to give staff opportunities for innovative teaching methods.[44] However, the impact of the Miller Report was limited. Options for third-year LLB students gradually increased to embrace more legal topics and other topics such as criminology and the sociology of law, as well as guided research. By the second half of the 1980s some twenty-five third-year optional courses were listed in prospectuses. But not all courses drew sufficient interest to be taught in any given

---

41. The other members were the Dean (Dafydd Evans up to 1987, and then Peter Rhodes), the Head of the Department of Law (Bob Allcock up to mid-1986 and then Ray Wacks), Johannes Chan, Michael Olesnicky, Sarah Nield, Edward Tyler, and three successive third-year student members: Francoise Lam See-man, Audrey Leung, and Rico Chan Wai-kwok. Wesley-Smith to Rhodes, 1 November 1989, HKUA: Board of the Faculty of Law – Minutes (1989).

42. LLB Review Working Party, Minutes of a meeting on 29 May 1985, HKUA: Board of the Faculty of Law – Minutes (1985).

43. The other members were Rodney Griffith and Peter Rhodes.

44. Report of the Working Party on the LLB Degree Curriculum, 5 December 1979, HKUA: Board of the School of Law (1979).

year. Their development was also constrained by the need to cope with expanding student intake and by the view that some third-year courses (such as Business Associations, Evidence and Procedure, and Family Law) were essential for admission to the PCLL.[45] The unit-based system did not materialize.[46] As for a four-year LLB, 'the Board of the School of Law recognised the practical, political and financial difficulties and no serious attempt was made to implement the idea.'[47]

Wesley-Smith's working party revived the idea of a four-year LLB. The expansion of traditional subjects and the emergence of new subjects needed a longer degree, the report argued. The narrow focus of the existing curriculum led students to see law 'as an independent body of knowledge isolated from other disciplines.' The working party believed it would benefit the legal profession and society at large if the curriculum reflected 'the dual nature of the LLB degree as both a qualification for the practice of law and a means of becoming an educated person.'[48] Students could study law in relation to other disciplines. They could have more opportunities to develop research, writing, and reasoning skills. Existing subjects could be taught in a more leisurely fashion, easing students' workload, 'which we have no doubt is too heavy.' Students who found law not to their liking could more easily transfer to other degrees. Teachers could teach more subjects in which they had expertise, reinforcing their research. In short, the working party envisaged a broad-based degree that 'would produce better-educated citizens, more aware of the social context of law, better able to adapt to social and legal change, and better equipped to serve society whether as lawyers or as professionals in other occupations.'[49]

The prospects for a four-year LLB seemed brighter in the late 1980s than a decade earlier. They were already the norm in Australia, Singapore, and Malaysia and were increasingly common in the UK. In Hong Kong, some other professional disciplines – medicine, dentistry, and architecture – required five years. In 1986 the HKU Senate resolved that it wished to extend the three-year undergraduate degree to four years, with a common foundation year.[50] However, any such change required UPGC funding. Although sympathetic,

---

45. See, for example, Willoughby to Evans, 12 November 1980, & Willoughby to all staff, 9 June 1981, HKUA: Board of the School of Law (1980 & 1981).

46. LLB Review Working Party Report (November 1988), HKUA: Board of the Faculty of Law (1988), 20.

47. Wesley-Smith to the Attorney General, the Law Society of Hong Kong & the Hong Kong Bar Association, 24 October 1985, HKUA: Board of the Faculty of Law (1986).

48. LLB Review Working Party Report (November 1988), HKUA: Board of the Faculty of Law (1988), 5.

49. LLB Review Working Party Report, HKUA: Board of the Faculty of Law (1988), 11–13.

50. The Education Commission was then also considering the structure of tertiary education and the entry point for students. At this time, HKU took in students after two years of sixth form – i.e. after Secondary 7, mainly on the basis of 'A' level results – for degrees generally lasting three years. The Chinese University took in students after either Secondary 6 or Secondary 7 for degrees usually lasting four years, including 'a general and cultural education' in the first year. In 1988 the commission recommended that Secondary 7 should be the entry point for all tertiary institutions and that the length of first-degree courses should in principle be the same for all subjects, though it was

the UPGC declined for the time being to give its support. The idea received no support from the legal profession: the Bar Association, Law Society, and ACLE offered no views; the Attorney General declined to endorse a proposal that would add another year to the six years already required for training as a solicitor.[51] The Faculty had to accept there was 'little likelihood of it being achieved in the immediate future.'[52]

The LLB review was more successful with proposals that were within the capacity of the Faculty to deliver. The Faculty Board quickly endorsed the principle advanced by the working party that the LLB should provide 'a liberal education in the law.'[53] Some existing compulsory 'core' courses in the first two years were reorganized or replaced, and some, such as the Law of Trusts, became optional. Two new subjects were added: a half-year course on Legal Writing and Research and a full-year course, Law and Society, reflecting the emphasis on liberal education. In the third year, compulsory Jurisprudence was split into half-courses on Legal Theory (compulsory) and Law, Justice, and Ideology (optional).[54] The compulsory dissertation had been replaced in 1988 with an optional course of Guided Research. Rising student numbers had made it difficult to avoid duplicating topics and maintain consistent standards. Administering the scheme, with up to 150 students looking for a topic every year, had become a source of discontent among students and teachers.[55]

The reduction of compulsory courses in the second and third years increased the scope for optional courses. The review revived the idea of a unit structure system. Under the new curriculum introduced in 1990, full-year courses were each given two units and half-year courses one unit. Students were required to pass in subjects totalling at least twenty-seven units (twenty-five from 1992): sixteen were to be from the compulsory subjects in years one and two, and the rest from optional courses. Already under the old curriculum the number of optional courses had increased to twenty-six (eleven full-year, fifteen half-year)

---

generally opposed to a four-year degree. 'University educational policy', 5 January 1987, HKUA: Board of the Faculty of Law (1988); LLB Review Working Party Report (November 1988), HKUA: Board of the Faculty of Law (1988), 7–11; Education Commission (Hong Kong), Report No. 3 (1988), Chapter 3.

51. UPGC, *Interim Report for the 1988–91 Triennium, July 1988 to December 1989*, 21; Gillanders to Deans, 29 August 1989, & Report of the working party on educational policy, June 1989, HKUA: Board of the Faculty of Law (1989).

52. LLB Curriculum Committee: Review of the degree of LLB curriculum, 2 February 1990, HKUA: Board of the Faculty of Law (1989).

53. Some had reservations. See, for example, Stephen Nathanson, 'The Purpose of Legal Education', 24 *HKLJ* (1994), 315–19, which argued that mixing general with professional purposes in an undergraduate degree was confusing to teachers and students and that the sole purpose of legal education was to educate students for legal practice. Minutes of the Board of the Faculty of Law, 10 January 1989, HKUA: Board of the Faculty of Law (1989).

54. LLB Curriculum Committee: Review of the degree of LLB curriculum, 2 February 1990, HKUA: Board of the Faculty of Law – Minutes (1989).

55. Annual Reports of the Dissertations Committee, 1985–1986, 1986–1987, Dissertations for the Degree of LLB, 30 November 1987 & 29 January 1988, Minutes of meeting on 9 December 1987, HKUA: Board of the Faculty of Law – Minutes (1986, 1987, & 1988).

by the time of the submission of the Wesley-Smith Report in 1989, even if only ten were actually taught that year. The report envisaged a broader range of options, though, with a few exceptions, it did not specify what they should be: the idea was that they should follow the interests of teachers and the changing demands of Hong Kong's legal environment. A further reform, in 1992, reorganized most full-year optional courses into half-year, one-unit courses.[56] Under a general university reform phased in from 1998, courses were allocated credits – 12 for full-year courses, 6 for half-year – and students were required to pass in subjects totalling 180 credits.[57]

As a result of these reforms, by 1999 the prospectus listed nearly seventy optional courses, thirty of which were offered that year. These were divided into two overlapping lists: a list of a dozen or so broad topics, such as Criminology, Comparative Law, Economic Analysis of Law or Legal Fictions (the first law and literature course, introduced in 1996)[58], from which at least one was to be taken; and a longer list of mostly specialized topics, from which the remaining courses were to be chosen. The longer list ranged from Alternative Dispute Resolution to the Use of Chinese in Law, and included established areas of law, such as Evidence, Trusts, and Family Law, as well as newer topics such as Planning and Environmental Law and the Child and the Law. Although private law subjects continued to dominate, there was a wider range of options on public law, such as Human Rights Law, the Hong Kong Basic Law, and Public International Law. It was now possible for a student to approach the LLB mainly as a preparation for practice by taking the black-letter-law options or, by focusing on the broader topics, to see the degree mainly as a liberal education. In practice, 'quasi-compulsory' options such as Evidence and Company Law, tended to draw the largest enrolments, partly because they were required for entry to the PCLL. The first Basic Law course, in 1990, had to be abandoned when only three students enrolled. The course on the PRC legal system was also cancelled that year for lack of interest.[59] The course on Human Rights attracted a healthy enrolment of thirty.

---

56. The exceptions were Guided Research and Human Rights Law (the latter on the insistence of its teacher, Nihal Jayawickrama), which continued to be two units.

57. A few – such as Chinese Language and Communication and Moot Court – were allocated three credits, and one – Legal Skills – had nine credits.

58. The course, developed by William MacNeil, focused on representations of the law in literature, philosophy, cinema, and television, with topics on Plato, Sophocles, Dickens and Kafka, films such as 'Witness for the Prosecution' and 'Judgment at Nuremberg', a sampling of TV series such as 'Rumpole of the Bailey' and 'L.A. Law', and (observed the course outline) 'possibly that series that was stranger than fiction, the OJ Simpson trial'. Assessment was through a tutorial presentation, a critical essay, and a final open-book examination.

59. A lecturer in the Faculty rejected suggestions that students had shunned the courses for political reasons. *SCMP*, 30 July 1990.

Mixed Degrees

The unit-based system enabled more flexible curriculum development and made it easier for the Law Faculty to collaborate with other faculties in designing mixed or joint degrees. This idea had been suggested as far back as 1965 in the report by overseas experts on establishing a law school in Hong Kong.[60] It was raised again when proposals for university-wide foundation studies were discussed in the late 1980s.[61] A decade later, after discussions with the other faculties concerned, a working party chaired by the Dean, Albert Chen, recommended two mixed-degree programmes: the Bachelor of Business Administration (BBA) (Law) and the Bachelor of Social Sciences (BSocSc) (Government & Laws), which were introduced in 1999 despite initial concerns among some faculty members that graduates would be qualified neither in law nor in the other discipline. The programmes were designed to recognize the important role of law in business and government. They also took into account views that the demand for lawyers was declining and the possibility that a new mixed degree in law and accountancy at City University might draw prospective applicants away from HKU.[62]

Unlike the four-or five-year joint honours degrees in other parts of the world, the new mixed degrees were initially three-year programmes with a roughly equal number of law courses and courses from the other faculty, as well as a general education element. The BBA (Law) had a greater component of compulsory law courses, and students were required to take courses in contract law, tort, company law, and various other relevant topics. The BSocSc (Government & Laws) had fewer compulsory courses and more electives. Graduates of the two programmes could also proceed to a self-funded fourth year of study in the Faculty of Law leading to a second degree of LLB, making them eligible for admission to the PCLL programme. Despite gruelling workloads, the mixed degrees were popular. In the first year they were offered the BBA (Law) attracted 850 applications for 25 places, and the BSocSc (Government & Laws) 984 for 20 places.[63] Places were gradually increased over the years. Following the introduction of four-year degrees in the early twenty-first century, mixed-degree programmes were extended to five years and upon graduation students received two degrees. New programmes were added, such as the Bachelor of Engineering in Civil Engineering (Law) and LLB mixed degree in 2004 and the BA in Literary Studies and LLB mixed degree in 2011.[64]

---

60. Report by Cowen, Guest, and Pannam: HKUA: Registry File No. 2/1/19/2 Part 2, encl. 222.

61. Foundation Studies, 17 October 1989, HKUA: Board of the Faculty of Law (1989).

62. Combined Undergraduate Degree, 26 May 1998, & Minutes of the Board of the Faculty of Social Sciences, 3 June 1998, HKUA: Board of the Faculty of Law (1998); Albert Chen, interview with the author, 12 March 2018.

63. Faculty of Law, 2001–2004 Triennium: Academic Development Proposal, 8 October 1999, HKUA: Board of the Faculty of Law (2000).

64. For the development of the former see Albert T. Yeung, Thomas Ng, L. George Than, & Peter K. Lee, 'HKU's double professional civil engineering and law programme', *Proceedings of Institution of Civil Engineers: Management,*

The Master of Laws, 1986

While the trend in LLB reform was towards a broader education for undergraduates, the taught LLM, introduced in 1986, offered graduate students possibilities for specialization. Regulations for a thesis-based LLM degree were approved as early as 1969.[65] Two candidates were admitted for the degree in 1970: one, Peter Wesley-Smith, transferred to a PhD degree; the other transferred to a Master of Philosophy but did not complete. In the late 1970s the Faculty embarked on plans for a new kind of LLM similar to those offered in the UK and North America: a part-time, course-based degree aimed at practitioners, covering subjects relevant to their work, such as, banking, insurance, international trade, and intellectual property law.[66] The programme was devised by a committee chaired by Peter Rhodes, with advice from Roy Goode, a visiting professor from Queen Mary College, London. Chinese law was added as a main field of study. Students were required to take four courses, or three courses and a dissertation, over one academic year (full-time) or two academic years (part-time).[67]

Over 120 applicants applied for the first LLM intake in 1986 and 22 were admitted, all part-time and several of them law graduates from HKU. Six courses were offered in the first two years: Credit and Security Law, International Travel Law, International Commercial Transactions, Securities Regulation, and two on Chinese law (Trade and Investment, and Economic and Civil Law in the PRC). Many of the dissertations were on topics relating to the rapidly expanding legal system in China. Courses were taught on campus by full-time members of the Faculty with assistance from practising lawyers. The programme was financed by student fees and private donations. Classes were small and were held after normal working hours on weekday evenings, from 6 p.m. to 9 p.m. They were on such a tight schedule that one teacher, Peter Rhodes, recalls having to take orders for sandwiches beforehand so that students got something to eat.[68] After three hours of intensive teaching, the classroom often looked like 'the aftermath of a football match.'[69] Carol Tan, on a teaching exchange from Keele University in 1993, was anxious about having to step in to teach Civil and Economic Law in the PRC while the course's teacher, Edward Epstein,

---

Procurement and Law, Vol, 163 No. 2 (2010), 77–85.

65. Report of Delegated and Non-Controversial Business for the meeting on November 18, 1969, Minutes of meetings on 17 February & 17 November 1970, HKUA: Board of the Faculty of Social Sciences – Minutes (1969 & 1970).

66. Background to proposals for Law in the Triennium 1981–1984, HKUA: Board of the School of Law (1979).

67. Minutes of meetings of the LLM Committee on 24 & 27 March 1986 & Annual Report of the LLM Committee, HKUA: Board of the Faculty of Law (1986).

68. Peter Rhodes, interview with the author, 22 February 2018; Rhodes, 'Educating today's law students for tomorrow's Hong Kong', *Law Society of Hong Kong Gazette*, June 1988.

69. Minutes of a meeting of the LLM Committee, 16 May 1989, HKUA: Board of the Faculty of Law (1989).

was on leave. She expected a critical audience. But the students were 'too exhausted from their labours in town to comment.'[70] Despite the long hours, the pass rate was high. One early fruit was a book on the expanding field of aviation and travel law, drawing on research projects in the LLM programme.[71]

The LLM attracted a steady stream of students over the years, many well established in the profession and most of them part-time. From the early 1990s, new courses were added, for example on Shipping Law, Comparative and Transnational Insolvency Law, and International Dispute Resolution. The LLM expanded to cover topics such as Human Rights, East Asian Law, the Basic Law, Environmental Law, and Construction Law. In 1999, when it had an enrolment of over ninety, the LLM consisted of four streams: a general LLM and specialized LLMs in Chinese Commercial Law, Corporate and Financial Law, and Human Rights. Funded by the Asia Foundation, the Human Rights programme took 'as a central focus the experiences of people across the region,' said Yash Ghai. It attracted students from all over the region. At one seminar, said the programme director, Andrew Byrnes, 'we had 12 students around the table, with 12 different nationalities.' This gave rise to debates on issues such as monarchies and democratic principles, 'where our Western republicans were taken aback by some of the views expressed by our colleagues from Thailand, Nepal and Cambodia.'[72] From 1993 the Faculty organized specialized Postgraduate Diplomas, initially on Commercial Law and the Law of the PRC and, from 1995, on Public Law. Admission requirements were the same as for the LLM – a recognized undergraduate law degree or admission to professional practice. Students attended the same courses but were required to take only two rather than four.

The Master and Diploma of Common Law Programmes, 1997

The first LLM programme at HKU was designed in part to introduce practitioners in Hong Kong to the legal system of Mainland China. The Master of Common Law (MCL) and related Postgraduate Diploma in Common Law, launched in 1997, worked in the other direction. They were designed for law graduates from non-common law jurisdictions, particularly Mainland China, who wished to acquire knowledge of the common law. This was, wrote the new Dean, Albert Chen, in 1996, a recognition that the legal system of the PRC would soon become a dual system, with socialist Chinese law on the Mainland and common law in the Hong Kong SAR. Hong Kong was an ideal place for Mainland lawyers to learn about the common law at a time when China was 'striving to borrow from Western

---

70. Carol Tan, recollection in *Thirty Years*, 96.

71. Gary Heilbronn (ed.), *Essays on Aviation and Travel Law in Hong Kong* (Hong Kong: Hong Kong University Press, 1990).

72. *Faculty of Law Newsletter*, November 1999 & August 2000.

experience in the construction of its young legal system.' 'Our vision,' wrote Chen, is 'to turn the Faculty of Law at HKU into a centre of excellence for the study of Common Law not only for local students but also for scholars from all over mainland China.' The new degree, he added, would also address perceptions that the law school at City University was more energetic in adapting to changing circumstances: in 1995 it had launched a joint master's degree in Chinese law with Renmin University.[73]

In fact, the Faculty of Law at HKU had been teaching Mainland students for some years. In 1979 a mature student from China was admitted as an external LLB student for one academic year.[74] In June 1985, in an initiative led by Edward Tyler, eighteen teachers from the Faculty gave a two-week course on Hong Kong commercial law at Zhongshan University in Guangzhou to forty students from across China.[75] Similar programmes were organized in the following years. In 1987 the Faculty enrolled three young law teachers – one each from Nanjing and Renmin Universities and the Chinese University of Political Science – in the LLB programme for a year in 1987–1988. The aim was to give them insights into Hong Kong law which they could pass on to their students. 'I learned a lot from them,' recalls Alison Conner, who organized the programme with Edward Epstein.[76] Similar programmes were held in other years, and in the early 1990s two PhD candidates were admitted from China, though they did not complete. Other Mainland scholars studied at the Faculty without pursuing a degree. Among these, Wang Zhenmin, a visiting scholar from Renmin University 1993–1995, played a key role in re-establishing the law school at Tsinghua University on returning to Beijing and served as dean there from 2008: his experiences at HKU and the friendship of Faculty staff were an inspiration to him in this.[77] In 2016 Wang became head of the legal department of the Liaison Office of the Central People's Government (CPG) in the Hong Kong SAR.

Many of these activities were sponsored by outside bodies. The Zhongshan University programme was funded by the Hong Kong Pei Hua Education Foundation.[78] The first external students from China were financially supported by law firms in Hong Kong, and the PhD candidates were funded by Li Ka Shing scholarships. In framing the proposals for the new MCL degree, the Dean, Albert Chen, urged the creation of special scholarships to cover the initial ten places, since existing postgraduate scholarships and studentships were not available for primarily course-based degrees. These were secured from the HKU

73. Chen to Cheng Yiu-chung, Vice-Chancellor, 24 August 1996, HKUA: Board of the Faculty of Law (1996).

74. Minutes of meeting on 12 September 1979, HKUA: Board of the School of Law (1979).

75. *SCMP*, 3 June 1985; Rhodes, 'Educating today's law students for tomorrow's Hong Kong', *Law Society of Hong Kong Gazette*, June 1988.

76. *Law Society of Hong Kong Gazette*, May 1987 & June 1988; *SCMP*, 4 July 1987; Alison Conner, interview with the author, 17 July 2017.

77. 王振民，'我的港大生活' [Wang Zhenmin, 'My Life at HKU'], *Faculty of Law Newsletter*, Spring 2004.

78. Established by Hong Kong businessmen in 1982 with the aim of helping China train professionals.

Foundation and other donors, including the Legal Education Trust Fund, and, later on, the Department of Justice.[79] Entry into the programme was extremely competitive, and early students included law teachers, judges, and government officials from Mainland China as well as master and doctoral graduates from China's leading law schools.[80] Among them were He Xin, a future professor in the Faculty, and Liu Chunhua, a future deputy director-general and legal counsel in the CPG Liaison Office in Hong Kong.

Students in the Postgraduate Diploma in Common Law programme were required to pass eight half-year courses in one year of full-time of study. These could be any courses offered by the Faculty of Law, but students were encouraged to take some LLB courses so as to learn something of the reasoning and methodology of the common law. Some went on to fulfil the Master of Common Law requirements: these consisted of the coursework under the diploma programme and a dissertation, to be submitted a year after the coursework. Since this required research and writing after the candidate had left full-time study in the Faculty and, in most cases, Hong Kong, most students preferred to conclude their studies at the diploma level.[81]

Research Degrees and the Doctor of Legal Science, 1998

Despite some isolated successes, research within the Faculty of Law for the university's standard postgraduate degrees – the PhD and the Master of Philosophy – had 'a dismal record' according to Peter Wesley-Smith, one of only four PhD candidates to have completed their degrees in the Faculty's first thirty years.[82] Two Master of Philosophy students graduated in the same period. Few students had been able to complete dissertations to an acceptable standard, a problem shared by law schools elsewhere. Disappointing performances by promising PhD candidates from Mainland China had been one of the justifications for the MCL programme.[83] But even law students trained in the common law found 'the lonely struggle with a long dissertation' difficult. 'The fact is that writing a PhD requires a student to undertake a piece of research and writing of a size and complexity which far exceeds anything he or she has ever done before,' wrote Jill Cottrell, Associate

---

79. Albert Chen to Cheng Yiu-chung, Vice-Chancellor, 24 August 1996, & Kwan to Chen, 3 September 1996, HKUA: Board of the Faculty of Law – Minutes (1996); Albert Chen, interview with the author, 12 March 2018.

80. Faculty of Law, 2001–2004 Triennium: Academic Development Proposal, HKUA: Board of the Faculty of Law – Minutes (1999).

81. Albert Chen, interview with the author, 12 March 2018.

82. The other three were Alan Tse Chung, on Hong Kong's bilingual legal system (1996), Zhou Wei, on Marxism and human rights (1998), and Physer Leung Kwan-yuen, on a critical theory of law (1999). Wesley-Smith, 'Epilogue', in *Thirty Years*, 107.

83. Chen to Cheng Yiu-chung, Vice-Chancellor, 24 August 1996, HKUA: Board of the Faculty of Law – Minutes (1996).

Dean for Research, in a report in 1997. In any case, observed another report three years later, 'the demand in Hong Kong for postgraduate legal education has been minimal.'[84]

The solution proposed by Cottrell was a different kind of doctoral degree along the lines offered by law schools in North America and Australia: the Doctor of Legal Science, abbreviated as 'SJD' (*Scientiae Juridicae Doctor*). The degree was open to holders of an LLM or an LLB with at least upper second-class honours. The minimum period of study was three years full-time or five years part-time. Candidates had to take eight half-year courses, or their equivalent, usually from the LLM programme, and a compulsory course on Advanced Research Methodology. They then had to complete a 50,000-or 60,000-word dissertation, which accounted for two-thirds of the requirement for the degree and was judged by the same standards as a PhD. Like the MCL, the SJD was designed partly with students from non-common law jurisdictions in mind. Most of the candidates have been from Mainland China, with some from Thailand, India, and the Netherlands. Most of the theses completed in the first twenty years of the SJD have been on non-Hong Kong topics or on Hong Kong topics seen from a comparative perspective. Several have been on aspects of PRC law, with topics ranging from arbitration and intellectual property to education rights and historical human rights discourse. The SJD has also helped a growing body of experts on Hong Kong constitutional law in Mainland institutions advance their research.[85]

The Postgraduate Certificate in Laws

The majority of postgraduates in the Faculty continued to be students, mainly of Hong Kong origin, taking the PCLL in preparation for legal practice in Hong Kong. Intake for the PCLL grew more rapidly in the late 1980s and early 1990s than that for the LLB; in the mid-1990s annual admissions exceeded 200. From 1991, another hundred or so students were taking the PCLL at HKU SPACE, a programme identical to that in the Faculty and taught mainly by Faculty staff. City University was also admitting fifty or sixty students a year to its PCLL programme. Whereas in the early years the PCLL at HKU had been reserved mainly for HKU's own law graduates, the programme now accepted growing numbers of graduates with law degrees from other universities – many through external degrees at HKU SPACE – and students who had taken either the Common Professional Examination (CPE) of England and Wales or the Common Professional Examination (CPEC) of Hong Kong. The CPE was a one-year course for degree holders in non-law disciplines intending to practise law. It was introduced in England in the early 1980s and taught externally from the early 1990s as a part-time two-year programme at HKU SPACE

---

84. Cottrell, Proposal for a new doctoral degree for Law Degree, HKUA: Board of the Faculty of Law – Minutes (1997); Faculty of Law: Submission for the Review Panel, (January 2000) Volume 1, 5.

85. Yang Xiaonan, interview with the author, 19 September 2017.

in association with Manchester Metropolitan University. Its local equivalent, the CPEC, was offered jointly by the Faculty of Law and SPACE as a one-year full-time course. Students who passed either the CPE or CPEC on their first attempt were guaranteed a place in the SPACE PCLL programme.[86]

The Faculty of Law had expected that LLB graduates from the City Polytechnic hoping to enter the legal profession would join the PCLL programme at HKU. Accordingly, in the late 1980s plans were developed to expand intake to 250 or even 295 by the mid-1990s – the estimated maximum capacity of the new premises in the K.K. Leung Building. Somewhat to the Faculty's surprise, the UPGC, following advice from ACLE, decided in 1989 that a separate PCLL programme should be established at the City Polytechnic for its own LLB graduates. This reflected the government's belief in the need to rapidly increase the supply of lawyers. Largely to satisfy the professional bodies (which were talking about introducing their own qualifications), it was nevertheless agreed that there would be a common curriculum and common admission requirements, with oversight by an Advisory Board appointed by ACLE under the chairmanship of Patrick Chan (LLB 1974), then a district judge. Thus, as the head of the HKU programme, Edward Tyler, put it, the two institutions would 'not be able to go off on a frolic of their own.'[87] There were nevertheless some differences in teaching and assessment methods. Applying the latest ideas in professional legal education, the City Polytechnic emphasized practical skills and 'learning by doing', whereas HKU tested knowledge of the substantive law largely through final examinations.[88] Common examinations for the two programmes were introduced in 1999 but were abandoned the following year amid concerns in the Faculty that they would stultify curriculum development and 'inevitably lead to the lowering of standards' at HKU.[89]

With two institutions now teaching the PCLL, the professional bodies had wished for greater control than was possible through a mere advisory board. 'It's a professional qualification and we want to make sure that it's granted to the right people who have attained

---

86. The CPEC was suspended in 1999.

87. Established in 1991, the committee, which came to be known as the Joint Examination Board, was more or less inactive by the end of the century. *SCMP*, 11 February 1988; PCLL Committee: Annual Report, 1989–1990, HKUA: Board of the Faculty of Law – Minutes (1990); Paul Redmond and Christopher Roper, *Legal Education and Training in Hong Kong: Preliminary Review: Report of the Consultants* (August 2001), 175.

88. Some HKU staff expressed concern about 'unnecessary polarization' between the two courses. Insisting that the system at HKU had been successful, Gary Heilbronn described the approach at City Polytechnic as a 'dubious formula': *SCMP*, 28 October 1990. For accounts of the special features of the City Polytechnic PCLL see Neil Gold, 'Professional Legal Education for Tomorrow's Lawyers: The Evolution of the Postgraduate Certificate of Laws at the City Polytechnic of Hong Kong', 9 *Journal of Professional Legal Education* (1991), 45–57, & *New Gazette*, November 1991.

89. Michael Wilkinson, Report from the Department of Professional Education, *Faculty of Law Newsletter*, November 1999.

the right levels,' said the chairman of the Bar Association, Anthony Rogers QC, in 1991.[90] But too much external control was 'clearly incompatible with the autonomy of the two institutions,' Tyler and others argued.[91] Nevertheless, uncertainties over the PCLL in the late 1980s, the need to co-ordinate curriculums, and objections from the profession made it difficult to introduce reforms. Although some proposals emerged in the 1990s, no great change was introduced 'because the proposed reforms did not receive the endorsement of the Advisory Committee on Legal Education,' the Faculty reported in 2000. 'Since the PCLL is directly tied to the system for professional qualification as lawyers in Hong Kong, changes in the PCLL curriculum are almost impossible without the support of the legal profession.'[92] If the professional bodies felt that the curriculum or standards did not meet the needs of the profession they could withdraw recognition, a measure considered by the Bar Council in 1992 when it found that minimum standards in the new PCLL programme at the City Polytechnic fell below those at HKU.[93] The desire by the profession for greater control over the PCLL was to become a burning issue later in the century and beyond.

In outline the PCLL curriculum at HKU was the same in 2000 as it was in 1991. Its core full-year subjects – Conveyancing and Probate Practice, Revenue Law, Commercial Law and Practice, and Civil and Criminal Procedure – stretched back to the early 1970s, when the PCLL was first taught. Although some course names had been changed over the years and content had been adapted to accommodate changes in the law, the syllabuses remained remarkably consistent.[94] Three other subjects had been added since the 1970s: Professional Practice (introduced in 1980 as The Lawyer and His Practice), from which Accounts and Advocacy were split off into separate courses in 1984 and 1992 respectively; a two-week summer school in advocacy, conducted by barristers from England, had already been introduced in 1988. By the 1990s these three additional subjects were all half-year courses.

The new subjects emphasized skills and practice. Increasingly, the more traditional subjects, without reducing the element of substantive law, did the same. In the late 1980s, for example, the courses in Commercial Law and Practice and Conveyancing were completely revamped with objectives stating what skills and transactional knowledge students

---

90. *SCMP*, 3 April 1991.

91. PCLL Committee: Annual Report, 1988–1989, HKUA: Board of the Faculty of Law – Minutes (1989).

92. Faculty of Law: Submission for the Review Panel, (January 2000) Volume 1, 5.

93. At the insistence of both the Bar Association and the Law Society, the examinations for the first City Polytechnic PCLL programme were reset to bring them in line with standards set by HKU. Only twenty-one of the sixty-three students passed. A further twenty passed in resits and most of the rest retook the course the following year. Students were reportedly so outraged by the last-minute changes that one attempted to take the matter to court. *SCMP*, 3 April 1991 & 11 June, 3 August & 2 November 1992; Bar Association, *Annual Statements* 1991–1992 & 1992–1993.

94. The course descriptions for three of the subjects – Conveyancing and Probate Practice (originally Property Law), Revenue Law, and Commercial Law and Practice – were identical in 2000 with those in 1974, except for the addition of the topic of insolvency to the Commercial Law and Practice course.

were expected to acquire. This reflected a trend in professional legal education throughout
the common law world, in which the skills and techniques required for legal practice were
given increasing emphasis.[95] Problem-based learning, pioneered by Stephen Nathanson in
the Commercial Law and Practice course and adopted by some other teachers, encouraged
students to develop problem-solving skills by presenting them with real-life or simulated
legal challenges ranging from drafting documents to client interviews. Deriving from new
teaching methods in medicine, management, and architecture, problem-based learning
was a shift from traditional teacher-centred learning through lectures and tutorials to student-centred learning, both independently and in small groups. This required students to
participate actively, to be responsible for their learning, and to tackle problems that could
not be solved only with previously learned knowledge – though, as Nathanson pointed
out, they could not be addressed without the relevant legal knowledge.[96]

The exercises in these courses required high-quality materials and laborious preparation by teachers: one four-hour legal drafting exercise took Nathanson and a colleague a
hundred hours to design. Preparing for a tutorial was 'like preparing for a motion or an
appeal – you have to be sure to sell the main points but you'd also better be prepared for
anything,' observed his colleague, David Murphy, a former partner in a large Toronto law
firm.[97] Learning skills relied on intensive small-group sessions, guided by detailed teaching
plans. This was assisted by audiovisual presentations of lawyers at work, some produced
jointly by the Faculty and practitioners.[98] In 1989, after moving to its new premises in the
K.K. Leung Building, the Faculty acquired a range of new audiovisual equipment, including portable cameras and a film-editing system, enabling student exercises to be recorded
and given feedback from teachers. This and other forms of 'micro-teaching' depended on

---

95. One of the earliest educationalists to highlight this trend was Professor William Twining in a paper given at
the Ninth Commonwealth Law Conference held in Hong Kong in 1983 (published as Twining, 'Preparing Lawyers
for the Twenty-First Century', 3 *Legal Education Review* (1985), 8–9). The discussion gave rise to an 'acrimonious
debate' about the direct teaching of professional skills 'in which it was apparent that neither side had any empirical
basis for their assertions about the value or effectiveness of such training.' It nevertheless led to the establishment
of programmes in Canada and elsewhere in which skills were given prominence. William Twining, 'Developments
in Legal Education in the Commonwealth: Beyond the Primary School Model', in Wacks (Ed.), *The Future of Legal
Education and the Legal Profession in Hong Kong*, 50.

96. Murray Gordon, 'Interview with Stephen Nathanson of the University of Hong Kong: Problem-Based Learning
and Problem-Solving', 11 *Journal of Professional Legal Education* (1993), 137–43; Stephen Nathanson, 'Changing
Culture to Teach Problem-Solving Skills', 14 *Journal of Professional Legal Education* (1996), 143–58; Michael
Littlewood, 'Professional Legal Education in Hong Kong', 8 *Journal of Professional Legal Education* (1990), 50–2.

97. *New Gazette*, December 1989.

98. The collaborations began in 1987–1988 with recordings of members of staff and practitioners playing roles in the
examination of witnesses and interviews between solicitors and clients. For example, one video, entitled 'Acquisition
of Private Companies', was written and presented by Christine Booth of the Faculty of Law and Tony Wales of the
firm Turner Kenneth Brown. PCLL Committee, Annual Report 1986–1987, HKUA: Board of the Faculty of Law –
Minutes (1989); *Law Society of Hong Kong Gazette*, February 1989.

an army of instructors drawn from the permanent staff of DOPLE and a growing list of practitioners teaching part-time. Numbering over a hundred in some years, the practitioners were an essential link between the Faculty and the actual practice of law in Hong Kong, helping to ensure the relevance of teaching materials and the maintenance of standards. Others from the profession performed a variety of functions as course consultants, external examiners, and advocacy judges. Among them were experienced lawyers and senior judges, including many graduates and a few former staff of the Faculty itself.

Holders of HKU LLB honours degrees continued to be eligible for automatic admission to the PCLL programme up to 1992, after which holders of third-class or pass degrees had to compete with non-HKU graduates for places: with the decline in the number of thirds and passes awarded (a source of disquiet in the professional bodies),[99] this had no impact on most HKU students wishing to go on to the PCLL. But intense competition for the limited, albeit increasing, quota for non-HKU LLBs produced other problems. A policy of relying partly on the date of application for allocating places to eligible 'overseas-qualified' applicants led to complaints. This culminated in an unfortunate episode on Saturday 13 January 1990, the day on which applications to the PCLL opened. Several applicants queued overnight to obtain application forms. 'Some were then displaced by latecomers who pushed and shoved their way into the queue causing general disorder and lack of harmony.' The 'January 13 Incident' prompted a flood of complaints and letters to newspapers calling for more PCLL places and criticizing both the applications policy and the priority given to HKU LLB graduates. A 'random selection' for certain categories of eligible 'overseas-qualified' applicants was immediately introduced.[100]

The PCLL was again the focus of controversy when, during the early hours of Sunday 12 May 1991, burglars broke into staff offices on the third, fourth, and fifth floors of the K.K. Leung Building, shattering the glass panels of four doors. They took away seventy-one scripts from the Accounts examination held in January. The scripts were either unmarked or provisionally marked as 'fail'. The police were called in but the culprits were never found. Most likely they were looking for the script of a candidate who feared he or she had done badly in the exam. But other questions remained unanswered – for example, whether the Accounts exam (which usually had a high pass rate) was the real target or whether, as was rumoured, the burglars had really been looking for the scripts of the Revenue Law exam, which had a low pass rate. The biggest question was why so many scripts had been left unmarked for so long. A re-examination was held for the affected candidates, many of

---

99. Redmond & Roper, *Legal Education and Training in Hong Kong: Preliminary Review: Report of the Consultants* (August 2001), 177.

100. In the event, places were found for virtually all non-HKU applicants in 1990 with first-or second-class degrees, and random selection was only used to select third-class degree holders. Report on PCLL Admissions 1990 & PCLL Selection Procedures and Criteria, HKUA: Board of the Faculty of Law – Minutes (1990); *SCMP*, 29 January, 2 & 5 February & 3 September 1990.

whom were indignant about having, through no fault of their own, to resit an examination they had taken nearly five months before.[101]

Students

Despite the occasional disruptions, the majority of PCLL graduates from HKU – more than in any other discipline – found the programme to be relevant to their work. Nearly all went into the legal profession, usually as solicitors. A small minority went into government or other fields, or pursued further studies. Most secured job offers earlier than other graduates did, usually before they completed the PCLL, helped in some cases by summer internships under a scheme organized by the student Law Association. Surveys of HKU graduates in the late 1980s and early 1990s showed PCLL graduates to be among the most satisfied in their new jobs and – with the exception of pupils for the Bar, who did not receive salaries – among the best paid.[102]

Spotting law students was never a difficult task, wrote Charles Chau (LLB 1997). 'When you see some smart young men and women either dressing conservatively in black suits, or smoking heavily at the bench outside the K.K. Leung Building, it is relatively safe to assume that they are members of the Law Faculty.'[103] Homogeneity in appearance disguised much diversity in motivation and outlook. Nevertheless, annual surveys of new undergraduates, starting in 1985, allow some generalizations to be made about law students at the start of their academic studies in the last decade or so of the twentieth century.[104] New law students tended to be the most self-confident of all categories of students. In most years they reported the highest self-ratings in spoken and written English, Putonghua, and written Chinese, and they usually had the highest self-assessments in independence, communication skills, leadership ability – in fact, in practically all skills except sport and computer skills, where they generally reported themselves to be of middling ability. They were more widely travelled than students in other categories and were – by far – the most regular readers of newspapers, with the *South China Morning Post* at the top of the list, followed by *Ming Pao* and, from the late 1990s, the more anti-establishment *Apple Daily*. Except for sport and religion, they awarded themselves some of the highest ratings for

---

101. The overall pass rate for the PCLL examinations in May 1991 declined to 50 per cent, from 59 per cent the previous year, attributable to a drop in the pass rate for students from other institutions from 88 per cent to 41 per cent. The Head of DOPLE, Michael Wilkinson, insisted there was no connection between this and the theft. Many candidates were allowed to retake the exam later in the year, bringing the overall pass rate up to 85 per cent. Minutes of meeting on 12 June 1991 & Statement Re Stolen Exam Scripts, 17 May 1991, HKUA: Board of the Faculty of Law – Minutes (1991); *SCMP*, 17, 18, & 24 May & 4 & 12 June 1991; *New Gazette*, August 1991.
102. Appointments Service, HKU, *Graduate Employment Surveys 1985–94*.
103. Charles Chau Chi-chung, 'Man in Black' in *Thirty Years*, 88.
104. Office of Student Affairs, HKU, *Profiles of New Students*, (annual) 1985–2000.

participation in extracurricular activities, such as hobbies, cultural pursuits, academic societies, and political activities.

The objective data suggests that law undergraduates were justified in their self-confidence. In the 1980s and 1990s entrants to the LLB were markedly and consistently higher than the HKU average in their examination scores for English and Chinese and in their 'A' level results generally, and well above average scores for entrants to the City Polytechnic law programme. Applicants placing law among their first choices declined dramatically in the early 1990s, a trend attributed to the increase in places in other disciplines, anxieties about the legal profession after 1997, and 'the length and portability for immigration purposes of the LLB curriculum.'[105] From the mid-1980s the Faculty and the profession were concerned about an apparent deterioration in the quality of students' use of English. This was a university-wide – indeed territory-wide – issue, given international prominence when the new head of the Department of English, Roy Harris, delivered an inaugural lecture in 1989 provocatively entitled 'The worst English in the world?'[106] The Faculty appointed English-language instructors from 1986 and considered introducing its own English exam for applicants for both the LLB and PCLL.

Despite these concerns, the quality of new law undergraduates relative to other undergraduates was not only sustained but actually improved. In the last few years of the twentieth century LLB students ranked highest in the whole of HKU in average 'Use of English' scores and came within the top 25 per cent in 'A' level results. New LLB students also scored high in Chinese language.[107] By the end of the century the Faculty could report that 'the LLB programme has been attracting some of the best students in Hong Kong.'[108] The late 1990s saw record numbers of LLB graduates awarded first-class honours – nine in 1997 and 1999 and as many as thirteen in 1998.

---

105. Annual Report by the Faculty of Law, HKU, to the Australian Law Teachers' Association (1992), 158; Minutes of meeting of the Admissions Committee, 18 January 1991, HKUA: Board of the Faculty of Law – Minutes (1991). Applicants from school-leavers to HKU who placed law in their top three choices dropped from over 5,000 in the late 1980s to under 500 in the mid-1990s, stabilizing at around 600 or 700 in the later years of the decade. Some of the decline may have been influenced by the introduction of the computerized Joint University Programmes Admissions System in 1990, which unified and streamlined the admissions procedures for all of Hong Kong's universities, making it unnecessary for prospective students to make separate applications and follow separate admissions procedures for each institution. The Faculty also accepted applications outside the joint admissions system from applicants who had not gone through Hong Kong's school system. Figures for most years are in the annual LLB Admissions Reports, HKUA: Board of the Faculty of Law – Minutes.

106. *University of Hong Kong Gazette (Supplement)*, 24 April 1989; *SCMP*, 22 May 1989; *New York Times*, 16 April 1989.

107. The 1999 LLB intake ranked fifth among forty-three programmes, but two of the four programmes ranking higher were the mixed-degree programmes introduced by the Faculty itself. University of Hong Kong: Faculty of Law, 'Submission for the Review Panel' (January 2000), Vol. 1, 9.

108. Faculty of Law: 2001–2004 Triennium: Academic Development Proposal, HKUA: Board of the Faculty of Law – Minutes (2000).

Because of their strong 'A' level results and high scores in English and Chinese, law students were among the least limited in their choice of degree and among the most single-minded in their career plans, with 80 or 90 per cent accepting offers because law was their first choice; few if any 'accepted the offer somewhat reluctantly.' Like students in medicine, architecture, and other professional subjects, about half chose the subject primarily because it led to their desired career; another third or so chose it mainly because of a strong interest in the subject. The great majority – around 70 or 80 per cent in the late 1990s – planned to go into law as a career, with government a distant second choice. Naturally, the determination to go into practice influenced students' choices of LLB courses and their decisions to go on to the PCLL. This made it all the more important that curricula should be relevant to professional needs; for the same reason, it also strengthened arguments for broadening horizons and developing the LLB as a 'liberal education in the law.'

Like most other new undergraduates, the majority of law students – well over 85 per cent – were school-leavers between the ages of eighteen and twenty. Although, following general trends, the Faculty admitted more students from lower-income families, it had the largest proportion of students from higher-income families: over 60 per cent in 1997, for example, were from families with a monthly income of over $20,000, compared with 52 per cent in the next-highest Faculty (Business) and 42 per cent for all new students. Along with Medicine, Business, Architecture, and Dentistry, the Faculty also had the largest proportions of students whose parents worked in the professions, business, or management. These figures are set against rising levels of prosperity in the 1980s and 1990s, with increasing real incomes, higher rates of home ownership, declining family sizes, and a shift in parental occupations from industrial to white-collar jobs. Nevertheless, by 2000 under 40 per cent of new undergraduates (52 per cent for law students, compared with 44 per cent in 1985) had their own rooms and desks at home: this, combined with insufficient accommodation in university halls, made the provision of study spaces in the Law Library, the centre of student life, all the more essential.

Most strikingly, the proportion of women admitted to study law far exceeded the university average. In 1985 the ratio of women to men admitted to the Faculty of Law was 59:41, compared with 30:70 in 1984 and a university-wide ratio of 37:63. In 1994, when the number of women admitted to HKU exceeded men for the first time (at 54:46), the ratio for the Faculty of Law was as high as 69:31. Only the Faculties of Arts and Education, each with a ratio of about 86:14, had higher proportions of women. In every year from 1985 the majority of entrants to the LLB were women. By the late 1990s they outnumbered men by more than two to one. It seemed that 'a career in law was no longer regarded by male sixth formers as being as attractive as other careers,' the Faculty Board concluded in 1995.[109] Whatever the

---

109. Minutes of meeting on 13 December 1995, HKUA: Board of the Faculty of Law – Minutes (1995).

reasons, the decision by so many women to pursue legal studies was to change the face of a profession – and an academic discipline – traditionally dominated by men.

One of these female students, Alice Lee (LLB 1990) came to study law almost by accident after discovering that over half her classmates at the Diocesan Girls' School had put law as first choice in their university applications. At HKU she found it hard to adapt to the lecture and tutorial system and the lack of feedback from teachers in a curriculum geared entirely towards exams. Even so, the courses on Personal Property and Land Law, and an optional course on Intellectual Property, sparked a lifelong interest in these subjects. An uninspiring summer internship with a small firm in Mong Kok sealed her resolve not to become a lawyer. Instead, Lee was one of a tiny minority of graduates from her year who did not go straight into the PCLL. She gained a place at Oxford University to take a Bachelor of Civil Law degree, a highly academic programme requiring intellectual engagement with the law – in many ways the opposite of the PCLL. She deferred taking up an offer to read for a D.Phil. at Oxford and returned to HKU to take the PCLL (her 'fourth year') at the request of her mother. The PCLL, Lee recalls, was 'a nightmare', 'the worst year in my whole life.' Only the support of classmates stopped her from quitting. Halfway through her PCLL, two teaching positions in the Faculty fell vacant. Lee successfully applied for one of them and was put in charge of the Land Law course. She has taught in the Faculty ever since, specializing in her early interests, land law and intellectual property, and taking part in the creation of Hong Kong's bilingual legal system.[110]

Although some found time for extracurricular activities, the workload of LLB students continued to be 'horrifyingly heavy,' recalled Charles Chau, who still found time to serve as a student representative on the Faculty Board. Students had to read 'tons of duplicated materials,' stuffed into their pigeonholes, in preparation for tutorials. It was a 'nightmare' just to go through them, let alone understand them. 'You were under peer-group pressure to study hard. Competition was keen, but we were always prepared to help each other.'[111] The heavy workload was a common complaint, although it was 'nothing compared to the workload at law firms,' observed Belinda Wong (LLB 1988).[112] While other undergraduates could treat their first year as a 'year-long holiday,' the examination results in all three years for LLB students counted equally towards their final class of honours, observed Angie Li (LLB 2001). 'To be honest,' added her classmate Nicholas Mak (LLB 2001), 'being hardworking is merely the bare minimum requirement for survival here.'[113]

---

110. Alice Lee, interview with the author, 13 April 2018.

111. Charles Chau, 'Man in Black' in *Thirty Years*, 88–91. Chau went on to take the PCLL (1998) and an LLM at Cambridge University (1999) before going into practice as a solicitor in Hong Kong, specializing in financial and commercial law.

112. Belinda Wong Sheung-yu in *Thirty Years*, 75.

113. Interview with Angie Li and Nicholas Mak by Simon Wong, HKU Faculty of Law, *Prospectus 1999–2000*, 70.

Angie Li and Nicholas Mak, vice-chairmen of the Law Association, were interviewed for the Law Faculty's 1999 student prospectus as part of an initiative to make the publication more than 'a collection of professors' biographies and programme outlines.' They had many positive things to say about student life. Research assignments were 'intellectually exciting,' said Angie Li, although it was a pity they did not count more towards final results. And tutorials were 'a thrill too,' requiring students to take 'a really active role in discussion and problem solving,' even if preparation was demanding. Above all, many of the staff were 'really good teachers,' able to make 'apparently dry subjects lively, challenging and thought provoking.' Nicholas Mak praised the personal tutor system, a feature of the law school since the 1970s, in which each student was assigned a personal tutor to give guidance and advice and to help deal with problems and weaknesses.

Naturally, attitudes towards individual teachers varied according to the difficulty of the course, qualities such as confidence, helpfulness, approachability, and – since law was now taught in many varieties of English – comprehensibility. Teaching in the LLB programme continued to rely mainly on lectures and small-group tutorials. Students welcomed efforts to move beyond traditional lecturing, for example in the lively diagrammatic slides used by Sarah Nield in Land Law.[114] From the early 1980s students evaluated courses by rating the pace and content of lectures and tutorials, and the preparedness and clarity of teachers. The Faculty was one of the first in HKU to implement such a scheme, which it organized in collaboration with student representatives on the Faculty Board. When the scheme was reviewed in the late 1980s there was much debate about how questionnaires should be framed and whether evaluations should be published.[115] There were also concerns that students in some courses gave unfairly negative assessments simply because they were not prepared to be challenged. Centralized and extended in the 1990s, the process exercised a disproportionate influence, encouraging teachers 'to abandon rigour in favour of the natural desire of students for an easy life,' said Peter Wesley-Smith.[116] Conversely, some LLB students were concerned they were 'assessed tightly' and given heavier workloads compared with students in other disciplines, or were not given feedback on assignments and examinations promptly or in sufficient detail.[117]

---

114. Alice Lee, interview with the author, 13 April 2018. For other comments by students on individual lecture styles, see in particular reminiscences by Paul Lam (LLB 1990) 'The Life of an LLB Student in the Late 80s,' *Law Media*, 1999, Vol.1.

115. Student Evaluation of Teaching, 3 April 1989, HKUA: Board of the Faculty of Law – Minutes (2000).

116. Wesley-Smith, 'Epilogue', *Thirty Years*, 103; Peter Wesley-Smith, interview with the author, 23 October 2017.

117. In the mid-1990s students, with the support of a majority of the Faculty Board, also requested disclosure of their examination marks (as opposed to just the grades) and details of guidelines for assessment. Resisted by the Senate at first, this was made possible from 1997 under the influence of the Data Protection (Privacy) Ordinance, which came into force the previous year. Report on the review of the Faculty of Law (draft, 2000), 8, Student

From 1994 student research found a new outlet in the *Hong Kong Student Law Review*. This student-edited journal was published annually until 2006 and was widely distributed to the legal profession in Hong Kong and law schools around the world. One of its aims was 'to promote academia as a career option for Hong Kong law students.' The *Student Law Review* contained articles by law students from both HKU and City University, including dissertations from the guided research course in the LLB programme. The last issue of the earlier student journal, *Justitia*, had appeared in 1986, not long before the abolition of compulsory dissertations under the LLB, from which it had drawn much of its material. Like *Justitia*, the *Student Law Review* was scholarly, topical, and occasionally provocative. Early volumes included articles on new consumer protection laws (Aster Camille Elms, LLB 1993), judicial accountability (Biby Chan, LLB 1995) and – in a pre-echo of an actual legal challenge in 1997 – whether the establishment by the Chinese government of an unelected Provisional Legislative Council outside of the provisions of the Basic Law to straddle the 1997 handover would lead to a legal vacuum in Hong Kong (Stephen Law, LLB 1995).[118] The bumper 1997 commemorative edition – nearly 200 pages long – contained articles on subjects ranging from the right of abode (Catherine Siu, LLB 1996) to international breaches by the UK government in the treatment of ethnic minorities in Hong Kong (Neeta R. Dadlani, LLB 1997). From 2000, second-year students were appointed as student editors of the *Hong Kong Law Journal*, helping, among other things to prepare the tables of cases and legislation.[119]

Mooting

Other opportunities for law students to demonstrate their skills before a wider audience came in the mooting competitions held both locally and internationally. A moot usually takes the form of a mock appeal hearing, in which participating teams present written and oral arguments on the law applicable to a fictional problem before a panel of judges. The

---

Access to Examination marks and procedures, 5 January 1995, & Practice Regarding the Implementation of the Data Protection (Privacy) Ordinance, 23 June 1997, HKUA: Board of the Faculty of Law – Minutes (1995, 1997 & 2000).

118. Stephen Law Shing-yan, 'A Legalistic Approach to Hong Kong's Potential Legal Vacuum', 2 *Hong Kong Student Law Review* (1995), 92–121. The article concluded that the Provisional Legislative Council and its legislation might be justified by invoking the doctrine of necessity, as developed by recent common law decisions elsewhere. The question of a legal vacuum was later raised in *HKSAR v Ma Wai Kwan, David and others* [1997] HKLRD 761, a trial for conspiracy to pervert the course of justice begun on 16 June 1997 and resumed on 3 July, shortly after the establishment of the Hong Kong SAR. Counsel for the defence argued that the Reunification Ordinance, providing for continuity in the legal system and proceedings, which had been passed by the Provisional Legislative Council in the early hours of 1 July, had not been validly enacted because the council had not been elected as required by Article 68 of the Basic Law. The question was referred to the Court of Appeal, which, though it heard arguments based on the doctrine of necessity, found other reasons for rejecting the claim.

119. *Faculty of Law Newsletter*, August 2000.

aim is to develop drafting and advocacy skills and self-confidence in an adversarial setting similar to that of a real court. Participation in internal mooting competitions continued to be compulsory for third-year LLB students at HKU. From the mid-1980s these annual competitions were open to voluntary participation by second-year students and, a few years later, first-year students. The moots were usually held in the Supreme Court in January. The sixteen best performers went on to semi-finals and a final, usually held in the Senate Room at HKU, where the winner and runners-up received prizes sponsored by law firms and the Bar.[120] Judges were drawn from the legal profession, the Judiciary, and Faculty staff. Sir Ti Liang Yang, Chief Justice 1988–1996 and Chairman of the HKU Council, was a keen supporter. The growing number of students presented considerable organizational challenges in setting problems and finding judges: for the compulsory moots spread over three evenings in January 1994, for example, no fewer than eighty-nine judges presided over moots in thirty-five courtrooms in the Supreme Court building.

Internal mooting competitions were the training ground for larger competitions. For HKU, these began with the Commonwealth Law Mooting Competition, inaugurated in Hong Kong in 1983, and later included other regional or specialized moots, such as the LAWASIA International Moot Competition and the Red Cross International Humanitarian Law Moot Competition. In 1985 the Faculty sent its first team to the oldest and most prestigious contest, the annual Philip C. Jessup International Law Moot Court Competition, originally a purely American event but from 1970 thrown open to teams from around the world. Participants argue hypothetical legal disputes between nations according to the procedures of the International Court of Justice. HKU's first Jessup team beat France and Lesotho but lost by a small margin to Belgium and Germany, coming twelfth out of twenty-four teams in overall performance and seventh in oral advocacy: two Hong Kong team members, Mary Wan (LLB 1984) and Johnny Mok (LLB 1985), were judged to be among the top twenty oralists. The overall champion was the National University of Singapore.

Unlike the National University of Singapore, a frequent champion or runner-up, the HKU teams have not so far been among the outright winners in the Jessup international round, although in some years they came close, ranking third in 1987, fifth in 1998, fourth in 2000, and third in 2004. Several team members have been cited among the best oralists, notably Angelina Lai (1987), Ferheen Mahomed (1987 & 1988), Lawrence Ng (1988), Michael Cheng (1989), P.J. Long (2000), and M. Wentworth (2001); and in 2006 a team consisting of Zabrina Lau, Tim Parker, Kay Seto, Yvonne Shi, and Megan Yeung won the Baxter Prize for the Best Applicant's Memorial. Jessup was the ultimate test for law students, recalls Roda Mushkat, one of the early organizers of the HKU teams. It was never

---

120. From 1984 the finals were videotaped: recordings for 1984–2002 may be found on the 'HKU Scholars Hub' website.

difficult to find a team, 'and they did so well – maybe it was beginners' luck.'[121] Brian Baillie, a co-ordinator of the PCLL advocacy course and a Jessup co-ordinator in the 1990s was also impressed by the standard of oral argument 'given that for the vast majority of students English is a second language, and common law principles are not naturally a part of their educational or cultural background.'[122] Staff devoted a good deal of time to preparing students. A half-course for the Jessup challenge and other international moots, following the practice in American universities, was introduced in 1999.[123]

The international round of the Jessup competition was usually held in Washington DC. Travel and accommodation expenses for the three-or five-member mooting teams and their coach were covered by donations from the legal profession, the *Hong Kong Law Journal*, and Faculty staff and alumni. From 1987 a large part of the expenses was covered by the proceeds of annual raffles and 'Jessup auctions', in which students bid for prizes donated by members of staff. These ranged from aerobic demonstrations and trips to Kowloon Walled City to the privilege of shaving off the beards – and sometimes the leg hair – of volunteers from the male staff. Jessup auctions took place less frequently from the mid-1990s as teams from newer law schools began to represent Hong Kong; they ended when university funds were earmarked for international moots. Since the Jessup international competition only accepted one team from each region, regional heats were held from 1990 to determine which team should go to Washington. In 1995, 1996, and 1999 the City University team won the regional heats. The HKU team won the regional heats and represented Hong Kong in all nine years from 2000 to 2008 and in 2015, 2017, 2018, and 2019.

Headwinds in the Late 1990s

By the time of its thirtieth anniversary in 1999 the Faculty was flourishing. During the first thirty years, 2,460 students had graduated with LLBs. Some 741 full-time and 162 part-time students were now enrolled in eight taught programmes, including joint or mixed degrees, masters' degrees, and postgraduate diplomas. Another twenty-one postgraduates were pursuing research degrees. Law students were winning a disproportionately high number of university scholarships and were notably successful in gaining scholarships for post-graduate studies overseas. Among them were some of Hong Kong's first Rhodes Scholars – Sandra Fan (the first, 1986) and Ferheen Mohamed (the third, 1988). Graduates were transforming the legal profession into a body firmly rooted in Hong Kong, with a growing number of women and a capacity to function bilingually. Others had entered business,

---

121. Roda Mushkat, interview with the author, 5 September 2017.

122. Brian Baillie, recollection in *Thirty Years*, 86.

123. Curriculum Planning Committee, minutes of meeting on 7 November 1986, HKUA: Board of the Faculty of Law – Minutes (1987).

politics, journalism, or the civil service. They maintained fellowship through a flourishing Law Alumni Association. In the Friends of the Faculty scheme, launched in 1995, graduates joined with other members of the profession to fund seminars, publications, student activities, and collaborations with other law schools. Donations from law firms and individuals supported prizes, scholarships, teaching, and research.[124] These included the US$1 million donation in 1989 from Anna Pao Sohmen and Helmut Sohmen to establish the chair in public law in memory of the shipping magnate Sir Y.K. Pao, a $5 million gift in 1997 from the barrister Leslie Wright for creating the Hong Kong-China Legal Fund, and a sixfold increase in 1997, from $50,000 to $300,000, in the annual scholarship donated by the solicitor Peter Vine.[125]

The forty-seven-strong permanent teaching staff, thirty-one of whom were on tenured terms, had expertise in a wide range of legal fields as well as experience in legal education and practice in five continents. About half had joined since the last big anniversary in 1989, attracted by the Faculty's reputation and the opportunities for research in a city undergoing fundamental legal change. A growing number – thirteen in 1999 – were from Hong Kong and another five were from Mainland China. A further thirty or so part-time teachers, all legal practitioners, assisted in teaching the PCLL. The Faculty was one of the most active centres of research in the university. Its publications, conferences, and other activities were influential in Hong Kong and beyond. The Centre for Comparative and Public Law, formed in 1995, was particularly productive. A second research centre, the Asian Institute of International Financial Law, was established in 1999. The Faculty, concluded an academic review in 2000, 'continued to enjoy virtual monopoly and recognized leadership in the provision of legal education in Hong Kong' and was 'able to consistently admit students of high quality ... compared with those applying to other Faculties of the University.'[126]

The Faculty's achievements were highlighted by the first Chief Justice of the Hong Kong SAR, Andrew Li, in a speech at a dinner on 4 June 1999 for participants in two of the eleven conferences held to mark the Faculty's thirtieth anniversary.[127] Li spoke of the varied curriculum and the benefits to students of being taught by 'a galaxy of staff who are rich in their diversity and qualifications from many jurisdictions.' He spoke of the contributions by

---

124. One law firm offered to donate a sea-going junk to the Faculty. 'We earnestly debated whether we should accept it, but didn't,' recalls Peter Wesley-Smith: interview with the author, 27 October 2017.

125. After serving as a lieutenant-colonel with the Judge Advocate General's Department during and after World War II, Leslie Wright (1926–1998), an Irishman, was admitted to the Bar in Hong Kong in 1947 and practised mainly in the field of mergers and acquisitions. Minutes of meetings on 10 September 1997 & 9 April 1999, HKUA: Board of the Faculty of Law – Minutes (1997 & 1999); SCMP, 7 September 1947 & 25 February 1998.

126. Report on the review of the Faculty of Law (draft, 2000), 4, HKUA: Board of the Faculty of Law – Minutes (2000).

127. The conferences were on Comparative Private Law and International Financial Architecture. The address is reproduced in Thirty Years, 1–2.

academic lawyers. 'They are independent from all centres of power, public or private. In the exercise of their academic freedom, their teaching and research as well as their commentaries on executive and legislative action and judgments of the courts play a very important part in the development of our jurisprudence and our legal system.' He stressed the value of legal education as a preparation for many careers and urged that curricula 'should not be driven purely by the requirements of professional practice.' He also emphasized the importance of educating students in the 'moral and ethical values that underlie our legal system' at a time when the 'business pressures of a fiercely competitive market place have had the tendency of eroding the traditions of what should be an honourable profession.' And he pointed to widespread concern about the quality of entrants to the profession, one of the challenges posed by wider access to tertiary education.

Andrew Li knew the Faculty well. As a young barrister, he was an honorary lecturer in the School of Law in the late 1970s and early 1980s. Beginning with Audrey Eu (LLB 1975) and her brother Benjamin Yu (LLB 1978), he was pupil master to some of its graduates. He chaired the UPGC 1989–1993 at a time of massive university expansion. At the Opening of the Legal Year in January 1999, Li, now Chief Justice, had already spoken very specifically about the community's expectations of the legal profession. He raised 'the widespread concern' about 'the quality of new entrants to the profession,' stressing the need to enhance the quality of LLB programmes. He also suggested admitting fewer students to the PCLL programmes, raising entry standards, lengthening programmes to include more teaching of skills and electives appropriate to each branch of the profession, and perhaps increasing fees.[128] These comments, along with remarks by leaders of the legal profession at the same ceremony, spurred the commissioning of a full-scale review of legal education in Hong Kong – an idea that lawyers had been urging for some time.

The review – discussed more fully in Chapter 7 – was prompted partly by the concerns about quality raised by Chief Justice Li. It was also driven by concerns about an oversupply of lawyers and by austerity campaigns in the wake of the Asian financial crisis 1997–1998. It came after several years of paring away of the Faculty's resources as a result of new university policies and UGC reviews. These reflected broader trends towards greater accountability in the public sector and the rise of 'new managerialism', with its stress on value for money, performance management, business plans, external assessments, and greater central control.

Trends towards centralization began to emerge in 1993, when the Vice-Chancellor, Wang Gungwu, introduced a new system for the triennial allocation of funds, moving from historic accounting (based on what a faculty had received in previous years plus more for new or expanded activities) to a system of functional accounting applying 'unit cost

---

128. Chief Justice's Address at the Opening of the Legal Year, 11 January 1999, Hong Kong Judiciary website.

relativities.' A formula was adopted based on the number of students and research performance, and a multiplier was designed for each discipline based on historic experience in
universities elsewhere, mainly the UK, which, as some Faculty members pointed out, had
a tradition of underfunding legal education. The multiplier proposed for the Law Faculty
was the lowest in the university; it ignored the recent transition to a liberal education in
the LLB and the need for intensive teaching of the PCLL. Astounded by this peculiar
reformulation of historic accounting and by the 'neo-colonial' reference to British models,
the Dean, Peter Wesley-Smith, and the Head of Law, Albert Chen, argued successfully for
parity with the Faculties of Arts and Social Sciences. But Law continued to be among the
worst-funded faculties. The problem deepened when, three years later, Wang's successor,
Cheng Yiu-chung, introduced a system of 'top-slicing' the UGC grant to HKU, reserving
funds for central allocation to special schemes, and providing less money for the day-to-
day work of individual faculties.[129]

From the late 1990s the Faculty of Law faced the prospect of further cuts in budgetary
provision as part of a general reduction in UGC funding and plans by the Vice-Chancellor
to reduce the number of law student places. Projections in 1996 and 1997 envisaged reductions in student intake and cuts in staff as high as 20 per cent or even 25 per cent, spread
over two trienniums. In the event, the cuts were not so deep. Student numbers were kept up
through the introduction of the mixed degrees and an expansion of postgraduate degrees.
Reductions in UGC funding were cushioned by private donations, income from continuing legal education (including Law Lectures for Practitioners), self-funding by students in
some programmes, and retention by the Faculty of a greater share in income from SPACE
for teaching its PCLL cohorts.[130] Unlike the Faculty's own PCLL students, PCLL students
from SPACE were entirely self-funded, paying a tuition fee of $104,000 compared with
$42,000 for Faculty students, though they followed the same curriculum and were taught
in the same way.

The Faculty's own PCLL programme came under scrutiny. In late 1999 the UGC asked
why any of HKU's PCLL places should be publicly funded. A few weeks later, in March
2000, newspapers reported remarks from the UGC chair Alice Lam, that the UGC was
planning to withdraw funding from certain postgraduate programmes, including the
PCLL, that had a 'high productivity value' for students or did not, like medicine, serve a
special social need.[131] Concerted efforts by the two law schools, the profession, and the

129. Wesley-Smith, 'Good Dean, Rotten Teacher' & Chen 'Reminiscences of Deanship' in Faculty of Law, University
of Hong Kong, *Building for Tomorrow on Yesterday's Strength*, 13–14; Peter Wesley-Smith, interview with the author,
27 October 2017; Albert Chen, interview with the author, 12 March 2018.
130. HKU, 'Report on the review of the Faculty of Law' (April 2000), 10, HKUA: Board of the Faculty of Law –
Minutes (2000); Albert Chen, interview with the author, 12 March 2018.
131. 'Funding for the PCLL Programme', 4 March 2000, HKUA: Board of the Faculty of Law – Minutes (2000).

Judiciary persuaded the UGC that withdrawal of funding would present real difficulties for young LLB graduates hoping to complete their formal legal education. It would, as the lawyer-legislator Margaret Ng put it, result once again in a legal career 'reserved for the well-to-do.'[132] Henry Litton, now a Permanent Judge of the recently established Court of Final Appeal and chairman of ACLE, stressed that the PCLL was an integral part of a lawyer's basic training: it was seen by students as their 'fourth year' and had, he said, been designed as such; even the few LLB students who did not intend to practise law went on to take it so that their legal education was complete. It would, he added, 'be a highly retrograde step' and one damaging to the rule of law, 'to go back to the days when the legal profession was, in practical terms, only open to the financial elite.'[133]

The UGC decided to defer the question of funding the PCLL until after the review of legal education. The details of the report and its impact on the Faculty are discussed in Chapter 7. In the meantime, Chapter 6 examines the Faculty's role in the momentous changes affecting Hong Kong during its transition from British colony to Special Administrative Region of the People's Republic of China.

---

132. Margaret Ng, Chairman, Legislative Council Panel on Administration of Justice and Legal Services, to Alice Lam, 24 March 2000 (and similar letters from other prominent lawyers), HKUA: Board of the Faculty of Law – Minutes (2000).

133. Litton to Alice Lam, 22 March 2000, HKUA: Board of the Faculty of Law – Minutes (2000).

Chapter 6

The Faculty and the Transition, 1984–1999

The planned return of Hong Kong to Chinese rule in 1997 presented exceptional challenges. Decolonization required a more complete dismantling of constitutional links than most other former British colonies had experienced. The creation of the Hong Kong Special Administrative Region (SAR) of the People's Republic of China (PRC) envisaged an unparalleled relationship between a communist sovereign power and a city held up as a paragon of capitalism. Promises of 'a high degree of autonomy' in the Joint Declaration 1984 required an urgent strengthening of institutions in a crown colony which, alone among Britain's overseas possessions, had no experience of representative government, still drew many of its civil servants and judges from overseas, and enjoyed only an embryonic civil society. Nevertheless, despite doom-laden predictions, the transition from colonial rule to SAR status took place peacefully and smoothly on 1 July 1997.

Severing constitutional links with Britain required adaptation and localization of laws and treaties and the substitution of a Court of Final Appeal (CFA) in Hong Kong for the Privy Council in London. Despite the emphasis on continuity between British and Chinese rule, this was an age of reform. Great projects, undertaken with urgency and against formidable difficulties, transformed the legal landscape. The successful introduction of bilingual laws and justice – seen by some as a near-impossibility – was accompanied by rapid localization of the legal profession and the Judiciary. A Bill of Rights, enacted in 1991 as a measure to secure Hong Kong's freedoms after 1997, had the more immediate effect of sweeping away oppressive colonial laws and fostered a rights-based legal culture.

The Basic Law for the Hong Kong SAR, promulgated by the Chinese government in the same year, became both the fulcrum for a smooth transition and a source of disagreements. Foremost among the latter was a prolonged dispute over how the new CFA should be constituted, which scuppered plans to establish the court before 1997, and controversies about where the ultimate power to interpret the Basic Law should lie, culminating in a constitutional crisis in 1999. Some of the controversies gathered momentum during a phase of rapid but short-lived democratization of the Legislative Council, initiated by Hong Kong's last Governor, Chris Patten, without agreement from China. They also took place at a time of ferment within the legal profession and reforms in many areas of Hong Kong law that had little or nothing to do with the transition through 1997.

Staff and graduates of the Faculty of Law at HKU participated in all of these processes. This chapter focuses on their involvement in two projects that were to fundamentally change Hong Kong's legal system: the Bill of Rights, which entrenched in local law international standards of human rights, and which succeeded in part because of Faculty expertise and advocacy; and the Basic Law, which prescribed the constitutional arrangements for Hong Kong beyond 1997, and became a subject of intensive analysis. A final section examines controversies in Hong Kong's fast-expanding legal profession. The chapter begins with a brief survey of the growth of legal research in the Faculty and beyond, and its contribution to an emphasis on the rule of law during the transition period.

The Expansion of Legal Research

One of the objects in establishing the law school at HKU was to produce scholarly research on Hong Kong law, not only for students but also for the wider legal community. This had got off to a slow start. In a survey in the late 1970s Peter Wesley-Smith dwelt on the paucity of literature on Hong Kong law, the reliance on English textbooks, and the 'tiny size of the potential market' for works specifically on Hong Kong.[1] In his inaugural lecture as Professor of Law in 1989 he catalogued the many ways in which his 'mild-mannered' crusade for reforms in the *Hong Kong Law Journal* had failed to influence either the legal profession or the courts. Early efforts by teachers to generate legal literature were not always appreciated. The *Journal* was notoriously undersubscribed. The multi-author surveys produced for the Faculty's twentieth anniversary in 1989 received mixed reviews: one critic acknowledged that half of *The Future of the Law in Hong Kong* consisted of stimulating chapters, but said that the 'single unifying factor' of the chapters in the rest of the book was their pointlessness and lack of imagination; a companion volume, *The Law in Hong Kong 1969–89*, was dismissed by another reviewer as 'more an indictment against legal scholarship, or its absence,

---

1. The survey was prepared for a seminar on legal literature in small jurisdictions organized by William Twining in Toronto in 1978. Wesley-Smith, *Legal Literature in Hong Kong* (1979).

in this territory' than a 'vista of legal academic achievement.'[2] Five years later, to the dismay of Faculty members, the first Research Assessment Exercise (RAE), commissioned by the University and Polytechnic Grants Committee (UPGC), found too many edited volumes, too much 'textbook-type output', and too few articles in international journals; it assessed output in Law as below the HKU average.[3]

These appraisals were perhaps unduly harsh. The RAE report, opaque about its methods and vague in its observations, prompted an indignant response from the Faculty, which concluded that the exercise was 'fundamentally flawed.' Law and legal literature were largely territorial in nature, the Faculty pointed out. It could not be assumed that one type of legal research was necessarily superior to another, or that journals published in England and the US were as 'international' as some of them claimed to be. The 'automatic denigration' of textbooks and edited collections failed to acknowledge that scholars had only begun to study Hong Kong law twenty-five years earlier. Nor did it recognize the huge appetite for literature on Hong Kong law among practitioners, students, officials, and academics in other fields. Theoretical or comparative research was of great value. 'But much of the research labour of a Faculty engaged in the teaching of Hong Kong law – law in a jurisdiction with its own special characteristics – must be involved with Hong Kong law. Scholars from elsewhere are not going to do it.'[4]

After the slow start in the 1970s, law teachers at HKU, along with other academics and practitioners, produced legal literature in growing quantities. By the late 1980s the preconditions for producing works on Hong Kong had markedly improved. In the 1990s publications proliferated on all aspects of Hong Kong law, past, current, and prospective. The market within Hong Kong grew in tandem with the expansion of the legal profession and legal education. Hong Kong and Chinese law became topics of global interest during a time of rapid reform. From the 1980s local publishers took a growing interest in legal literature. International publishers started to focus on Hong Kong: among these, Oxford University Press and Longmans published several works on Hong Kong law. Legal publishers such as Butterworths and Sweet & Maxwell brought out series and serials on Hong Kong law. The scope of law reporting expanded. Encouraged by more widely available research funding and the RAE, Hong Kong academics published widely in international journals. The Faculty itself became a prolific publisher of new research in key areas of law.

From the 1980s Faculty members produced textbooks covering large swathes of Hong Kong law, often for the first time. Topics included revenue law (Peter Willoughby, 1981),

---

2. Reviews by Mark Findlay & Andrew Raffell, *The Lawyer*, December 1989 & January 1990: Findlay and Rafell were teachers at the new law school at the City Polytechnic.

3. Antony Leung, UPGC Chairman, to Vice-Chancellor Wang Gungwu, 22 June 1994, HKUA: Board of the Faculty of Law – Minutes (1994).

4. Wesley-Smith to Spooner (draft), October 1994, HKUA: Board of the Faculty of Law – Minutes (1994).

family law (Leonard Pegg, 1981, Athena Liu, 1999), personal injuries (Robyn Martin & Peter Rhodes, 1982), constitutional law and legal system (Peter Wesley-Smith, 1983 & 1987), intellectual and industrial property law (Michael Pendleton, 1984), tenancy law (Malcolm Merry, 1985), tort (Robyn Martin, 1987), conveyancing (Sarah Nield, 1988), contract law (Carole Pedley-Chui, 1988, Betty Ho, 1989), criminal law and procedure (Gary Heilbronn, 1990, Michael Jackson, 2003), business law (Anne Carver, 1991), the Chinese legal system (Albert Chen, 1992), taxation law (Andrew Halkyard & Jefferson VanderWolk, 1993), conveyancing (Judith Sihombing & Michael Wilkinson, 1994), professional conduct of lawyers (Michael Wilkinson & Michael Sandor, 1996), company law (Philip Smart, Katherine Lynch, & Anna Tam, 1997), and land law (Say Goo, 1998). Faculty members collaborated on multi-author volumes on current legal topics, for example, the Basic Law (Albert Chen & Peter Wesley-Smith, editors, 1988), civil liberties and human rights (Raymond Wacks, editor, 1988 & 1992), and the three collections for the twentieth anniversary in 1989. Such enterprises were encouraged by the Dean, Peter Rhodes, as a quick way of generating legal literature and launching younger scholars into publishing.[5] The late 1980s also saw substantial works in Chinese, beginning with topical books on Hong Kong's legal system and the Basic Law (Albert Chen, 1986) and human rights during Hong Kong's transition (Albert Chen & Johannes Chan, 1987), and including a Chinese edition of Betty Ho's book on contract law (1990).

The pace of publication accelerated in the 1990s and extended to new or developing areas of law, such as privacy law, anti-discrimination laws, alternative dispute resolution, financial law, environmental law, and construction law. A survey of the published research of Faculty members during the four-year period 1996–1999 listed over 120 journal articles or book chapters and a dozen books, not including new editions, editorships, professional manuals, or contributions to conferences and seminars.[6] The second and third RAEs in 1996 and 1999, conducted more transparently than the first, found great improvements in the Faculty's output, and awarded scores well above the HKU and sector-wide averages.[7] Strong results in the RAEs produced more funding for future research projects: the 1996 exercise led to the allocation of two research fellow posts 'as reward.'[8] By early 2000, Faculty members were holding nearly fifty ongoing research grants on topics ranging from contested confessions in Hong Kong courts to globalization and Chinese law.[9]

5. Peter Rhodes, interview with the author, 23 February 2018.
6. Faculty of Law: Submission for the Review Panel, (January 2000), Appendix 22.
7. UGC Research Assessment Exercise 1999: Results for Law Cost Centre, 15 May 2000, Annex II, HKUA: Board of the Faculty of Law – Minutes (2000).
8. Minutes of meeting on 10 September 1997, HKUA: Board of the Faculty of Law – Minutes (1997).
9. Faculty of Law: Submission for the Review Panel, (January 2000), Appendix 21.

The 1999 RAE panel noted that academics from the two law schools had 'published almost all the leading treatises on Hong Kong law.' One of the schools had 'managed to reach an internationally respectable level of performance.'[10] Apart from producing academic works, teachers continued to contribute to magazines such as the *Law Society of Hong Kong Gazette* and its successor, the *New Gazette*. They joined with practitioners to compile large-scale reference works, such as *Hong Kong Current Law* (1984–1993),[11] the *Annotated Ordinances of Hong Kong* (1995–) and *Halsbury's Laws of Hong Kong* (1995–), a multi-volume statement of the law modelled on the English original first published in the early twentieth century. As technology advanced, the Faculty took a lead in building electronic databases of legal materials. These began with the Hong Kong Unreported Judgments Database (1990–1995), led by Gary Heilbronn, and the Law-On-Line Database (1991–1996), managed by JoJo Tam with the help of postgraduate students, covering Chinese law and Bill of Rights materials. Along with the official Bilingual Laws Information System (BLIS, introduced in 1991) and commercial databases such as LEXIS (which from 1999 included the *Hong Kong Law Journal*), these services made legal reference more accessible, comprehensive, and up to date.[12] At first, access to these databases was restricted to special terminals, including some in the Law Library at HKU, or CD-ROMs. But, starting with Law-On-Line and BLIS in the mid-1990s, some services were opened to free public access through the Internet. Some of the initiatives were later merged into the freely accessible database of judgments, legislation, and other materials launched in 2001 by the Hong Kong Legal Information Institute (HKLII).[13]

A City of Law: Disseminating Legal Research to the Wider Community

The web-based projects marked a stage in the opening up of legal information to the wider community. The process had its roots in unofficial efforts to provide cheap Chinese translations of the laws of Hong Kong earlier in the twentieth century, and in official pamphlets explaining new laws.[14] Early efforts by law teachers and students to inform the general

10. UGC Research Assessment Exercise 1999: Results for Law Cost Centre, 15 May 2000, Annex II, HKUA: Board of the Faculty of Law – Minutes (2000).

11. Renamed the *Hong Kong Law Digest* 1989–1993.

12. Graham Greenleaf, Philip Chung, Andrew Mowbray, Ka Po Chow, & K.H. Pun, 'The Hong Kong Legal Information Institute (HKLII): Its Role in Free Access to Global Law via the Internet', 32 *HKLJ* (2002), 401–27: Greenleaf was a visiting professor at HKU. For a survey of Hong Kong legal literature in the late 1990s see Jill Cottrell, *Legal Research: A Guide for Hong Kong Students* (Hong Kong: Hong Kong University Press, 1997).

13. This and other more recent web-based initiatives are discussed in Chapter 8.

14. Foremost among the translations were those by Ma Yuen and a team of translators from the *Wah Kiu Yat Po*: these were consolidated into two unofficial Chinese editions of the ordinances of Hong Kong, in 1936 and 1950, the first of which contained essays on Hong Kong's legal system and endorsements from Chinese barristers: 馬沅編：香港法例彙編 (1936 & 1953).

public about the law had included radio broadcasts and newspaper articles and exhibitions and other activities organized by the HKU Law Association. These efforts expanded in the 1980s and 1990s. Teachers engaged closely with newspapers, writing letters, opinion pieces, and accessible articles on their areas of interest, and making themselves available to reporters for informed comment.

Various civic bodies, formed in the late 1970s and monitored at first as 'pressure groups' by a nervous colonial government, targeted shortcomings and abuses in the law. These included the Society for Community Organization, the Association for the Promotion of Public Justice, founded by Elsie Elliott and Andrew Tu, and the Hong Kong Observers, whose early members included Christine Loh, Anna Wu (LLB 1974), Frank Ching, and Leung Chun-ying.[15] Newspapers employed journalists with legal qualifications to analyse developments in the law. Among these were HKU graduates Margaret Ng (BA 1969, MA 1975, PCLL 1988), a columnist for *Ming Pao* and the *South China Morning Post*, and Kevin Lau (LLB 1986), who wrote on legal topics for the *Hong Kong Economic Journal* 1989–1995 and then became an editorial writer for *Ming Pao*.

Encouraged to study law by his elder brother's schoolmate James To (LLB 1985), Kevin Lau had enjoyed the more theoretical LLB courses, such as Sociology of Law, Jurisprudence, and Civil Liberties – subjects which his more practical classmates found less appealing. Reading books by Denning and other jurists had shown him that practising law was not just about making money but also about helping people. Yet the formalities surrounding the legal profession made him hesitant about joining it. Having obtained his LLB, he went on to the PCLL at HKU, worked as an assistant for Martin Lee QC, the first representative of the legal functional constituency on the Legislative Council, and took an LLM at the London School of Economics. After seeing first-hand the punishing daily routine of a classmate now working as a junior barrister, Lau postponed plans for pupillage and took up journalism instead. This launched him on a newspaper career during a dramatic period in Hong Kong politics.[16]

The intense focus on law by the press during the transition was 'all because we lived in a period of rapid and major changes in our legal system,' Lau recalls. Throughout the 1990s, he adds, journalists usually asked 'the two Chans' (Albert Chen and Johannes Chan) for comments on current legal issues.[17] Other lecturers also contributed to a broader understanding of the law through comments to the press, participation in public seminars, and service on official committees and NGOs. Raymond Wacks, Head of the Department of Law 1986–1993, was a presenter of RTHK's English-language 'The Week in Politics'. A list

---

15. For government monitoring of these and other groups see Suzanne Pepper, *Keeping Democracy at Bay: Hong Kong and the Challenge of Chinese Political Reform* (Lanham: Rowman & Littlefield, 2008), 176–9.

16. Kevin Lau, interview with the author, 1 March 2018.

17. Kevin Lau, interview with the author, 1 March 2018.

from the late 1990s records Faculty participation in over fifty official and non-official bodies, ranging from the Law Reform Commission and the Central Policy Unit to the Council of the Red Cross and the Human Organ Transplant Board.[18] Professional bodies, such as the Bar Association, the Law Society, and the Hong Kong branch of JUSTICE, also intensified their research and advocacy on legal issues, particularly in relation to the problems of the transition. Lawyers participated widely in policy formulation.

The more people understood the law, the better the chance for securing Hong Kong's legal system, said the Chairman of the Bar Association, Robert Tang QC, in 1990. 'We need education at homes and schools to inculcate into the people of Hong Kong as well as potential lawyers an understanding of our legal system and the importance of the rule of law.'[19] Senior officials – including British ministers on their now frequent visits – engaged more widely with the press and the public. In 1991 RTHK produced a series of thirteen TV programmes explaining how different laws affected the public, concluding with a one-hour public forum in which Johannes Chan debated human rights with Andrew Wong, a legislator, and Simon Li, a retired judge and a member of the Basic Law Drafting Committee.[20] In 1992 the government's Committee on the Promotion of Civic Education took on responsibility for human rights education. Several legal experts, including Johannes Chan (1992–1995) and Benny Tai (1995–2003), were appointed to it. The committee commissioned teaching kits, games, and other materials for schools, many of which unfortunately remained in teachers' drawers or in dark corners of libraries.[21] The professional bodies made special efforts to promote understanding of the law. In the first annual 'Law Week', organized by the Law Society in April 1991, over 200 lawyers, judges, lecturers, and students took part in school visits, court tours, seminars, and other activities culminating in a variety show on TV.[22] New NGOs, such as the Hong Kong Human Rights Commission (founded in 1988) and the Hong Kong Human Rights Monitor (founded in 1995), promoted law reform through advocacy and public education. Political parties, forming in the late 1980s and early 1990s as representative government expanded, all stressed the importance of the rule of law.

Representative government came late to Hong Kong, partly because officials came to believe that the Chinese government would not tolerate elections in the colony[23] but also

---

18. Performance Profile for the Assessment of the Faculty (draft), HKUA: Board of the Faculty of Law – Minutes (1994).

19. Speech at the Ceremonial Opening of the Legal Year, 8 January 1990, Hong Kong Bar Association, *1989/90 Annual Statement*, Appendix IV.

20. *SCMP*, 27 April 1991.

21. Benny Tai, interview with the author, 12 October 2018.

22. *New Gazette*, April & June 1991.

23. For a discussion of how this belief came to dominate British official views see Steve Tsang Yui-sang, *A Modern History of Hong Kong* (Hong Kong: Hong Kong University Press, 2004), 206–7.

because there was no strong public demand for it. This sustained an idea that Hong Kong people were 'apathetic' about politics and fed into a still more pernicious view, prevalent among business elites, that they were not ready for democracy. With the opening of negotiations on Hong Kong's future in the early 1980s the government embarked on a gradual progress towards representative government. In 1982, district boards – local advisory bodies – were created in Hong Kong's eighteen districts with unofficial majorities and some elected members. In 1985, for the first time, twenty-four of the Legislative Council's fifty-seven members were returned by an electoral college or by functional constituencies representing business and professional sectors; the rest were appointed. In 1991 direct elections in geographical constituencies were held for eighteen of sixty seats on the council; of the remainder, twenty-one were elected by functional constituencies, eighteen were appointed, and three were ex officio. Greater accountability made all unofficial members, elected or appointed, more ready to challenge policies and criticize government performance.

The agreements between Britain and China envisaged a 'legislative through-train', in which the same Legislative Council would bridge 1997. However, in 1994–1995 the through-train was derailed when Governor Patten proposed a massive extension of the franchise of existing functional constituencies and new functional constituencies with large electorates. As a result, the elections in 1995 were to be on a near-democratic basis. This arrangement breached secret understandings between Britain and China limiting the pace of reform. Against opposition from the Chinese government, Patten secured passage of his reforms in 1994. But, in response, the National People's Congress (NPC) appointed a Preliminary Work Committee and then a Preparatory Committee to make plans for the Hong Kong SAR. The Preparatory Committee appointed a Provisional Legislative Council, which, holding session across the border, existed in parallel with the colonial legislature before becoming an interim legislature on 1 July 1997. Patten's reforms were reversed and more limited elections to a new Legislative Council took place in mid-1998.

The reforms in the 1980s and 1990s radically changed the composition and operation of the Legislative Council. Pro-democracy members came to dominate proceedings, particularly after the 1995 elections. The council took on a more parliamentary style. Sittings were longer. Genuine, sometimes heated, debate replaced scripted ritual. Scrutiny of bills and policies was opened up to public participation. Members with legal qualifications included several from HKU. Among these were the solicitor Chung Pui-lam (PCLL 1977); two of the earliest LLB graduates, Moses Cheng (LLB 1972), an independent, and Albert Ho (LLB 1974), a leading member of the Democratic Party; James To (LLB 1985) and Andrew Cheng (PCLL 1992), both members of the Democratic Party; and Margaret Ng (PCLL 1988), an independent. Along with some half a dozen other lawyer-members of these years – notably Martin Lee, Ronald Arculli, and Simon Ip – they were energetic in debate and committee work.

Through this process of democratization the Legislative Council achieved greater legitimacy and relevance in the last decade of British rule. In partnership with a liberalizing administration, the council experienced a golden age, vigorously proposing, debating, and passing laws which improved many aspects of life. But its impact was limited. Some of its enactments – for example the electoral reforms of 1994, or the removal of certain restrictive provisions in the Societies and Public Order Ordinances, were cancelled by the non-adoption in 1997 of provisions deemed to be in conflict with the Basic Law, or repealed by the Provisional Legislative Council.[24] And, despite plans for continued democratic reform after 1997, including ultimately the election of the Chief Executive by universal suffrage, functional constituencies, some with narrow franchises, have continued to return half of the Legislative Council. Chief Executives have been nominated and elected by a small election committee appointed by the Central People's Government (CPG).[25]

In the absence of full democracy, or a democratic tradition, faith in the future settled on a cluster of values encapsulated in the rule of law, an idea which permeates the Joint Declaration and Basic Law, has deeper roots in Hong Kong, and is seen daily in action in the courts. Modern jurists have defined the rule of law as embracing several core principles: the law must be accessible and intelligible; it should apply equally to all; questions of legal right and liability should be resolved by application of the law and not by discretion; officials should exercise their powers within the law and not unreasonably; means should be provided for resolving bona fide civil disputes without prohibitive cost or inordinate delay; the law should be adjudicated fairly, and as far as possible in public, by an independent and impartial judiciary aided by an independent legal profession; in criminal trials the accused should be presumed innocent until proved guilty, told clearly the nature of the accusation, and given legal representation, time to prepare a defence, and the opportunity to call witnesses and examine prosecution witnesses; the law should adequately protect human rights.[26]

There were some who held that the rule of law required a democratically elected legislature to avoid repressive laws which judges had no choice but to enforce.[27] There were others whose research suggested that the rule of law had shallower roots in Hong Kong

---

24. For the non-adoption of legislation see Chen, 'Legal Preparation for the Establishment of the HKSAR: Chronology and Selected Documents', 27 *HKLJ* (1997), 405–31.

25. The intricate selection system is explained in Simon Young & Richard Cullen, *Electing Hong Kong's Chief Executive* (Hong Kong: Hong Kong University Press, 2010).

26. This is a precis of the eight principles set out by Lord Bingham, former Chief Justice of England and Wales. Bingham's analysis, much of it historical, has become a key point of reference in the common law world, not least in Hong Kong. T.H. Bingham, *The Rule of Law* (London: Allen Lane, 2010).

27. See, for example, the speech by the Chairman of the Bar Association, Robert Tang QC, at the Opening of the Legal Year in 1989, Hong Kong Bar Association, *Annual Statement 1988–89*, Appendix I.

than some enthusiasts claimed.[28] Nevertheless, the concept of the rule of law became both a central feature of the rhetoric of British withdrawal and a focus of hopes for a stable, prosperous, and free Hong Kong beyond 1997. The last British Governor, Chris Patten, described the rule of law as 'perhaps this community's most prized possession ... the very essence of our way of life.'[29] Businessmen saw the protection of private property and the enforceability of contracts under the rule of law as essential for Hong Kong's status as an international city. Those with liberal views looked to it as a means of holding officials to account, a tool for promoting equality, and a guardian of rights and freedoms. Those who stressed order understood it simply as obedience to the law. 'We strive for liberty but not at the expense of the rule of law,' said Tung Chee-Hwa in his first speech as Chief Executive of the Hong Kong SAR.[30] The rule of law, in its shades of meaning, thus became a rallying cry across the political spectrum.

Academics tried to find out what people understood by the rule of law. A survey in 1987–1988 found little difference in attitudes between people in Hong Kong and people in Norwich, an English city. Traditional ideas had given way to 'an overwhelming insistence on legal rights and resorts to the courts to settle disputes by the Chinese population.'[31] Another survey, in 1996, found much support for the idea of equality before the law, and for the presumption of innocence, but noted that 38 per cent of respondents thought that 'in adjudicating major cases, judges should defer to the views of the executive authorities.' Hong Kong Chinese, the survey concluded (mistakenly, as it turned out), 'may be readier to stand up against encroachments affecting legal equality and due process than interference with the rights-based autonomy of law.'[32] Some saw the growing attention to the rule of law and the rise of Hong Kong as a 'city of law' as an acceptance that democracy, which had played virtually no part in colonial rule, would develop only slowly after 1997. More and more, political discourse dwelt on the protection of the rights and freedoms guaranteed by law. Increasingly, law became a substitute for politics.[33]

---

28. For example, Peter Wesley-Smith, 'Anti-Chinese Legislation in Hong Kong' in Ming K. Chan (ed.), *Precarious Balance: Hong Kong Between China and Britain 1842–1992* (Armonk, New York: M.E. Sharpe, 1994), Lethbridge, *Hard Graft in Hong Kong: Scandal, Corruption, the ICAC* (1985), & Ming K. Chan, 'The Legacy of the British Administration of Hong Kong: A View from Hong Kong', *China Quarterly* (1997), 567–82.

29. Patten, Policy Address, *Hong Kong Hansard*, 11 October 1995.

30. *SCMP*, 2 July 1997.

31. Berry Fong-chung Hsu & Philip W. Baker, 'Law and Opinion in Hong Kong in the Late 1980s', 20 *HKLJ* (1990), 345–66.

32. Kuan Hsin-chi, 'Support for the Rule of Law in Hong Kong', 27 *HKLJ* (1997), 187–205.

33. For an analysis see Carol A. Jones, 'Politics Postponed: Law as a substitute for politics in Hong Kong and China' in Kanishka Jayasuriya (Ed.), *Law, Capitalism and Power in Asia: The rule of law and legal institutions* (London: Routledge-Cavendish, 2007), & Carol A. Jones, *Lost in China? Law Culture and identity in Post-1997 Hong Kong* (Cambridge: Cambridge University Press, 2015).

The Hong Kong Bill of Rights Ordinance and the Faculty of Law

Much of the discussion of the rule of law focused on the Hong Kong Bill of Rights Ordinance 1991, which enacted in local law most of the provisions of the International Covenant on Civil and Political Rights (ICCPR). Members of the Faculty of Law were involved in the conception, implementation, and promotion of this ordinance, perhaps the single most important piece of domestic legislation of late colonial Hong Kong. Various Faculty members urged its introduction. They helped shape its form and content. They took part in drafting related legislation on discrimination and privacy. They promoted understanding of the Bill of Rights through conferences, lectures and publications, and timely reports of the many judicial decisions arising from this novel and far-reaching legislation.

The ICCPR was adopted by the United Nations (UN) in 1966 along with the International Covenant on Economic, Social and Cultural Rights (ICESCR). The two covenants came into force in 1976. In the same year the UK extended the covenants to its colonies, including Hong Kong, albeit with reservations: for example, the right to self-determination in the ICCPR was not extended to Hong Kong; rights relating to freedom of movement, expulsion, and citizenship were qualified, partly to maintain restrictions on immigration into the UK; and the right to vote was qualified by a reservation not to establish an elected Executive or Legislative Council. Whereas the ICESCR set out rights to education, work, and other common goods based on a principle of 'progressive realization', the ICCPR defined rights and freedoms that were to be protected by law and enforceable in the courts. Among these were fundamental rights such as freedom of expression and freedom of association, detailed rights relating to criminal justice, such as the presumption of innocence and trial without undue delay, and general principles stating that the rights enshrined in the covenant applied equally to everyone without distinction.[34]

Under common law an international treaty only has force within a jurisdiction if it is implemented through domestic law. Signatories to the ICCPR undertook to 'develop the possibilities of judicial remedy' for citizens to enforce their rights under the covenant. They were required to submit progress reports to the UN Human Rights Committee. However, although justiciable bills of rights were included in the constitutions of former British colonies and some dependent territories,[35] no attempt was made to apply the ICCPR in Hong Kong law. The official view was that most, if not all, of the rights in the ICCPR were protected by existing law. Common law and equity offered 'an abundant number of remedies which safeguarded the rights of the citizen,' said Sir Michael Hogan, a former Chief Justice of Hong Kong (1955–1970) and a member of the UK delegation to the UN Human Rights Committee when it discussed the first report on Hong Kong in

---

34. ICCPR, adopted by the UN General Assembly on 16 December 1966 and entering into force on 23 March 1976.
35. Nihal Jayawickrama, 'The Bill of Rights' in Wacks (ed.), *Human Rights in Hong Kong*.

1979. The committee asked questions about reversals of the presumption of innocence in some legislation, curbs on the right of assembly, and the sentencing of minors to detention centres.[36]

There was little awareness at this time of Britain's obligations under the ICCPR. In 1983, for the first time, the ICCPR was cited in the Legislative Council by the Attorney General, Michael Thomas QC, in a debate on the imprisonment of debtors, a practice maintained in Hong Kong in breach of Article 11 of the covenant: the law was amended, though it fell short of satisfying Article 11.[37] Then, in the Joint Declaration of 1984, the Chinese government stated that the ICCPR and ICESCR, as applied to Hong Kong, would remain in force after 1997. This undertaking aroused interest not only in how the ICCPR would be applied in the future – particularly since China itself was not yet a signatory – but also in how far existing laws conformed with the covenant. Academics, journalists, civic groups, and lawyers began to call for an enforceable bill of rights, either as part of the Basic Law or as a freestanding law.

In a speech in June 1985, Albert Chen, recently appointed as a lecturer in the Faculty of Law, proposed that a bill of rights should be included in the future Basic Law of the Hong Kong SAR in a manner similar to that adopted by former British colonies in their constitutions upon independence; his views were soon echoed by another young lecturer, Johannes Chan.[38] In August, Henry Litton QC, now a candidate for the legal constituency in the Legislative Council elections, called for a Hong Kong bill of rights codifying rights and freedoms under common law without waiting for the Basic Law.[39] Politicians, journalists, and academics detected breaches of the ICCPR in existing laws and even in new laws and measures – for example, the contentious Legislative Council (Powers and Privileges) Bill

---

36. *Yearbook of the Human Rights Committee 1979–1980*, I, 169–89; Jayawickrama, 'Hong Kong and the International Protection of Human Rights', 134–6.

37. Article 11 states that no one shall be imprisoned 'merely on the ground of inability to fulfil a contractual obligation.' In Hong Kong, under an old rule, a debtor could be imprisoned for up to a year at the behest of a judgment creditor through a writ obtained from the Supreme Court Registry. In 1983, a year of economic instability, 423 men and women were imprisoned in this way. The solicitor and legislator Peter C. Wong led a campaign to abolish the practice. Under reforms enacted in 1984 a civil debtor could only be imprisoned by order of a court, and only if it was satisfied he was deliberately avoiding his obligations. A new provision also enabled a court to prohibit a debtor from leaving Hong Kong; it took into account support from judges for the old system and representations from business interests against too liberal a system. *Hong Kong Hansard*, 8 June, 26 October, 10 November, & 7 December 1983, & 11 January 1984; Ordinance No. 1 of 1984; Peter Morrow, 'The Crumbling Walls of the Debtors' Prison', 14 *HKLJ* (1984), 195–205.

38. *SCMP*, 21 June & 14 October 1985.

39. This idea was markedly different from a Bill of Rights based on the ICCPR, and Litton was later to express considerable scepticism about the Bill of Rights Ordinance. He lost the election to Martin Lee. *SCMP*, 16 August 1985 & 3 April 1990.

(1985),[40] a recasting of the law against publishing false news (1987),[41] new Film Censorship Regulations (1987) with powers to ban films deemed damaging to relations with other territories, and the Obscene Articles Tribunal (1987) with its ill-defined powers and decisions appealable only on points of law.[42]

Three events propelled debate on a bill of rights. First, early drafts of the Basic Law, published in 1986 and 1987, left the task of implementing the ICCPR to the future Hong Kong SAR. Instead, the drafts included a general statement of rights and freedoms modelled on those in the Chinese Constitution. This fell short of recommendations by legal scholars.[43] The debate intensified, drawing in other scholars, notably Nihal Jayawickrama, since 1985 a lecturer in law at HKU and a leading figure in the Hong Kong branch of JUSTICE.[44] His speech at a meeting of JUSTICE in December 1987 criticizing the draft Basic Law prompted the Attorney General, Michael Thomas, to invite lawyers and academics to a series of secret round-table discussions. Among the participants were Jayawickrama and Johannes Chan, as well as HKU graduates Anna Wu (LLB 1974) and Eric Au (LLB 1979). The consensus was that a justiciable, constitutionally entrenched bill of rights was necessary *before* 1997 to educate the public, enable jurisprudence to be built up, and aid in a smooth transition. Denis Chang QC, Chairman of the Bar Association, and Johannes Chan together produced two options: a short draft, which by reference to the covenant simply incorporated the ICCPR into Hong Kong law; and a longer bill of rights tailoring the ICCPR to Hong Kong's needs, with additional provisions, for example on academic freedom. The

---

40. Among the proposals were the criminalization of defamation of the council and an offence of 'intentional disrespect' to members. These and other offending provisions were taken out during passage of the bill. *Hong Kong Hansard*, 15 May & 12 & 26 June 1985; Ordinance No. 35 of 1985.

41. The government proposed to transfer and modify the offence of publishing false news 'likely to alarm public opinion or disturb public order' from the Control of Publications Consolidation Ordinance 1951 to the Public Order Ordinance. Unlike the 1951 provision, the new provision did not require proof of intent or malice. Opponents feared this might catch publishers who were merely negligent. Against opposition from journalists and lawyers, the Legislative Council passed the measure, voting down an amendment by Martin Lee to add the element of intent. The provision was, however, repealed in 1989. Litton, 'The Public Order (Amendment) Ordinance: Alarming the Public', 17 *HKLJ* (1987), 136–8; *Hong Kong Hansard*, 11 March 1987; Ordinances Nos. 15 & 16 of 1987.

42. The intricate controversies surrounding these last two measures are discussed in Albert Chen, 'Some Reflections on the "Film Censorship Affair"' & Johannes Chan, 'The Control of Obscene and Indecent Articles Ordinance 1987', 17 *HKLJ* (1987), 352–9 & 288–306.

43. Chen, 'A disappointing draft of Hong Kong's bill of rights', 17 *HKLJ* (1987), 133–6; Jayawickrama, 'The Basic Law and human rights', *Law Society of Hong Kong Gazette*, August 1988.

44. Born into a family of lawyers in Ceylon, Jayawickrama had been Permanent Secretary to the Ministry of Justice under the Bandaranaike government 1970–1977 and had taken part in drafting the 1972 Constitution, under which Ceylon became a republic and was renamed Sri Lanka. After the change of government in 1977, Jayawickrama was convicted of various politically motivated charges. He received a free pardon in 1986, but in the meantime civil penalties prevented him from practising law in Sri Lanka. He embarked on an academic career, obtaining a PhD in the international law of human rights from the University of London. Interview in *The Island* (online), 4 November 2001.

discussions ended when Thomas retired in March 1988. His successor, Jeremy Mathews, was less enthusiastic. For a while, the official position was that the round-table discussions had never taken place.[45]

Secondly, as international interest in the Hong Kong transition grew, the pace of reporting to the UN Human Rights Committee quickened. The second official report on Hong Kong, considered in November 1988, received far more careful attention than did the first. It was accompanied by submissions from NGOs, such as the Hong Kong branch of JUSTICE and the Hong Kong Journalists Association, which sent observers to the meetings. The committee grilled UK representatives on various human rights issues, such as self-determination, the death penalty, and the treatment of Vietnamese refugees, and asked why the ICCPR had not been enacted in local law. It requested a third report within a year. In anticipation of this, the Hong Kong government set about repealing laws in conflict with the ICCPR, including judicial corporal punishment, mandatory sentencing, and the false news provisions in the Public Order Ordinance. It announced plans to decriminalize homosexual acts and review police powers. In contrast to the silence surrounding its first report nine years earlier, it tabled the second report in the Legislative Council. In December 1988 the press revealed that the former Attorney General had left behind a draft bill of rights.[46]

The third, decisive event was the violent suppression of student protests in Beijing on 4 June 1989. This shattered faith in the future for many people in Hong Kong. Calls mounted for measures to boost confidence and strengthen protections of freedoms beyond 1997. The scope for action at this late stage of colonial rule was limited. Most of the measures that were adopted either speeded up processes already in train, such as constitutional reform and expansion of tertiary education, or confirmed projects that had been contemplated for some time, such as a new airport off Lantau Island, an idea first mooted in the 1970s. The boldest initiative, and one that would have an immediate impact, was announced by the Foreign Secretary, Sir Geoffrey Howe, on 4 July 1989: Hong Kong was to have 'a Bill of Rights entrenching essential freedoms' that would 'form part of the existing law and be able to continue after the transfer of sovereignty.'[47] A 'White Bill' was issued for public consultation in March 1990 and a bill was introduced in the Legislative Council in July 1990. After months of scrutiny, the Hong Kong Bill of Rights Ordinance was enacted on 8 June 1991.[48]

---

45. Johannes Chan, interview with the author, 20 June 2018; Jayawickrama, 'The Bill of Rights' in Wacks (ed.), *Human Rights in Hong Kong*.

46. Johannes Chan & Kevin Lau, 'Some Reflections on the Human Rights Committee's Hearing of the United Kingdom Second Report on Dependent Territories, held November 4–5, 1988 in Geneva', 20 *HKLJ* (1990), 150–77; Jayawickrama, 'Hong Kong and the International Protection of Human Rights', 136–9; editorial, 17 *HKLJ* (1987), 136–8; *Hong Kong Hansard*, 14 December 1988 & 11 January 1989.

47. UK Hansard, HC Deb 5 July 1989 vol 156 cc309.

48. Ordinance No. 59 of 1991.

The decision to apply the ICCPR in Hong Kong law was widely welcomed: the White Bill drew over 800 submissions, mostly in support.[49] A lively debate took place about what form the Bill of Rights should take and how the challenges of delivering it in such short order should be met. How, for example, could it be entrenched above all other laws, including future laws, in a way that would survive 1997? Should the bill protect rights between citizens as well as those between citizen and the state? Would repeal of existing laws that breached the ICCPR undermine law and order? Should the legislature or the courts decide these questions? And should a human rights commission be created to ensure compliance? These questions were complicated by uncertainty about how the final version of the Basic Law would deal with the ICCPR and by Chinese official opposition to any radical change to Hong Kong's legal system. Under the Joint Declaration 'the previous system remains unchanged in 1997,' said Lu Ping, Deputy Secretary-General of the Basic Law Drafting Committee. 'Under the current legal system, all laws enjoy equal status.'[50] Chinese officials issued statements reserving the right to repeal the Bill of Rights after 1997. There were doubts in Hong Kong too, not just from law enforcers but also among some lawyers. 'With the uncertainties of 1997 before us, is it worth unshackling the courts from the discipline of law as we know it?' asked Henry Litton, now a firm sceptic. 'Is it wise to throw the courts into the arena of "international jurisprudence" and expect them to survive with any degree of credibility?'[51]

The White Bill came with a proposal to insert two new provisions in the Letters Patent, the constitutional instrument in force until 30 June 1997 and superior to all local ordinances: a requirement that the ICCPR, as applied to Hong Kong, should be implemented through the laws of Hong Kong; and another that no new law should restrict rights and freedoms in a way that was inconsistent with the ICCPR as applied to Hong Kong. This form of entrenchment, making no direct mention of the Bill of Rights, echoed a provision in the final version of the Basic Law (Article 39) adopted by the NPC in April 1990. It drew on proposals from experts connected with the Faculty of Law. Nihal Jayawickrama, in a draft 'Hong Kong Charter of Rights' that had gained currency in 1989, had proposed entrenching the charter in the Letters Patent.[52] At a press conference in Hong Kong by the new Foreign Secretary, Douglas Hurd, the journalist Kevin Lau suggested 'mirror-imaging'

---

49. *An Introduction to the Bill of Rights Ordinance 1991* (Government Printer, 1991), 2.

50. Quoted in Jayawickrama, 'The Bill of Rights', 74.

51. Litton, letter to the editor, *SCMP*, 6 June 1990. Now a retired judge of the CFA and an honorary professor in the Faculty of Law, Litton has recently developed this argument in the light of experience in a collection of essays, *Is the Hong Kong Judiciary Sleepwalking to 2047? Have Abstract Principles Smothered an Effective Legal System?* (Hong Kong: Sherriff Books, 2019).

52. Jayawickrama's draft incorporated provisions from both the ICCPR and the ICESCR. He proposed a provision in the Letters Patent protecting the charter from amendment or repeal except by a prescribed majority in the Legislative Council. Jayawickrama, 'The Bill of Rights', 71.

the Letters Patent with Article 39. Prominent barristers backed the idea. Officials in Whitehall pursued it, consulting, among others, Johannes Chan, then in London pursuing doctoral studies while on leave from HKU: his proposals for entrenchment in an article in the *New Gazette* were much studied by officials in the Foreign and Commonwealth Office.[53] Another strategy to ensure the Bill of Rights survived 1997, also recommended by Chan, was the decision to incorporate word for word in the Bill of Rights Ordinance all of the ICCPR as applied to Hong Kong: this became Part II – the meat of the ordinance – entitled 'The Hong Kong Bill of Rights.'

The main purpose of the Bill of Rights Ordinance was to offer assurance to Hong Kong people that their rights would be protected beyond 1997. However, in empowering the courts to strike down laws that were inconsistent with it, the ordinance had a wide and deep impact during its six years of operation before 1997. The advantages of this were that it allowed the courts to develop jurisprudence and purged the legal system of laws that failed to meet international standards of human rights, placing Hong Kong in a better position than some other ex-colonies left burdened with repressive colonial legislation. The difficulties arose first, in uncertainty about how many laws would be struck down in this way, and secondly, from concerns that key tools for handling long-standing problems – corruption, drug abuse, and triads, for example – would be rendered inoperative. The 1990 White Bill proposed a freeze period of two years after commencement of the ordinance to allow time to review existing legislation for consistency with the Bill of Rights. During the freeze all pre-existing statute law would be immune from challenges.

This proposed blanket freeze was received with dismay by many, particularly since the British government had extended the ICCPR to Hong Kong as long ago as 1976 and had 'studiously maintained to the United Nations that all laws in Hong Kong are in conformity with the Covenant.'[54] Some saw no merit at all in a freeze: it would be almost impossible for the government to repeal all conflicting provisions in a short time, said Nihal Jayawickrama; in any case it should be for the courts to decide such matters. Johannes Chan, now advising Executive and Legislative Councillors on the bill, noted that during a three-year freeze period for the Canadian Charter of Rights and Freedoms several provinces had simply done nothing. He suggested a one-year freeze for only some ordinances. 'The bill has been conceived primarily as a bulwark against 1997 and beyond,' said his colleague Andrew Byrnes. 'One senses that the government is concerned to limit its impact before then.'[55]

---

53. Kevin Lau, interview with the author, 1 March 2018; Johannes Chan, interview with the author, 20 June 2018; transcript of Hurd's press conference, *Daily Information Bulletin* (Supplement), 16 January 1990; *SCMP*, 17 & 25 January & 11 March 1990; *New Gazette*, March 1990.

54. Ronald Arculli, speaking in the debate on the White Bill, *Hong Kong Hansard*, 27 June 1990.

55. *SCMP*, 28 December 1989; *The Lawyer*, April 1990.

Andrew Byrnes had joined the Faculty of Law in 1989. A graduate of the Australian National University, with LLMs from both Harvard and Columbia, he had developed an interest in human rights, especially the rights of women: one of his early contributions to public debate was to ask why the British government had not extended to Hong Kong the 1979 UN Convention on the Elimination of all Forms of Discrimination against Women.[56] Byrnes joined the debate on the Bill of Rights, defending it against critics and urging the creation of a human rights commission to enforce it. In October 1990 the Legal Department took the unusual step of seconding him for a year to advise on how far existing statute law complied with the Bill of Rights.[57] Following this, the proposed blanket two-year freeze was dispensed with. Instead, six key ordinances relating to law and order were exempted from the effects of the Bill of Rights for one year to allow time for amendment.[58] Otherwise, the bill came into force immediately on enactment, on 8 June 1991. However, as a result of lobbying by business groups and some lawyers, the final version, unlike the White Bill, bound only the government and public authorities, and not private citizens in their relations with each other.[59]

The six frozen ordinances – the 'dirty half-dozen' as Raymond Wacks called them[60] – were amended in 1992. Restrictions were placed on the once-extensive police powers of stop, search, and arrest. Various presumptive offences were removed or modified. Certain offences, such as loitering, no longer placed the burden of proof on the accused. By late 1995 another thirty or so ordinances had been amended to align them with the Bill of Rights. For example, the licensing of public assemblies and processions under the Public Order Ordinance was replaced with a notification system; provisions allowing discretionary control by the government of broadcasting were modified; and all Emergency Regulations, which had not been used for several years, were repealed (but not the Emergency Regulations Ordinance itself). Under the influence of the Bill of Rights, homosexual acts between consenting male adults were decriminalized (1991) and capital punishment was formally repealed (1993).

Some experts believed that the various legislative amendments under the Bill of Rights were just the tip of a large iceberg. Research suggested that some 170 provisions, perhaps as

---

56. *SCMP*, 22 & 29 October & 3 & 23 December 1989.

57. A year earlier the Legal Department had also enlisted the help of a Canadian federal judge, Barry Strayer, on a three-month contract to advise on the bill. *SCMP*, 27 October 1990.

58. The Immigration Ordinance, Societies Ordinance, Crimes Ordinance, Prevention of Bribery Ordinance, ICAC Ordinance, and Police Force Ordinance.

59. *Hong Kong Hansard*, 5 June 1991; Byrnes, 'The Hong Kong Bill of Rights and Relations Between Private Individuals' in Johannes Chan & Yash Ghai (Eds.), *The Hong Kong Bill of Rights: A Comparative Approach* (Hong Kong: Butterworths Asia, 1993), 83–8.

60. Raymond Wacks and Andrew Byrnes (Eds.), *Human Rights in Hong Kong* (Hong Kong: Oxford University Press, 1992), 10.

many as 288, spread across the statute book, reversed the burden of proof, in conflict with the right to be presumed innocent (Article 11).[61] The government took a cautious view, preferring to be guided by judicial interpretation, an approach which, some said, shifted too much of the burden to the courts.[62] The government decided not to follow the practice elsewhere of creating a human rights commission, which might have eased this burden. Instead, parties could invoke the Bill of Rights in any court and at any stage in proceedings. The Bill of Rights, said Sir Derek Cons, a Vice-President of the Court of Appeal, at a conference hosted by the Law Faculty in 1991, was a 'gateway to an uncharted sea': litigation arising from it would result in trials being unduly delayed, which in itself would be a breach of the Bill of Rights. Elsewhere, Henry Litton warned that the Bill of Rights would be 'the port of first asylum for every lawyer whenever a client has a grievance to ventilate.'[63]

These predictions were partly borne out by a deluge of Bill of Rights arguments in the lower courts, frequent adjournments, uncertainty while decisions were tested in the higher courts, and what the barrister Gerard McCoy described as a flourishing 'grey market in unreported decisions' as lawyers, 'groping in the dark', tried to understand different approaches by different courts.[64] Some district judges refused to grant 'stop orders' preventing people from leaving the territory if they had not paid their taxes, in conflict with the right to liberty of movement under Article 8.[65] The district judge Bernard Downey (a former HKU law lecturer) declared that the power given to the District Court to prohibit a judgment debtor from leaving Hong Kong was repealed because it too breached Article 8.[66] Magistrates ruled that certain presumptive offences, for example under the Gambling Ordinance or Dangerous Drugs Ordinance, breached the right to be presumed innocent (Article 11).

---

61. The lower figure is from Philip Dykes, then assistant solicitor general, *SCMP*, 12 November 1991. The higher figure is cited by the barrister Gerard McCoy, 'Problems in the area of litigation', in Andrew Byrnes and George E. Edwards (Eds.), *Hong Kong's Bill of Rights: the First Year* (Hong Kong: Faculty of Law, HKU, 1993), from computer-generated research.

62. *Hong Kong Hansard*, 19 February 1992; Lugar-Mawson, 'Judicial perspectives in interpreting the Bill of Rights,' in Byrnes and Edwards (Eds.), *Hong Kong's Bill of Rights: the First Year*, 42.

63. Cons, Keynote Address, Hong Kong Bill of Rights Conference 1991, quoted in Johannes Chan, 'Undue Delay in Criminal Trials and the Bill of Rights', 22 *HKLJ* (1992), 2–19; *SCMP*, 3 April 1990 & 21 June 1991.

64. *New Gazette*, April 1992.

65. Anthony Au-Yeung, 'Taxation and the Bill of Rights' in William Fong, Andrew Byrnes, and George E. Edwards (Eds.), *Hong Kong's Bill of Rights: Two Years On* (Hong Kong: Faculty of Law, HKU, 1994).

66. The decision was reversed by the Court of Appeal, which held that the Bill of Rights did not apply to disputes between private citizens, and that in any case the provision did not breach Article 8, since it was necessary for the protection of the rights of others and, in deterring creditors from taking the law into their own hands, might also be necessary for the protection of public order – a restriction permissible under Article 8. *Tam Hing-yee v Wu Tai Wai* (1991) 1 HKPLR 261.

One of these cases led to the first judgment on the Bill of Rights by the Court of Appeal. In *R v Sin Yau Ming*, the defendant was charged with possessing unlawful drugs for the purpose of trafficking. He had been found with ninety-five grams of pure heroin. Under the Dangerous Drugs Ordinance, any amount more than a half gram was presumed to be for trafficking. The maximum penalty was a $5 million fine and life imprisonment. During Sin's trial the judge reserved for the Court of Appeal the question of whether the presumptive offences in the ordinance were consistent with Article 11 of the Bill of Rights. In September 1991 the Court of Appeal decided they were not and held them to have been repealed. This landmark judgment affirmed the unique status of the Bill of Rights and set out principles for applying it. The Bill of Rights was to receive 'a generous and purposive' interpretation, said the Vice-President, William Silke. While the interests of the individual had to be balanced against those of society, there should be 'a bias towards the interests of the individual.' And, since the Bill of Rights was almost identical with the ICCPR, the courts should look to decisions of supranational tribunals and jurisdictions with constitutionally entrenched bills of rights, and go beyond 'the dicta of the common law inherent in our training' to adopt an 'entirely new jurisprudential approach.'[67]

Sin Yau Ming showed a 'generous receptivity to jurisprudence from outside the United Kingdom' and a 'liberal attitude' that helped 'bring Hong Kong human rights standards up to international standards.'[68] The judgment set the tone for a series of successful challenges under the Bill of Rights on questions of criminal law and procedure, affirming, for example, the right to examine witnesses, the right not to be compelled to testify against oneself, and the prohibition on retrospective offences. Other cases addressed long delays in criminal cases coming to trial and the right to bail. Access to legal advice was improved in line with Article 11(2)(d) (the right to free legal assistance where the interests of justice require it) by expanding the Duty Lawyer Scheme and giving the Director of Legal Aid greater discretion to grant legal aid in Bill of Rights cases even if applicants did not meet the means test.[69]

Staff in the Faculty of Law helped advance understanding and implementation of the Bill of Rights in practical ways, through holding workshops and conferences, producing law reports and commentaries, participating in law drafting, and representing litigants in challenges brought under the Bill of Rights. First, the Faculty held frequent workshops and conferences on the Bill of Rights, bringing together not only academics but also practising lawyers, judges, and civil servants. These events were opportunities to share experience on issues such as the impact of the bill on criminal investigations or financial regulation. A wide range of voices was heard, including police officers tasked with adapting procedures to

---

67. *R v Sin Yau-ming* (1991) 1 HKPLR 88. Amendments were later made to the Dangerous Drugs Ordinance to remove the presumptive provisions. Ordinances No. 52 of 1992 & 62 of 1994.

68. Johannes Chan, in the *New Gazette*, January 1992.

69. Ordinance No. 43 of 1995.

conform with the bill, social workers assisting people in protecting their rights, and judges and lawyers from places with established human rights laws. Proceedings were published by the Faculty itself, in the *Hong Kong Law Journal*, and in collections such as Johannes Chan and Yash Ghai's influential edited book *The Hong Kong Bill of Rights: A Comparative Approach* (1993), a work aimed at assisting the Judiciary with international approaches to human rights legislation.[70]

Occasionally, the impact was immediate. In June 1991, during two Legislative Council debates, Martin Lee cited international experts on human rights who had attended a large HKU-hosted conference only the week before. One debate was on a motion calling for the implementation of the death penalty, which, though it remained on the statute book, had not been enforced since 1966. Citing, among other documents, a letter to legislators from conference participants in opposition to the death penalty, Lee secured an amendment of the motion so that it called for the *abolition* of the death penalty, which passed by a large majority. Two years later, in 1993, legislation was enacted to this effect. This was, suggested the *Commonwealth Law Bulletin*, 'one of those rare occasions when an international conference may have played some practical part in local lawmaking by reason of the coincidence of its concerns with proposals for law reform in the legislature.'[71]

Momentum from conferences and publications on the Bill of Rights was a key stimulus in the creation in 1995 of the Faculty's Centre for Comparative and Public Law, with Andrew Byrnes as its first director. By then, the Faculty was already providing training in human rights to students not only from Hong Kong but also from other parts of Asia. Partly to reflect this, the new LLM in human rights, launched in 1999, had a special focus on international and regional issues.

Secondly, as the Bill of Rights played out in the courts, the Faculty embarked on its own programme of law reporting and commentary. From October 1991 a regular *Bill of Rights Bulletin*, edited by Andrew Byrnes and Johannes Chan and published by the Faculty, contained reports of cases, analysis of new legislation, and editorial comment. The reports covered not only judgments in the higher courts but also decisions in the District Court and magistrates' courts, where the Bill of Rights was often invoked. Readers were invited to fax in information on new cases on a form included in early issues. The aim, wrote the editors, was 'to help judges, practitioners and others to keep up to date with the rapidly evolving case law under the *Bill of Rights*.'[72] In 1993, Andrew Byrnes, Johannes Chan and

---

70. Johannes Chan, interview with the author, 20 June 2018.

71. *Hong Kong Hansard*, 26 June 1991; 17 *Commonwealth Law Bulletin* (1991), 1105–6. The other debate was on legislation requiring permits for soliciting donations in public places for election campaigns and other purposes. Citing international experts at the conference, Lee argued that the legislation was in conflict with the recently enacted Bill of Rights Ordinance. Lee was less successful in this debate: the legislation was passed.

72. *Bill of Rights Bulletin*, October 1991.

George Edwards, a research officer, launched the *Hong Kong Public Law Reports*, a formal series of reports and other documents tracing in detail jurisprudence on the Bill of Rights.[73]

Thirdly, Faculty members helped legislators draft other laws to ensure that key principles in the Bill of Rights were made applicable both to the private and public sectors. Article 1 states that the rights recognized in the bill shall be enjoyed without distinction of any kind, 'such as race, colour, sex, language, religion, political or other opinion, national or social origin, property, birth or other status.' Article 22 states that the law shall prohibit any discrimination and guarantee to all persons equal and effective protection against discrimination on any ground. The Heung Yee Kuk – the representative body of indigenous villagers – had campaigned for exemption for 'traditional' rights, such as male-only inheritance of land in the New Territories, exclusion of women in rural elections, and a policy under which male villagers received land for building houses (the 'Small House Policy'). The campaign not only failed but prompted women's groups to lobby for anti-discrimination laws covering all aspects of life, including employment, where sex discrimination was rife. Action in such cases was inhibited by the exclusion of inter-citizen disputes from the purview of the Bill of Rights and the high cost of litigation. Proponents of change were also frustrated by the official view that discrimination was not a serious problem.[74]

Women's groups joined together to campaign for change. The movement gained support from an increasingly assertive Legislative Council. In 1991 the Council unanimously passed a motion by Emily Lau calling for the UN Convention on the Elimination of all Forms of Discrimination against Women (CEDAW) to be extended to Hong Kong: this was done in 1996. In 1994, against fierce, often violent opposition, another legislator, Christine Loh, led a successful campaign to abolish male-only succession to landed property in the New Territories.[75] In parallel, a third legislator, Anna Wu, produced two private member's bills aimed at combating discrimination on a wide range of grounds – sex, marital status,

---

73. *Hong Kong Public Law Reports* (Hong Kong University Press, 1991–1994). In 1995 this commercially successful series was taken over by Butterworths. It now runs to more than twenty volumes.

74. The discussion here draws on Petersen, 'Equality as a Human Right: The Development of Anti-Discrimination Law in Hong Kong', 34 *Columbia Journal of Transnational Law* (1996), 335–88.

75. Research by Carol Jones, Carole Petersen, and Carla Howarth had revealed that, as a result of a court ruling in 1970, the prohibition on female inheritance applied to *all* residents of the New Territories, the majority of whom by the 1990s were non-indigenous people living in new towns. In 1993 the government introduced legislation to reform the system for non-indigenous inhabitants. Christine Loh proposed an amendment to extend this to indigenous inhabitants, which was passed by an overwhelming majority. In 1996–1997, indigenous villagers of the New Territories, claiming to be an ethnic minority, challenged the legislation on the ground that Article 23 of the Bill of Rights guaranteed the rights of minorities to enjoy their own culture and practise their own religion. The Court of Appeal found against the villagers, ruling that their claim was 'wholly untenable' in an age in which 'the elimination of all forms of discrimination against women was a policy to which all civilized nations subscribed.' *Lau Wong Fat v Attorney General* [1997] HKLRD 533; Ordinance No. 55 of 1994; *Tang Kai-chung and another v Tang Chik-shang and others* [1970] HKLR 276; Petersen, 'Equality as a Human Right,' 368–72.

pregnancy, family responsibility, disability, sexuality, race, age, and political and religious conviction. Private members' bills were a rarity in Hong Kong. This was the first such bill seeking to establish a whole new area of policy. Drawing on Australian models, Wu was aided by her assistants, Eric Chow and Adam Mayes, and by two law lecturers from HKU, Andrew Byrnes and Carole Petersen, who was then at HKU SPACE but who in 1999 joined the Faculty of Law. At conferences organized by the Faculty, Wu and her team consulted civic groups and officials, hoping that the government would work with her on the bill.

The Governor's permission was needed for private member's bills requiring public expenditure. Wu therefore drafted two bills: one, the Equal Opportunities Bill, needed no new expenditure and could be enforced through the courts; the other, creating a human rights and equal opportunities commission and a tribunal to enforce the first bill, required expenditure. Governor Patten refused Wu permission to introduce the second bill. She proceeded with the first bill on its own, introducing it in the Legislative Council in 1994 and giving an undertaking to the government to drop the corresponding parts of the bill in favour of any government bill on equality. This she did when the government produced two bills, starting with the Sex Discrimination Bill, modelled on an English act, and continuing with the Disability Discrimination Bill. Both were enacted in 1995 in place of Wu's bill.[76] They covered only two grounds of discrimination and exempted or delayed action in some areas, including rural elections and the Small House Policy. The legislation nevertheless established an Equal Opportunities Commission, tasked with working towards the elimination of discrimination. Other ordinances followed to prohibit discrimination on grounds of family status (1997) and race (2008). Legislation on the other categories covered by Wu has yet to be introduced. Wu served as the second chairperson (1999–2003) of the Equal Opportunities Commission. One of the highlights of her tenure was a successful action brought by the commission against the Director of Education, ending an allocation system for admission to secondary schools in place since 1978 that was systematically weighted against girls.[77]

The other new legislation arising out of the Bill of Rights was the Personal Data (Privacy) Ordinance, enacted in 1995. Article 14 of the Bill of Rights provides for protection against arbitrary or unlawful interference with privacy, which the UN Human Rights Committee has interpreted to include data protection. In 1989 the Law Reform Commission established a subcommittee to examine this question at a time of rapid change in ways of acquiring and exploiting personal data, particularly through the use of computers. The subcommittee met no fewer than fifty-six times, received nearly one-hundred submissions, and heard from experts in other jurisdictions. One of its members was Raymond Wacks, Professor of Law and Legal Theory at HKU and a leading expert on the subject: his book *The Protection*

---

76. Ordinances Nos. 67 & 86 of 1995.
77. *Equal Opportunities Commission v Director of Education* [2001] 2 HKLRD 690.

of Privacy (1980) was the first work on the subject in England. The subcommittee's report, delivered in 1994, became the basis for the 1995 ordinance, which, unlike earlier legislation in many other jurisdictions, applied to computerized as well as manually held data, and to the private as well as the public sector.[78] In the mid-1990s a course on Privacy and Data Protection was added to the LLM programme at HKU.

The fourth contribution by Faculty members to the Bill of Rights was in litigation. One of the Faculty's leading human rights scholars, Johannes Chan, qualified as a barrister in Hong Kong and practised for a year before joining the Faculty of Law as a lecturer in 1985. He was on study leave in London when plans for a Bill of Rights were announced. Wishing to contribute at this historic time, he cut short his studies and returned to Hong Kong. Chan had embarked on an academic career partly with the aim of bridging the gap between town and gown through combining scholarship and teaching with occasional advocacy in the courts.[79] From the early 1990s he appeared in several cases that tested laws or executive acts against the Bill of Rights. Among the earliest were criminal trials for presumptive offences as well as judicial reviews of classifications by the Obscene Articles Tribunal, refusals to grant right of abode under the Immigration Ordinance, and rejections of nominations of district board candidates under the Electoral Provisions Ordinance.

In 2003 Johannes Chan became Hong Kong's first honorary Senior Counsel, or 'academic silk', in recognition of his scholarship and his work in the courts. In most of his early cases, as a junior barrister, he was led by Queen's Counsel. As in all such cases, the objective was to persuade the court. But in one case he first had to convince his own leader, the eminent Charles Ching QC, of the merits of advancing a Bill of Rights argument. In 1994 Ming Pao Newspapers Ltd and three of its editors were prosecuted for breaching section 30(1) of the Prevention of Bribery Ordinance, which forbade disclosure of the details of an ICAC investigation or the identity of a person under investigation. Along with other newspapers, *Ming Pao* had reported on allegations of blatant bid-rigging in a land auction. It had also reported in general terms on steps taken by ICAC officers to meet reporters who had covered the auction. Ching had prepared his case on the basis that no details of the investigation had been disclosed and the report had not prejudiced the investigation. When Chan suggested adding a defence of freedom of expression under Article 16 of the Bill of Rights, Ching was reluctant: it was 'a sign of weakness' to rely on the Bill of Rights – or the 'Bill of Wrongs' as he called it. He nevertheless agreed, and it was the Bill of Rights argument that won the case. The magistrate rejected all the defence's arguments except the Bill of Rights point: section 30(1) of the Prevention of Bribery Ordinance, he ruled, was inconsistent with Article 16 and was therefore repealed. The ruling was overturned on

---

78. Law Reform Commission of Hong Kong, *Reform of the Law Relating to the Protection of Personal Data* (1994); Ordinance No. 81 of 1995; Wacks, 'Data Privacy: Reforming the Law', 26 *HKLJ* (1996), 149–51.

79. Chan, *Paths of Justice*, 14 & 20; Johannes Chan, interview with the author, 20 June 2018.

appeal but a further appeal to the Judicial Committee of the Privy Council, where Chan appeared with Anthony Lester QC, resulted in qualified victory for both sides. The Judicial Committee found that section 30(1) was a proportionate and permissible restriction on freedom of expression. But it also ruled that it could only apply if the disclosure referred to a specific person. Since the *Ming Pao* report had made no such reference, no offence had been committed.[80]

The Judicial Committee's opinion on the *Ming Pao* case, delivered in 1996, contained a vigorous affirmation of freedom of expression as one of the essential foundations of a democratic society. It also cited jurisprudence from the European Court of Human Rights.[81] Three years earlier, however, when considering the Bill of Rights for the first time, the Judicial Committee had urged caution. The courts in Hong Kong had ruled presumptive offences in two ordinances to have been repealed by the Bill of Rights. One of these, having in one's possession 'anything which may be reasonably suspected of having been stolen or unlawfully obtained' without being able to give a satisfactory explanation, dated back to the early years of the colony, when it had been used to convict people found in the streets with petty objects which the police believed, but could not prove, to have been stolen. In this case the accused, Lee Kwong-kut, had been found with $1.76 million in cash. Lee was acquitted by a magistrate on the ground that the offence put the burden of proof on the accused and was incompatible with the Bill of Rights. Both the Court of Appeal in Hong Kong and the Judicial Committee upheld the decision. As a result, 386 others had their convictions quashed. The other case, heard at the same time, involved a new offence of assisting drug traffickers to retain the proceeds of their crime. The Judicial Committee reversed the finding in Hong Kong that section 25 of the Drug Trafficking (Recovery of Proceeds) Ordinance 1989 conflicted with the right to be presumed innocent. In delivering the opinion, Lord Woolf urged a sense of proportion. 'While the Hong Kong judiciary should be zealous in upholding an individual's rights,' he said, 'it is also necessary to ensure that disputes as to the effect of the Bill are not allowed to get out of hand.' Otherwise, 'the Bill will become a source of injustice rather than justice and it will be debased in the eyes of the public.'[82] This advice, contrasting with the progressive tone set by the Court of Appeal

---

80. *Ming Pao Newspapers Limited and Others v. The Attorney General of Hong Kong* (Hong Kong) [1996] UKPC 12. There is a personal account of the case in Johannes Chan, *Paths of Justice* (Hong Kong: Hong Kong University Press, 2018), 23–9.

81. Albeit somewhat vaguely in the view of Johannes Chan: Chan, 'Hong Kong's Bill of Rights: Its Reception of and Contribution to International and Comparative Jurisprudence', 47 *International and Comparative Law Quarterly* (1998), 317–20.

82. *The Attorney General of Hong Kong v. Lee Kwong-kut and The Attorney General of Hong Kong v. (1) Lo Chak-man and (2) Tsoi Sau-ngai* (Hong Kong) [1993] UKPC 20.

in *Sin Yau Ming*, encouraged judges to take a more conservative approach.[83] The number of Bill of Rights cases, and their success rate, declined. Judges warned lawyers against bringing 'half-baked' Bill of Rights cases to court.[84] The *Bill of Rights Bulletin* observed a tendency among judges towards 'a somewhat parochial reaffirmation of the Bill of Rights as embodying little more than existing common law guarantees.'[85]

In 1995 the Chief Justice, Sir Ti Liang Yang, privately remarked to Zhang Junsheng, Deputy Director of the New China News Agency, that the Bill of Rights had undermined Hong Kong's legal system. When Zhang disclosed the remark to the press, controversy erupted at a time when Chinese officials were speaking of plans to water down the bill. Yang's attempts to explain the remark only deepened the controversy. In empowering the courts to repeal legislation, the Bill of Rights failed to preserve the demarcation between the Judiciary and the Legislature, he said. The power to repeal also gave rise to a practical difficulty if two magistrates held different views on the same issue in different cases. 'The resulting chaos need not be specified.' Another senior judge, Benjamin Liu, in an article in *Ming Pao*, said that Yang's views were shared by many judges. Government officials, lawyers, and scholars strongly disputed them. Peter Wesley-Smith described the 'chaos' comment as a 'nonsense argument.' Magistrates often held different views but their decisions did not bind other courts. Judges in Hong Kong had always had the power to strike down legislation inconsistent with acts of parliament or the Letters Patent, he said.[86]

The Basic Law and the Court of Final Appeal

Despite the threats from Chinese officials and a promise by Sir Ti Liang Yang in his campaign for election as Chief Executive to revise it,[87] the Bill of Rights Ordinance remained in force after 1997. The only parts that did not survive the transition were the provisions repealing legislation that was inconsistent with the Bill of Rights and requiring future legislation to

---

83. Johannes Chan, 'Hong Kong's Bill of Rights: Its Reception of and Contribution to International and Comparative Jurisprudence', 47 *International and Comparative Law Quarterly* (1998), 306–36.

84. Godfrey JA, echoed by Litton JA, in *Kwan Kong Co. Ltd v Town Planning Board* [1996] HKCA 563.

85. Editorial, *Bill of Rights Bulletin*, June 1996.

86. *SCMP*, 13–24 November 1995; *Ming Pao*, 16 November 1995; Wesley-Smith, 'Judicial Review of Legislation in Hong Kong', 26 *HKLJ* (1996), 1–2. Wesley-Smith had, however, concluded in an earlier article that 'the scope of the Letters Patent is so wide that in fact the Hong Kong courts have not yet discovered an ordinance which can be pronounced bad as ultra vires': 'Legal Limitations upon the Legislative Competence of the Hong Kong Legislature', 11 *HKLJ* (1981), 3–31. Various statements in the controversy are in George Edwards and Johannes Chan (eds.), *Hong Kong's Bill of Rights: Two Years Before 1997* (Hong Kong: Centre for Comparative and Public Law, Faculty of Law, HKU, 1995), Appendixes A to E.

87. Both he and another former judge, Simon Li, lost the election to the businessman Tung Chee-hwa. *SCMP*, 31 October 1996.

be construed so as to be consistent with the ICCPR as applied to Hong Kong.[88] These were declared by the Standing Committee of the NPC to be in contravention of the Basic Law. The changes had no material effect, since the Basic Law both requires the ICCPR to be implemented through the laws of Hong Kong and empowers the courts to interpret the Basic Law. Moreover, the Basic Law echoes many of the provisions in the Bill of Rights and sets out other rights and freedoms – for example, freedom of choice of occupation, the right to strike, the right to social welfare, and freedom to engage in academic research. In a further provision that has no counterpart in the Bill of Rights, the Basic Law also requires the Hong Kong SAR to protect the right of private ownership of property. It states that the capitalist system shall remain unchanged for fifty years, and it further requires the SAR to strive for balanced budgets, to provide an appropriate environment for maintaining Hong Kong as an international financial centre, and to safeguard the free flow of capital within, into, and out of Hong Kong.[89]

These and other policy principles prompted the constitutional expert Yash Ghai to observe that the Basic Law prescribes a 'special kind of capitalism' for Hong Kong, one which reflects its history and differentiates it from the socialist system of Mainland China, but which also inhibits the high degree of autonomy promised in the Basic Law and promotes a system that is 'hostile to democracy and favours a strong executive distanced from popular pressures.'[90] The Basic Law, reflects Ghai, is 'full of irony.' The PRC paid a great compliment to Britain by entrenching the system that Britain had established, despite its resentment of British rule in Hong Kong. 'By elevating the market to the highest principle, professedly the most ardent of communist states promulgates the most extensive charter of capitalism that exists anywhere.'[91]

Ghai's analysis appears in his book *Hong Kong's New Constitutional Order: The Resumption of Chinese Sovereignty and the Basic Law*. First published in 1997, and frequently cited in the courts, this work has become a classic text. The first Sir Y.K. Pao Professor of Public Law at HKU, Ghai was born into an Indian family in Kenya in 1938 – then a highly segregated society. The sufferings of Asians and Africans under British rule left him with 'an aversion to colonial rule' and led him to explore the legal mechanisms used to sustain colonial rule. By the time he joined the Faculty of Law at HKU in 1989 he had helped draft the constitutions of newly independent countries such as Seychelles, Papua New Guinea, Vanuatu, and the

---

88. Decision of the Standing Committee of the NPC on treatment of the laws previously in force in Hong Kong in accordance with Article 160 of the Basic Law of the Hong Kong SAR, 23 February 1997.

89. *The Basic Law of the Hong Kong Special Administrative Region of the People's Republic of China.*

90. Yash P. Ghai, *Hong Kong's New Constitutional Order: The Resumption of Chinese Sovereignty and the Basic Law* (Hong Kong: Hong Kong University Press, 1997, second edition 1999), 138–40, & Ghai, 'The Rule of Law and Capitalism: Reflections on the Basic Law' in Raymond Wacks (Ed.), *Hong Kong, China and 1997: Essays in Legal Theory* (Hong Kong: Hong Kong University Press, 1993), 344.

91. Ghai, *Hong Kong's New Constitutional Order*, 493.

Solomon Islands. He later advised on constitutions in over a dozen countries, ranging from Fiji to Iraq.[92] In 2001 he was invited by the President of Kenya to chair the Constitution of Kenya Review Commission at a time when Kenya was close to civil war. Ghai asked for twelve months' leave from the Faculty. Johannes Chan, Head of the Department of Law, gave him eighteen: 'How often do our colleagues receive a phone call from the president of their country?' Ghai brought the opposing factions together, and a new constitution, emphasizing human rights and social equity, was promulgated in 2010.[93]

The drafting of the Constitution of Kenya was a highly participatory process culminating in a referendum in which 67 per cent of voters endorsed it. The drafting of Hong Kong's Basic Law had limited participation and did not lead to a referendum. 'I have the fear that a lot of people in Hong Kong will think that the Basic Law is not a constitution of their own making – that it has been forced on them,' Ghai said shortly before it was promulgated. 'There are very many provisions that they disagree with. I think that's a bad start.'[94] A Basic Law Drafting Committee, formed by the NPC in June 1985, consisted of fifty-nine members – thirty-six from Mainland China and twenty-three from Hong Kong, including businessmen (the biggest group), politicians, academics, priests, and lawyers. A larger Consultative Committee, comprising 180 members, all from Hong Kong, was more broadly representative. It received 73,000 submissions during the first phase of consultation. But its influence was limited. With the hardening of attitudes in 1989 more conservative views prevailed. Two members of both the Drafting and Consultative Committees, the Reverend Peter Kwong and Louis Cha, resigned in May 1989. Two others, Martin Lee and Szeto Wah, the most outspoken among the drafters, were expelled later in the year for their 'antagonistic stand' towards the Chinese government.[95]

The task of the Basic Law Drafting Committee was to set out in a national law the system prescribed for the Hong Kong SAR in the Joint Declaration. The main points of contention centred on how the Basic Law dealt with matters left unclear in the Joint Declaration and on perceived inconsistencies between the two documents, particularly where they seemed to erode the high degree of autonomy promised for Hong Kong. Among the most hotly debated issues were the systems for electing the Chief Executive and the Legislative Council, which were only vaguely stipulated in the Joint Declaration: in the end, a gradualist

---

92. Ghai trained as a lawyer at Oxford and Harvard, and was called to the Bar by Middle Temple. He helped establish the Faculty of Law at the University of East Africa at Dar es Salaam in 1963–1973. He then taught at Yale Law School, Uppsala University, and Warwick University before joining the Faculty of Law at HKU in 1989. Ghai, Research Statement on the Ethnicity and Democratic Governance Project website, Queen's University at Kingston, Ontario, & 'A Journey Around Constitutions: Reflecting on Contemporary Constitutions' in HKU Faculty of Law, *Building for Tomorrow on Yesterday's Strength* (2004), 36–49.

93. Chan, *Paths of Justice*, 15.

94. *New Gazette*, March 1990.

95. *SCMP*, 23 May & 1 November 1989; Ghai, *Hong Kong's New Constitutional Order*, 56–61.

approach was adopted, with universal suffrage as the ultimate aim, but with no timetable for achieving it.

Another issue was who should interpret the Basic Law. The first draft vested this power in the Standing Committee of the NPC, reflecting a distinction in Chinese law between interpretation and adjudication – a distinction that does not exist in common law. The Joint Declaration did not mention interpretation of the Basic Law but stipulated that final adjudication would be vested in the courts of the Hong Kong SAR. In the end, after much debate, a compromise was reached: the Hong Kong courts were authorized to interpret provisions in the Basic Law that were within the autonomy of the SAR, while provisions concerning affairs that were the responsibility of the CPG or concerning relations between the Central Authorities and the SAR were to be referred to the Standing Committee.[96] Before making an interpretation, the Standing Committee was required to consult its committee on the Basic Law: the first Hong Kong SAR Basic Law Committee, appointed on 1 July 1997 included among its legal experts Albert Chen from the Faculty of Law at HKU, who has remained a member ever since. In 2010 Chen was awarded a Silver Bauhinia Star by the Hong Kong SAR government in recognition of his contributions to the development of law in Hong Kong, 'particularly his balanced views on issues involving the Basic Law to facilitate constructive discussion in the community.'[97]

Interpretation by the NPC's Standing Committee was to be a point of friction in some cases after 1997. But even before 1997 a disputed interpretation led to the shelving of one of the key elements of the 'judicial through-train', the creation of a court of final appeal in Hong Kong before 1997. The Basic Law provided for a Court of Final Appeal (CFA) to be established in the Hong Kong SAR with the power of final adjudication. By any standards this was a remarkable devolution of power, virtually without precedent even in the most loosely federated of countries. Furthermore, only the Chief Justice and the Chief Judge of the High Court (formerly the Supreme Court) were required to be Chinese citizens and permanent residents of Hong Kong with no right of abode in any foreign country. The CFA could invite judges from other common law jurisdictions to sit on appeals. Apart from some changes in nomenclature,[98] the creation of the CFA was to be the only important change in the judicial system. All other provisions emphasized continuity. Mechanisms for ensuring judicial independence were maintained and strengthened. Judges were to continue to be appointed on the basis of their judicial and professional qualities and could be recruited from other common law jurisdictions. They could continue to serve through 1997 – as indeed most of them did.[99]

---

96. Basic Law Article 158; Ghai, *Hong Kong's New Constitutional Order*, Chapter 5.

97. Hong Kong SAR Government, press release '2010 Honours List', 1 July 2010.

98. The Supreme Court was renamed the High Court, and the High Court (the lower division of the Supreme Court) was renamed the Court of First Instance.

99. Basic Law, Articles 80–96.

The British and Hong Kong governments intended the CFA to take over the functions of the Privy Council for Hong Kong several years before 1997 so that it could gain legitimacy, develop jurisprudence, and promote confidence in the judicial system. In 1991 the Sino-British Joint Liaison Group – the body negotiating details of the transfer of power – agreed that the CFA would consist of the Chief Justice, three other Hong Kong judges, and a fifth judge who might be either a serving or retired local judge or a judge from another common law jurisdiction. Neither the Basic Law nor the Joint Declaration specified the precise composition of the CFA but simply stated that it 'may as required invite judges from other common law jurisdictions.'[100] Critics claimed that any limit on the number of overseas judges breached this provision. A bitter dispute ensued between the professional bodies and Hong Kong and British officials. In December 1992 Simon Ip, the representative of the legal functional constituency on the Legislative Council, moved a motion calling for the CFA to have greater flexibility to invite overseas judges in accordance with the Joint Declaration and the Basic Law. The motion was passed by a large majority.[101]

This was, as the journalist Frank Ching observed, 'the first time in history that the Hong Kong legislature had stood up to oppose an agreement reached by Britain and China on the future of Hong Kong.' It was another four years before new proposals were put forward. These were announced in May 1995 by the Preliminary Working Committee of the Preparatory Committee for the Hong Kong SAR – the body appointed by the NPC after the rift with Governor Patten over constitutional reform. Although they were more detailed, the proposals kept the 1992 formula: for each hearing, the CFA was to consist of the four permanent judges and a fifth judge drawn from a panel of up to thirty Hong Kong and overseas non-permanent judges (NPJs). The CFA was to be established on 1 July 1997. The plan became the basis for a revised agreement by the Joint Liaison Group, achieved after tense negotiations in which the Chinese side argued for further restrictions and British officials, fearing a judicial vacuum, threatened unilateral action, even if that risked dismantling the court in 1997. As the sense of urgency grew, the desire for a solution within Hong Kong increased, although the Bar Association maintained its opposition and academics continued to have misgivings.[102] In July 1995 the Legislative Council passed the Hong Kong Court of Final Appeal Ordinance by thirty-eight votes to seventeen, providing for the CFA to be established on 1 July 1997. A motion of no confidence in Patten, accusing him of U-turns on the CFA, was defeated, but it was the first no-confidence motion against a governor in

---

100. Basic Law, Article 82.

101. *Hong Kong Hansard*, 4 December 1991; Alison Conner, 'Final Appeal Court Proposal Stirs Controversy in Hong Kong', *East Asian Executive Reports*, 15 November 1991; Young, Da Rosa, & Ghai, 'Genesis of Hong Kong's Court of Final Appeal' in Simon Young & Yash P. Ghai, *Hong Kong's Court of Final Appeal: The Development of the Law in China's Hong Kong* (Cambridge: Cambridge University Press), 2014.

102. See, for example, Mushkat, 'The Joint Declaration and the CFA Agreement', 26 *HKLJ* (1996), 277–81.

Hong Kong's history. Moved by members of the Democratic Party, allies of Patten on most other issues, it was proof that parliamentary politics had arrived in Hong Kong.

Opposition to the limit on overseas judges had been a matter of principle. But it also reflected practical concerns that Hong Kong lacked the judicial talent to form a credible CFA – all nine justices of appeal were due to retire before 1997 – and that local judges would be more easy to control. These concerns faded when appointments to the CFA were announced. They vanished entirely as the new court rapidly gained a reputation for independence and efficiency. Andrew Li, the first Chief Justice of the Hong Kong SAR, earned widespread respect for his principled approach to the rule of law and skilful management of the Judiciary in difficult times. He provided 'clear and firm leadership' and 'put together a formidable team of both local and foreign judges,' concluded Yash Ghai in his introduction to a survey of the CFA's first thirteen years, edited by him and his colleague in the Faculty, Simon Young.[103]

The first permanent judges of the CFA, in addition to Chief Justice Li, were Henry Litton, Charles Ching, and Kemal Bokhary, eminent barristers with a combined experience at the Hong Kong Bar of over eighty years before they joined the bench in the years leading up to 1997. Each had connections with the Faculty of Law: Ching had been an external examiner for the PCLL; Bokhary, like Andrew Li, had been an honorary lecturer; and Litton had been a member of the Faculty Board. In 2000 Ching and Litton retired and their places were filled by Patrick Chan, the first Chief Judge of the High Court of the Hong Kong SAR (1997–2000) and a leading expert on the use of Chinese in the courts, and Robert Ribeiro, who had joined the Judiciary in 1999. Ribeiro had begun his career as a lecturer in the Department of Law at HKU 1972–1980. Patrick Chan (LLB 1974) was the first HKU law graduate to be appointed to the CFA; the second, Andrew Cheung (LLB 1983) was appointed in 2018 after serving for seven years as Chief Judge.

The CFA has two panels of NPJs: overseas NPJs and Hong Kong NPJs. The early overseas NPJs included former chief justices of Australia and New Zealand, British law lords, and other eminent judges from these jurisdictions. Chief Justice Li established the convention of inviting one overseas NPJ to sit with the four Hong Kong permanent judges on each hearing. The presence of some of the leading jurists in the common law world has brought many benefits. Working with the permanent judges, they have helped the CFA develop its own jurisprudence while remaining open to new developments in other jurisdictions. They have drawn on CFA judgments in interpreting the law in their own jurisdictions. And, because only one overseas NPJ sits on each case, they have never dominated the court. No matter where a judge comes from, said Sir Anthony Mason, the longest-serving NPJ

---

103. Ghai, 'Themes and Arguments' in Young & Ghai, *Hong Kong's Court of Final Appeal*, 23–4.

(1997–2015), he 'needs to see himself primarily as a Hong Kong judge, serving its community and seeing legal problems through a Hong Kong lens.'[104]

Within a short time the CFA gained the confidence of people in Hong Kong and acquired an international reputation for the quality of its jurisprudence. Given the delays in creating the court, and the unprecedented nature of Hong Kong's transition from colony to SAR, this was no small achievement. It came with its own difficulties. At the Faculty of Law's thirtieth anniversary dinner on 4 June 1999, Chief Justice Li spoke of Hong Kong's historic position 'in the early and exciting (perhaps sometimes too exciting) stage of a new constitutional order.' The parenthesis referred to an unfolding drama in the courts that was causing alarm in the legal profession. In January the CFA had ruled unconstitutional a law that restricted the right of abode in Hong Kong of Mainland-born children of Hong Kong permanent residents by requiring them to obtain permits under a quota system before entering the territory, even though they had a right of abode under the Basic Law. In the months leading up to July 1997, several thousand such children had entered Hong Kong illegally in expectation of enjoying this right – a right not extended to them under colonial rule. The SAR government was anxious that many thousands more would enter Hong Kong if restrictions were not imposed. In its judgment – its first on a constitutional issue – the CFA laid down general principles about its constitutional jurisdiction under the Basic Law, declaring that, within the high degree of autonomy conferred on the SAR, it was for the courts to determine whether an act of the NPC or its Standing Committee was inconsistent with the Basic Law.[105]

The judgment was welcomed by lawyers in Hong Kong as a robust statement of the rule of law. But the assertion of a power to declare invalid acts of the NPC brought to a head the question of who ultimately should interpret the Basic Law. Legal experts in Mainland China were outraged, accusing the court of putting itself above the sovereign power.[106] In February, at the request of the SAR government, the court reconvened to clarify that it did not question the authority of the NPC's Standing Committee to make its own interpretations of the Basic Law, as provided in Article 158 of the Basic Law.[107] On 26 June, at the

---

104. Quoted in Young & Da Roza, 'The Judges' in Young & Ghai, *Hong Kong's Court of Final Appeal*, 265.

105. *Ng Ka Ling and others v the Director of Immigration* (1999) 2 HKCFAR 4. William Clarke, a former law lecturer at HKU, was an instructing solicitor in this and several other right of abode cases.

106. New China News Agency press release carrying views of Professors Xiao Weiyun, Wu Jianfan, Shao Tianren, and Xu Chongde, 6 February 1999, in *Ta Kung Pao*, 7 February 1999, translated in Johannes Chan, Fu Hualing, & Yash P. Ghai (eds.), *Hong Kong's Constitutional Debate: Conflict Over Interpretation* (Hong Kong: Hong Kong University Press, 2000), 53–9.

107. *Ng Ka Ling and others v the Director of Immigration (No. 2)* (1999) 2 HKCFAR 141. For comments on this unusual development see Ghai, 'A Play in Two Acts: Reflections on the Theatre of the Law', 29 *HKLJ* (1999), 5–7, & Johannes Chan, *Paths of Justice*, 30–4: Chan, led by Clive Grossman SC, had represented the Bar Association in its unsuccessful application to intervene to oppose the government's request.

request of the SAR government, the Standing Committee issued the first such interpretation, reinstating the restrictions on the right of abode and the permit system which the CFA had earlier declared invalid.[108] Despite assurances from the SAR government that it would seek interpretations from Beijing only in rare cases, many in Hong Kong saw the intervention as a blow to 'one country, two systems.' In December 1999 fears of an even greater crisis were averted when the CFA upheld the validity of the June interpretation, declaring it binding on the courts in Hong Kong, and acknowledged that the Standing Committee of the NPC had a general power to make interpretations of the Basic Law without reference from the CFA. Some scholars saw this as an 'almost defeatist' retreat from the bold assertions in *Ng Ka Ling*.[109] Others regarded it as a tactical way of averting further curtailments of its jurisdiction,[110] or an attempt to achieve a 'golden mean', 'neither too proud nor too humble'.[111] In the light of later judgments by the CFA, the general view has emerged that it was one of a series of adjustments as the court ascertained its powers under an unprecedented new system – a stage, in Po Jen Yap's words, in 'the rise, retreat and resurgence' of independent judicial power.[112]

Further litigation on the right of abode followed as the courts heard representations on behalf of Mainland-born children still in Hong Kong. In the *Director of Immigration v Chong Fung Yuen*, involving a boy born in Hong Kong to parents visiting from the Mainland, the CFA held that the right of abode of 'Chinese citizens born in Hong Kong' in the Basic Law could not possibly mean that their parents were also required to have the right of abode or be settled in Hong Kong at the time of birth, as the Director of Immigration had argued.[113] In *Tam Nga Yin v Director of Immigration* (2001) the CFA held that the right of abode did not extend to Mainland-born children adopted by parents in Hong Kong.[114] In *Ng Siu Tung v Director of Immigration* (2002) – 'the case of the Five Thousand'[115] – the court considered claims by over 5,000 Mainland-born children who had been given assurances by the government that they would be dealt with in the same way as the parties in the original *Ng Ka Ling* case: under the Basic Law, judgments previously rendered were not affected by the Standing Committee's interpretation. The court found that, although the Standing

---

108. Interpretation by the Standing Committee of the NPC of Articles 22(4) and 24(2)(3) of the Basic Law, *Hong Kong Government Gazette*, LN 167 of 1999, 26 June 1999.

109. Johannes Chan, 'Basic Law and Constitutional Review: The First Decade', 37 *HKLJ* (2007), 420.

110. Benny Tai, 'Chapter 1 of Hong Kong's New Constitution' in Ming K. Chan & Alvin Y. So (Eds.), *Crisis and Transformation in China's Hong Kong* (Hong Kong: Hong Kong University Press, 2002), 205.

111. Albert H.Y. Chen, 'Constitutional Adjudication in Post-1997 Hong Kong', 15 *Pacific Rim Law and Policy Journal* (2006), 629.

112. Po Jen Yap, '10 Years of the Basic Law: the Rise, Retreat and Resurgence of Judicial Power in Hong Kong' 36 *Common Law World Review* (2007), 166–91.

113. *Director of Immigration v Chong Fung Yuen* (2001) 4 HKCFAR 211.

114. *Tam Nga Yin and others v Director of Immigration* (2001) 4 HKCFAR 251. Tam's counsel was Patrick Szeto (LLB 1994).

115. Kemal Bokhary, *Recollections* (Hong Kong: Sweet & Maxwell, 2013), 567–9.

Committee's interpretation had extinguished any immediate claim to a right of abode, about 1,000 of these claimants, who fell broadly into the same category as the parties in *Ng Ka Ling*, had been given a legitimate expectation in common law that they would be allowed to remain in Hong Kong: it therefore quashed the removal orders issued against them by the Director of Immigration. *Ng Siu Tung* was among several early CFA judgments that became influential throughout the common law world.[116]

The right of abode cases were heard amid campaigns by the government – seen by some as scaremongering – to drive home the impact on Hong Kong if restrictions were not placed on Mainland-born children eligible for the right of abode: the estimate soon reached 1.675 million children, requiring 242 new schools, 13 housing estates, and 11 hospitals.[117] Claimants' families and supporters kept vigil outside the courts. Children whose fate was in the balance filled the public galleries; some, naturally, fell asleep.[118] One litigant who did not attend any hearings was Agnes Tam Nga-yin, whose claim to the right of abode was rejected by the CFA in 2001 and who learned about her early life from press coverage of her case only a week before final judgment was given. Born in 1986 in a small village in Guangdong, Agnes was the fourth daughter of biological parents who could not afford to keep her. Adopted by a Hong Kong couple when she was only a few months old, she spent her early years in Shenzhen before entering Hong Kong on a travel visa in 1996. When the visa expired she stayed on as an undocumented child: 'No schooling. No socialization. No friends. It went on for a year and a half. I was constantly afraid of being caught by the police. I dared not go out during school hours. I didn't have much clue why I had to live like that because (I thought) I was a child of a Hong Kong couple.' Wishing to protect her, Agnes's mother had only told her that being born in Mainland China had made things complicated. With help from NGOs, Agnes started school in 1998 – 'the best years of my life.' The prospect of deportation when her case failed was devastating. But she was permitted to remain in Hong Kong after petitions from her teachers and schoolmates. Her experience inspired her to study law, and in 2006 she entered the LLB programme at HKU. Not wanting to be identified as 'Tam Nga-yin, the adopted child from the Mainland' she was relieved to find that her case, while significant, was not a focus of study in the course on Constitutional Law.[119]

---

116. *Ng Siu Tung and others v the Director of Immigration* (2002) 5 HKCFAR 1. For its impact see Andrew S.Y. Li & Hester Wai-San Leung, 'The Doctrine of Substantive Legitimate Expectation', 32 *HKLJ* (2002), 471–96, & P.Y. Lo, 'Impact of jurisprudence beyond Hong Kong', in Young & Ghai (eds.), *Hong Kong's Court of Final Appeal*, 600.

117. 'Assessment of Service Implication in Relation to the Judgment of the Court of Final Appeal on the Right of Abode Issue', 6 May 1999, in Chan, Fu & Ghai, *Hong Kong's Constitutional Debate*, 274–87; *SCMP*, 29 April–7 May 1999; *Hong Kong Hansard*, 28 April 1999; Minutes of a Special Meeting of the Legislative Council House Committee, 6 May 1999.

118. 'It's very boring and I don't know what they're talking about,' said one of the children in Ng Ka-ling's case while it was being heard by the Court of First Instance: *SCMP*, 19 September 1997.

119. Agnes Tam, interview with the author, 7 September 2018; *Ming Pao*, 25 July 2001.

Lawyers and the Transition

'How secure is our new legal order?' asked Raymond Wacks in his introduction to *The New Legal Order in Hong Kong*, published on the Faculty of Law's thirtieth anniversary in 1999 amid fears that 'the legal controversy currently enveloping Hong Kong' might soon be 'overshadowed by new calamities that arise as the fledgling SAR learns to fly.' The analysis in chapters by over twenty Faculty members pointed to work that remained to be done. But it also suggested there were 'few grounds for pessimism.' The common law was 'a hardy plant, difficult to uproot,' wrote Wacks. 'The culture and traditions of our system, whatever its imperfections, seem destined to endure for the next ten years, and well beyond.'[120] The interpretation of 26 June 1999, coming so soon after the establishment of the SAR, nevertheless came as a shock to many lawyers. Confidence in the survival of the common law received a jolt, wrote Jill Cottrell and Yash Ghai in a postscript to an otherwise largely optimistic article on the legal profession published in 1999. The interpretation was seen as 'a deadly blow to the standing of the Hong Kong judiciary.'[121] Some CFA judges talked about resigning but decided that the rule of law would be weakened if they were replaced by less independent judges.[122] Shortly after the interpretation, on 30 June 1999, about 600 lawyers, academics, and law students, all dressed in black, walked in silent procession from the High Court to the CFA: the aim, said the organizers, was to show respect for the rule of law, not to mourn its death.[123]

Lawyers held similar protests in 2005, 2014, and 2016 after other interventions from Beijing, and in 2019 against a bill proposed by the SAR government that would have enabled extraditions to Mainland China. Mute processions by men and women who relied on language for their livelihood became a Hong Kong SAR tradition. Many older traditions were retained after 1997. Royal insignia were replaced by the emblem of the SAR. Prosecutions were now brought by the Hong Kong SAR and not in the name of the Queen. Queen's Counsel appointed in Hong Kong were renamed Senior Counsel. The Attorney General was now called the Secretary for Justice. Otherwise, much remained the same. English continued to be used, particularly in the higher courts, despite an increase in cases heard in Chinese. Judges and barristers kept their horsehair wigs.[124] The courtroom

---

120. Raymond Wacks (ed.), *The New Legal Order in Hong Kong* (Hong Kong: Hong Kong University Press, 1999), 1 & 6.

121. Jill Cottrell and Yash P. Ghai, 'The Legal Profession and Transfer of Sovereignty: Hong Kong' in Rob McQueen and W Wesley Pue (Eds.), *Misplaced Traditions: British lawyers, colonial peoples* (Leichhardt: Federation Press, 1999).

122. *SCMP*, 8 September 2011; Bokhary, *Recollections*, 582.

123. *SCMP*, 1 July 1999.

124. Judges of the new CFA wear a simple black gown and lace jabot, but, like judges on the Judicial Committee of the Privy Council, do not wear wigs. A few years after 1997, magistrates, who had formerly worn standard business attire, began to appear in black gowns in court.

remained a 'haven of formalism', a theatre of elaborate etiquette and arcane language – 'May it please your Lordship...', 'I'm much obliged', and so on – at least for cases heard in English.[125] The ceremonial opening of the legal year continued much as before. Judges and lawyers chose to maintain these customs during this time not only of great legal change but also of massive growth in the legal profession.

In 1999 the number of lawyers in private practice in Hong Kong was nearly 5,500 – over twenty-two times the number in 1969, when the Department of Law at HKU was founded. In addition, there were over 300 government lawyers, about 170 judges and magistrates, and 100 or so full-time law teachers, bringing the number of actively employed legally qualified personnel to over 6,000. In the mid-1960s, when advancing arguments for a law school, the Attorney General, Maurice Heenan, had suggested a desirable lawyer-to-population ratio of 1:7,000; the ratio for Hong Kong at the time was about 1:12,000. By 1999 the ratio – at about 1:1,400 – far exceeded this yardstick, reflecting a more sophisticated society, a more diverse economy, and a more complex legal system than even Heenan's ambitious projections had envisaged.[126]

The number of practising barristers in private practice rose from 44 in 1969 to about 700 in 1999. The majority – over 80 per cent in 1999 – were men. Fifty-one were Senior Counsel with at least ten years' experience: Sir Oswald Cheung SC, who headed the list, had practised for forty-eight years. Another 30 per cent had over twelve years' experience, and 40 per cent had less than seven years'.[127] Men and women of Hong Kong origin accounted for about 70 per cent of the private bar in 1999, including many Senior Counsel.[128] Since the early 1990s most new entrants to the profession had taken the PCLL, either at HKU or City University. Insufficient places in solicitors' firms in the early 1990s had led to an increase in the number of local graduates seeking to become barristers.[129] A substantial minority of new entrants, including many from Hong Kong, had also joined the profession with qualifications from the UK and other Commonwealth countries: this second route to

---

125. Ng Kwai-hang, *The Common Law in Two Voices: Language, Law and the Postcolonial Dilemma in Hong Kong* (Stanford: Stanford University Press, 2009). This study compares trials in English and Chinese under Hong Kong's bilingual legal system: see especially Chapters 4 & 6. The old modes of address in English have proved difficult to translate into modern Cantonese and often appear ridiculous where they are attempted. One of Ng's themes is the comparative informality of trials held in Chinese, particularly in the lower courts, where the removal of linguistic barriers has introduced a new dynamic in the courtroom.

126. See Chapter 2.

127. Hong Kong Bar Association, *List of Practising Barristers* (March 1999) & Hong Kong Bar Association, *Annual Statement 1998/99*, Appendix I, & *Annual Report 1999*, 10.

128. The fifty-one Senior Counsel included about thirty who were Hong Kong-born and several others with Hong Kong connections that predated their entry into the private bar: among these were two former attorneys general, seven other ex-government lawyers, two sons of Hong Kong judges, and the grandson of a chief interpreter of the Supreme Court. Eleven of the fifty-one Senior Counsel held law degrees from HKU.

129. *SCMP*, 18 December 1992.

practice was reformed in 2003, when, to meet Hong Kong's obligations as a member of the World Trade Organization, the Bar was opened to lawyers qualified in any country, subject to their passing an exam and meeting other criteria.[130] Queen's Counsel from England and elsewhere continued to be admitted for specific cases, often against objections from the Bar Council.

Solicitors increased at an even faster rate: in 1969 there were fewer than 200; in 1999 there were 4,726 in active practice. Two-thirds of these, most with PCLLs from HKU or City University, had been admitted in the 1990s. A growing number of new admissions – nearly half in the late 1990s – were women. In addition, there were over 600 trainee solicitors – the new term for articled clerks from 1991. About 78 per cent of solicitors in 1999 were of Chinese ethnic origin.[131] Apart from sheer numbers, the contours of the profession had changed. Solicitors' firms – numbering 610 in 1999 – had become larger while the proportion of sole practitioners had declined. In addition to serving Hong Kong's own varied needs, many were providing legal services to businesses in Mainland China. Several of the larger UK firms had set up branches in Hong Kong. Firms from over a dozen other countries had registered under the system introduced in 1994. Registered foreign lawyers were not allowed to practise Hong Kong law. However, another scheme, similar to the later scheme for barristers, allowed solicitors from other jurisdictions to practise in Hong Kong on passing an exam and meeting other criteria. The first Overseas Lawyers Qualification Examination, held in late 1995, attracted 135 candidates from 12 jurisdictions, including the PRC and Japan. Solicitors with UK qualifications were exempted until December 1997, when the automatic right of admission enjoyed for the previous 153 years came to an end.[132]

The professional bodies increased their support for the rising numbers of new or prospective entrants. In 1994 the Bar Association undertook a review of pupillage, led by Anselmo Reyes, a former law lecturer at HKU (1986–1988), which formulated minimum standards and a 'canon' of work that every pupil should encounter.[133] In the same year the Bar Association established a special committee on young barristers to promote professional development. In 1999 the association expanded its continuing professional education to include an Advanced Legal Education programme of lectures and seminars, organized

---

130. The Barristers Qualification Examination, set by the Bar Association and held annually from 2004. Lawyers from overseas seeking admission as barristers were also required to have practised for at least three years in their own jurisdictions. Legal Practitioners (Amendment) Ordinance, No. 42 of 2000; Barristers (Qualification for Admission and Pupillage) Rules 2003.

131. Law Society of Hong Kong, *Annual Report 1999*, 14–15.

132. Administered by the Law Society, the exam varied according to whether the applicant was from a common law or non-common law jurisdiction. Applicants were required to have had five years' experience in their own jurisdictions. Various exemptions applied according to experience and qualifications. Overseas Lawyers (Qualification for Admission) Rules 1994; Law Society of Hong Kong, *Annual Report 1995*, 38–9 & *Annual Report 1997*, 9.

133. Hong Kong Bar Association, *Annual Statement 1994/1995*, 36–7.

by Carol Chen (LLB 1982). An initiative by the chairman for that year, Ronny Tong (LLB 1972), resulted in the admission of academic and student members with the aim of ensuring 'that there is new blood in our younger generation to continue our work.'[134] In 1991, following developments elsewhere in the world, the Law Society implemented a points-based scheme of mandatory continuing legal education, initially for trainee solicitors and solicitors in their first year, and later for other solicitors. In 1998, when it was remodelled as Continuing Professional Development, the scheme embraced some 900 accredited courses, arranged by the Law Society or by firms with their own in-house training. The Faculty of Law, which had for many years provided continuing legal education, became one of the accredited providers.[135] Another initiative by the Law Society was the founding of the Advocacy Institute of Hong Kong in 1993, aimed at raising standards of advocacy through skills-based workshops.[136]

Lawyers sat on the Law Reform Commission's subcommittees and other advisory bodies. They participated in politics, some as candidates in elections. Pro bono work flourished, as lawyers gave free advice to charitable organizations and people in need, including the growing numbers of Vietnamese boat people held in difficult and dangerous conditions in closed camps until a scheme of repatriation was implemented in the 1990s for those not granted refugee status. Solicitors and barristers took part in the expanding Duty Lawyer Service, providing representation at low cost to defendants in the magistrates' and juvenile courts, and advised other members of the public through the Free Legal Advice Scheme. Through their professional bodies, they commented on the many proposals for changes in the law in the 1980s and 1990s. 'In all the years that lawyers have flourished in Hong Kong,' said the Attorney General, Michael Thomas, in 1988, 'I doubt whether so many private lawyers have ever before devoted their time so whole-heartedly to public business.'[137]

Much of this public business consisted of quiet committee work aimed at reforming the law, improving the legal system, and ensuring a smooth transition. But a great deal of it was also contentious and highly visible. The long standoff over the CFA and the widespread dismay over the intervention in the right of abode episode were the largest of the conflicts. Barristers were also concerned about the legitimacy or otherwise of the Provisional Legislature and plans for the non-adoption or repeal of certain legislation deemed to be

---

134. Hong Kong Bar Association, *1999 Annual Statement*, 7

135. *New Gazette*, November 1990; *Hong Kong Lawyer*, September 2008; 'Continuing Legal Education', 4 March 1999, HKUA: Board of the Faculty of Law – Minutes (1999).

136. The institute got off to a rocky start when the Bar Association, seeing it as a move towards extending rights of audience of solicitors, declined to give support. The Chief Justice, who had initially agreed to be its patron, then also withheld his support. *SCMP*, 18 & 20 January 1993.

137. Speech by Michael Thomas QC at the Ceremonial Opening of the Legal Year, 11 January 1988, *Law Society Gazette*, February 1988.

politically unacceptable.[138] These were matters of fundamental principle affecting Hong Kong's future freedoms, on which the Bar Council would not compromise. Generally, and with some exceptions,[139] the Bar as a whole was more politically engaged, while solicitors took a more practical approach and, having links with Mainland businesses, tended to be more accommodating of the official Chinese perspective. 'All in all,' observed Cottrell and Ghai in their survey of the profession in 1999, 'the Bar has presented itself as far more a potential protector of the common law and of human rights than the solicitors.'[140]

While relations between Hong Kong and the CPG loomed large in the debates among lawyers, some of the most acrimonious controversies were about domestic issues. The dispute between the Law Society and the government over the admission of foreign lawyers simmered for years before a compromise was agreed. In the mid-1990s, a time of escalating property prices, the government proposed to abolish 'scale fees', under which solicitors charged for conveyancing according to the value of the property. The Law Society dug in its feet, arguing that that price wars would erupt – even that legal education would become less attractive to young people and the rule of law would be threatened. Scale fees were eventually abolished in 1997, shortly before the Asian financial crisis of that year triggered a sharp decline in property prices and transactions.[141] Among other issues between the profession and the government during this decade were calls for an independent legal aid agency, resisted by the government, and a policy by the Legal Department, following audit criticisms, of reducing fees for prosecutions briefed out to barristers.

The two branches of the profession were also at loggerheads with each other on various turf issues. In 1993 the Law Society published proposals for a fused legal profession, following the practice in many other jurisdictions, arguing that it would reduce costs and make

---

138. These included removal of the entrenchment provisions in the Bill of Rights Ordinance and the reinstatement of restrictive provisions in the Societies and Public Order Ordinances that had been repealed in the light of the Bill of Rights. The Bar Association insisted that the only criterion for non-adoption of any existing law should be that it contravened the Basis Law. Hong Kong Bar Association, *Annual Statement 1996/1997*, 59–78.

139. In particular, a substantial 'rebel' element of younger solicitors opposed the Law Society's change of view over the CFA in 1995: *SCMP*, 22 January 1995; *New Gazette*, February 1995.

140. The differences were baldly illustrated when, in 1994, Martin Lee and Szeto Wah, prominent members of the Democratic Party, wished to sue Simon Li, a retired justice of appeal who was then a member of the Basic Law Drafting Committee and the Preparatory Committee, for defamation. Li had accused them of appealing to people to make a run on Mainland-funded banks after the 1989 Tiananmen Square incident. Nine of Hong Kong's leading solicitors' firms refused to take the case, some admitting they feared losing Mainland business. Lee and Szeto later shelved the case. Meanwhile, the Faculty of Law held a symposium entitled 'In Fear of China: Lawyers and the Public Interest', the proceedings of which were brought out in a Faculty publication: Raymond Wacks (Ed.), *The Right to Representation: Problems and Prospects* (Hong Kong: Faculty of Law, HKU, 1994). Cottrell & Ghai, 'The Legal Profession and Transfer of Sovereignty: Hong Kong', 133–6; *SCMP*, 21, 25, 28, & 29 July 1993 & 4 February 1996; Minutes of the meeting on 8 September 1993, HKUA: Board of the Faculty of Law – Minutes (1993).

141. These and other controversies are discussed in Cottrell & Ghai, 'The Legal Profession and Transfer of Sovereignty: Hong Kong'.

justice more efficient. Barristers rejected this: some claimed that if it were to happen their 'more outspoken branch of the profession would be wiped out.'[142] The Bar also opposed extending rights of audience to solicitors in the higher courts. These disputes at least prompted a reasoned pamphlet debate, concluding in attempts by the Attorney General to encourage a general discussion of the future of legal services.[143] But relations reached a nadir when a quarrel between the two branches over the official Chinese translation of the word 'barrister' delayed by over a year the first authentic translation of the Interpretation and General Clauses Ordinance (Cap. 1), the source of key legal definitions and an essential part of the Bilingual Laws Programme.[144] By late 1995, relations had worsened to such an extent that, in the words of Johannes Chan, 'the two branches of the profession could hardly co-operate on any issue.'[145] Even the united opposition to a limit on the number of overseas judges on the CFA, which had prompted a rare joint statement by the two professional bodies in 1991, had broken down as the Law Society changed its stance and supported the 1995 bill.

Quarrels between the two branches, along with instances of touting and outright fraud by some lawyers, led to what the president of the Law Society described as 'a diminution of the respect with which the profession is held by the public.'[146] Legal services were said to be among the most expensive in the world: the cost of litigation was 'absolutely disgraceful', far exceeding that in London, complained one judge in 1996, while standards of competence were falling.[147] The disputes merged with other anxieties about the quality of the legal system at the very time when the rule of law was being proclaimed as the mainstay of Hong Kong's way of life. A series of scandals, large and small, plagued the Judiciary and the Legal Department, prompting resignations and culminating in the conviction of the Deputy Director of Prosecutions, Warwick Reid, on corruption charges.[148] As caseloads

142. The opposite had happened during the brief fusion of the profession engineered by barristers in 1858–1864, which prompted a flight of attorneys from Hong Kong: see Chapter 1.

143. Law Society of Hong Kong, *The Future of the Legal Profession* (1993); Hong Kong Bar Association, *The Future of the Legal Profession* (1994); *Consultation Paper on Legal Services* (1995). Under amendments to the Legal Practitioners Ordinance in 2010, solicitors with at least five years' practice and sufficient experience of litigation became eligible to apply for the right of audience as 'solicitor-advocates' in the High Court and Court of Final Appeal. Ordinance Nos. 52 of 1995 & 2 of 2010. Earlier, in 1995, solicitors with ten years' practice also became eligible to serve as High Court judges.

144. The traditional translation of 'barrister' in Hong Kong is 大律師, meaning literally 'big lawyer'. Solicitors (known simply as 律師 – or 'lawyer') did not like this. Various alternative terms were proposed, but in the end the old terms were retained. *SCMP*, 19 & 28 August, 28 & 30 October 1990, 13 May 1991, 9 June 1992, 29 November 1993.

145. Chan, 'To Change of Not to Change: The Crumpling Legal System' in Nyaw Mee-kau & Li Si-ming (Eds.), *The Other Hong Kong Report 1996*, 19.

146. Anthony Chow, President's Report, Law Society of Hong Kong, *Annual Report 1999*, 7.

147. Godfrey JA, in a speech at the Inside Asia Conference, reported in *SCMP*, 28 April 1996.

148. Judges resigning in the late 1980s included Denis Barker, who had presided over the catastrophic Carrian trial; the flamboyant Miles Jackson-Lipkin, who had lied about his age in *Who's Who* and had been seen on public

increased and proceedings became more complex, waiting times for trials were longer than ever, peaking in the mid-1990s. The delays and inefficiencies of the courts became a political issue and a matter that engaged the Bill of Rights. The government sent in one of its ablest administrative officers, an early HKU law graduate, Alice Tai (LLB 1974), as the first Judiciary Administrator, to help the Judiciary modernize.

In contrast to the fears about a legal brain drain in the aftermath of Tiananmen, the view in the 1990s was that the legal profession as a whole had grown too rapidly and was now oversupplied – that there was, as one observer remarked, 'a shortage of good lawyers but in general an oversupply of lawyers.'[149] The problem was exacerbated by the property market slump triggered by the Asian financial crisis 1997–1998, which forced solicitors' firms to lay off staff.[150] But concerns about numbers and quality had begun some years earlier. In 1995 the chair of the Bar Association, Gladys Li QC, acknowledged 'very basic problems' among junior barristers, some of whom were 'not able to express themselves at all in court, either in English or Chinese.' The problem, she said, was rooted in the fact that some law graduates had enrolled as barristers simply because quotas for trainees in solicitors' firms were full. Many were unable to make a living.[151]

Two years later, the solicitor Simon Ip, a member of the Advisory Committee on Legal Education (ACLE), pointed to what many in the profession also saw as a decline in standards of English among trainee solicitors, stemming, he suggested, from a lowering of the average grades of students entering the two law schools. 'Because the universities in Hong Kong have more places to fill, their admission criteria is lower.' This resulted in 'mediocre solicitors doing mundane work while the big-ticket international cases are handled by overseas lawyers.'[152] Echoing this, international firms in Hong Kong preferred to recruit graduates from overseas law schools because local schools did not produce enough graduates of the standard they required.[153] Some observers also noted inflation in the degrees awarded: forty-four out of the sixty-one first-class LLBs from HKU from 1972 to 1999 were awarded in 1995–1999; only 4 per cent of graduates in the same years received thirds or passes, compared with 35 per cent in 1972–1976. The solicitors' profession was increasingly

occasions wearing medals for active service to which he was not entitled (an offence under the Army Act); and Patrick O'Dea, who had been caught reading the novel *Lady Chatterley's Lover* while hearing arguments in court. After a dramatic escape from Hong Kong, Warwick Reid was extradited from the Philippines and, in exchange for immunity from further prosecution for corruption offences, pleaded guilty to being in control of assets disproportionate to his emoluments under section 10(1)(b) of the Prevention of Bribery Ordinance. He was ordered to pay $12.4 million to the Crown and sentenced to eight years' imprisonment, later reduced to seven.

149. David Sai Hong Woo, quoted in Redmond & Roper, *Legal Education and Training in Hong Kong: Preliminary Review: Report of the Consultants* (August 2001), 91.

150. Anthony Chow, President's Report, Law Society of Hong Kong, *Annual Report 1999*, 7.

151. *SCMP*, 26 February & 23 March 1995.

152. *SCMP*, 9 February 1997.

153. Redmond-Roper Report, 82.

concerned about the 'genuineness' of the lower seconds – the largest class – awarded by the two universities.[154]

In the light of these concerns, the professional bodies considered measures to maintain standards. The improvements in continuing professional education and pupillage standards in the 1990s were part of this. Other ideas included English-language competency tests, separate entrance examinations for admission to the profession, and limits on the number of new entrants.[155] In 1997 the Law Society commissioned its own 'mini-study' of legal education. In 1998, after the society had lobbied interested parties, ACLE unanimously recommended a full-scale review of legal education 'in order to maintain the integrity of public confidence in the legal profession and to prepare lawyers for the demands of practice in the 21st century.'[156] The outcome of this review is discussed in the next chapter.

---

154. Redmond-Roper Report, 177; Lester Huang, Chairman, Legal Education Committee, Law Society of Hong Kong, 'Review of Legal Education and Training in Hong Kong', 26 March 2001, HKUA: Board of the Faculty of Law – Minutes (2001).

155. *SCMP*, 26 February; Ip to Litton, 12 March 1996, HKUA: Board of the Faculty of Law – Minutes (1996).

156. Anthony Chow, President's Report, Law Society of Hong Kong, *Annual Report 1999*, 7; Redmond-Roper Report', 4–6; Patrick Moss to Percy Ma, 12 April 1999, LC Paper No. CB(2)1693/98–99(05).

Chapter 7

A Special Standing in the World

The Faculty in the Twenty-First Century

By the end of the twentieth century the Faculty of Law had established itself as one of the leading law schools in East Asia. Its graduates were making their mark in a city that was no longer a backwater of English law but a flourishing jurisdiction, where common law intersected with China's civil law system, and where the courts grappled almost daily with fundamental questions under a new constitutional order. Faculty members and alumni were at the forefront of research in Hong Kong law. The Faculty now also contained the largest concentration of expertise on Chinese law outside Mainland China. Thanks to its extensive library, its partnerships with other universities, and its climate of free inquiry, it had become a magnet for research students from across the country and beyond.

'We aspire to be one of the best law schools in the world,' wrote Johannes Chan shortly after beginning his second term as Dean in 2005. 'We set ourselves to compete with the top law schools overseas, not just the local or even regional ones.'[1] With this in mind, the Faculty fixed its sights on building a more international profile. The staff and student body became more diverse. Partnerships with other universities gave students opportunities to take courses outside Hong Kong and brought large numbers of exchange students to the Faculty. Research projects focused increasingly on transnational questions and issues of global interest, clustered in seven broad areas of strategic development: public law and human rights; comparative Chinese law; commercial, corporate, and financial law; World Trade Organization (WTO) and international economic law; intellectual property and

---

1. Johannes Chan, interview in *Faculty of Law Newsletter*, Autumn 2005.

information technology; dispute settlement and negotiation; and professional legal education. This strategy brought unexpected recognition when, from 2012 onwards, the Faculty was consistently ranked among the top twenty law schools in the world. In 2012 the Faculty marked another milestone when it moved into its own building on HKU's new Centennial Campus.

These achievements came during a turbulent time for Hong Kong as financial crisis, social division and political disputes produced uncertainty, hardship and confrontation. The role of Faculty members in these processes is discussed in Chapter 8. This chapter explores the Faculty's institutional development in the first two decades of the twenty-first century, when it opened up to the world and reformed its curricula to meet the highest international standards. It begins with the Redmond-Roper Report of 2001, a harshly critical evaluation of Hong Kong's system of legal education – and of its legal profession – which concluded that much of it was not fit for purpose. Its key recommendation – to take practical legal training out of the universities – had far-reaching implications for all of the Faculty's teaching and research, confronting it with something approaching an existential crisis. Out of crisis came opportunity. The Faculty kept its legal training role by radically reforming the PCLL programme. Taking up other recommendations in the report, the Faculty also extended its LLB degree to a four-year programme, adding a much wider range of courses to reflect its increasingly global outlook.

Legal Education at the Turn of the Century: The Redmond-Roper Report

Paul Redmond was Dean of the Faculty of Law at the University of New South Wales. Christopher Roper was Director of the Centre for Legal Studies in Australia when the consultancy began, and was appointed Director of The College of Law Alliance while the review was in progress.[2] The review was initiated by the Law Society but its coordination was taken over by the Department of Justice in 1999, with funding from the government, the professional bodies, HKU, and City University. A steering committee chaired by the Solicitor General, Bob Allcock, a former law lecturer at HKU, was composed of representatives from the profession, the two law schools, the government and the Judiciary, and two lay members. The Faculty of Law at HKU was represented by Albert Chen (Dean) and Michael Wilkinson (Head of the Department of Professional Legal Education (DOPLE)). The consultants began their work in January 2000, issued a consultation paper in September,

---

2. The College of Law Alliance was a potential provider of the legal practice course recommended by Redmond and Roper as a replacement for the PCLL. At the request of the Steering Committee, Roper disclosed this potential conflict in the final report. Department of Justice, 'Consultation Paper on Legal Education and Training in Hong Kong: Preliminary Review', November 2000, Legislative Council Panel on Administration of Justice and Legal Services, LC Paper No. CB(2)338/00–01 (05); Redmond-Roper Report, 7.

and submitted their final report in August 2001. They made three visits to Hong Kong, held meetings with over sixty organizations and individuals, and received fifty-five written submissions. In a related study, GML Consulting Limited was tasked with identifying trends that would influence the future demand for legal services.[3]

The reports came at a time of mounting criticisms about the quality of recent law graduates and amid claims that, after decades of shortages, Hong Kong now had too many junior lawyers chasing after too little work. These concerns came in the wake of the Asian financial crisis 1997–1998, which damaged businesses and livelihoods across the region. The crisis had a prolonged impact on Hong Kong. Dramatic but unsuccessful speculative attacks aimed at breaking the peg between the Hong Kong dollar and the US dollar were followed by several years of debilitating deflation, high unemployment, plunging property prices, and retrenchment. The year 1998, observed the president of the Law Society, was one that many lawyers would prefer to forget. Solicitors' firms cut staff and engaged in price wars 'to gain a share of what was left of the conveyancing market.' The following year was even worse, as recession – which was to last until 2003 – began to take its toll, forcing some firms to close.[4]

At HKU, budget cuts, reductions in student and staff numbers, a move to fixed-term contracts for newer staff (in case of further cuts), and a drying up of promotion prospects had undermined morale and limited the Faculty's scope for development.[5] In a climate of austerity and encroaching managerialism the Faculty was increasingly required to justify its methods and output. The periodic Research Assessment Exercises (RAEs), which had an impact on funding, impressed on staff the importance of research and publication, preferably on topics of international interest: 'the only crucial factor is research performance,' a pro-vice-chancellor told staff at one promotion seminar.[6] The Faculty's research scored better than university and sector averages in the 1999 RAE. But an otherwise largely positive academic review by the university in 2000 bluntly concluded that, in its key function of educating students for legal practice, 'the Faculty's perception of professional needs was misdirected, and in obliging itself to be influenced by this perception the Faculty had curtailed its academic effectiveness to provide legal education in Hong Kong.'[7]

---

3. Redmond-Roper Report, 3–6; GML Consulting Limited, *Study on the Manpower Needs of the Legal Services Sector of Hong Kong, Final Report* (2001).

4. Anthony Chow, President's Report, Law Society of Hong Kong, *Annual Report 1998 & 1999*.

5. *Legal Education and Training in Hong Kong: Preliminary Review, Consultation Paper* (September 2000) (hereafter, 'Redmond-Roper Consultation Paper'), 78.

6. Faculty of Law, *Submission for the Review Panel* (2000), I, 25, & 'Department of Law: A Summary' in Redmond-Roper Consultation Paper, 5.

7. HKU, 'Report on the review of the Faculty of Law' (April 2000), para. 6.7, HKUA: Board of the Faculty of Law – Minutes (2000).

Redmond and Roper were concerned with teaching, not research. They were asked to assess the current system of legal education and training, to advise on a system best suited to the needs of Hong Kong in the twenty-first century, and to recommend improvements. Although tasked with assessing strengths as well as weaknesses, they drew a largely negative picture of the state of legal education and the legal profession in Hong Kong. This set the scene for their recommendations for radical changes to the professional stage of legal education in Hong Kong. The consultation paper, issued in September 2000, seemed to be 'pre-occupied with comments and criticisms of the PCLL curriculum,' observed one Faculty member.[8]

The consultants heard that students in Hong Kong were less motivated than students elsewhere and took a narrow, utilitarian approach to their education, directed mainly at passing exams. Rote learning, a characteristic of Hong Kong's schools, extended into the universities, where students still expected to be spoon-fed.[9] The continued reliance on lectures, tutorials, and examinations was an impediment to active learning and critical thinking. Insufficient resources and the pressure on teachers to research and publish had discouraged innovation in teaching. Budget cuts and mixed messages from university management had undermined staff morale.[10] Within the profession, legal services were too expensive, and the needs of the poor and 'sandwich class' were left unmet.[11] English-language proficiency, essential for an understanding of the common law, was declining.[12] Newly trained lawyers had difficulty communicating with their clients and lacked knowledge outside their own field of practice. There was an absence of a culture of service to the community and a feeling that law existed only to serve economic development.[13] An unhealthy preoccupation with conveyancing had spoilt many lawyers, who had lost the ability to to develop other areas of law when conveyancing collapsed in the late 1990s.[14] For all these reasons, the larger law firms in Hong Kong preferred to recruit lawyers trained overseas.[15]

The consultancy was framed as a *preliminary* review, but plans for a further review were not pursued. As a result, although it made 160 recommendations, many of its prescriptions

---

8. Minutes of meeting on 14 September 2000, HKUA: Board of the Faculty of Law – Minutes (2000). The consultation paper stressed that it was merely reporting views and not necessarily agreeing with them. However, as the City University Law School pointed out, the reliance on perceptions that were not necessarily backed up by evidence was problematic: 'it is an unwise policy maker who would proceed on the basis of perception alone.' City University of Hong Kong School of Law, Response to Consultation Paper, November 2000, in David Smith to Legislative Council Panel on Administration of Justice and Legal Services, 18 April 2001, LC Paper No. CB(2)1321/00–01, Appendix 1, 2.
9. Redmond-Roper Consultation Paper, 9–10 & 66–7.
10. Redmond-Roper Report, 251–4; Redmond-Roper Consultation Paper, 78–9.
11. Redmond-Roper Report, 58 & 72.
12. Redmond-Roper Consultation Paper, 10, 17.
13. Redmond-Roper Consultation Paper, 17; Redmond-Roper Report, 296–8.
14. Redmond-Roper Consultation Paper, 24; Redmond-Roper Report, 72.
15. Redmond-Roper Report, 70.

were vague or dependent on further study. There was, for example, little on the content of the LLB, which the consultants believed to be a matter for each university. Much was said about the need to move towards active learning – crucial to the success of a reformed LLB – but how this might be achieved was to be left to a proposed further working group. The consultants were, however, clear in their recommendations on several key issues: the question of numbers, access to the profession, training in values and ethics, the future or otherwise of the PCLL, and the creation of a more robust and representative governance framework to set benchmarks and spearhead reform.

Drawing on the separate study on future demand for legal services, the consultants concluded there was no oversupply of lawyers in Hong Kong. The need for solicitors and law graduates generally was likely to increase as a result of economic expansion, the importance of the rule of law, the emergence of new areas of law, the opening of China to legal services, and a greater readiness of Hong Kong people to seek legal advice and take disputes to the courts.[16] The dramatic decline in conveyancing as a source of income, the consultants observed, could well be a necessary corrective for the legal profession 'to keep pace with where Hong Kong is now going, and thus continue to have a role to play.'[17] The real issue was 'quality, not numbers.'[18] One of the concerns in the profession was that there was a 'through-train' to legal practice, in which entry into a law school equated with exit into the legal profession. A perceived failure by the law schools to weed out those who should not graduate had led both the Law Society and the Bar Association to consider setting their own examinations – measures which the consultants believed could be seen, and perhaps used, as protectionist mechanisms to control numbers rather than quality.[19]

In examining the numbers question, the consultants highlighted some striking facts. Fewer graduates with law degrees were now going into law as a profession: only 68 per cent of those graduating with Hong Kong LLBs in 1996 were now in practice, and 28 per cent of graduates completing the PCLL in 1997 did not proceed to pupillage or a trainee solicitor contract.[20] Moreover, the two law schools in Hong Kong were now educating only a minority – less than 30 per cent in 1996 – of those taking the academic stage of their legal education in Hong Kong; the remainder were studying for external law degrees, mostly at HKU SPACE, which had over 5,000 law students at various levels. In 2000–2001, 1,260 SPACE students were enrolled in the external University of London LLB programme – several times the number of LLB students at HKU and City University; another 350 were

---

16. GML Consulting Limited, *Study on the Manpower Needs of the Legal Services Sector of Hong Kong,* Chapter 1; Redmond-Roper Report, 90–2.

17. Redmond-Roper Report, 87.

18. Redmond-Roper Report, 85.

19. Redmond-Roper Report, 80–1.

20. Including those graduating with external degrees through HKU SPACE. Redmond-Roper Report, 83.

enrolled in the English Common Professional Examination (CPE) course.[21] This was 'an unusual state of affairs for a developed legal and educational system such as Hong Kong.'[22] Combined with graduates who had studied overseas, it rendered pointless any plan to control entry to the profession by reducing numbers in the two law schools.[23]

The division of law undergraduates between HKU SPACE and the two law schools raised questions about access to legal education. Although entry into full-time University Grants Committee (UGC)-funded LLBs at the two law schools was open to all Hong Kong school-leavers, those with higher socio-economic status and access to the best English-medium schools inevitably had a competitive advantage.[24] Most SPACE courses were part-time: it was ironic, remarked the consultants, that the only way to study law part-time in Hong Kong was through courses essentially in English law. SPACE courses, run on commercial lines, were financed by the students themselves, who were mostly mature students, many from less affluent families: some hoped to enter the legal profession, others simply wished to improve prospects in their current job.[25] To increase access, the consultants recommended introducing a part-time LLB at one or other of the two law schools. They also recommended the introduction of a six-month conversion course for persons seeking to enter vocational training on the basis of law degrees other than a Hong Kong LLB or the English CPE: its main purpose would be to fill gaps in Hong Kong law not covered by overseas law degrees.[26]

Questions of equity and access also applied to the PCLL. Although the external London LLB graduates with Honours 2:2 degrees or above (and even some with thirds or passes) were guaranteed places on the SPACE PCLL programme, taught by the Faculty of Law, they paid over two and a half times the fee paid by HKU's own UGC-funded PCLL students to be taught in the same way by the same teachers: this uneasy cohabitation produced complaints about poor value for money and raised doubts about the viability of 'small-group sessions.'[27] The guarantee of places for most graduates from HKU and SPACE presented a further problem of access: there was intense competition for the few remaining places among law graduates returning from study overseas, many of whom, despite having obtained jobs with large international firms, were unable to obtain the PCLL qualification

21. Redmond-Roper Report, 261–2.

22. Redmond-Roper Report, 232.

23. Redmond-Roper Report, 91–2.

24. Redmond-Roper Report, 256–9.

25. The total cost for a student of taking a three-year part-time London LLB at SPACE ($63,000) was about half that for a full-time LLB at HKU or City University, where the amount payable by a student for all three years, even with UGC-funding support, was $126,300. Redmond-Roper Report, 263.

26. Redmond-Roper Report, 239–42.

27. SPACE students paid the full fees of $104,000 for the full-time PCLL, compared with $42,100 paid by HKU students: Redmond-Roper Report, 177 & 191.

necessary to enter practice.[28] The consultants made no recommendations to address this problem: for other reasons, they proposed to abolish the PCLL entirely and replace it with a new qualification.

Redmond and Roper examined the concerns raised about the PCLL. Some – such as inconsistent treatment of those seeking places, or its availability only as a full-time course – were already being addressed.[29] But others were fundamental, and, they believed, fatal. The purpose of the PCLL was unclear: intended to provide practical instruction, in reality it was 'primarily an additional year of law studies – with a distinct academic emphasis in its goals, content, teaching methods and assessment.' The division between the LLB and the PCLL was artificial: topics that were part of the LLB in other jurisdictions were taught in the PCLL in Hong Kong. The PCLL lacked coherence: instead of offering a holistic programme for developing the ability to be a practising lawyer, it was simply a combination of seven subject-centred courses, with 'no overall schema for the systematic development of skills.' Teaching and assessment methods were inadequate, relying mainly on lectures and examinations, some with a heavy emphasis on multiple-choice questions. Development of more interactive teaching was inhibited by lack of funding and by the PCLL's placement within universities: this, the consultants believed, was inappropriate for what was, in effect, vocational preparation, since the pressure on university teachers to develop careers as academics distanced them from the day-to-day practice of law and made their teaching of practice 'increasingly "book learnt" and quite possibly outdated.'[30]

Redmond and Roper concluded that 'the PCLL does not provide, nor is capable of providing, the essential element of practical training which enables academic training to be used in practical ways.' It was a 'house divided against itself.'[31] It was 'frozen in time', not because there was any great attachment to it, but because, taught by universities, it was seen by the profession 'as that part of the legal education process which is in their particular domain.'[32] They dismissed efforts at reform from within, notably in plans advanced by Stephen Nathanson of HKU for a skills-based structure 'reflecting a coherent theory of legal practice.'[33] Instead, they proposed replacing the PCLL with a new sixteen-week 'legal practitioners course' (LPC) to be taught at a separate institution governed with strong representation from the profession. The LPC was to be an intensive course to develop the skill of 'lawyering', meaning 'the *bringing together* of knowledge and understanding of substantive and procedural law, general and legal skills, and professional and ethical attitudes – in

28. Redmond-Roper Report, 265.

29. Redmond-Roper Report, 261.

30. Redmond-Roper Report, 185–195.

31. Redmond-Roper Report, 185, 186.

32. They did, however, note how City University's attempts to introduce an innovative PCLL in the early 1990s had been harshly criticized.

33. Redmond-Roper Report, 195, 184, 188.

order to be able *to do* what is required of a lawyer in various aspects of practice.' It would be funded by the UGC, built around practical exercises, and taught mainly by practising lawyers using innovative methods. Students would be assessed according to whether they 'could do' rather than by exams.[34]

The consultants recommended that all substantive law subjects taught in the PCLL should be 'folded into' a reformed LLB, lasting four years instead of three. About a quarter of the syllabus of the new LLB would consist of non-law subjects from the humanities and social sciences, taught mainly in the first two or three years. This would strengthen the role of the degree as an education for non-lawyers. An emphasis on generic skills as well as core professional skills would encourage students to think logically, creatively and critically. A system of active learning would place 'a strong and rigorous' emphasis on the use of English, which would be a factor in assessing work; English-language skills could also be strengthened by exchange programmes and other forms of immersion.[35] To counter what many saw as a decline in ethical standards under the pressure of market forces, they recommended greater emphasis on ethics and values, clinical legal experience, internships with community and government agencies, and a mandatory pro bono work requirement.[36]

The consultants made recommendations on training beyond the universities. These included reforms to training during pupillage and trainee solicitor contracts, and improvements to the Law Society's mandatory Continuing Professional Development scheme and the Bar Association's Advanced Legal Education programme, which they advised should be mandatory.[37] They were particularly critical of existing governance arrangements for legal education, which they found to be fragmented and lacking a structure in which all stakeholders could play a role: the various requirements for admission were set (indirectly) by the universities, the Legal Practitioners Ordinance, and the professional bodies. This, combined with the conservatism of ACLE, where stakeholders tended to protect their own interests, tended to inhibit reform, particularly of the PCLL. The Joint Examination Board, set up in 1991 to oversee the PCLL in the two law schools, was practically defunct. The consultants therefore recommended the creation of a legal qualifying council, modelled on similar bodies elsewhere, with prescriptive rather than merely advisory functions. The council would set, monitor and govern the process of education and qualification for admission to practice, taking over some of the existing powers of the professional bodies under the Legal Practitioners Ordinance.[38]

---

34. Redmond-Roper Report, 197–210 & Appendix F.
35. Redmond-Roper Report, Chapter 7.
36. Redmond-Roper Report, Chapter 14.
37. Redmond-Roper Report, Chapter 8.
38. Redmond-Roper Report, Chapter 16.

Several of these recommendations encountered resistance. For example, the Law Society opposed the idea of a legal qualifying council, preferring instead to see a strengthening of the Advisory Committee on Legal Education (ACLE). The resulting Standing Committee on Legal Education (SCLET), established in 2005, was a compromise. It took on some of the responsibilities suggested by the consultants for a legal qualifying council, but had only advisory functions and took away none of the powers of the professional bodies. It nevertheless proved to be more energetic and transparent than the ACLE, addressing a concern of the steering committee that the momentum for reform should continue after the consultants had done their work.[39]

By far the most contentious recommendation was to replace the PCLL with the proposed LPC taught outside the universities. The Bar Association had reservations about the idea. There was no consensus in favour of it even within the Law Society. The Faculty of Law was strongly opposed. It was not convinced that a sixteen-week course taught by an institution yet to be created would be an adequate substitute for the year-long PCLL. The Faculty argued that the PCLL provided a uniform standard for entrants to the profession, took in students of diverse backgrounds, and did in fact contain useful components of practical skills. It feared there would be insufficient funding to extend the LLB to four years to absorb some of the PCLL courses. It also pointed out that the consultants had given no serious consideration to proposals for reforming the PCLL, drawn up by Stephen Nathanson and submitted early in the consultancy.[40]

The arguments were aired in public before the Legislative Council's Panel on Administration of Justice and Legal Services, chaired by Margaret Ng. They were hammered out in private at stormy discussions in the Faculty Board, where the Law Society's representative, Lester Huang (LLB 1982), was quizzed on the proposed LPC and

39. Established through amendments to the Legal Practitioners Ordinance, SCLET consists of seventeen members appointed by the Chief Executive after nomination by various stakeholders, including the Chief Justice, the Secretary for Justice, the Secretary for Education, the professional bodies, and the universities, as well as two members of the public. There was some continuity in membership between the Steering Committee on the Review of Legal Education and Training and the early SCLET. The first chairman of SCLET was the Solicitor General, Robert Allcock (2005–2007), who was succeeded by Christopher Chan (2007–2010), a former Registrar of the Court of Final Appeal, Patrick Chan (2010–2017), and Robert Tang (2017–). SCLET publishes detailed annual reports and statistics on its website. Review of Legal Education and Training in Hong Kong: Second Progress Report to the Legislative Council Panel on Administration of Justice and Legal Services, LC Paper No. CB(2)2351/01–02(02), Legislative Council website.

40. Albert Chen to all members of the Faculty, 12 February 2001, HKUA: Board of the Faculty of Law – Minutes (2001); Chen, Further Submission to the Consultants on the Review of Legal Education in Hong Kong, 6 March 2001, LC Paper No. CB(2)1307/00–01(03), & Chen, Submission to the Steering Committee on the Review of Legal Education: The PCLL and its Reforms, 20 August 2001, LC Paper No. CB(2)2344/00–01(04) Legislative Council website; Albert Chen, interview with the author, 8 August 2018.

the 'accusatory' tone of the society's submission on the subject, which had been put on the Internet.[41] Abolishing the PCLL threatened to remove from the Faculty a large part of its responsibilities, with potentially disruptive effects on other degrees, research capabilities, relations with the profession, and student and staff morale. As one senior judge had predicted, tinkering with the sensitive subject of legal education would lead to 'blood all over the place.'[42] 'It was a life-and-death issue,' recalls Wilson Chow, the first full-time Hong Kong-trained teacher of the PCLL, who became Head of DOPLE in 2005.[43]

The Faculty put forward a counterproposal: radical reform of the PCLL into a more skills-based programme along the lines it had already proposed to the consultants, and greater involvement of the profession in curriculum planning and oversight. The parallel HKU SPACE PCLL was abolished in 2001 and admissions to the PCLL were centralized. Through a series of discussions, successive Deans, Albert Chen and Johannes Chan, and their colleagues gained the support of the Chief Justice, the Department of Justice, senior lawyers, and the Legislative Council Panel. The law school at City University made common cause. By the end of 2001 the steering committee had reached consensus that the PCLL should not be abolished but should instead be reformed into a course with generally similar aims to those for the proposed LPC, and with greater supervision by the profession and other stakeholders. The Law Society reserved its position, acquiescing in the reform of the PCLL as an interim measure pending a decision on whether to implement the reforms recommended by the consultants. The steering committee gave its support to a four-year LLB and other proposals, and made representations to the UGC for extra resources to enable them to be implemented as soon as possible. Progress was fast – so fast, in fact, that the steering committee decided that a contemplated second review was unnecessary.[44]

The next large-scale review – the 'Comprehensive Review of Legal Education and Training' – took place in 2015–2018 under the auspices of SCLET. The consultants were former vice-presidents of the Court of Appeal, Woo Kwok-hing and Anthony Rogers (successive chairmen), and two overseas academics, Tony Smith and Julian Webb.[45] This consultancy saw its role as 'primarily to consolidate, sustain and strengthen.' It concluded

41. Lester Huang was chairman of the Law Society's Legal Education Committee and a member of the steering committee for the consultancy. Minutes of meeting on 11 April 2001 & Law Society's submission, 26 March 2001, HKUA: Board of the Faculty of Law – Minutes (2001).

42. Johannes Chan, 'Building upon a Noble Tradition' in Faculty of Law, HKU, *Building for Tomorrow on Yesterday's Strength*, 25, 16.

43. Wilson Chow, interview with the author, 28 September 2018.

44. Minutes of meeting on 28 January 2002 (extract), Legislative Council Panel on Administration of Justice and Legal Services, LC Paper No. CB(2)2351/01–02(01); Review of Legal Education and Training in Hong Kong: Progress Report, January 2002, LC Paper No. CB(2)987/01–02(03), Legislative Council website; Albert Chen, interview with the author, 8 August 2018.

45. Woo resigned in October 2016 to become a candidate in the Chief Executive elections. Tony Smith, Professor of Law at the University of Wellington, was a former chairman of the Faculty of Law at the University of Cambridge.

that legal education and training in Hong Kong represented 'a considerable success story. University law schools have grown, diversified and developed. They have become much more autonomous, multi-functional, institutions. Today they operate increasingly within their own norms of appropriate teaching, research and scholarship, rather than as a "service industry" for the profession.'[46] The recommendations for the law schools were targeted mainly at improving access, establishing uniform outcomes and standards, and improving quality assurance for the PCLL, which, following the opening of a third law school, at the Chinese University of Hong Kong in 2004, was now taught at three universities. Other recommendations focused on improving training at the pupillage and trainee solicitor stages.

One other issue took up the consultants' attention. This was a proposal for a common entrance examination (CEE) for graduates seeking to enter into a trainee solicitor contract in Hong Kong. A reversion to pre-1972 practice, the idea was taken up by the Law Society in 2012 with the aim of ensuring consistency in standards among prospective solicitors. It reflected a belief that, despite greater monitoring by the profession, a 'quality' problem existed in assessment standards for the PCLL. There were also concerns about a 'bottleneck', which, owing to insufficient places, prevented some able students from finding a place on a PCLL course. In January 2016 the Law Society announced its intention to proceed with plans to introduce a CEE some time after 2021, saying it had statutory powers to do so under the Legal Practitioners Ordinance and Trainee Solicitors Rules.[47] In April 2016 it specified that the proposal was for centralized assessment *within* the PCLL for core PCLL subjects, to be set and marked by the Law Society.[48] In 2018 the Law Society advocated a Law Society Examination, outside of the PCLL and coexisting with it, as an alternative route of entry into the solicitors' profession for those unable to gain places on PCLL programmes.[49]

Julian Webb, Professor of Law at the University of Melbourne, was formerly director of the UK Centre for Legal Education at the University of Warwick.

46. Standing Committee on Legal Education and Training, *Comprehensive Review of Legal Education and Training in Hong Kong: Final Report of the Consultants* (2018) (hereafter 'Comprehensive Review Report'), 57, 154.

47. This claim is disputed: see Johannes Chan, 'The Law Society's Power to Introduce a Common Entrance Examination', 48 *HKLJ* (2018), 1–10.

48. Most common law systems have moved away from centralized examinations towards 'distributed assessment', in which course providers mainly design and make their own assessments, as in Hong Kong. However, India, New Zealand, Nigeria, South Africa, some US states, and by default (since there is only one course provider) Singapore have centralized assessment. There have also recently been moves towards centralized assessments in England, although a wholly centralized assessment system has yet to be implemented. Background note by SCLET, 3 December 2013, LC Paper No. CB(4)219/13–14(01); Submissions of the Law Society of Hong Kong on the Common Entrance Examination, LC Paper No. CB(4)899/15–16(01), Legislative Council website; Comprehensive Review Report, 106–110 & Annex 7.

49. *SCMP*, 25 May 2018.

Other stakeholders, including the Bar Association, generally do not share the Law Society's concerns about quality and standards.[50] The three law schools point out that their PCLL programmes work to common benchmarks set by the profession; they suggest that problems of consistency and quality could be dealt with by further improvements in monitoring.[51] The Comprehensive Review concluded that an adequate case for a CEE had not yet been made. While it did not rule out some limited written common examination for core courses, provided it was integrated into the PCLL and not imposed from outside, the review rejected any idea of a CEE as the only test of competence for prospective trainee solicitors at the end of the PCLL. It recommended a moratorium on CEE development pending further benchmarking for the PCLL and agreement among stakeholders on whether the idea of common assessment should be pursued.[52]

In the decade after the 2001 Redmond-Roper Report, law studies at HKU were subjected to the most thoroughgoing reforms since the creation of the Department of Law in 1969. The PCLL was transformed from a set of compulsory courses mainly on substantive law into a more skills-based programme, with a range of electives and greater involvement of the profession in course design and monitoring. The LLB was extended to four years in 2004, with a wider range of optional courses and more emphasis on analytical skills. Double degrees were extended to five years and new forms of double degrees were introduced. A two-year Juris Doctor (JD) programme was introduced in 2009 to prepare non-law degree holders and holders of law degrees from non-common law jurisdictions for admission to the PCLL. Teaching methods have been developed to make the learning experience more active, and students are now assessed by other means than just exams. Hong Kong's two other law schools have also made reforms. In 2007 a separate Conversion Examination was introduced for applicants to the PCLL with law degrees from other common law jurisdictions to align their knowledge base with that of applicants with Hong Kong law degrees. The reforms at HKU put into practice many of the recommendations in the Redmond-Roper Report. Benchmarked against those in the world's leading law schools, the resulting programmes offer a wide range of courses to meet the needs of an increasingly diverse student population.

Curriculum reform on this scale required careful co-ordination, new resources, and dialogue with a more active system of external oversight. Student expectations, staff capabilities, and university policies also had to be accommodated. For two academic years, 2004–2006, the new and old LLBs coexisted while the last cohort of students taking the three-year degree finished their studies. The PCLL reforms were implemented in phases

---

50. Comprehensive Review Report, 113.

51. Joint submission from the three law schools to the Legislative Council Panel on Administration of Justice and Legal Services, 9 December 2013, LC Paper No. CB(4)234/13–14(01), Legislative Council website.

52. Comprehensive Review Report, 105, 116, 119, 122, & 123.

over five years, with the final phase in 2008 timed for the first intake of graduates from the four-year LLB and other entrants who had taken the recently introduced Conversion Examination. Despite the complexities, the reforms were implemented smoothly with the support of the legal profession and the UGC.

To provide the more intensive teaching required by the new programmes, the number of full-time teaching staff was increased from about fifty at the turn of the century to over eighty in 2019, including teaching consultants skilled in pedagogical methods. Most were recruited in 2006–2012 as part of the university-wide Centennial Recruitment Plan to prepare for the general introduction of four-year undergraduate degrees and to improve research competitiveness.[53] The new staff have strong credentials in research, teaching, and practice. Several have doctorates or other research degrees. Others have experience of legal practice in Hong Kong. Four – Malcolm Merry, Anselmo Reyes SC, Alexa Lam, and Lee Aitken – returned to the Faculty after many years in private practice or public service. The additional staff have enabled the Faculty to build on its traditional strengths and to develop expertise in emerging areas of law, such as intellectual property and information technology, international economic law, medical ethics, and alternative dispute resolution. This has enabled the Faculty to gain international recognition for its research output. It has also made it possible for the Faculty to offer students an impressive choice of courses in practically all areas of legal study.

The New Four-Year Bachelor of Laws, 2004

The new LLB, introduced in 2004, finally put into practice an idea dating back to the 1960s, when the overseas advisors on the planned law school at HKU suggested that the LLB should be a four-year degree, with its early stages devoted partly to courses in non-law subjects and critical thinking. Similar recommendations were made in the Miller Report (1979) and the Wesley-Smith Report (1988), though without much confidence they would be implemented. With its twin aims of providing foundational legal knowledge and a liberal education, the new four-year LLB was a natural progression from the reformed three-year LLB of the 1990s. Its curriculum was developed under successive Heads of the Department of Law, Johannes Chan (1999–2003), Roda Mushkat (2003–2005), and Michael Jackson (2005–2008). The compulsory 'core' subjects in law remained largely intact. Absorbing about half of the 240 credits required for the LLB, these were now taken mainly in the first two years, along with a larger component of transferable skills: the centrepiece was a five-part Legal Research and Writing course, spanning the first two years and inculcating skills such as statutory interpretation and case analysis. First-year students were required to take

---

53. Minutes of meeting on 23 November 2005, HKUA: Board of the Faculty of Law – Minutes (2005).

courses in English and Chinese and Critical Reasoning & Analysis (developed with the help of the Department of Philosophy) and a broadening course from another discipline, as well as the established course in Law & Society. The PCLL courses in substantive law were gradually transferred to the new LLB, either as compulsory courses (such as Commercial Law) or as optional courses (such as Business Associations or Conveyancing).[54]

Most of the rest of the third and fourth years were given over to optional courses, or 'electives'. In 2004–2006 the electives were redesigned and expanded in preparation for entry into the third year by the first batch of students in the four-year LLB programme. The number of electives grew from about 75 in 2004 to over 220 by 2018–2019, although not all are taught every year. They comprise a wide range of topics, from Animal Law to World Trade Organization Law. They embrace well-established subjects, such as Labour Law and Banking Law, and innovative topics such as Heritage Law, Digital Copyright, Space Law, Climate Change Law, and Online Dispute Resolution. Large clusters of courses deal with Chinese law, international trade and economic law, and commercial, corporate, and financial law. This has allowed specialized LLBs to be awarded to students who take a prescribed minimum of credits in these three areas. In public law and human rights, areas of strength since the 1990s, courses increasingly focus on regional and global topics – for example, Law, Governance and Development in Asia, Comparative Constitutional Law, and Business and Human Rights, which focuses on multinational enterprises.

The trend towards an international understanding of legal topics is one of the most striking aspects of the optional part of the curriculum. Hong Kong law is not neglected: much of it is covered by the compulsory courses, and some electives are strongly Hong Kong focused. But most electives stress regional, international, and comparative perspectives. This trend is a reflection partly of the increasingly transnational, cross-border nature of much modern law, particularly in an open city such as Hong Kong. It also addresses the diverse interests of students, the growing number of exchange students in the third and fourth years, and the increasingly international outlook of students from Hong Kong, many of whom spend one or more semesters at law schools overseas. In one course – Law, the Individual and the Community: a Cross-Cultural Dialogue – the class meets in parallel with classes taking the same course in universities in North America, Asia, and Europe, engaging with a 'global classroom' through web-based discussion groups on topics such as the death penalty, parent-and-child relationships, and freedom of expression.[55]

Many elective courses are also cross-disciplinary, examining legal topics in their broader social, political, and philosophical context and addressing the interests of students taking the popular double-degree programmes with other faculties, who now outnumber students taking the LLB on its own. In addition to joint-degree programmes established

54. Under the 'Land Law III' course.
55. Faculty of Law, HKU, 'Syllabus for the Degree of Bachelor of Laws 2018–19', Faculty website, 81.

in the 1990s – the Bachelor of Business Administration (BBA) (Law) and the Bachelor of Social Sciences (Government & Laws)[56] – a new double degree in Law and Literary Studies (Bachelor of Arts & LLB) was introduced in 2011 as a reflection of the importance, on the one hand, of rhetoric and oratory in the law and, on the other, of legal themes in many great works of literature. Developed by Marco Wan and his colleagues in the Faculty of Law and the School of English, the programme was one of the first of its kind in the world and is the only one in East Asia. Courses in this programme are fully integrated and draw on new research: they range from the intertwined relationship between law and literature in England before 1600 to recent film representations of law and the legal system. The programme attracts a select group of students with a wide variety of backgrounds and interests and very high standards of English and Chinese. 'HKU is a leading centre for interdisciplinary research in law and the humanities,' observes Wan. 'It is immensely exciting to investigate how the law intersects with other disciplines concerned with our intellectual heritage, including literature, history, philosophy, and film.'[57] The focus on law and literature complements a growing interest within the Faculty in legal history: since 2000, courses on this subject have been taught by Humphrey Ko (LLB 1991) and Michael Ng (LLB 1993), both of whom hold doctorates in history.

The new LLB curriculum includes courses on clinical legal work. When urging more training in this area, Redmond and Roper had commended HKU for introducing a social justice summer internship programme in 2001, under which law students pair with NGOs or public agencies to study sociolegal issues in Hong Kong.[58] More recent initiatives have included internships in Mainland China and other places in the region. Clinical programmes, designed with the help of Stacy Caplow of Brooklyn Law School, have been introduced with the aim of cultivating an ethos of public service.[59] Some provide practical experience in specialized areas such as disability rights, refugee law, and global migration. The general Clinical Legal Education (CLE) course gives students the opportunity to participate in real cases. A revival on a larger scale of a scheme for PCLL students in the 1970s, the scheme is directed by Eric Cheung (LLB 1986), an experienced litigation solicitor who joined the Faculty in 1996: some of the cases helped by the scheme are discussed in Chapter 8.

Students in the clinical education programmes are assessed mainly according to the quality of their work portfolios, their professional attitudes, and their competence in

56. The Bachelor of Engineering (Civil Engineering and Laws) was discontinued in 2012 because it proved impossible to fit the curriculum, with its new common core elements, into five years. Message from the Dean, *Faculty of Law Newsletter*, Summer 2009.

57. Marco Wan, interview with the author, 30 November 2018.

58. Redmond-Roper Report, 144–152 & 307–8.

59. Stacy Caplow, 'Clinical Legal Education in Hong Kong: A Time to Move Forward', 36 *HKLJ* (2006), 229–58.

handling cases. Other electives rely mainly on research papers as well as on class participation. Some include practical exercises, such as fieldwork or blog and video assignments. Although examinations (some of them take-home exams) still play a role in compulsory subjects and in the more knowledge-based electives, this is a shift from the predominantly exam-oriented system of the old three-year LLB, where, despite a trend towards continuous assessment, in-hall exams still accounted for 60 or 70 per cent of assessment. The growing variety addresses the recommendation in the Redmond-Roper Report that assessment methods should reflect the teaching and learning goals of each course. The greater emphasis on substantial written assignments and class participation takes into account the report's emphasis on active learning and research and writing skills.[60]

Introduced in 2004, the four-year LLB predated the general introduction of four-year degrees in Hong Kong's universities in 2012. The change in 2012 was achieved by shortening secondary school curriculums by one year, replacing the Hong Kong Certificate of Education Examination (in Year 5) and 'A' levels (in Year 7) with a new Hong Kong Diploma of Secondary Education Examination (HKDSE), usually taken in Year 6.[61] Students therefore enter university a year earlier than before. Partly to compensate for the loss of a year of secondary education, universities in Hong Kong have introduced 'common core' courses for undergraduates in their first two years, to be taken alongside subjects in their own discipline. Structured under four cross-disciplinary 'areas of inquiry',[62] the common core courses are intended to broaden students' intellectual and social perspectives, help develop creative, critical, collaborative, and communications skills, and foster friendships across the faculties – in brief, they 'create a relationship with your own future, that of others, and that of the larger world.'[63] The Faculty of Law offers some of these courses: for example, the Rule of Law in a Globalizing World is taught by Benny Tai, and the Rule of Law in Contemporary China is taught by Albert Chen, Yongxi Chen, and Eric Ip. The common core courses account for 36 of the 120 credits for the first two years. A further 36 of 120 credits for the third and fourth years are devoted to 'free electives', which may be taken in any faculty.

To accommodate the common core courses, adjustments had to be made to the existing four-year LLB, for example, by halving the length of the courses on Law & Society and

---

60. Redmond-Roper Report, 167–8.

61. The HKDSE is divided into compulsory subjects, such as Chinese and English language, mathematics, and liberal studies; subject-based electives; applied learning electives; and other languages. Even before 2012 the Faculty was admitting students under the Early Admissions Scheme, which enabled those with outstanding Hong Kong Certificate of Education Examination results to enter university without taking 'A' levels. In 2008, for example, Early Admissions Scheme students taking the LLB and its various double-degree programmes accounted for half of HKU's Early Admissions Scheme intake. Message from the Dean, *Faculty of Law Newsletter*, Summer 2009.

62. Scientific and Technical Literacy, Humanities, Global Issues, and China: Culture, State and Society.

63. 'Introducing the Common Core @ HKU', HKU Common Core website, 2018.

Legal Research and discontinuing the Faculty's own custom-made course on Critical Reasoning & Analysis. The Faculty, recalls Fu Hualing, Head of the Department of Law (2008–2011), made these changes reluctantly after long negotiations. Coming soon after SCLET designated additional core LLB subjects as prerequisites for admission to the PCLL, the changes further reduced the scope for elective courses.[64] The general introduction of four-year undergraduate programmes in 2012 also produced considerable logistical challenges: in 2012 the university, including the Faculty of Law, took in twice the usual number of undergraduates that year in two cohorts – students with 'A' levels and those leaving school a year earlier with the new HKDSE.

With the introduction of university-wide four-year undergraduate degrees in 2012, HKU took the opportunity not only to revitalize curriculums but also to emphasize its support of 'innovative pedagogies, especially those incorporating the use of technology-supported and student-centred learning.'[65] Teaching skills are not a conventional part of an academic's training, and, among all disciplines, law is known for its pedagogical conservatism. Teachers quite naturally tend to follow the style and methods of the teachers they most admired in their own undergraduate days. While elective courses, with their smaller class sizes, allow flexibility in teaching methods and greater class participation, lectures and tutorials continue to be the standard format for the compulsory LLB courses. Some teachers have nevertheless been able to work within this format using imaginative methods. Technological aids in the form of web-based 'Moodles' allow course materials to be placed online and enable communication between students and teachers outside class and formal office hours.[66] Workshops, resource centres, and other university-wide initiatives have focused on improving teaching methods – or rather, *learning* methods – moving away from passive, teacher-centred learning towards active student-centred learning, in which students actively engage with the learning process and teachers become facilitators rather than merely instructors. Student-centred learning blends individual projects with collaborative teamwork, drawing on new technology and relying less on assessment through closed-book examinations. The HKDSE, with its emphasis on critical thinking and its more varied assessment methods, has also encouraged students to be more participatory: it has made students much more vocal than before, observes Daisy Cheung (LLB 2011), whose courses in medical law provide ample scope for debates on ethical issues.[67]

Interest among law teachers in developing the teaching and learning experience date back to the 1990s, when Jill Cottrell, Alice Lee, Janice Brabyn, Katherine Lynch, and others organized workshops on the subject. The impact was limited, and most of their colleagues

---

64. Fu Hualing, interview with the author, 7 November 2018; SCLET Annual Report 2007.

65. 'Strategic Themes for 2009–2014: Enhancing the Student Learning Experience', HKU website.

66. A 'Moodle' is a modular object-oriented dynamic learning environment.

67. Daisy Cheung, interview with the author, 18 October 2018.

continued to teach along traditional lines, replicating their own experiences as undergradu-ates. Among the earliest to experiment with new methods was Benny Tai (LLB 1986), whose participation in a week-long intensive workshop organized by the Australian Law Teachers' Association entirely changed his approach to teaching. After joining the Faculty in the early 1990s he made use of Harvard Graphics – a precursor of the now-ubiquitous PowerPoint – which allowed him to introduce cartoons and other illustrations to bring out the essential issues of a case. He divided his 150-strong Constitutional Administrative Law class into groups and introduced specially designed games, including a 'very complicated' board game on judicial review.[68] These and other innovative teaching methods earned him recognition as one of the first recipients of a University Teaching Fellowship, in 1996–1997.

University teaching fellowships and awards are awarded to a handful of staff every year. Since their introduction in 1996, eight members of the Faculty of Law have been recognized in this way, some more than once.[69] The most prolific among these is Rick Glofcheski, who was also one of the first recipients of the Hong Kong-wide UGC Teaching Award in 2011. A member of the Faculty since 1989, Glofcheski has transformed learning methods not only in his elective courses but also in the compulsory course on Tort Law, which, with its enrol-ment of up to 300 students, 'is where creativity is really needed.' Each student is required to keep a 'media diary', recording events in the news that resonate with the tort law issues they are studying. These might range from a sudden reversal of direction of an escalator in a shopping mall to threats of defamation actions by a Chief Executive. Another requirement is a photographic essay analysing a 'tort environment' according to legal principles – for example, a construction site with multiple breaches of safety regulations. Glofcheski is emphatic that questions in the final, open-book exam, should address real-life incidents in Hong Kong, and not the clichéd or 'ridiculously hypothetical questions' traditionally set in this area of law: thus, students are asked about objects falling from high-rise build-ings or pedestrians crossing against a red light rather than 'cricket balls hitting greenhouses or snails in beer bottles.' In recent years Glofcheski has largely replaced lectures with the 'flipped classroom', held in the old Loke Yew Hall, which, unlike most lecture theatres, has flexible seating. Students do the readings and watch pre-recorded 'mini-lectures' on the class website beforehand. At class they are presented with a problem – usually a news report of a tort incident – and are then required to brainstorm in small groups, at the end of which each group produces a legal analysis of the problem with reference to the authori-ties. Glofcheski's unique methods have been of considerable interest to other university teachers and the subject of study by scholars of higher education.[70]

---

68. Benny Tai, interview with the author, 12 October 2018.
69. For a list of recipients see Appendix 3.
70. Rick Glofcheski, interview with the author, 8 October 2018.

The Reformed Postgraduate Certificate in Laws, 2003–2008

The four-year LLB provides great flexibility to undergraduates, including opportunities to specialize in a particular area of law or to take a minor in a non-law subject. It offers possibilities for students who decide they do not wish to become lawyers. For those who do, the PCLL continues to be the primary route – indeed almost the only one for fresh graduates seeking to enter the profession.[71] Despite increases in the number of places at HKU, from under 200 at the end of the twentieth century to over 400 in 2018,[72] and the introduction of a third PCLL at the Chinese University of Hong Kong in 2008, competition to get into the PCLL has been strong, partly owing to the return to Hong Kong of large numbers of law graduates educated overseas: nevertheless, some 60 per cent of first-choice applicants obtain admission to the programme.[73] Largely because of the high calibre of students, pass rates for the PCLL are now high, at well over 90 per cent, and about 90 per cent of PCLL holders obtain solicitors' training contracts or pupillages. The PCLL is therefore the main gatekeeper for entry into the legal profession. Some see it as a bottleneck, denying access to some competent candidates who are unable to gain a place, while practically guaranteeing a training place to those who obtain a PCLL. For this reason, pressure on the universities to increase places continues, and proposals for other routes of entry into the profession continue to be debated.[74]

In the meantime, in the wake of the Redmond-Roper Report, the PCLL has been transformed from a subject-based curriculum to one focusing more on skills. Admission procedures no longer practically guarantee a place to LLB graduates from HKU or HKU SPACE. A good 2:2 honours degree is now the minimum requirement; applicants are also required to have a recent pass at a specified level (usually 7 or above) in the International English Language Testing System. HKU LLB graduates still make up most of the intake.[75] A policy from 2001 of charging the same fees for both self-funded and UGC-supported places addressed the 'inequity' identified in the Redmond-Roper Report. But this had to be abandoned in 2005 when the UGC decided against cross-subsidies of this kind.[76] To

---

71. The other routes are the Overseas Lawyers Qualification Examination and the Barristers Qualification Examination.

72. Of these, 325 were full-time and 92 part-time. In addition, in 2017 the City University of Hong Kong admitted 201 to its PCLL programme and the Chinese University of Hong Kong admitted 174, bringing the total admissions to the three PCLL programmes to 792: SCLET Annual Report 2017.

73. The rate varies from one law school to another: the success rate for applicants to HKU has risen over the past few years: for the 2018–2019 PCLL it was 66.8 per cent.

74. These issues are examined in Chapter 5 of the Comprehensive Review Report (2018).

75. The proportion of HKU law graduates in the PCLL intake in recent years range from just over half in 2010 and 2011 to about two-thirds from 2012 to the present.

76. Under this arrangement the annual tuition fee was $55,000 for all students. When it ended, the old differentials were reinstated, with a fee of $42,000 for UGC-funded places and $95,000 for self-funded places. Albert Chen, The

broaden access, a part-time PCLL, spread over two years and with classes outside working hours, was designed by a team led by Richard Wu and introduced in 2005. The first cohort of fifty-eight represented 'an amazing diversity of background and age.'[77]

In a further initiative to extend access to the PCLL, in 2009 a full-time two-year JD programme was launched in 2009 to equip holders of non-law degrees with a foundation in common law subjects, including, optionally, all the prerequisites to apply for admission to the PCLL: the law schools at City University and the Chinese University of Hong Kong had already introduced their own JD programmes with larger intakes than at HKU. The JD degree at HKU was benchmarked against similar programmes offered by other leading law schools and was designed with advice from experts from Harvard Law School and Melbourne Law School.[78] The programme admits about forty students a year: they are taught separately from LLB students in an intimate environment that encourages interaction. The first year of the JD attracted about 360 applications; more than half of the 44 admitted had degrees from overseas institutions.

The curriculum for the reformed PCLL programme was introduced in phases from 2003 to 2008 to allow co-ordination with the reforms to the LLB and a larger staff complement to be built up. The reforms were drawn up by a task force led by Stephen Nathanson and consisting of Felix Chan, Eric Cheung, Richard Wu, Jessica Young, and Wilson Chow. They began their work before the Redmond-Roper Report was finalized and set out their blueprint in an article in the *Hong Kong Law Journal* in 2002: this envisaged a coherent framework for legal practice structured around areas of practice, a systematic teaching of skills through a problem-based curriculum, and a 'feedback' culture in which students were expected to assist each other and adopt a professional attitude towards learning.[79] The task force received advice from overseas experts such as Judy Smith of the TC Beirne School of Law at the University of Queensland and Phil Knott of the Nottingham Law School at Nottingham Trent University. In addition, Edward Chan SC (LLB 1972) and Wong Yan Lung SC of the Hong Kong Bar Association spent three days in the Faculty going through each course and offering detailed advice on areas for improvement. Several new staff with considerable experience in legal practice helped develop and implement the new PCLL. Among those recruited during this decade of reform (2001–2010) were Lee Aitken, Farzana Aslam, Alice Chan, Michelle Cheng, Nigel Davis, Emma Gooding, Keith Hotten, Norman Hui, Stephane Hui, Julienne Jen, Dave Lau, Gary Meggitt, Vandana Rajwani, Bernard Siu, Amanda Whitfort, and Jessica Young.

Introduction of a Mixed Mode Funded PCLL in the Faculty of Law, 16 May 2001, HKUA: Board of the Faculty of Law – Minutes (2001); Dean's Message, *Faculty of Law Newsletter*, Spring 2005.

77. Michael Wilkinson, 'The New Part-time PCLL', *Faculty of Law Newsletter*, Spring 2006.

78. SCLET Annual Report 2010, 41.

79. Stephen Nathanson, Wilson W.S. Chow and Felix W.H. Chan, 'The University of Hong Kong's New PCLL,' 32 *HKLJ* (2002), 381–99.

The changes began with the transfer of parts of Revenue Law to the LLB and the renovation of some other courses with greater emphasis on transactional knowledge and lawyering skills. After an absence of several years, the course in Trial Advocacy was reintroduced, now taught mainly by practitioners. A range of elective courses was introduced for the first time in 2008. These were initially part of an experiment in streaming in 2004–2007 aimed at enabling students to take practical exercises relevant to either a barrister's work (the litigation-oriented stream) or a solicitor's practice (the transactions-oriented stream). The final phase came in 2008, when the first graduates from the four-year LLB and the new Conversion Examination entered the PCLL. By now, most of the substantive law formerly taught in the PCLL had been moved to the LLB. Applicants to the PCLL must have already acquired competence in eleven core areas of law, ranging from contract to equity, as well as in three areas of Hong Kong law: constitutional law, the legal system, and land law. The PCLL courses now focus on the skills required of a lawyer, such as problem solving, document analysis and issue identification, drafting, case management, interviewing, negotiation, and mediation. In the first semester the emphasis is on essential procedural and transactional knowledge, taught in four compulsory core practice areas.[80] In the second, apart from a compulsory course in Professional Practice and Management (dealing with ethics and professional conduct), students take three electives from up to twelve practice areas broadly divided into two lists, litigation-specific and transaction-specific.[81] Classes are divided into large-group sessions, in which students are introduced to the subject matter, sometimes with demonstrations of legal processes and skills by practitioners, and small-group sessions, of ten to fifteen students, in which they carry out exercises, some based on real-life cases.

About twenty full-time staff in DOPLE design, administer, and teach the PCLL programme. Most have experience as barristers or solicitors, and some have themselves taken the PCLL at HKU. The full-time staff are assisted by over a hundred part-time teachers from the legal profession, many of them also graduates of HKU, who contribute up-to-date practical experience to the design and teaching of courses. Instructions for tutors have become more detailed, and each course has its tutors' meetings at which objectives, teaching methods, and student reactions are shared and discussed. The small-group sessions, which previously (as tutorials) often took the form of 'mini-lectures', now require more active involvement by students before and during class, where they work together and learn from each other through discussion and group drafting of legal documents. Assessment is still mainly by examinations, now mostly 'open-book'. To assess interviewing techniques a 'standardized client' scheme has been implemented since 2013, based on an

---

80. Civil Litigation, Criminal Litigation, Corporate and Commercial Transactions, and Property Transactions.
81. Completion of the course in Trial Advocacy and one other course from a litigation-specific list of electives are required by the Bar Association for those wishing to join the Bar.

initiative by the Glasgow Graduate School of Law (which drew on the experience of some US and Australian law schools and methods used in medical training). Under the scheme, lay persons enlisted and trained by DOPLE role-play as clients and give assessments after they have been interviewed by students.[82]

The Faculty has a long tradition of engaging practising lawyers as teachers, course consultants, and external examiners. Participation by the profession deepened with the reform of the PCLL. Special committees of the Law Society and Bar Association set benchmarks common to all the PCLL programmes and monitor quality. The same member of the Judiciary serves as the chief examiner of all three programmes. In addition, the HKU programme is externally assessed by one examiner nominated by the Law Society and another by the Bar Association. An academic board has been established for each PCLL, consisting of members from the profession, the university, the Judiciary, and the Department of Justice, as well as lay members. Each board has subcommittees on curriculum, admissions, and human resources. HKU has only 40 per cent of the representation on its Board, meaning that the Faculty has lost ultimate control of the PCLL, a difficult compromise to sell to the university but one that has worked well.[83] Anna Wu (LLB 1974) has chaired the HKU Academic Board since its creation in 2003.

The Faculty and the Wider World: Exchanges and Other Partnerships

'I would not be surprised if you feel you are in a foreign country when you visit the Faculty these days,' wrote the Dean, Johannes Chan, in the Faculty's newsletter in 2007. 'We admit about 100 LLB students each year, and each semester we typically admit about 90 exchange students coming from all over the world. Every tutorial group or seminar becomes an international class.' Similar numbers of HKU law students travel in the opposite direction to take one or two semesters in universities overseas. Degree programmes, particular at the postgraduate level, attract students from over twenty different jurisdictions. The Faculty has co-organized annual summer programmes in Hong Kong with Duke University and Santa Clara University. It has a regular stream of distinguished visitors and hosts a growing number of international conferences, which students are encouraged to attend: the largest, the fifth Annual Conference of the International Society of Public Law (ICON-S) in June 2018, jointly organized by the International Society of Public Law and the Faculty's Centre for Comparative and Public Law, attracted over 700 participants. Teams from the Faculty take part in a dozen or so international mooting competitions, often returning with prizes and distinctions.

---

82. Wilson Chow, interview with the author, 28 September 2018.
83. Johannes Chan, interview with the author, 20 June 2018.

Student exchange partnerships – now numbering over eighty, and including some of the world's leading law schools – allow students to gain credits towards their degrees from courses taken in other universities. 'Buddy programmes' pair students in the Faculty with exchange students to help introduce them to Hong Kong life. Exchanges offer opportunities to broaden horizons, hone language skills, forge friendships with overseas peers, and live independently. 'Everyone benefits,' observes Scott Veitch of his classes in the theory and philosophy of law. 'Students from other parts of the world bring fresh perspectives to class and take home new ideas from a city where the role of law in society is fiercely debated. Almost without exception our own students return from their exchanges intellectually enriched and full of enthusiasm about their time abroad.'[84] Some of the Faculty's partnerships have been taken further: since 2008 the Faculty has signed agreements with the University of Zurich, King's College London, University College London, the University of British Columbia, the University of Pennsylvania, and the University of New South Wales for dual degree programmes in which students earn a law degree from both HKU and the partner university.[85] The Faculty also continues to work closely with the Universities of Melbourne and Toronto and has annual research conferences with the law schools in Singapore. The Faculty was a founding member of the Asian Law Institute in 2003, an initiative of the National University of Singapore which now has over fifty members.

In 2003, after intensive competitive bidding, the WTO designated the Faculty of Law at HKU as its partner university in the Asia-Pacific region for three consecutive years to hold its training courses for senior government trade officers. The Faculty was chosen because of its high standards of teaching and its excellent library. The first three-month Regional Trade Policy Course took place in June 2004 with participants from thirty-two countries and trainers from the WTO, HKU, and other institutions. The initiative was part of the East Asian International Economic Law and Policy Programme, founded in 2003 under the Asian Institute of International Financial Law (AIIFL) at HKU and led by Donald Lewis, Mattheo Bushehri, and Henry Gao. The programme was a regional leader in research and knowledge exchange in international trade policy, law and regulation, holding conferences, hosting visiting scholars, officials and students, and generating research on topics such as regional economic integration and the growth of arbitration work.

---

84. Scott Veitch, interview with the author, 26 September 2018.

85. The nature of the degrees varies. In the University College London partnership students spend their first two years at University College London and their final two years at HKU, on the successful completion of which they obtain an LLB degree from each university. In the Pathways Programmes with King's College London and the University of New South Wales, LLB students spend their first three years at HKU and their fourth year at the partner institution, and upon successful completion obtain an LLB from HKU and an LLM from the partner institution. The partnership with the University of Zurich follows a similar pattern. The arrangement with the University of British Columbia enables students to obtain an LLB from HKU and a JD from the University of British Columbia in a programme lasting five years. Under the University of Pennsylvania programme, JD students from each university spend a third year in the LLM programme at the partner university.

The Faculty and the Nation: Relations with Mainland Chinese Institutions

The impetus for founding the East Asian International Economic Law and Policy Programme – and a focus of its activities – was the accession of China to the WTO in 2001. This liberalization of China's trade and investment relations with the rest of the world has stimulated demand for legal services, which WTO rules require to be opened to China's trading partners on a level playing field. In 2003, under the Closer Economic Partnership Arrangement between the Mainland and Hong Kong, the Chinese government made commitments to open up legal services to Hong Kong firms and lawyers: for example, Hong Kong permanent residents with Chinese citizenship are eligible to acquire legal qualifications in Mainland China; Mainland law firms may employ Hong Kong legal practitioners; and representative offices of Hong Kong law firms on the Mainland are allowed to work in association with Mainland law firms. Since many foreign law firms still prefer to use Hong Kong as a base, these measures have boosted Hong Kong's role as a gateway to China.[86] China's entry into the WTO stimulated a series of lectures and conferences at the Faculty of Law, mostly under the auspices of the AIIFL. It also spurred several large-scale research initiatives, notably the founding of the East Asian International Economic Law and Policy Programme in 2003 with an $8.5 million grant from the University Development Fund, at the time the largest amount of public funding ever granted to the Faculty. WTO-related issues have also been the focus of collaborative projects with institutions in Mainland China, many of them held under the auspices of the Hong Kong-Shanghai Institute for World Trade and China Development, a joint venture between Fudan University and HKU started in 2001.

Since the late 1990s the Faculty has extended its links with universities and institutions in Mainland China. '"One country, two systems" means the co-existence of two legal systems, but it should not mean complete isolation of one legal system from another,' said the Dean, Johannes Chan, in 2003.[87] On the contrary, the Faculty has 'a unique role to play in facilitating interaction, understanding and collaboration between the two different legal worlds.' This role was acknowledged in the 1980s with the introduction of courses in PRC law for Hong Kong students in the LLB and the new LLM. The Master of Common Law (MCL) and Doctor of Legal Science (SJD) degrees, introduced in the 1990s, have proved particularly successful in attracting students from Mainland China – so much so that when the Faculty celebrated its fortieth anniversary in 2009–2010 three anniversary dinners were held, one in Hong Kong, one in Beijing, and one in Shenzhen. By then the Faculty had over 600 graduates from the Mainland, including many in senior government positions and as many as 99 judges in the Shenzhen People's Court alone. The two-year JD course

---

86. Anthony W.K. Chow, 'Cross-Border Practice: The Hong Kong Perspective,' *Hong Kong Lawyer*, January 2009.

87. Message from the Dean, *Faculty of Law Newsletter*, Spring 2003.

introduced that year for non-law degree holders has also proved to be popular with graduates from the Mainland.

Student exchange agreements have been made with several leading Mainland law schools. Collaborative teaching arrangements include an agreement with Tsinghua University in 2004 for graduates of HKU's four-year LLB programme to obtain a second law degree at Tsinghua, and a further agreement with Tsinghua Law School in 2013 for Faculty members to provide intensive training in the common law to Mainland judges and prosecutors. The HKU-Peking University double master's degree in law, begun in 2011, builds on a partnership with Peking University going back to the creation of the Peking University-HKU Legal Research Centre in 1998, which has held a conference every year since then, alternately in Beijing and Hong Kong, except in 2003.[88] The Faculty also participates in an annual cross-strait conference, which brings together legal scholars from institutions on the Mainland, Taiwan, Macau, and Hong Kong. Under a partnership between the Faculty and Dalian Maritime University sponsored by the Hong Kong SAR government and the shipping industry, students from Hong Kong attend annual summer programmes and internships in maritime law; students from Dalian undergo a year's training in law or other subjects at HKU, and some stay on to work in Hong Kong. Staff from the Faculty have also taken part in a rule of law programme in Beijing, taught successively at Renmin University and Peking University, and in annual HKU-University College London-Peking University seminars on the rule of law.

The building of partnerships with institutions elsewhere in China was boosted by the recruitment of staff of Mainland origin and the appointment of associate deans with responsibility for Mainland affairs, beginning with Zhang Xianchu (2002–2014) and continuing with Fu Hualing (2014–2019). Joining the Faculty on 1 July 1997, Zhang and Fu were among several teachers who moved to HKU in the 1990s to escape the internal quarrels then afflicting the law school at City University. Zhang is a graduate of the China University of Political Science and Law in Beijing, where he also taught for three years in the 1980s before taking his MCL and JD at Indiana University School of Law at Bloomington. Among other initiatives, he and Peter Feng, who joined the Faculty in 1993, were instrumental in establishing the annual Peking University-HKU conference, one of the longest collaborations between a Hong Kong and a Mainland law school.[89] Fu was an undergraduate at the Southwest University of Political Science and Law in Chongqing, which was one of the first universities to revive the teaching of law and political science in the wake of the Cultural Revolution. Taught by teachers who had only recently returned

88. The outbreak of severe acute respiratory syndrome (SARS) that year in Hong Kong and Beijing forced organizers to cancel plans.

89. Peter Feng (Feng Xiang 馮象) left the Faculty in 1999. He is now the Mei Ru'ao Chair Professor in Law at the School of Law, Tsinghua University, and a distinguished literary scholar, specializing in producing Chinese translations of biblical and other texts.

from re-education in the countryside, he began his studies there at the age of sixteen with classmates from different backgrounds – workers, peasants, soldiers – ranging in age from fourteen to forty-five. Upon graduation he taught there for two years, while simultaneously learning English from scratch, before taking a master's degree at the University of Toronto and a doctorate in jurisprudence at Osgoode Hall, Toronto. Among the recent initiatives developed by Fu and other colleagues are short training courses in Hong Kong for lawyers from the Mainland in special topics such as laws against discrimination and sexual violence, and regular summer and winter camps for law students from HKU at Fudan and Donghua Universities in Shanghai, which include visits to law firms: in a city in which legal services are growing rapidly in size and sophistication, these visits are eye-openers for those used to viewing China from a purely Hong Kong perspective.[90]

Mainland law students at the Faculty of Law have been supported by scholarships and other funding from the Hong Kong SAR government, the Sun Hung Kai Properties-Kwoks' Foundation, the Chow Tai Fook Charity Foundation, the Leslie Wright Hong Kong-China Legal Fund, and other external bodies. A variety of other activities, ranging from visits from Mainland scholars to seminars and conferences, have been supported by the Legal Education Fund, which was founded in Hong Kong in 1988. This remarkable private initiative has been managed almost single-handedly over the past thirty years by one of its founders, Cecilia Chen.[91] As a manufacturer of stainless steel products with no previous connection with the law, Chen was one of the first Hong Kong entrepreneurs to outsource work to factories on the Mainland in the late 1970s. Various disputes over quality control and parallel sales made her realize how different the two legal systems were and how difficult it then was to resolve cross-border disputes. Determined to do something about it, she resigned from her work at the factory and devoted her time to promoting legal education and contacts between Hong Kong and the Mainland. Chen and her husband, Donald Chow, formed the Legal Education Fund, financing it themselves for the first ten years, and then raising additional funds from friends and supporters.[92]

Building on a growing network of relations with senior judges, lawyers, officials, and academics, the Legal Education Fund played a pioneering role in promoting understanding between Hong Kong and Mainland China in legal affairs. Chen began by bringing well-established Mainland legal scholars to Hong Kong, usually on attachments to universities of about six months and including visits to the Judiciary and government agencies: over 200 scholars have been supported in this way since 1988; many have become judges, deans

---

90. Zhang Xianchu, interview with the author, 6 October 2018; Fu Hualing, interview with the author, 7 November 2018.

91. Originally known as The Legal Education Trust Fund until its incorporation as the Legal Education Fund Ltd in 2011.

92. Cecilia Chen, interview with the author, 15 August 2018.

of law schools, and senior officials in the National People's Congress and other government bodies. The fund has sponsored study groups of judges and professors, dozens of lectures and seminars, a series of anti-corruption training programmes in Beijing, publications, and donations of law books and materials to Mainland and Hong Kong universities. In one innovative event in 2007, two identical court cases, one civil, the other criminal, were decided in two days of parallel mock trials, one under Hong Kong law, the other under Mainland law, with judges, lawyers, scholars and students playing various parts. The mock trials attracted an attendance of over 800; over 3,000 DVDs of the event were sent to law libraries throughout China. Since the late 1990s the fund has organized annual summer exchange programmes, bringing over 600 Mainland law students to Hong Kong for structured one-week visits and, since 2004, taking a similar number of Hong Kong law students on six-week exchanges to Mainland China, where they attend lectures at host universities, visit government departments, and take part in court internships under the mentorship of judges.[93]

Student Pathways

With the reforms to the LLB and PCLL, the introduction of double degrees, and the many opportunities for exchanges and internships, law students at HKU now have more options than ever before. 'Students today have a much bigger awareness that they need to get their act together and make strategic choices of teachers and courses,' observes Daisy Cheung (LLB 2011), a former student in the Faculty, now a teacher. 'We used to be more clueless as a group, but now students are coming to me in their first year to talk about internships and life plans.'[94] The paths students take in their careers are moulded by their choices at university. In this section we examine how the experiences of a handful of recent law graduates – in class, in extracurricular activities, and in exchanges and internships – shape their decisions.

While most law graduates still enter the legal profession, a substantial minority decide to follow other paths. Among these are the graduates – some with double degrees – who make use of their legal knowledge in public service or business and others who move away from law altogether. Agnes Tam (LLB 2010), introduced in Chapter 6, embarked on legal studies after having herself been at the centre of a prominent court case. It was the philosophy of law, more than its practical application, that most interested her. She was inspired by theories of justice and law taught in Anne Cheung's classes, and by working with Amanda Whitfort and various NGOs on animal rights and welfare. On graduation she decided not to take up the offer of a place on the PCLL and joined People for the Ethical Treatment of Animals as their legal advisor and first cruelty case officer in Asia. This encouraged her to

---

93. HKU students began joining the exchanges and internships in 2010. Website of the Legal Education Fund Ltd; Cecilia Chen, interview with the author, 15 August 2018.
94. Daisy Cheung, interview with the author, 18 October 2018.

think deeply about moral contradictions in the treatment of other animals by humans: in 2012 she started graduate studies, first with a Master of Science in political theory at the London School of Economics, and then at Queen's University at Kingston (in Ontario, Canada), where she is currently working on a PhD on the subject of moral progress.[95]

Geoffrey Yeung (BBA 2012, LLB 2014) started his studies at HKU just as Agnes Tam was entering her final year. An alumnus of Diocesan Boys' School, Yeung had applied for business and economics programmes in Hong Kong and the US. He chose the double degree at HKU because it gave him more options. Like several others from his school, he joined through the Early Admissions Scheme on the strength of his Hong Kong Certificate of Education Examination results, entering university just after turning 18. He found the LLB more demanding than the BBA, mainly because of the large quantity of reading. But he enjoyed the LLB most, particularly the electives in Media Law, Multiculturalism and the Law, and Equality and Non-Discrimination. Imaginatively taught, these courses introduced him to the works of two legal philosophers that were to have an influence on his later graduate studies – Iris Marion Young at the University of Chicago and Sandra Fredman at Oxford. The courses were also directly relevant to his various extracurricular projects: a summer internship with the United Nations Development Programme in Beijing, for example, and involvement in the Pink Alliance, a lesbian, gay, bisexual, and transgender advocacy group. This was at a time when UN CEDAW hearings in Geneva were focusing on Hong Kong issues, including the treatment of lesbian, bisexual, and transgender women. After passing his PCLL, Yeung went to Oxford University on a Rhodes Scholarship, taking a Bachelor of Civil Law (2016) and a Master of Philosophy in Law (2017). He decided to return to Hong Kong to train for the Bar because he wanted to work 'in the community I have always worked for.' He is currently a barrister in Denis Chang's Chambers. 'One of the lasting influences of HKU is the fact that the Faculty care about what is happening in Hong Kong, not necessarily because of any political leaning,' reflects Yeung. 'You see teachers standing up for principles and ideals. This makes an impression on students. And that is one of the reasons why you see a lot of such people in the legal profession.'[96]

Another double-degree graduate, Tony Lau Hon Yiu, was among the first batch of HKDSE students to enter HKU, after studying at Queen's College, one of Hong Kong's oldest secondary schools. He joined the five-year Bachelor of Social Sciences (Government & Laws) programme in 2012 to satisfy his own interests in politics and to meet his parents' expectations that he should take a degree leading to entry into one of the professions. He had little idea of how the legal profession worked, but a summer internship as a marshal for the High Court judge Anselmo Reyes gave him an excellent opportunity to see the law in action before starting university: this was shortly before Reyes left the Judiciary to return to

---

95. Agnes Tam Nga-yin, interview with the author, 7 September 2018.
96. Geoffrey Yeung, interview with the author, 29 September 2018.

HKU as a professor of law. Lau found the politics courses more interesting than the black-letter law courses, and tended to do better in them, but he also enjoyed courses that sparked lively discussions, such as Law and Society, Government and Law, Multiculturalism and Law, Alternative Dispute Resolution, and Media Law. In early 2016 he went on a semester-long exchange at the University of St Andrews in Scotland, taking advanced international relations courses. His summers were devoted to a variety of internships – with lawyers in Hong Kong and London, an NGO in Toronto, a Member of Parliament at Westminster, and an assistant district officer in the Yau Tsim Mong District Office. Seeing first-hand the workings of government in Yau Tsim Mong made him more determined to pursue law as a career. After graduation in 2017 he went on to obtain the PCLL in 2018. 'An education at HKU really changed my horizons, not just through what I learned from it but also through the networks it helped me develop, particularly in the legal profession,' says Lau. Now a trainee solicitor in a firm specializing in commercial work in Hong Kong and Mainland China, he is considering the possibility of further academic study.[97]

Cheung Ting also entered HKU in 2012, the year of the double cohort. She had studied first at St Paul's Convent School and had taken her 'A' levels at the Hang Seng School of Commerce, focusing mainly on business-related subjects. Although Cheung's main interest was in languages, her mother hoped she would enter one of the professions. Out of curiosity about legal English, Cheung decided to explore law. After joining the LLB programme at the Faculty of Law at HKU (her first choice), she came to realize that law was difficult, and the workload heavy. Although she enjoyed the more practical, real-life subjects, such as tort law and criminal law, she felt quite lost by her third year. 'Unlike some of my classmates, I wasn't in love with law,' she recalls. But she kept her hesitation to herself: the impression was 'if you don't become a lawyer you are a loser.' While her third-year classmates were already embarking on internships with large law firms, in 2015 she took a summer programme in Spanish at the University of California, Berkeley; during the last two years of the LLB she also devoted most of her non-law electives to a minor in Japanese. For two summers she interned with the UN in New York, working with units reviewing administrative decisions made by the organization. Along with voluntary work in Hong Kong with Amnesty International and the Asian Migrant Centre, this helped her realize that it was not law she disliked but the idea of profit-making in private practice. Her real interests were in human rights law and public service. After a more enjoyable time taking the PCLL, she joined the Department of Justice in 2017 as a trainee solicitor, the only position for which she applied: her training consists of a structured two-year programme in a variety of different roles, ranging from law drafting to prosecuting at the Eastern Magistrates' Courts. Her plan is to study international law at the postgraduate level overseas.[98]

---

97. Tony Lau, interview with the author, 16 August 2018.
98. Cheung Ting, interview with the author, 22 September 2018.

A Family of the Law and Justice: Students and the Legal Community in Hong Kong

'Even if you do not pursue a career in the law – I hope you do, but even if you do not – you will always be a part of this family of the law and justice,' said Kemal Bokhary, shortly after his retirement as a permanent judge of the Court of Final Appeal, to LLB graduands at their graduation ceremony in 2012.[99] At that time the number of practising lawyers in Hong Kong was approaching 10,000. The larger family of which Bokhary spoke extended to politics, business, government, the arts, and many other walks of life. From the early days of the Department of Law these connections – ranging from student summer internships with law firms to scholarships and prizes – have always been strong and productive. In more recent years they have become more extensive and more structured, drawing both on personal relationships and on an annual programme of workshops, lectures, and ceremonies that bring together students, teachers, and members of Hong Kong's wider legal community.

A driving force has been the HKU Law Alumni Association, founded in 1989 and established as an unincorporated body in 2001. By 2001, HKU had produced nearly 3,000 LLBs and about 4,000 PCLLs, rising to over 6,000 and over 9,500 respectively in 2018. The Faculty's longest-serving teacher, Michael Wilkinson, estimated he had 'probably taught 60 to 70 per cent of all lawyers in Hong Kong' in his thirty-five years at HKU – including (though not at HKU) the SAR's first Chief Justice, Andrew Li.[100] In such a compact jurisdiction HKU's law graduates come into frequent contact with each other, and friendships formed at university have matured and developed over long careers. The Law Alumni Association has helped them not only to maintain contact with each other but also to forge connections with students before they graduate. The association has been particularly energetic in recent years under the successive presidencies since 2001 of Priscilla Wong (LLB 1982), Kenneth Kwok (LLB 1972), Lucy Yen (LLB 1972), Elaine Liu (LLB 1987), and Kelvin Tang (LLB 2011).

In addition to organizing social events, raising funds, and maintaining a much-admired Law Alumni Choir, the HKU Law Alumni Association has worked with the Faculty on several initiatives to prepare students for professional life. Among these have been informal gatherings, the HKU Law Alumni Lecture Series, talks on topics such as 'the first day in practice', job interview workshops, and a thriving mentorship programme. Mentorships began in the late 1990s. They were placed on a regular footing in 2002 under a plan devised by the association with the help of the Associate Dean, Richard Wu (LLB 1984), and the

---

99. Address by Bokhary NPJ, 3 November 2012, *Faculty of Law Newsletter*, Summer 2013. For some, 'family of the law' has a more literal meaning: all five members of the Hui family – Thomas and Rosemary (parents), and Lawrence, Frederick, and Angela – have obtained PCLLs from HKU: *Faculty of Law Newsletter*, Spring 2007.

100. Andrew Li was a member of Wilkinson's first tutorial group at Fitzwilliam College, Cambridge in the late 1960s. Michael Wilkinson, interview in *Hong Kong Lawyer*, July 2018.

Faculty's first development officer, Carol Chen (LLB 1982). The mentorship programme matches students and alumni in small groups, bringing them together for dinner talks, outings, and other events. It fosters students' educational, social, and personal growth through supportive relationships with their mentors. On its launch in 2002, the scheme immediately attracted nearly 500 students and over 100 experienced solicitors, barristers, and judges. Starting as a one-year programme, in 2015 the formal mentorship relationship was extended to four years to enable students to build relationships throughout the whole of their first degree.

Whether through the Law Alumni Association, the Friends of the Faculty scheme, or in a purely individual capacity, alumni and other supporters have made generous financial donations to the Faculty, enabling it to embark on new initiatives that cannot be financed from its regular operating budget. In 2004 the Alumni Association formed its own charitable arm for the purpose of raising and disbursing funds for scholarships, prizes, and financial assistance to students. In 2010 the association's president, Lucy Yen (LLB 1972), presented the Faculty with $424,212 raised by the association for the HKU Law Alumni Association Scholarship; this was immediately increased to $1,164,130 through matching grants from the government and the Stanley Ho Alumni Challenge. Donations from alumni and other benefactors have funded five named professorships in Law since HKU introduced its endowed professorship scheme in 2005. In 2007 an early alumnus, Paul K.C. Chung (LLB 1977) endowed the Professorship in Jurisprudence, which has been held since 2010 by Scott Veitch. Most recently, in 2018, another alumnus, Warren Chan SC (LLB 1977), endowed the Professorship in Human Rights and Responsibilities to mark the Faculty's fiftieth anniversary, with Fu Hualing as its first holder. In addition, friends of the Faculty have endowed three other professorships: the Harold Hsiao-Wo Lee Professorship,[101] held in Company Law by Philip Smart (2007–2008) and in Trust and Equity by Lusina Ho (2011–); the Cheng Chan Lan Yue Professorship in Constitutional Law (originally endowed quasi-anonymously as the Chan Professorship),[102] held since 2007 by Albert Chen; and the Kerry Holdings Professorship in Law,[103] held by Michael Tilbury (2010–2015) and Douglas Arner (2017–). These named professorships are in addition to the Sir Y.K. Pao Chair in Public Law, founded in 1989 and held successively by Yash Ghai (1989–2006), Hurst Hannum (2006–2009), Anthony Carty (2009–2016), and David Law (2016–).

---

101. Endowed by Mrs Christina Lee in memory of her husband, the late Harold Hsiao-Wo Lee, a co-founder of Television Broadcasts Ltd.

102. 'Not donated by himself or me!' the Dean, Johannes Chan assured readers when announcing the appointment in the *Faculty of Law Newsletter*, Spring 2008. The professorship was endowed by Christopher Cheng Wai Chee, a businessman, philanthropist and member of several public bodies, including the Council of HKU. It was named after his mother, Cheng Chan Lan Yue.

103. Kerry Holdings is a global business organization, headquartered in Hong Kong, with subsidiary companies engaged in property management, logistics, and other activities.

Generous support from outside has also enabled the Faculty to organize lectures, conferences and other programmes, and to invite eminent scholars and jurists. Many of these are one-off events targeting issues of current interest, such as the Sixth Asian Law Institute Conference in 2009, which attracted some 300 scholars from around Asia, or the International Colloquium on Law and Literary Studies held in 2010 in advance of the launch of the new double degree. Others take the form of regular lecture series which are open to the public. The annual Hochelaga Lecture Series was founded in 1999 with funds donated anonymously to commemorate the life and interests of the donor's father.[104] Speakers have included internationally renowned jurists and scholars, such as the Chief Justice of Canada, Beverley McLachlin (who in 2018 was appointed a non-permanent judge of Hong Kong's Court of Final Appeal), the philosopher Kwame Anthony Appiah, and Lord Pannick QC, a leading English barrister who has appeared in many public law cases in Hong Kong.

Recognizing Hong Kong's unique position as the only common law jurisdiction in China, the Common Law Lecture Series, inaugurated in 2005 and organized with the assistance of the Hong Kong Judiciary, presents lectures by distinguished judges from Hong Kong and overseas. The speakers so far have included permanent and non-permanent judges of the Court of Final Appeal in Hong Kong and other senior judges from Australia, New Zealand, and Singapore. In the inaugural lecture Sir Anthony Mason, a non-permanent judge of the CFA and a former Chief Justice of the High Court of Australia, spoke on the role of the common law in Hong Kong. Other topics have ranged from vexatious litigants (Robert Ribeiro, 2005) to the duty to give reasons in administrative law (Michael Kirby, 2012).

Funds, scholarships, and prizes have been founded to remember Faculty members and alumni. Memorial funds for prizes and other purposes were established in memory of two of the Faculty's pioneer teachers, in 2006 for the late Dafydd Evans, the first Head and Dean, and in 2000 for the late Peter Willoughby, the first Head of DOPLE. In 2008 the Philip Smart Memorial Fund was founded in memory of Philip St John Smart, who had died at the age of forty-six, to support a research prize, research activities, and financial assistance to students. An expert on corporate law, Smart had taught in the Faculty since 1985; his book *Cross-Border Insolvency* (1991) was the first in the world to address a subject that has since become an important area of study.[105] Colleagues contributed essays in his memory to a tribute issue of the *Hong Kong Law Journal* in 2009. Another much-respected teacher, Betty Ho, who taught contract law at HKU 1988–2002, is remembered in the Betty

---

104. Hochelaga was the name given by sixteenth-century French explorers to an Iroquoian village near modern Montreal.

105. Philip Smart, *Cross-Border Insolvency* (London: Butterworths, 1991). In 2004 Smart's book was described in the High Court of England and Wales as 'the leading' book in the field: *Re Herlan Edmunds Engineering Pty Ltd* [2004] EWHC 2260.

Ho Prize in Law, founded by her brother, Gallant Ho, in 2012, and the Betty Ho Essay Prize on Contract Law, set up by her students, colleagues, and friends in 2014. Memorial funds to support lectures and other activities have also been established in the names of alumni whose careers were cut short by premature death. Among these are Eric Au (LLB 1979), a principal crown counsel and a pioneer in bilingual legislation, who died aged thirty-nine in 1992, and Jerome Chan (LLB 1974), a Court of First Instance judge and a proponent of the use of Chinese, who died at the age of forty-six in 1997.

Public lectures, conferences, seminars, moots, prize-givings, open days, and other events make for a crowded calendar. As the Faculty has matured and grown in size various ceremonies and traditions have taken root. Some, such as the annual graduation ceremonies, are an established feature of university life. Others, like the first PCLL High Table Dinner in 2007, 'an old tradition newly recreated',[106] draw on student culture in Hong Kong. Annual high table dinners, like orientation camps and other events, have been fixtures in the Law Association's calendar from its earliest years. The Faculty now holds its own graduation ceremonies for LLB graduates. Opening ceremonies or receptions are also held for new intakes to the LLB, LLM, and PCLL and research postgraduate programmes. The guests of honour on these occasions are usually distinguished alumni and other members of Hong Kong's 'family of the law and justice,' who give inspirational speeches and reflect on their own days as students.

A Permanent Home and a Symbol of the Rule of Law: The Cheng Yu Tung Tower

Up to 2012, the Faculty's graduation ceremonies were held in the Loke Yew Hall in HKU's Main Building, an Edwardian baroque structure completed in 1912 shortly after the founding of the university. Since 2013 these and other large-scale events have been held in the Grand Hall of the new Centennial Campus, a large extension to the west of the main campus completed in 2012 to mark the university's centenary. At the western edge of the new campus, on a steep mountainside among trees and gardens, stands the Cheng Yu Tung Tower, housing the Faculty of Law. Once again, the Faculty has its own building. But, unlike the disused terrace of houses on Caine Road allocated to the fledgling law school in 1969, the Cheng Yu Tung Tower is a permanent home, a state-of-the-art facility that has been custom designed over several years of consultation and careful thought. The new building was financed in part by a $400 million donation from the businessman Cheng Yu-tung (1925–2016), founder of the Chow Tai Fook Charity Foundation. It is a dignified symbol of the Faculty's role in the university and Hong Kong, and the focal point of its

---

106. A comment by Wilson Leung (PCLL 2006), one of the organizers of the first PCLL High Table. The PCLL Class of 2005–2006 was a particularly active and cohesive group: one of its other productions was a lively yearbook – the first and so far the only publication of its kind for the PCLL at HKU.

many activities. The opening of an MTR station at HKU in 2014 also brought the Faculty much closer to the community of lawyers in Central and Admiralty, turning a journey that could once take up to an hour into one of a mere ten minutes.

The Faculty of Law had been asking for its own building for some years, partly to provide additional space for its expanding programmes but also to recognize the fact that 'a separately identifiable Law Building carries a symbolic value symbolizing the importance of the rule of law in this community.'[107] In 2003 the Faculty commissioned the Faculty of Architecture to conduct a feasibility study of whether it could move into the former Old Halls – two low-rise buildings at the eastern end of the campus dating back to 1914–1915 and originally used as student accommodation. The conclusion was that the Old Halls would not meet the Faculty's needs. The exercise nevertheless gave a good idea of what the Faculty wanted in its new home when, two years later, the university drew up its expansion plans.[108]

In 2005–2006 four concepts for the new campus were produced by four Hong Kong architectural firms, each designed to meet the challenges of a steep 42,000-square-metre space on the site of an old waterworks and to make the most of its wooded landscape. The Faculty produced its list of requirements and invited ideas from teachers, students, alumni, and friends. They responded with photographs of other law schools, old and new, advice on facilities, and imaginative sketches, including a futuristic impression of the students' common room resembling something from Star Trek. A feng shui master, Louis Wong (PCLL 2002), stressed the importance of the elements of earth and wood to the legal profession and recommended a brick-built classical structure rather than a modern glass building. The Chairman of the Hong Kong Bar Association, Rimsky Yuen SC (LLB 1986), recommended a modern style that would appeal to the international commercial world. One early alumnus, Suffiad Azizul Rahman (LLB 1973), a judge of the Court of First Instance, suggested 'cold grey stone walls' reflecting dignity, integrity, and solemnity.[109] Johannes Chan, who as Dean was closely involved in design of the Cheng Yu Tung Tower, was determined that it should not be a 'matchbox' style building of the kind that dominates much of the university and its environs.

The design eventually chosen for the Centennial Campus was by Wong & Ouyang (HK) Ltd. It consists of three connected towers around a central courtyard with extensive underground facilities, including the magnificent Grand Hall, and is linked to the old campus by a double-level pedestrian 'University Street'. Two of the towers accommodate the Faculties of Arts and Social Sciences, along with other facilities. The third tower, on the far western edge, houses the Faculty of Law. Harmonizing with the design of the other towers, this is a

---

107. *Faculty of Law Newsletter*, Spring 2006.

108. Johannes Chan, Message from the Dean, *Faculty of Law Newsletter*, Summer 2013.

109. *Faculty of Law Newsletter*, Spring 2007.

semi-cylindrical, eleven-storey building of glass and brick-coloured tiles. The Law Library occupies the first two floors. The top (eleventh) floor contains a light-filled academic conference centre. The other floors consist of classrooms, conference rooms, staff offices, and a variety of specialized facilities, including mooting chambers, nineteen advocacy laboratories, a clinical legal education centre, common rooms, and other facilities for students and for the Faculty's research centres. The large moot court, in an adjoining structure next to the tower, can accommodate 400 people.

The Faculty moved into its new home in June 2012. A dedication ceremony on 8 November was presided over by the former Chief Justice, Andrew Li, now since 2010 an Honorary Professor of Law and, once again, a teacher in the Faculty. A few days earlier, on 30 October 2012, a dedication ceremony took place for the new Lui Che Woo Law Library. The main donor, the businessman and philanthropist Lui Che Woo, then in his eighty-fourth year, was the guest of honour. A long-standing benefactor of the Faculty, Lui had made a substantial donation to HKU in 1997, when the old law library in the K.K. Leung Building was named in his honour. The new library, greatly enlarged, with 1,856 square metres of floor space, houses discussion rooms, study carrels, and a collaborative area, with strong collections of materials from Hong Kong, Mainland China, the UK and the Commonwealth, and other jurisdictions in the Asia-Pacific region.

The Faculty's Administrative Staff

The complicated process of planning and moving to the new home in Cheng Yu Tung Tower could not have been achieved without the support of a dedicated team of administrative staff, who are essential to the life and success of the Faculty. The administrative staff, now numbering about fifty, support the Faculty in two main offices: the Faculty Office, which helps develop new plans and initiatives and co-ordinates the Faculty's work with the broader policies of the university; and the General Office, which helps manage the day-to-day operations of the Faculty. The Faculty Secretary, Vivian Wong, who heads the Faculty Office, joined the Faculty of Law in 1997. Several other staff have been with the Faculty for even longer, and four have received rare long-service awards: Henley Chan (2008), Cecilia Chan (2015), and Raymond Lam (2018), each for thirty-five years of service, and Monnie Leung (2015) for forty years. In an important sense, therefore, the administrative staff are custodians of the Faculty's institutional memory, maintaining continuity and traditions while working with the academic staff and students to address the rapidly developing needs of university education and research.

The administrative staff are involved, usually behind the scenes, in every aspect of the Faculty's work, from the policies and procedures for admitting students through to the organization of graduation ceremonies and alumni affairs. They organize budgets, timetables, examinations, recruitment exercises, and publications, and provide information technology and other forms of practical support, including help with resolving problems encountered by students. During the past two decades of root-and-branch reform in the Faculty and the university as a whole, they have also helped manage the complex processes of curriculum reform and quality assurance, including the RAEs and academic reviews, and the forging of partnerships with other law schools around the world. 'One of the important roles of the administrative staff is to help translate the university's institutional objectives into policies and practices that work for the Faculty, while at the same time respecting the individual approaches of teachers and the expectations of students,' reflects Vivian Wong. 'At a time of increasing competitiveness with other universities, this is a challenging and endless task.'[110] The recognition given to HKU around the world, in particular to the Faculty of Law, suggests that this task is being accomplished with a considerable degree of success.

A Special Standing in the World

In their report on legal education in Hong Kong in 1965, Zelman Cowen, Clifford Pannam and Anthony Guest described the proposed law school at HKU as an 'exciting project.' The school would, of course, fill a vital educational and professional need. There was also, they conjectured, 'a real possibility that it could develop into a law school with a special standing in the world.' They suggested that this would arise from Hong Kong's ideal position for developing research in Chinese law, both historical and contemporary. They could hardly have envisaged the enormous changes that have taken place in China and in Hong Kong's own legal system since the 1960s. Nor could they have predicted that, within fifty years of their report, the Faculty of Law at HKU would rank with their own universities of Melbourne and Oxford among the top law schools in the world.

University ranking systems have drawn mixed responses from academics. For some, along with RAEs and performance targets, they are part of the commoditization of academic life in a world obsessed with lists and ratings. For others, particularly students, they are a useful – though not infallible – indicator of what a university has to offer. Systematic worldwide rankings began to appear in 2004, when the *Times Higher Education Supplement* partnered with Quacquarelli Symonds, a global higher education company, to produce their annual World University Rankings. The partnership ended in 2009, but the two organizations have each continued to produce their own annual rankings. Other organizations, notably the Academic Ranking of World Universities, originating in the Shanghai Jiao Tung University, also carry out ranking exercises.[111] Ranking systems adopt

---

110. Vivian Wong, interview with the author, 11 February 2019.
111. The Faculty of Law at HKU has been ranked in the 51st–75th range in its most recent rankings, in 2017 and 2018.

various indicators such as academic reputation, teaching quality and research output.[112] Recently, the Quacquarelli Symonds survey has also ranked subjects within universities.

In the first two World University Rankings surveys HKU ranked 39th (2004) and 41st (2005) in the world. In 2007 and 2008 HKU shot up to 18th place, and first in Asia. Over the past decade it has ranked between 20th and 30th in the world – 25th in the latest rankings for 2019. HKU's surge to prominence in 2007 was greeted with a mixture of reassurance and scepticism: it put the university 'in a chilling position as we must strive our best to maintain and improve our global reputation,' observed the Dean of the Law Faculty, Johannes Chan.[113] When the Faculty of Law at HKU was ranked 31st in the first Quacquarelli Symonds survey of the world's law schools in 2011, he described it as 'a nice encouragement' but also 'a reminder that we should work harder.'[114] In 2013 the Faculty rose to 20th place in the world and first in Asia. Since then it has consistently been 18th or 19th in the world, jostling with the National University of Singapore for first place in Asia.

'What is the true measure of a Law School?' asked Michael Hor, a Malaysian-born graduate and former professor of the National University of Singapore, shortly after his appointment as Dean of the Faculty of Law at HKU in 2014. Hor had a long association with the Faculty, having taught there as a visiting professor in 2008 and during a sabbatical from the National University of Singapore in 2013. His answers to this question lay in careful curriculum design, teachers with ability, the success and contributions of alumni in their careers, co-operation with other institutions, and research into questions that grip Hong Kong, China, Asia, and the world – in brief 'the advancement of knowledge and understanding, and the cultivation of such virtues as selflessness, integrity and the belief in the inherent dignity of all humankind everywhere.' Hor went on to describe the Faculty's ultimate mission as being 'to nurture and impart the best in Hong Kong society, with its unwavering commitment to human rights and to the welfare of its phenomenal economy, and its legal system, underpinned by the rule of law and the independence and impartiality of its legal institutions.' It was the Faculty's responsibility 'to provide and maintain a liberal forum for the study and discussion on conflicting views on matters of public importance, and to deepen our engagement with China by being a different yet constructive presence in Chinese society.'[115]

The next chapter explores how the Faculty has sought to fulfil this mission through research and engagement with the issues confronting Hong Kong in recent years.

---

112. The Quacquarelli Symonds survey consists of six categories: academic reputation (40 per cent), employer reputation (10 per cent), faculty/student ratio (20 per cent), citations per faculty (20 per cent), international faculty ratio (5 per cent), and international student ratio (5 per cent).

113. *Faculty of Law Newsletter*, Spring 2008.

114. *Faculty of Law Newsletter*, Autumn 2011.

115. Michael Hor, Dean's Message, HKU Faculty of Law website.

Plate 36 The Faculty of Law team at the Peking University-HKU Legal Research Centre's annual conference in Beijing in 2006. From left to right: Johannes Chan, Rebecca Lee, Amanda Whitfort, Zhang Xianchu, Jessica Young, Thomas Cheng and Albert Chen.

Plate 37 A visit by law students from Hong Kong to the Supreme People's Procuratorate in Beijing in 2018 as part of a tour organized by the Legal Education Fund. (Picture courtesy of Ms Cecilia Chen)

Plate 38   Singing the Faculty of Law anthem at the graduation ceremony, Loke Yew Hall, 14 November 2009.

Plate 39   The Faculty's longest-serving teacher, Professor Michael Wilkinson, Head of the Department of Professional Legal Education 1991–1993 and 1997–2005, Chair of the Faculty Board 2006–2015, and HKU's Public Orator, presides over the Faculty's Graduation Ceremony, 14 November 2009.

Plate 40 Trial by Jury: a production of the Gilbert and Sullivan operetta by the Law Alumni Choir in 2012. Front row, from left to right: Janette Sham, Heusen Yip, Bethany Choi, David Yam, Rayne Chai, May Chan, Jonathan Chan, Jeffrey Sham and Helen Cheng.

Plate 41 The Law Alumni Choir perform at a concert on 17 November 2018 to celebrate the Faculty's fiftieth anniversary.

Plate 42 A poster for Senior CLIC (Community Law Information Centre), an online service for senior citizens launched by the Faculty in 2013 – a service provided by the Community Law Information Centre, which since 2007 has also included Family CLIC and Youth CLIC.

Plate 43 Clinical legal education: a scene from RTHK's 'A Legal Journey', a six-part series produced for the Faculty of Law's fiftieth anniversary, first broadcast in March 2019. The scene shows a reconstruction of an interview of a client by students. (Picture courtesy of RTHK)

Plate 44 The Cheng Yu Tung Tower, the Faculty's home since 2012, at the western edge of HKU's Centennial Campus.

Plate 45 The dedication ceremony for the $400 million donation from Dr Cheng Yu-tung for the Faculty of Law's building on the new Centennial Campus, 19 March 2008. Opened in 2012, the building was named the Cheng Yu Tung Tower in recognition of this support. From left to right, Professor Johannes Chan, Dean, Dr Henry Cheng, Managing Director of New World Development Co. Ltd, Dr Cheng Yu-tung, founder of the Chow Tai Fook Charity Foundation, Dr Victor Fung, Chairman of the HKU Council, and Professor Lap-Chee Tsui, Vice-Chancellor.

Plate 46 Professor Scott Veitch with Paul K. C. Chung (LLB 1977) at the inauguration of the Paul K. C. Chung Professorship in Jurisprudence, 2010.

Plate 47 Professor Fu Hualing with Warren Chan SC (LLB 1977) at the inauguration of the Warren Chan Professorship in Human Rights and Responsibilities in 2018.

Plate 48 The Hon. Andrew Li, Chief Justice of the Hong Kong SAR 1997–2010 and an Honorary Professor in the Faculty, speaks at the Faculty's Graduation Ceremony on 30 November 2018.

Plate 49 The Chief Justice of the Court of Final Appeal, the Hon. Geoffrey Ma Tao-li (right), and his colleague on the Court of Final Appeal, the Hon. Robert Ribeiro PJ, after receiving their honorary LLDs from HKU, April 2019.

Plate 50 The mass demonstration on 16 June 2019 calling for the complete withdrawal of a controversial bill that would allow extraditions from Hong Kong to jurisdictions, including Mainland China, with which Hong Kong has no extradition treaties. The government's attempt to rush the bill urgently through the Legislative Council triggered the gravest political crisis since the establishment of the Hong Kong SAR in 1997. (Picture courtesy of Cora Chan)

Chapter 8

Contemplation and Action

Faculty and Society in a Changing World

In his inaugural lecture as HKU's first Professor of Legal Practice, on 20 May 2014, Anselmo Reyes reflected on how much the university had changed since he left the Faculty of Law in 1988 to pursue a career as barrister and later as a judge of the Court of First Instance. HKU was now 'a vibrant and variegated institution,' 'a place "full of noises, sounds and sweet airs, that give delight and hurt not,"' he said, borrowing a description of Prospero's island in Shakespeare's *The Tempest*. The university and the Faculty of Law had been transformed 'from an introverted, parochial institution to a gregarious, generous-spirited community of scholars.' Reyes saw his role as 'to engage with the concerns of everyday life and to suggest how law can be applied in practical ways to alleviate those concerns.'[1] He started the Faculty's Judicial Studies Programme, an initiative launched in 2013 to help build capacity among judges in Asia through training and conferences. The programme is based on the belief that, in an increasingly complex world, where judges have to deal with many specialist issues, the old method of learning on the job is no longer adequate. At a time of chronic shortages of judges and challenges to judicial independence, the programme seeks to bridge the gap between academy and judiciary – to send to judges the message that 'you are not alone.'[2]

In recent years the Faculty has engaged increasingly with judicial topics, a reflection of the important role of the courts under Hong Kong's post-1997 constitutional order and the

---

1. Anselmo Reyes, 'The Future of the Judiciary: Reflections on Present Challenges to the Administration of Justice in Hong Kong,' text reproduced in 44 *HKLJ* (2014), 429–46.
2. *The University of Hong Kong Bulletin*, March 2017, 31–2.

growing interest in comparative judicial studies. These activities have produced a stream of articles and books, ranging from a multi-author study of Hong Kong's Court of Final Appeal (CFA) under its first Chief Justice, Andrew Li (1997–2010), edited by Yash Ghai and Simon Young, to a recent study by Po Jen Yap of the relations between courts and political power in Asia.[3] Another key work, *The Law of the Hong Kong Constitution*, edited by Johannes Chan and Chin Leng Lim, has contributions from over twenty Faculty members. Cora Chan (Bachelor of Social Sciences (Government & Laws) & LLB 2005) has written extensively on proportionality and judicial deference in human rights adjudication in Hong Kong and the UK.[4] He Xin has co-authored a book on the decision-making process of Chinese courts.[5] Two recently appointed Faculty members – David Law, the Sir Y.K. Pao Professor of Public Law, and Ryan Whalen – make use of data analysis to understand judicial thinking in other jurisdictions. Within Hong Kong, Michael Wilkinson sat on the Working Party on Civil Justice Reform (2001–2004), a comprehensive review of civil procedure aimed at increasing efficiency in the courts: the many rules, practice directions, and judicial decisions arising from this exercise have become a key focus of recent editions of *Civil Procedure in Hong Kong*, an authoritative professional guide by Wilkinson and his colleagues Eric Cheung and Gary Meggitt.[6] Most recently, another Faculty member, Shahla Ali, has published a groundbreaking study of court mediation in ten jurisdictions.[7]

This survey of recent projects on judicial topics – together with the Judicial Studies Programme and the ongoing training of judges from Mainland China – is a mere sample of the Faculty's impact on a wide range of legal issues through research, external training, and public engagement. The Faculty's Legal Scholarship Blog – an online chronicle of research since 2014 – lists dozens of subjects that have attracted the attention of Faculty members, including access to justice in China (Anne Cheung and Michael Ng), WTO rules and conflicts (Zhao Yun and Chin Leng Lim), academic freedom (Fu Hualing, Michael Davis, and Carole Petersen), and women's rights (Puja Kapai and Kelley Loper). The blog covers books, journal articles, newspaper reports, conferences, and other activities in which

---

3. Simon Young & Yash P. Ghai, *Hong Kong's Court of Final Appeal: The Development of the Law in China's Hong Kong* (Cambridge: Cambridge University Press), 2014; Po Jen Yap, *Courts and Democracies in Asia* (Cambridge: Cambridge University Press, 2017).

4. Two of her articles on these subjects have won prizes: Cora Chan, 'Deference, Expertise and Information-Gathering Powers,' *Legal Studies*, Vol. 33 No. 4 (2013), 598–620, (winner of 2012–2013 HKU Research Output Prize), 'Proportionality and Invariable Baseline Intensity of Review' (2013) 33(1) *Legal Studies*, 1–21 (winner of 2012 Society of Legal Scholars Best Paper Prize).

5. Ng Kwai Hang and He Xin, *Embedded Courts: Judicial Decision-Making in China* (New York: Cambridge University Press, 2017).

6. Michael Wilkinson, Eric T.M. Cheung and Gary Meggitt, *Civil Procedure in Hong Kong Sixth Edition* (Hong Kong: LexisNexis, 2017).

7. Shahla F. Ali, *Court Mediation Reform: Efficiency, Confidence and Perceptions of Justice* (Cheltenham: Edward Elgar Publishing Ltd, 2018).

Faculty members contribute to scholarship and community affairs. The hundreds of postings since 2014 show that, while the Faculty may indeed be a place full of noises and sounds, it is not, like Prospero's island, disconnected from the world around it. There is much to be said for the 'need of the academic to rise above the hubbub and hurly-burly of the "real world" in order to contemplate the deeper and more lasting aspects of life and living,' wrote the Dean, Michael Hor, in 2016. But 'an institution which has little or no effect on the society or the world it is found in is bound to struggle with the question of what it is there for.' The Faculty of Law, he was proud to say, was 'very much out there with shirt-sleeves folded' in projects combining 'contemplation and action' that 'touched the lives of people in Hong Kong, Asia and the world.'[8]

Yet, like Prospero's island, the Faculty is surrounded by storms. Law can be a contentious matter, affecting as it does practically all of human activity, private and public. Since 1997 the law and the courts have played a larger role than ever before in holding the balance between citizen and state. The Basic Law not only safeguards citizens' rights and freedoms but also lays down the system of government and the fundamental policies for Hong Kong. Crucial to the full implementation of the Basic Law – and, many have argued, to the vitality of the rule of law – is the policy that the Chief Executive and the legislature should ultimately be elected by universal suffrage in accordance with democratic procedures. Progress towards this objective has been beset with tension as the SAR government has attempted unsuc-cessfully to square the aspirations of many Hong Kong people for genuine democracy with the determination of the Central People's Government (CPG) that Hong Kong should not become a base for subverting the rest of China. In 2014 this tension reached a climax in the 'Occupy movement', a prolonged street protest against proposals for a restricted system for electing the Chief Executive from 2017: the failure of both sides to come to terms put an end to hopes of any form of universal suffrage for the time being. Because one of its members, Benny Tai, was an architect of the Occupy movement, the Faculty found itself at the centre of the fiercest political storm in its history.

This final chapter examines the various parts played by Faculty members in the civil society of modern Hong Kong through research, advocacy, and occasional activism. It explores the controversies over political reform against a background of growing friction in the implementation of 'one country, two systems' and rising concerns about freedom of expression and academic freedom in particular. Taking examples from current and recent research projects, it examines how the work of Faculty members has influenced the development of law and policymaking – and how in some cases it has not. Hong Kong is a unique place, enjoying, under its separate legal system, many rights and freedoms that are not extended to the whole of the country to which it belongs. As an open, cosmopolitan city it is also exposed to the same challenges that affect people everywhere: these include

---

8. Michael Hor, introduction to Faculty of Law, HKU, *Knowledge Exchange and Impact* (2016).

the globalization of trade and finance amid rapid technological change; environmental degradation; growing gaps between rich and poor; disillusion with traditional governing elites; and periodic financial and political crisis.

Twenty-First-Century Hong Kong

On 2 July 1997, one day after the establishment of the Hong Kong SAR, a debt and currency crisis erupted in Thailand. It spread quickly throughout East Asia, bursting bubbles that had been inflated by rampant speculation and crony capitalism. Foreign lenders withdrew credit, currencies collapsed, asset prices plummeted, and businesses went bankrupt. In Hong Kong, speculative attacks in 1997–1998 aimed at breaking the link between the Hong Kong and US dollar were defeated. But in 1998 the economy shrank for the first time since GDP statistics began in 1961. The next five years saw high unemployment, colossal falls in property values, and general deflation. In 2003, when unemployment reached a peak of 7.9 per cent, Hong Kong was one of the cities worst affected by severe acute respiratory syndrome (SARS), a mysterious viral disease originating in Guangdong Province. SARS killed 299 people, caused widespread alarm, and for a few weeks turned Hong Kong into a ghost town. The end of the SARS outbreak heralded the beginning of economic recovery. But it was also followed by a protest by some 500,000 people on 1 July 2003 against the government's plans to introduce national security legislation. The protest stopped the legislation and led to resignations by senior officials. But a pervasive mood of discontent had set in. This has continued to the present, culminating most recently in mass demonstrations in 2019 against proposed legislation that would allow the extradition to Mainland China of people alleged to have committed offences against Mainland law.

Much of the discontent springs from growing economic inequality and social injustice. Despite a return to economic growth, full employment, and gains in productivity, the average real wages for most workers, particularly younger workers, have not kept pace with inflation or with real GDP growth.[9] The gap between rich and poor has widened.[10] After plunging by 66 per cent in the early 2000s, property prices have since risen to nearly twice their level during the bubble of the mid-1990s. Yet public housing programmes were drastically cut after the Asian financial crisis 1997–1998.[11] Despite nearly full employment, over

---

9. For an analysis see John D. Wong, 'Between two episodes of social unrest below Lion Rock', in Michael H.K. Ng and John D. Wong (Eds.), *Civil Unrest and Governance in Hong Kong: Law and Order from Historical and Cultural Perspectives* (Abingdon: Routledge, 2017), 101–6.

10. The Gini coefficient for households, a measure of wealth inequality, rose from 0.453 in 1986 to 0.518 in 1996 and 0.539 in 2016, a record high for Hong Kong and one of the highest in the world.

11. An ambitious plan by the Hong Kong SAR's first Chief Executive, Tung Chee-hwa, to build 85,000 new units a year was abandoned when private property values plummeted after the Asian financial crisis. By 2012 the annual average supply of new units was 62 per cent lower than in 1997.

1.3 million people – nearly a fifth of the population – now live in officially defined poverty, many paying exorbitantly to rent cubicles in dilapidated private buildings – Hong Kong's 'hidden slums'.[12] A policy of retrenchment after the financial crisis and an ingrained official reluctance to spend money on social services, despite a massive accumulation of fiscal reserves, have worsened their plight. In contrast, the government has devoted considerable resources to business-friendly policies and costly infrastructure projects, the benefits of which have been doubted: among these are large-scale reclamations, a bridge across the Pearl River estuary, and a high-speed rail connection to the Mainland.

The failure to address the basic needs of a hard-working, peaceable population in one of the world's wealthiest cities has deepened disillusion with government and politics. Successive chief executives and their principal officials have mismanaged Hong Kong, argues a recent study by Leo Goodstadt. The city's survival has been threatened by disastrous policy decisions. Good governance has collapsed.[13] A close identification between the governing class and business has led to allegations of cronyism. A former Chief Executive, Donald Tsang (2005–2012), was convicted of misconduct in office by failing to declare a conflict of interest; the conviction was quashed by the CFA on the ground that the jury had been misdirected.[14] Tsang's deputy, Raphael Hui, was convicted of accepting millions of dollars in bribes from a property developer. A ministerial system, introduced to make government more accountable, has placed inexperienced people in positions of great responsibility; some have proved incompetent. Persistent conflict between an unelected executive and a partially democratic Legislative Council has resulted in legislative paralysis in many policy areas; this is aggravated by the prohibition on a serving Chief Executive from being a member of a political party.[15]

Increasingly, the burden has fallen on the courts, which have been asked to decide questions that might otherwise have been resolved by the other branches of government. The surge in judicial reviews – a major topic of research at the Faculty's Centre for Comparative and Public Law (CCPL) – has been linked by some experts to a 'democratic deficit', a lack of confidence in the political process, or simply 'plain bad governance.' It represents a 'negative verdict' on Hong Kong's 'democratic development, or more accurately, the lack of it,' concludes Johannes Chan.[16] Many of these actions, nevertheless, have been test cases

---

12. Oxfam Hong Kong, *Hong Kong Inequality Report* (2018), 9.

13. Leo F. Goodstadt, *A City Mismanaged: Hong Kong's Struggle for Survival* (Hong Kong: Hong Kong University Press, 2018). Goodstadt, an economist and former journalist, was head of the Hong Kong government's Central Policy Unit 1989–1997. He was an honorary law lecturer at HKU 1979–1985.

14. In the interests of justice, the CFA decided not to order a retrial, noting that Tsang had already served a prison sentence for the offence for which he would have been retried. *HKSAR v Tsang Yam-kuen, Donald* [2019] HKCFA 24.

15. The prohibition is in the Chief Executive Election Ordinance, Cap. 569, section 31.

16. Philip Dykes, 'The Functions of Judicial Review in Hong Kong' & Mark Daly, 'Judicial Review in the Hong Kong Special Administrative Region' in Christopher Forsyth, Mark Elliott, Swati Jhaveri, Michael Ramsden, &

in which disputes between citizen and state have been adjudicated for the first time under the Basic Law on issues ranging from town planning and the award of TV franchises to access to social welfare and the status of transgender persons. 'Some day you will be telling your grandchildren that you were a law student when these foundational cases were being decided,' Carole Petersen, Director of the CCPL 2001–2004, would tell her Constitutional Law class. 'We wish we lived in less interesting times,' was the response from one student.[17]

Academic Freedom: Faculty and University in the Hong Kong SAR

The Basic Law of the Hong Kong SAR states that educational institutions 'may retain their autonomy and enjoy academic freedom' and may continue to recruit staff and use teaching materials from outside Hong Kong.[18] Like most other institutions, the Faculty of Law passed through 1997 with little change. In the prospectus for the year, the Dean, Albert Chen, reflected with pride on 'the distinguished scholars who teach here, the competent and dedicated administrative and clerical staff who work here, the outstanding graduates who were educated here, and, above all, the bright conscientious and earnest students who are currently gathered here to learn about the law, about Hong Kong, China and the world, and about Life itself.'[19] Although a few teaching staff left for various reasons in 1996, only one departed in 1997: Nihal Jayawickrama, one of several human rights experts in the Faculty, told the press that he had been let go because of his political views.[20]

Many doubted Jayawickrama's claim, and over the next few years the Faculty's expertise in human rights and public law was in fact strengthened with several new appointments, including Fu Hualing, Carole Petersen, Robyn Emerton, Simon Young, Puja Kapai, Richard Cullen, Kelley Loper, Po Jen Yap, Cora Chan, Michael Davis, and Eric Ip. But the story merged with other concerns about academic freedom. A plan by the Vice-Chancellor, Cheng Yiu-chung, to transform HKU into a 'world-class' university aroused anxieties among staff, particularly when one of his consultants began to talk of redundancies, though

---

Anne Scully-Hill (Eds.) *Effective Judicial Review: A Cornerstone of Good Governance* (Oxford: Oxford University Press, 2010); Johannes Chan, 'Administrative Law, Politics and Governance: The Hong Kong Experience' in Tom Ginsburg and Albert Chen (Eds.), *Administrative Law and Governance in Asia: Comparative Perspectives* (London & New York: Routledge, 2008), 142.

17. Carole Petersen, interview with the author, 6 December 2017.

18. Basic Law, Article 136.

19. Message from the Dean, Faculty of Law, HKU, *Prospectus, 1997–1998*, 3.

20. Jayawickrama had reached the retirement age of sixty. His application to extend his appointment beyond retirement was rejected by the university, which at the time rarely granted such extensions. Jayawickrama, one of many outspoken human rights advocates, believed that his provocations of the Chinese government – for example, by encouraging students in his class to discuss whether Tibet had a valid claim for self-determination – were behind the decision. *SCMP*, 8 June 1997.

it also received much support.[21] The plan envisaged greater emphasis on research, more centralized management, and a performance-based system of budgeting, tenure, and promotions. It came while Hong Kong's higher education system was under scrutiny after the expansion of the early 1990s, and when universities were grappling with globalization, technological advance, and rising expectations. Two territory-wide reviews, in 1996 and 2002, stressed the importance of research, quality over quantity, and the need for Hong Kong's universities to compete on the international stage.[22]

The 2002 review – by Lord Sutherland, Vice-Chancellor of the University of Edinburgh – concluded that the old ways of running Hong Kong's universities through elected deans and dispersed governance were no longer suited to managing substantial public funds or building world-class universities. It favoured a centralized system similar to that of universities in the US, the UK, and Australia, and expressed a preference for appointed deans. Sutherland advised that each university should review its management structures. At HKU this came with the *Fit for Purpose* review of 2003, which recommended that deans should be appointed by the Vice-Chancellor and that the university's Council should be regarded as its de facto supreme governing body, with a higher ratio of lay to university members.[23] The system of appointed deanships on five-year terms was introduced in 2003. It allows full-time 'executive' deans to be recruited from outside the university after searches in which faculty staff take part. It also makes the deans part of the university's management team and – formally at least – accountable to the Vice-Chancellor rather than the faculties. As before, heads of departments are appointed by the Vice-Chancellor after consultation with the dean.

Some in the Faculty of Law saw the advent of appointed deans as a retrograde step.[24] The change was mitigated by making the chairmanship of faculty boards an elected position – the first elected chairman in the Faculty of Law was Michael Wilkinson (2006–2015) – and by selecting as first appointed Dean someone who already had the confidence of the Faculty. Johannes Chan served as both an elected Dean (2002–2005) and the first appointed Dean (2005–2014) of the Faculty. He saw no great change in style or functions, except that as appointed Dean he found himself working more closely with the university,

---

21. *SCMP*, 27 July 1997.

22. UGC, *Higher Education in Hong Kong – A Report by The University Grants Committee* (October 1996); Stewart R. Sutherland, *Higher Education in Hong Kong: Report of the University Grants Committee* (2002).

23. HKU, *Fit for Purpose: A review of governance and management structures at The University of Hong Kong* (February 2003). The review panel was convened by Professor John Niland, a former Vice-Chancellor of the University of New South Wales and a member of the UGC. Its other members were Professor Neil Rudenstine, a former President of Harvard University, and the Chief Justice, Andrew Li.

24. For critical analyses see Carole J. Petersen and Jan Currie, 'Higher Education Restructuring and Academic Freedom in Hong Kong' *Policy Futures in Education*, Vol. 6 No. 5 (2008), 589–600, & Carole J. Petersen and Alvin Y.H. Cheung, 'Academic Freedom and Critical Speech in Hong Kong: China's Response to Occupy Central and the Future of "One Country, Two Systems"', *North Carolina Journal of International Law and Commercial Regulation*, Vol. 42, No. 3 (2016), 1–64.

acting effectively as its legal advisor on many issues.[25] A prolonged search for a successor also required him to stay on for an extra year: feeling he had already served for long enough, he had negotiated only a three-year term for his second appointment. Chan was the longest-serving Dean of the Faculty of Law. His successor, Michael Hor (2014–2019), from the National University of Singapore, was the first Dean to be appointed from outside the Faculty.

Critics of the new governance arrangements point to the fact that the Governor, and since 1997 the Chief Executive, is chancellor of each of Hong Kong's publicly funded universities and appoints a proportion of members of their councils, including the chairs.[26] This arrangement, reflecting the involvement of the government in the founding and early development of HKU, drew on practices in British India; it exists in few other places. Governors in Hong Kong's later years as a colony tended to treat the position as a largely ceremonial one, relying, for example, on lists submitted by HKU for appointing lay members to seats on the University Council, and using the University Grants Committee (UGC) as a buffer between government and universities. Since 1997, chief executives have generally preferred to select their own appointees, some of whom lack expertise and are unclear about their roles.[27] They have also been more ready to intervene in university business, sometimes to the detriment of academic autonomy.

On 7 July 2000 the Director of HKU's Public Opinion Programme (POP), Robert Chung, revealed in an article in the *South China Morning Post* that he had received from the Chief Executive, Tung Chee-hwa, through a 'special channel', a clear message that his polls on the Chief Executive's popularity and the government's credibility were not welcomed.[28] Chung and his team had been tracing opinion on these issues since the early 1990s. Tung's ratings in 2000, at just over 50% support, were not especially low compared with those of his successors, but they were declining.[29] A week after his article appeared, Chung

---

25. Johannes Chan, interview with the author, 20 June 2018.

26. Following the changes recommended in the *Fit for Purpose* report in 2003, the Chancellor appoints seven lay members to the Council of HKU, one of whom he or she also appoints as Chairman; the Council appoints another six lay members; the Vice-Chancellor and Treasurer are ex officio members (the latter, usually a banker, is appointed by the Council); two are elected by the Court, four by teachers, and one each by non-teaching university employees, undergraduate students, and postgraduate students. Out of a total membership of twenty-four, sixteen members are lay (i.e. non-academic) members from outside the university. For the functions of the Chief Executive as Chancellor and the Council, and comparisons with practices elsewhere, see HKU, *Report of the Review Panel on University Governance* (February 2017), Chapters 5 and 6.

27. Petersen and Cheung, 'Academic Freedom and Critical Speech in Hong Kong,' 20–21; Sir Howard Newby, *Governance in UGC-funded Higher Education Institutions in Hong Kong: Report of the University Grants Committee* (Hong Kong: UGC, 2015), 19–20.

28. *SCMP*, 7 July 2000.

29. Tung's ratings declined to a low of 42.3 per cent in the second half of 2003. Those of his successors, Donald Tsang and Leung Chun-ying, dropped to below 40 per cent towards the end of their terms, in 2012 and 2016 respectively.

revealed that the 'special channel' was the Vice-Chancellor, Cheng Yiu-chung, who had sent a message to him, via the Pro-Vice-Chancellor, Wong Siu-lun, that Tung was unhappy with the polls and that they should be discontinued. Cheng confirmed that one of Tung's assistants, Andrew Lo, had visited him about Chung's polling activities but denied he had asked Wong to exert pressure on Chung. Responding to outrage over these allegations, the Council of HKU appointed an independent investigation panel, chaired by Sir Noel Power, a former Vice-President of the Court of Appeal, and including the barrister Ronny Wong SC (a former HKU law lecturer) and Pamela Chan, the head of the Consumer Council. The panel not only confirmed Chung's allegations but also criticized Cheng and Lo for failing to disclose 'the full and truthful extent of what was said' in their meeting.[30]

The Council of HKU met on 1 September 2000 to consider the panel's report. A letter from forty-two of the university's chair professors (but not those in the Faculty of Law) stated that they did not feel the incident substantiated 'a conclusion of deliberate interference of academic freedom.' The Council agreed to release the report to the public but postponed a decision on whether to adopt it to a second meeting on 6 September. In the meantime a petition signed by more than half the university's academic staff urged the Council not to reject the report simply because it did not like its conclusions. Alumni groups called for the Vice-Chancellor and Pro-Vice-Chancellor to resign: under pressure from the (elected) deans, they stepped down on 6 September. Whether through government pressure, fear of a judicial review, or a belief that the resignations had settled the matter, the external members of the Council (then as now constituting a majority) opposed a motion by the university members to adopt the report. The Faculty of Law passed a near-unanimous motion calling on the Council to adopt it, observing that the crux of the issue was the application of academic freedom not only to the Robert Chung affair, 'but more prevalently in terms of resources allocation, promotion and contract renewal.' One of the Faculty's human rights experts, Carole Petersen, in her analysis of the Robert Chung incident, called for the links between the Council and the government to be reduced and for the Chancellor to be someone other than the Chief Executive.[31]

The Council never adopted the report. The Chief Executive continued as Chancellor of HKU and of Hong Kong's other universities. In 2003, following the proposals in the *Fit for Purpose* report, the university's statutes were amended to reduce the size of the Council: the majority of external members was retained, but ex officio membership of the deans of

---

In the second half of June 2019, after the mass demonstrations against the extradition bill, the support rating of the fourth Chief Executive, Carrie Lam (2017–) fell to 32.8%. HKU Public Opinion Programme website.

30. *Report to the Council of The University of Hong Kong by the Independent Investigation Panel* (2000); Carole J. Petersen, 'Preserving Academic Freedom in Hong Kong: Lessons from the Robert Chung Affair,' 30 *HKLJ* (2000), 165–76.

31. Petersen, 'Preserving Academic Freedom in Hong Kong: Lessons from the Robert Chung Affair'.

faculties was abolished. In 2011 the University of Hong Kong Ordinance was amended to formally designate the Council (and not, as before, the much larger Court) as the university's supreme governing body – a recognition of what in practice had long been the case but also a confirmation of its primacy in university affairs. Three years later the Council was to exert itself much more aggressively when it considered another controversial issue: the nomination for the position of Pro-Vice-Chancellor of the former Dean of Law, Johannes Chan, a scholar noted for his liberal views and, along with other members of the Faculty of Law, caught up in the conflicts arising out of 'one country, two systems.'

Friction under 'One Country, Two Systems'

Under 'one country, two systems' Hong Kong maintains its way of life and enjoys a high degree of autonomy as an SAR of the People's Republic of China (PRC). This 'grand experiment', as Albert Chen describes it, has for the most part worked well.[32] Its implementation has nevertheless involved some friction between the SAR and the rest of the country. The 1999 constitutional crisis over right of abode confirmed the power of the Standing Committee of the National People's Congress (NPC) not only to overrule interpretations of the Basic Law by Hong Kong's courts but also to make its own freestanding interpretations. Since the 1999 interpretation the Standing Committee has made four more interpretations: two on its own initiative, one at the request of the SAR government, and only one at the request of the CFA. These interventions have caused growing anxiety in the legal community. After the Asian financial crisis and SARS the Mainland authorities introduced measures to help Hong Kong, for example by relaxing restrictions on visits by Mainland residents to revive tourism, and by allowing Hong Kong's service industries greater access to the Mainland under the Closer Economic Partnership Arrangement. However, the arrangement did not deliver on its promises. The large increase in Mainland visitors, along with an influx of over 1.5 million migrants since 1997, has given rise to conflicts over resources and fears of 'mainlandization', which many in Hong Kong see as a threat to their identity.

Political friction between Hong Kong and the Mainland has also focused on two questions left unsettled by the Basic Law: national security laws and democratic reform. The first – the trigger for the mass protest on 1 July 2003 – is the requirement under Article 23 for the Hong Kong SAR to enact its own laws to prohibit treason, secession, sedition, subversion, and other acts affecting national security. The second is the ultimate aim, set out in Articles 45 and 68, that the Chief Executive and Legislative Council should be elected by universal suffrage.

---

32. Albert Chen, 'The Law and Politics of the Struggle for Universal Suffrage in Hong Kong, 2013–15,' 3 *Asian Journal of Law and Society* (2016), 189–207.

Article 23 and the 2003 National Security Bill

The idea that a regional government should be entrusted with enacting laws on national security is a mark of the high degree of autonomy conferred on Hong Kong. Yet such legislation was bound to be contentious given the importance attached to civil liberties and anxieties about extending state power. The National Security (Legislative Provisions) Bill, drawn up by the SAR government after open and intensive consultation, would have liberalized some of the laws inherited from colonial Hong Kong, notably those on sedition. But other parts of the bill – for example, on secession, disclosure of official secrets, and a power to ban organizations affiliated to bodies proscribed on the Mainland – raised concerns about human rights.[33] These concerns, along with a rush to enact the bill, sparked widespread opposition at a time of distress over the economy and SARS. The demonstration on 1 July 2003 not only halted the bill, as key supporters withdrew their backing; it was quickly followed by the resignations of the Secretary for Security, its main proponent, and the Financial Secretary, who had lost credibility in an earlier scandal.[34] In March 2005 the Chief Executive, Tung Chee-hwa, resigned shortly after President Hu Jintao had publicly criticized his administration for its inadequacies. The withdrawal of the Article 23 legislation and the collapse of Tung's administration demonstrated to many the power of mass protest.

The Faculty of Law was closely involved in the public debate on this proposed legislation. Its Dean, Johannes Chan, was a founding member of the Article 23 Concern Group, a coalition of politicians, lawyers, and academics. The Faculty's CCPL adopted Article 23 as a research project and held two conferences, in November 2002 and June 2003, where experts from Hong Kong and overseas analysed the National Security Bill and proposed amendments. Teachers, students, and alumni joined the march on 1 July. 'I felt proud being a member of the legal community,' said one alumna. 'Studying law is more than paving the way for a lucrative career.'[35] A book based on the 2002 conference had to be hastily revised to take into account the bill's demise. 'Why publish a book about a Bill that was not enacted?' asked one of its editors, Carole Petersen. The answer was that in the near future the government would likely introduce a new bill, using the 2003 bill as its starting point.[36] Yet none of Tung's successors has so far revived the legislation. More than twenty years after the establishment of the SAR, Article 23 remains dormant.

---

33. The provisions are analysed in Fu Hualing, Carole J. Petersen, and Simon N.M. Young (Eds.), *National Security and Fundamental Freedoms: Hong Kong's Article 23 Under Scrutiny* (Hong Kong: Hong Kong University Press, 2005).

34. He had purchased a brand new Lexus LS 430 car only weeks before proposing large increases in the first registration tax on new vehicles in his annual budget.

35. Rebecca Lee (LLB 2001), in *Faculty of Law Newsletter*, Autumn 2003.

36. Fu, Petersen, and Young (Eds.), *National Security and Fundamental Freedoms*, 3.

Democratic Reform

The other area of friction is the plan for democratic reform leading ultimately to universal suffrage 'in accordance with the principle of gradual and orderly progress.'[37] Under the Basic Law, the Chief Executive must be a Chinese citizen, be at least forty years old, have no right of abode in any foreign country, and have at least twenty years' residence in Hong Kong. Because of dual accountability to the CPG and the SAR, he or she is appointed by the CPG after elections or consultations in Hong Kong. Terms are for five years, to a maximum of two.[38] So far, under Annex I of the Basic Law, chief executives have been selected by an Election Committee designed to be representative of different sectors. Most of its members are elected by business, professional, and social sectors; others are members by virtue of their membership of the Legislative Council, or of the NPC as Hong Kong deputies, or of other bodies: the membership of the Election Committee was increased from 400 in 1996 to 800 in 2002, and 1,200 in 2010.[39] Despite a requirement that candidates receive a minimum number of nominations from Election Committee members,[40] some elections have been hotly contested. Those in 2007 and 2012 even took on the guise of popular elections, with campaign trails and televised debates (but no popular vote), when pro-democracy advocates, both law graduates of HKU, entered the contests: Alan Leong (LLB 1982) in 2007 and Albert Ho (LLB 1974) in 2012. Neither was successful.

The SAR's first elected Legislative Council, formed in 1998, consisted of 30 members elected by functional constituencies, 20 by geographical constituencies, and 10 by the 800-member Election Committee for selecting the Chief Executive. Corporate voting was restored for functional constituencies, reducing the number of eligible voters by 90 per cent. Proportional representation replaced the first-past-the post system introduced for geographical constituencies in the Patten reforms. Despite winning 66 per cent of the popular vote, pro-democratic parties won only twenty of the sixty seats (fifteen in geographical constituencies), down from twenty-nine in 1995; pro-establishment parties won forty. In accordance with the Basic Law, the ten Election Committee seats were reduced

---

37. Basic Law, Articles 45 and 68. For the legal and political context, see Cora Chan, 'Legalizing Politics: An Evaluation of Hong Kong's Recent Attempt at Democratization,' *Election Law Journal*, Vol. 16 No. 2 (2017), 296–305, Chen, 'The Law and Politics of the Struggle for Universal Suffrage in Hong Kong, 2013–15,' and Johannes Chan, 'A storm of unprecedented ferocity: The shrinking space of the right to political participation, peaceful demonstration, and judicial independence in Hong Kong,' *I-CON* (2018), Vol. 16 No. 2, 373–88.

38. In 2005, following the resignation of Tung Chee-hwa before he completed his term, the Standing Committee of the NPC, at the request of the Acting Chief Executive, issued an interpretation of the Basic Law to the effect that, if the office of Chief Executive becomes vacant before the expiration of the five-year term, the term of the next Chief Executive shall be for the remainder of the term of the previous Chief Executive.

39. Election Committee members serve for five-year terms. The early arrangements are analysed in Simon N.M. Young and Richard Cullen, *Electing Hong Kong's Chief Executive* (Hong Kong: Hong Kong University Press, 2010).

40. 50 in the first election in 1996, 100 in 2002, 2005 and 2007, and 150 in 2012 and 2017.

to six for the second Legislative Council (2000) and then to zero in the third (2004) and fourth (2008): they were replaced by directly elected geographical constituency seats, which had parity with the functional constituency seats in 2004 and 2008.[41] Provisions in the Basic Law make it difficult for members to amend government bills and almost impossible for them to introduce their own bills.[42]

The pattern set by the 1998 election continued up to 2008, with pro-democratic parties winning a majority of the geographical constituency seats and pro-establishment parties holding most of the functional constituency seats and a majority in the council as a whole. The pro-establishment parties (sometimes known as 'pro-Beijing' parties) consist of the Democratic Alliance for the Betterment and Progress of Hong Kong (DAB), the Federation of Trade Unions, the Liberal Party, and a few smaller parties. They have been successful in attracting support by addressing livelihood issues. Among the pro-democratic parties – now referred to as the 'pan-democrats' – the Democratic Party has gradually lost its share of votes both to the pro-establishment parties and to other, newer parties with reformist platforms. Among these is the Civic Party, established in 2006, and holding five or six Legislative Council seats since 2008. The party traces its origins to the Basic Law Article 23 Concern Group and its successor, the Article 45 Concern Group, formed to press for universal suffrage. Although drawing its membership from academics, social workers and other liberal-minded professionals, the Civic Party is very much a lawyers' organization. Four of its six founders – Audrey Eu SC, Alan Leong SC, Ronny Tong SC, and Margaret Ng, all at various times members of the Legislative Council – are barristers with LLBs or PCLLs from HKU. Other Civic Party legislators with a legal background are Tanya Chan (LLB 1994), Dennis Kwok (PCLL 2000), and Alvin Yeung.

The methods for forming the first three Legislative Councils after 1997 are set out in the Basic Law, which states that any changes after 2007 must be endorsed by a two-thirds majority of the Council, receive the consent of the Chief Executive, and be reported to the Standing Committee of the NPC for the record. A similar provision applies to the Chief Executive, except that changes require the *approval* of the Standing Committee.[43] In December 2007, in response to a public consensus that universal suffrage should first be implemented for the Chief Executive, preferably in 2012, the Standing Committee resolved

---

41. Legislative Council terms are four years, except for the first term, which was two years. Basic Law, Article 69 & Annex II.

42. Bills are introduced by Principal Officials, who are not members of the Council. Members may introduce bills not related to public expenditure, political structure, or the operation of government. Bills relating to government policies require the written consent of the Chief Executive. In addition, whereas passage of bills introduced by the government requires a simple majority vote by members present, passage of motions, bills, or amendments introduced by members requires a majority vote of each of two groups of members present: those returned by functional constituencies, and those by geographical constituencies and the Election Committee. Basic Law, Article 74 & Article II of Annex II.

43. Basic Law, Articles 45 & 68 & Annexes I & II.

that the Chief Executive could be elected by universal suffrage in 2017 and the Legislative Council could also be elected by universal suffrage at some time thereafter. Meanwhile, modest reforms in 2010 expanded the Election Committee to 1,200 and added 10 seats to the Legislative Council – 5 geographical constituencies and 5 'super seats' in a new functional constituency, giving a second vote to all voters ineligible to vote in other functional constituencies. The reforms were enacted only after the Chief Executive, Donald Tsang, agreed to substantial amendments to his original proposal.[44] The pan-democrat camp was split over whether to support the amended proposal, which was enacted with the support of the Democratic Party.

Donald Tsang was succeeded as Chief Executive in 2012 by Leung Chun-ying. One of the earliest issues to face Leung was the fate of a planned 'Moral and National Education' curriculum for schools, stressing national identity and promoting positive attitudes towards the Motherland. Opposition to the policy, centring on rallies and hunger strikes led by Scholarism, an organization of secondary-school students, was so great that Leung was forced to shelve the policy. This further example of people power, occurring soon after the 'colour revolutions' in the Middle East, emboldened activists to take to the streets to oppose other policies. At the same time, the Chinese government, under the new President, Xi Jinping, was intensifying its efforts to strengthen central authority, control information, and clamp down on dissent on the Mainland. It was now also turning its attention to Hong Kong, as consultations began on the method for electing its Chief Executive by universal suffrage from 2017.

On 10 June 2014 the State Council issued a White Paper on 'one country, two systems.'[45] The paper reviewed progress since 1997, reaffirmed China's commitment to the policy, and described the support given by the CPG to Hong Kong over the years. It also criticized the 'many wrong views' of those who failed to understand 'one country, two systems' as a holistic concept and neglected 'the fundamental objectives of maintaining China's sovereignty, security and development interests.' It stressed that China's central government 'has comprehensive jurisdiction over all local administrative regions, including the HKSAR.' The high degree of autonomy of the SAR was neither an inherent nor a decentralized power but 'the power to run local affairs as authorized by the central leadership.' Those who 'administrate' Hong Kong, including the judges, were responsible for 'safeguarding the country's sovereignty, security and development interests' and 'should above all be patriotic.' This apparent exhortation to judges to take on a political role prompted an indignant response from the Bar Association. The President of the

---

44. The amendments changed an original proposal that the electorate for five new functional constituency seats should be restricted to District Councillors into one based on universal suffrage.

45. 'The Practice of the "One Country, Two Systems" Policy in the Hong Kong Special Administrative Region,' reproduced in full in English in *SCMP*, 10 June 2014.

Law Society resigned on a vote of no confidence after expressing controversial views in support of the Chinese Communist Party. On 27 June some 1,800 lawyers held a silent march against the White Paper.[46]

On 31 August 2014 the Standing Committee of the NPC issued its decision on universal suffrage.[47] This confirmed that the Chief Executive could be elected by universal suffrage in 2017. But it placed a limit of two or three on the number of candidates, each of whom should be endorsed by over half of the members of a nominating committee the composition of which would be based on the existing Election Committee for the Chief Executive. Reflecting Article 45 of the Basic Law, this screening of candidates was explained as an institutional safeguard to ensure that the Chief Executive, who is accountable to both the SAR and the CPG, is a person 'who loves the country and loves Hong Kong.' However, while pro-establishment parties and some opinion polls generally supported this approach, many other groups, particularly the pan-democratic parties, insisted on 'civil nomination' by eligible voters and no limit on candidates, consistent with Article 21 of the Bill of Rights: this states that every citizen should have the right to vote and the right to be elected without unreasonable restrictions.

These questions were fiercely debated during the public consultation. In April 2014 the Faculty's CCPL held a panel discussion and a series of seminars on civil nomination and the various models put forward for electing the Chief Executive. Speakers included the Secretary for Justice, Rimsky Yuen SC (LLB 1986) and Audrey Eu, representatives of different political parties, and academics and other experts. Open to the public and streamed live on the Internet, these events attracted enormous media interest. Videos and other materials were placed on a special 'Design Democracy Hong Kong' website, where visitors were invited to submit their own models for electing the Chief Executive and the Legislative Council. Over 700 models were submitted, including proposals by Faculty members Albert Chen, Johannes Chan, Eric Cheung, Simon Young and Michael Davis, mostly designed to bridge the gap between civil nomination and the requirements of the Basic Law.[48]

---

46. 'White Paper on the Practice of "One Country, Two Systems" Policy in the Hong Kong Special Administrative Region: Response of the Hong Kong Bar Association,' 11 June 2014, Hong Kong Bar Association website; *SCMP*, 27 June 2014 & 19 August 2014.

47. Report on the Public Consultation on the Methods for Selecting the Chief Executive in 2017 and for Forming the Legislative Council in 2016; Decision of the Standing Committee of the National People's Congress on Issues Relating to the Selection of the Chief Executive of the Hong Kong Special Administrative Region by Universal Suffrage and on the Method for Forming the Legislative Council of the Hong Kong Special Administrative Region in the Year 2016.

48. CCPL, Faculty of Law, HKU, *Annual Report July 2013–June 2014*.

The Occupy Movement

A leading participant in the debate on electoral reform was Benny Tai (LLB 1986), an associate professor in the Faculty of Law and an expert on constitutional law. Long before official consultations began, on 16 January 2013, the day of Chief Executive Leung's first policy address, *Hong Kong Economic Journal* published an article by Tai outlining a plan to pressure Beijing and the SAR government into implementing genuine universal suffrage. Tai correctly anticipated that Leung would make no promises in his address. He doubted the efficacy of demonstrations against what he saw as Beijing's resistance to genuine universal suffrage. Instead, he advocated a carefully orchestrated plan of non-violent civil disobedience aimed at briefly paralysing Hong Kong's central business district to force Beijing to change its stance.[49] What happened did not quite follow Tai's blueprint. 'Occupy Central with Love and Peace' began in the Admiralty district on 28 September 2014 and lasted seventy-nine days. Tai and his co-organizers lost control as the protest took on a life of its own. Occupy not only failed to sway Beijing; it further polarized the community, provoking more extreme views and actions on both sides of the political divide, with consequences for both Benny Tai and the Faculty of Law.

A graduate of HKU, Benny Tai developed an interest in public affairs during his student days as External Secretary of the HKU Law Association and the Students' Union. He took part in visits by students to Mainland China, experiencing first-hand the optimism over the reforms of Deng Xiaoping. In 1987, while taking the PCLL, Tai was elected to the Basic Law Consultative Committee as a student representative. He formed an interest in constitutional law, started writing articles for *Ming Pao*, and worked with the politician Martin Lee. After a spell of teaching at City Polytechnic he took an LLM at the London School of Economics, where he wrote a thesis on 'one country, two systems.' On his return he joined the Faculty of Law at HKU to teach courses in public law. His public service continued with training for civil servants on judicial review and membership of the Bilingual Laws Advisory Committee and Committee on the Promotion of Civic Education (1995–2003): in 2001 the government awarded him a Medal of Honour for his contributions to civic education. Tai's special interest in educating younger people culminated in 2012 with his launch of the Rule of Law Education Project, an initiative to increase public understanding of the rule of law by training teachers, students, and community workers through a structured conceptual framework.

Benny Tai's plan for Occupy Central was founded on several principles: it required a large turnout and participation by leaders of public opinion; it was to be non-violent and sustained in a 'street carnival' style that would attract world attention; it was to be carefully timed and widely publicized in advance; it was to end as soon as the government showed

---

49. *Hong Kong Economic Journal*, 16 January 2013.

itself willing to sit down and discuss concrete measures for genuine universal suffrage; and participants had to declare they would accept the legal consequences of their actions. Tai drew his inspiration from historic campaigns led by Mahatma Gandhi and Martin Luther King Jr, and from recent 'occupy' protests in cities around the world (including Hong Kong) against the excesses of capitalism. The concept of civil disobedience was the topic of a lecture at the Faculty by the Israeli philosopher Joseph Agassi in November 2000.[50] Earlier, Roda Mushkat had included the subject in one of her courses.[51] But it had not been part of the early courses on civil liberties taught in the 1980s, and Benny Tai had scrupulously avoided the subject in his own courses.[52] Nevertheless, as the debate on political reform intensified, the planned Occupy Central became a talking point. The summer 2014 issue of the *Faculty of Law Newsletter* contained a special feature by student reporters on civil disobedience, carrying interviews with Benny Tai, Albert Chen, and Simon Young. There was a full range of views on the subject, noted the outgoing Dean, Johannes Chan, but the Faculty itself had no view, except to encourage students to engage with the issues and consider the arguments on both sides.[53]

The Occupy Central movement gathered momentum during 2014 with oath-takings, practical planning, a series of 'deliberation days' at which different forms of nomination were discussed, and a 'civil referendum' organized by the HKU Public Opinion Programme, in which nearly 80,000 people chose from a selection of three proposals, all with civil nomination. 'The whole idea of Occupy was not to occupy,' recalls Benny Tai; the prolonged preparations were intended to show strength and generate pressure without the need for action. When, therefore, the Standing Committee of the NPC announced its decision on electoral reform on 31 August 2014, Tai admitted the movement had failed.[54] Tai and the other leaders of Occupy, Chan Kin-man and Chu Yiu-ming, nevertheless planned a mass sit-in, possibly on a public holiday, causing minimum damage to the economy.

In September two groups that had come to the fore during the deliberations on Occupy – Scholarism and the Hong Kong Federation of Students – organized class boycotts by university and secondary-school students. On 26 September the leader of Scholarism, the seventeen-year-old Joshua Wong, and other protestors stormed 'Civic Square' near the new SAR government complex at Tamar near Admiralty, leading to seventy-eight arrests; the square had been fenced off with high railings since the national education protests, in which Wong had played a leading role. Two days later, in the early hours of Sunday 28

---

50. Agassi had been Head of the Department of Philosophy at HKU 1960–1963. Joseph Agassi, 'A Public Lecture on Civil Disobedience', 1 November 2000 (text in the Faculty of Law Library, HKU).

51. Roda Mushkat, interview with the author, 5 September 2017.

52. After the Occupy movement, however, he included the topic in his Common Core course on the rule of law. Benny Tai, interview with the author, 12 October 2018.

53. Message from the Dean, *Faculty of Law Newsletter*, Summer 2014.

54. Benny Tai, interview with the author, 12 October 2018; *SCMP*, 2 September 2014.

September, Benny Tai announced the start of Occupy Central outside the Tamar government complex. During the day large crowds gathered, blocking main roads nearby. Shortly before 6 p.m. the police began firing pepper spray and tear gas in an attempt to disperse the crowds. Tear gas has rarely been used in recent years in Hong Kong, and TV footage of familiar streets filled with smoke and young people reeling from its effects caused shock and anger; an analysis by Simon Young concluded that its use on this occasion was an excessive and ineffective response.[55] The tear gas not only failed to disperse the crowds but drew thousands more to the streets. The next day, after the police had backed off, the roads around the Tamar complex, including a section of Harcourt Road, the island's main highway, were still blocked by protestors. Other protest sites had formed at busy points in Causeway Bay and Mong Kok.[56]

The protest lasted seventy-nine days. The police retreated behind barricades. The roads around the Tamar government complex were turned into a self-regulating community of tents, open-air classrooms, and exhibitions. Students and their supporters created their own imaginative culture of protest, using international, Chinese, and colonial imagery but above all projecting a vibrant Hong Kong identity drawn from a bricolage of local popular culture. The movement was as much about questions of identity as it was about politics or law and order, argues Marco Wan, in his analysis of its artwork.[57] As the protest took on its own momentum, Occupy Central was transformed into the 'Umbrella Movement': used as a defence against pepper spray and tear gas, the umbrella had become the protest's symbol.

Hong Kong became the focus of international attention. Journalists from overseas were impressed by the self-discipline, resourcefulness, and civility of those taking part, particularly since this amorphous movement had no clear leadership. The charismatic young convener of Scholarism, Joshua Wong, along with office bearers of the increasingly divided Hong Kong Federation of Students, became the public face of the movement. Benny Tai and the other initiators of Occupy Central withdrew after one month. Tai returned to his teaching duties, though he continued to visit the site almost daily. 'No one was in charge,' he recalls. 'There was no decision-making process. In the end we all did our own thing.'[58] The Faculty of Law had left it to teachers to decide their own arrangements during the class boycott and Occupy: in response to student requests, many video-recorded their

---

55. In all, eighty-seven canisters of tear gas were fired that evening. Young's analysis, posted on the HKU Legal Scholarship Blog on 29 September 2014, was cited in the Legislative Council by the representative of the Legal Functional Constituency, Dennis Kwok: *Hong Kong Hansard*, 16 October 2014.

56. For a detailed account of the movement see Jason Y. Ng, *Umbrellas in Bloom: Hong Kong's Occupy Movement Uncovered* (Hong Kong: Blacksmith Books, 2016).

57. Marco Wan, 'The artwork of Hong Kong's Occupy Central Movement,' in Michael H.K. Ng and John D. Wong, *Civil Unrest and Governance in Hong Kong: Law and Order from Historical and Cultural Perspectives* (Abingdon: Routledge, 2017).

58. Benny Tai, interview with the author, 12 October 2018.

lectures and put them online.[59] After a week or so of absence, the students taking part in the movement generally managed to juggle attendance at classes with time at the protest site.

One law student, Yvonne Leung Lai Kwok (Bachelor of Social Sciences (Government & Law) 2015, LLB 2017), as President of the HKU Students' Union, took part in a televised debate on 21 October 2014 between student representatives and senior officials. The two-hour debate was polite but unproductive: the students rejected suggestions by the then Chief Secretary, Carrie Lam, that the nomination committee could be made more democratic, or that Hong Kong could 'pocket first' the decision of August 31 and plan for further reforms for the 2022 election. One of the highlights was an exchange between Yvonne Leung and the Secretary for Justice, Rimsky Yuen, in which she challenged his view that the decision of 31 August could not be changed.[60] An earlier TV production, 'The Class of 1986' (同班同學), shown by RTHK in August 2014, had traced the careers of some of the seventy-four LLBs who had graduated from HKU that year. From this vintage came not only the teachers Benny Tai and Eric Cheung but also the Secretary for Justice Rimsky Yuen, the Director of Public Prosecutions Keith Yeung, the High Court judges Anderson Chow, Patrick Li, and Lisa Wong, the Director of Broadcasting Roy Tang, the public law expert Stewart Wong SC, and the journalist Kevin Lau. Earlier in the year Lau had been the victim of a brutal chopper attack, which, though still unexplained, has been seen by some, including Lau, as an assault on press freedom.[61]

The seventy-nine-day Occupy protest was generally peaceful. Among the serious incidents of violence were mob attacks on protestors on 3 October; the beating up by policemen of a Civic Party member in a dark alley at Tamar on 15 October; a three-day confrontation in Mong Kok a few days later when police tried to reopen Nathan Road; and an attempt to escalate the protest at Tamar on 30 November by encircling the Chief Executive's Office, which led to clashes between police and protestors. By then public opinion was turning firmly against Occupy: support had never been high; now people felt it had gone on for too long and its chances of success were low.[62] Active opposition, including organized counterdemonstrations, increased. In late October taxi unions, minibus

---

59. Michael Hor, interview with the author, 2 November 2018.

60. A few months after the debate Leung applied unsuccessfully to the Court of First Instance for a judicial review of the government's proposals for political reform on the contention that it had wrongly regarded the decision of 31 August as legally binding on Hong Kong. *Leung Lai Kwok Yvonne v Chief Secretary for Administration*, HCAL31/2015, 5 June 2015.

61. Two of the attackers, who had been paid by a third party, were eventually caught, tried, convicted, and sentenced each to nineteen years' imprisonment. The judge observed that, although there was no direct evidence to show the attack was related to Lau's work as a journalist, it was important for members of the press to be adequately protected by the law. Lau had been replaced as Editor-in-Chief of *Ming Pao* only a few weeks before the attack. *SCMP*, 13 August 2015.

62. Support for Occupy Central, measured by the HKU Public Opinion Programme and the Chinese University of Hong Kong's Centre for Communication and Public Opinion Survey in 2013–2014, ranged between 20 and 40 per

operators, and other businesses began seeking court injunctions against those occupying public thoroughfares.[63] These were enforced by bailiffs from late November: the last of the clearances took place without resistance at Admiralty on 11 December and at the smaller protest site at Causeway Bay on 15 December. By then the momentum had already been lost. Benny Tai and other Occupy strategists had turned themselves in to the police on 3 December, following the principle of accepting the legal consequences of their actions.

The legal consequences for several prominent Occupy figures were prosecutions for public order offences, obstructing or assaulting police, inciting public nuisance, contempt of court in defying injunctions, and other offences. Various police officers were prosecuted for excessive use of violence. Proceedings moved slowly. The case against Joshua Wong and others for their part in the storming of Civic Square on 26 September 2014 was not tried until the summer of 2016. The magistrate, June Cheung (LLB 1999), convicted Wong of unlawful assembly and his co-defendants, Nathan Law and Alex Chow, of unlawful assembly and incitement; she imposed community service orders on Wong and Law and sentenced Chow to three weeks' imprisonment, suspended for one year, saying the court had to adopt a more understanding attitude towards student leaders, who were 'passionate and genuinely believing their political ideals.'[64] The Court of Appeal disagreed: in a review of sentence in 2017 – after Wong and Law had already served their community service orders – it imposed prison terms of six to eight months. Its Vice-President, Wally Yeung (LLB 1974), spoke of 'an unhealthy wind' blowing through Hong Kong and criticized 'certain people, including individuals of learning' who encouraged young people to break the law through their 'arrogant and conceited ways of thinking.'[65] On appeal, the Court of Final Appeal quashed the prison terms and reinstated the original sentences, while confirming the heavier sentencing guidelines set out by the Court of Appeal for future unlawful assembly convictions.[66]

Legislation on the electoral reforms under the decision of 31 August failed to secure the necessary votes. The old system of selecting the Chief Executive was retained for 2017. Political polarization deepened. As cases from the protests came up for sentence, judges and magistrates were denounced and threatened with violence for being too lenient or too severe to protestors or police officers. During the Chinese New Year holiday in February 2016 rioting broke out in Mong Kok – the worst since the 1960s – when 'localist' groups

---

cent, declining to below 20 per cent in November 2014, and to below 10 per cent in December 2014: Ng, *Umbrellas in Bloom*, 126–7.

63. Several were helped in this by CMK Lawyers, a firm owned by Maggie Chan (LLB 1991), a graduate of HKU and an elected member of the Wong Tai Sin District Council.

64. The suspended sentence for Chow took into account his plans to study overseas. *SCMP*, 2 September 2015 & 15 August 2016.

65. *Secretary for Justice v Wong Chi Fung and Others* [2017] HKCA 320.

66. *Secretary for Justice v Chow Yong Kang Alex and Others* [2018] HKCFA 4.

came out to defend unlicensed food hawkers who were the target of enforcement action. One police officer was hit in the head by a brick. Another fired warning shots into the air when he and his colleagues were surrounded by stone-throwing rioters. Some 130 police officers, reporters, and protestors were injured. Chinese officials blamed separatist elements. Student unions blamed the police and the divisive policies of the Chief Executive, Leung Chun-ying. Later that year six newly elected members of the Legislative Council were disqualified from taking their seats for adding words and slogans – some insulting to the PRC – to their oaths of office. While the Court of First Instance was hearing a government challenge to the Legislative Council President's decision to allow two of them to retake the oaths, the Standing Committee intervened with an interpretation of Article 104 of the Basic Law specifying requirements for oath-taking, which ruled out the possibility of a second chance.

Talk about self-determination or independence increased. The idea had never had currency in Hong Kong and was still limited to fringe groups. But it was anathema to the Chinese government and a departure from 'one country, two systems', a concept supported by all main political parties whatever their other differences. The negligible threat to national unity was exploited by the Chief Executive, Leung Chun-ying, as a rallying call for the pro-establishment camp.[67] In 2018 the SAR government banned a small but conspicuous group known as the Hong Kong National Party, whose goals included establishing an independent republic and abolishing the Basic Law. Influential voices in the Mainland and Hong Kong now urged the necessity of enacting national security legislation in fulfilment of Article 23 of the Basic Law. Some now regretted the defeat of the 2003 bill, particularly after the enactment of a new national security law in Mainland China in 2015 which, though it did not apply to Hong Kong, was far more severe than anything envisaged in 2003.

The Occupy movement had consequences for the Faculty of Law and some of its staff. The Faculty was condemned by the pro-Beijing press, which depicted it as a hotbed of dissent. A legislator and former President of the Law Society, Junius Ho (PCLL 1986), started an online petition calling for the removal of Benny Tai and threatened to sue the Council of HKU if it failed to launch an enquiry into his actions. The Vice-Chancellor, Peter Mathieson, rejected these demands, saying that HKU had its own procedures for dealing with infringements of university regulations and was not a 'surrogate courtroom'.[68] Whatever their personal views on Occupy, staff in the Faculty were united in defending Benny Tai's right to pursue his political activities as long as they did not affect his teaching

---

67. In his annual policy address in 2015, delivered a few weeks after the end of the Occupy protest, Leung cited the February 2014 issue of HKU's student magazine, *Undergrad*, in which the concept of independence had been discussed. The editor-in-chief of the magazine, a Government & Law student, countered that the article, along with a book on the subject published by *Undergrad*, was merely an academic analysis of issues connected with Hong Kong's history and identity. *SCMP*, 14 & 15 January 2014.

68. *SCMP*, 30 August 2017.

responsibilities. The campaign against Tai intensified when, at an academic forum in Taipei in 2018, he suggested that Hong Kong could consider independence or enter into confederation with other regions of China should the country become democratic in the future: Ho launched another petition urging the Department of Justice to prosecute him for sedition.[69]

In September 2017 charges were eventually brought against Tai and the cofounders of Occupy Central, Chan Kin-man and Chu Yiu-ming, for their role in the Occupy movement of 2014. They were tried in November and December 2018, and, in a verdict delivered in April 2019, were convicted of conspiracy to commit public nuisance; in addition, Tai and Chan were convicted of incitement to commit public nuisance. Tai and Chan were sentenced each to sixteen months' imprisonment, while Chu received a suspended prison sentence in view of his advanced age and his long record of service to society. Six others tried at the same time, including Tanya Chan, an alumna of the Faculty of Law, were also convicted of either incitement to commit public nuisance or incitement to incite public nuisance, or both: they received sentences ranging from prison terms to community service. Benny Tai and some of his co-defendants are appealing against their convictions.[70]

The Pro-Vice-Chancellorship Controversy

The full force of the pro-Beijing press was also brought to bear on the former Dean of the Faculty of Law, Johannes Chan. He had stepped down as Dean in July 2014 and was on sabbatical leave overseas when Occupy took place.[71] In late 2014, after a global search, a committee chaired by the Vice-Chancellor, Peter Mathieson, unanimously recommended Chan as the sole candidate for the vacant position of pro-vice-chancellor for academic staffing and resources. When this confidential recommendation was leaked to *Wen Wei Po*, a state-owned Hong Kong newspaper, both it and its partner-newspaper, *Ta Kung Pao*, embarked on a campaign of vilification against Chan and the Faculty.[72] Over the next few months the two newspapers published over 300 articles accusing Chan of sheltering Benny Tai, mishandling donations to the Faculty, and engaging in politics at the expense of the Faculty's research performance.[73] In other attacks, the email accounts of several staff were hacked into.

---

69. *SCMP*, 6 September 2017 & 16 August 2018.

70. Sentencing of Tanya Chan was postponed after she was found to be suffering from a brain tumour. She was sentenced in June to eight months' imprisonment, suspended for two years. *HKSAR v Tai Yiu Ting and others* [2019] HKDC 450 & 568; *SCMP*, 24 April & 10 June 2019.

71. Chan, *Paths of Justice*, 18–20.

72. *Wen Wei Po*, 26 November 2014.

73. The articles alleged that Chan, Tai, and Robert Chung of HKU's Public Opinion Programme had not followed university guidelines in handling anonymous donations totalling $1.45 million, some for the Occupy civil referendum and deliberation days, and including $300,000 for supporting conferences and seminars on constitutional

Amid protests by students, the Council of HKU repeatedly delayed a decision on Chan's candidacy. In September 2015, Convocation – the university's official alumni body – resolved by nearly 8,000 out of about 9,300 votes cast to call on the Council either to approve the appointment or to reject it, giving clear reasons. On 29 September 2014 the Council rejected Chan's nomination by twelve votes to eight in a secret ballot without stating reasons: leaks of the discussion suggested that there were concerns that Chan's appointment would divide the university, that he did not have a doctorate, and that he had failed to show sufficient sympathy towards a Council member who was allegedly injured during a storming of a Council meeting by students.[74] The government denied allegations that it had influenced the decision. In a statement a few days after the decision, the Emeritus Professor of Law, Yash Ghai, described the reasons, in particular the aspersions on Chan's academic record, as 'spurious and totally unbecoming the Council' and showing 'spite and vindictiveness'. The Faculty rejected the criticisms of Chan 'in the strongest possible terms', pointing out Chan's international reputation as a leading scholar in his field, his efforts to deepen ties with Mainland and overseas universities, and the high international rankings achieved by the Faculty during his time as Dean.[75]

The episode split the university, prompting protests and calls for the Chairman of the Council, Leong Che-hung, to resign. He was replaced in November 2015 by Arthur Li, a pugnacious former Secretary for Education appointed to the Council earlier that year by Chief Executive Leung Chun-ying. This raised once again the role of the Chief Executive as Chancellor. A review of governance commissioned by the Council in 2016 observed that 'in the deeply polarized politics of modern Hong Kong' the fact that the Chief Executive's powers as Chancellor 'could be used for political patronage has led to deep suspicion.' It recommended that the Chancellor should delegate to the Council most of his powers of

---

development and rule of law education, none of which was spent on Occupy-related activities. An audit report in March 2015 found that the $300,000 had been properly allocated for its stated purpose and made no criticism of Chan. However, a further 'elaboration' by the Audit Committee at the request of the Council found that Chan had failed to meet an 'expected standard' in handling the donation. Chan was not provided with proper disclosure for his response. He challenged the findings on legal and procedural grounds: this was rejected by the Council. The articles in *Wen Wei Po* and *Ta Kung Pao* also made much of prematurely leaked information from the 2014 Research Assessment Exercise (RAE) suggesting that the Faculty of Law was performing less well in research than its counterpart at the Chinese University of Hong Kong. Audit Committee, HKU, 'Report to the Council on a Matter of Public Concern as to Certain Donations Received by the University,' 11 March 2015 (HKU website); Johannes Chan and Douglas Kerr, 'Academic Freedom, Political Interference, and Public Accountability: The Hong Kong Experience,' 7 *Journal of Academic Freedom* (2016), 1–21.

74. Legal action by HKU resulted in injunctions against the dissemination of a secret recording made available to Commercial Radio and other disclosures of proceedings of the Council at which Chan's nomination was discussed, but the court refused to grant the university's extraordinary request for a blanket injunction on disclosure of all Council proceedings, past, present, and future. *The University of Hong Kong v Hong Kong Commercial Broadcasting Co. Ltd and Another* [2016] HKCFI 1130.

75. *SCMP*, 2 & 5 October 2015; HKU Faculty of Law, Press statement on 4 October 2015.

appointment. It also suggested that the Chief Executive as ex officio Chancellor might be replaced by an independent Chancellor to 'strengthen the autonomy of the University and achieve better separation of its governance from the politics of Hong Kong.' The Council has not pursued this idea.[76]

Research, Knowledge Exchange, and Social Impact

What makes a law school great, observed Johannes Chan in 2015, is 'the ability to attract and retain scholars of the highest calibre, and to admit and train excellent students.' This can only be achieved in an environment that respects and encourages diversity, he added. 'A university should be the place where any issues can be freely debated and argued' for it is only through 'open debates and arguments that advancement in knowledge can be made and the frontier of human understanding of the world can be expanded.'[77] His successor, Michael Hor, has also stressed the Faculty's duty to 'maintain a liberal forum' for discussing conflicting views on matters of public importance.[78] The Faculty has a tradition of giving staff freedom not only to design the courses they teach, and to develop new courses, but also to pursue their own research. Most recent new recruits, including staff near the beginning of their academic careers, come with strong research experience, mostly acquired through postgraduate research-oriented degrees.

According to the 2014 Research Assessment Exercise (RAE), fifty-six of the Faculty's academic staff were actively engaged in research: this represents most of the Faculty and accounts for over half of all legal research in universities in Hong Kong. RAE results are one of two main factors in the allocation of funding by the UGC; the other is success in obtaining external grants from the Research Grants Council, an advisory body under the UGC.[79] In the ten academic years up to 2018–2019 staff in the Faculty of Law have conducted Research Grants Council-approved research projects with a total budget of over $38 million and with topics ranging from the language and ideology of constitutions (David Law, 2017) to the implications of a land title registration system (Richard Wu, 2009). Some seventy postgraduate students are pursuing research, mostly at the PhD level. Although research can be a solitary activity, the Faculty's rich programme of conferences and other

---

76. The review panel was chaired by Professor Sir Malcolm Grant, Chancellor of the University of York. Its other members were Professor William C. Kirby of Harvard University and Peter Van Tu Nguyen SC, a former Hong Kong High Court judge. In an addendum, Nguyen stated his opposition to removing the Chief Executive from the Chancellorship, pointing out that the allegations of political interference were without foundation. HKU, *Report of the Review Panel on University Governance* (February 2017), 30–6 & addendum; *SCMP* 28 June 2017.

77. Johannes Chan, interviewed by Michael Wilkinson, *Faculty of Law Newsletter*, Summer 2015.

78. Michael Hor, Dean's Message, HKU Faculty of Law website.

79. The Research Grants Council's membership consists of local and international academics and lay appointees. Members are appointed by the Chief Executive of the Hong Kong SAR, who has delegated his power of appointment to the Secretary for Education: Research Grants Council, *Annual Report 2016–17*, 14.

activities encourages collaboration. Most of the Faculty's areas of research excellence are supported by dedicated centres: public law by the CCPL (established in 1995); comparative Chinese law by the Centre for Chinese Law (established in 2009); commercial and financial law, WTO law, and alternative dispute resolution by the Asian Institute of International Financial Law (established in 1999); and intellectual property and information technology by the Law and Technology Centre, founded in 2004 jointly with the Department of Computer Science.[80] A fifth centre, the Centre for Medical Ethics and Law, was founded in 2012 with the Faculty of Medicine, with donations from the WYNG Foundation and Dr Ron Zimmern, a pioneer in public health genomics and a nephew of Archibald Zimmern, the first Supreme Court judge appointed from the private Bar in Hong Kong.

Broad though their scope may be, neither the areas of excellence nor the dedicated centres can embrace the full breadth of the Faculty's research, which evolves according to the interests of staff, the changing needs of society, and the imperatives of the RAE. Recent RAEs have given weight to 'world leading' research. This tends to favour work that is comparative or theoretical or has transnational applications. As the Faculty observed in the first RAE in 1996, this presents challenges in the field of law, which is traditionally divided by jurisdiction. The Dean, Michael Hor, addressed this dilemma in 2015 by acknowledging that the Faculty's 'mission to contribute to the Hong Kong community … and the legal profession in particular might mean that it will sometimes be at the expense of doing more work with a global focus.' But, he added, 'it is a trade-off the faculty is proud to make.'[81]

Even so, the Faculty has made notable contributions to research with implications beyond Hong Kong. This reflects the globalization of many areas of law, the importance of comparative law in Hong Kong's own jurisprudence, and a growing interest in the Faculty in subjects that transcend boundaries, such as the philosophy of law. Recent examples include research into international law, comparative human rights, constitutions and courts in Asia, international financial regulation, WTO law, comparative intellectual property law, post-conflict justice, cross-border arbitration, comparative literature and the law, information technology and the legal process, and the regulation of cyberspace. Moreover, the next RAE, to be concluded in 2020 and covering the period 2013–2019, will include for the first time an element of 'research impact' that will recognize 'research of local relevance with high economic and social benefits.' The fifteen examples listed under law include widening access to justice or the political process, influencing law reform generally and on particular issues such as discrimination or the environment, contributing to a wider public understanding of the law, and providing expert advice to governments, regulators, and NGOs.[82]

---

80. Originally called the China Information Technology and Law Centre.

81. *SCMP*, 5 February 2015.

82. UGC: RAE 2020: Questions and Answers, & Panel-Specific Guidelines on Assessment Criteria and Working Methods for RAE 2020 (September 2018), UGC website.

In these and other areas of impact the Faculty has an abundant record of combining contemplation and action, as Michael Hor put it in his introduction to a booklet on the Faculty's knowledge exchange and impact in 2016.[83] 'Knowledge exchange', along with teaching and research, is one of three pillars underpinning activities at HKU: it is defined as 'engaging, for mutual benefit, with business, government or the public to generate, acquire, apply and make accessible the knowledge needed to enhance material, human, social, cultural and environmental well-being.' In recent years the university has promoted this activity by funding projects designated as knowledge exchange and awarding prizes for the best in each year: several have gone to members of the Faculty of Law. In law, as in other disciplines, knowledge exchange also extends beyond recognized projects to a wide range of activities. It takes various forms: advocacy and education, practical research in support of public policy formulation, dissemination of information on the law to the legal profession and general public, and support for individuals or groups in their encounters with the law. This section describes a few examples of these activities.

The Rights of Women and Minority Groups

Several projects have looked at the rights of groups in need of greater protection from the law. In a project in 2000–2003 under the auspices of the CCPL, Carole Petersen, Janice Fong and Gabrielle Rush examined enforcement by the Equal Opportunities Commission. Their substantial report – with its wealth of information on the nature of complaints – found that, although the commission had established several important precedents in the courts, the vast majority of cases were dealt with by conciliation, a confidential process which failed to satisfy the desire of many complainants for public hearings and more systematic remedies. The report argued that an equal opportunities tribunal should be established for this purpose.[84] Other studies examined debt bondage among migrant domestic workers, by Petersen and Peggy W.Y. Lee (in 2006), and migrant sex workers, by Petersen, Kelley Loper and Karen Laidler of HKU's Centre for Criminology (2003–2006), based partly on interviews with Mainland women imprisoned for immigration and other offences connected with their involvement in prostitution.[85]

Women and minorities have continued to be a central focus of the CCPL in recent years. Kelley Loper, now Director of the CCPL and of the LLM Human Rights Programme, has led research projects on refugee protection in East Asia and legal assistance for asylum seekers and torture claimants in Hong Kong; she has also served as chair of the board of

---

83. Faculty of Law, HKU, *Knowledge Exchange and Impact* (2016).
84. Carole J. Petersen, Janice Fong, and Gabrielle Rush, *Enforcing Equal Opportunities: Investigation and Conciliation of Discrimination Complaints in Hong Kong* (CCPL, HKU, July 2003).
85. Robyn Emerton and Carole J. Petersen, *Migrant Nightclub/Escort Workers: An Analysis of Possible Human Rights Abuses* (CCPL, HKU, April 2003).

the Hong Kong Refugee Advice Centre (now the Justice Centre Hong Kong) and has advised various bodies, including the UN High Commissioner for Refugees and Amnesty International. Her work has uncovered gaps in the law and she has argued strongly for comprehensive refugee legislation in Hong Kong.[86] Loper has also led projects on changing attitudes towards same-sex couples and the protection of the rights of people with disabilities, particularly in education. Research by Puja Kapai (LLB 2000), a former director of the CCPL, has influenced the development of policy on women's rights and the rights of persons with intellectual disabilities. Kapai's report on ethnic minorities in Hong Kong, which she presented to the Commission on Poverty in 2015, the first comprehensive investigation into the subject, threw light on gaps in policy and on the piecemeal measures that had failed minorities, including the Race Discrimination Ordinance (2008), which excludes certain government acts. The report also challenges a prevailing misperception that Hong Kong's ethnic minority population is a transient one.[87] In 2015 Kapai was awarded the US Department of State's International Women of Courage Award for her efforts in advocating for the rights of ethnic minorities and victims of domestic violence and human trafficking. She is currently convener of the HKU Women's Studies Research Centre.

Another area of research into the needs of special groups is children's issues. This once-neglected area of Hong Kong law has received attention recently with a series of Law Reform Commission reports, the establishment in 2018 of a Children's Commission, and a 'Children's Bill' to introduce a 'joint parental responsibility model' for custody and access by divorced parents.[88] These and other measures have been driven by a series of Children's Issues Forums, a collaboration between the law faculties of HKU and the Chinese University of Hong Kong, the Hong Kong Family Law Association, and other organizations. The forums, held so far in 2009, 2012, and 2015, have brought together judges, lawyers, officials, academics, social workers, and other professionals from Hong Kong and overseas to facilitate a comparative and multidisciplinary approach to improving the welfare and safety of Hong Kong's children. One of its leading members, Katherine Lynch, a founding director of the Faculty's LLM in Arbitration and Dispute Resolution, is a co-editor of three books from the forums. The forums have broadened their initial focus on resolving disputes relating to children into applying to Hong Kong advances made elsewhere in the world, including the movement away from concepts of custody, care, and control towards parental responsibility and ensuring the voices of children are heard. The 2009 forum

---

86. See, for example, Kelley Loper, 'Toward Comprehensive Refugee Legislation in Hong Kong? Reflections on Reform of the "Torture Screening" Procedures,' 39 *HKLJ* (2009), 253–9.

87. Kapai's paternal grandfather settled in Hong Kong in 1953. Born in India, she came to Hong Kong when only a few months old and attended a 'designated' (i.e. segregated) ethnic minority public-funded school, graduated from the Faculty of Law at HKU, and took her LLM at Harvard. Puja Kapai, *Status of Ethnic Minorities in Hong Kong 1997–2014* (CCPL, HKU, 2015).

88. Children Proceedings (Parental Responsibility) Bill.

resulted in a working group, chaired by the Justice of Appeal, Michael Hartmann, which led to fundamental changes in procedures for disputes relating to children in the courts. The 2012 and 2015 forums created the impetus for government action on recommendations in a 2005 Law Reform Commission report: soon after, the Children's Bill was put out for public consultation, and in 2016 the Children's Issues Forum held a roundtable discussion on the bill, a report on which was submitted to the government. Among the issues for the next forum, planned for 2020, will be the need for better inter-agency coordination in Hong Kong's child and family justice system.[89]

A related issue is the long-term welfare of persons with intellectual disabilities, a concern that weighs heavily on their parents, many of whom are anxious that care for their children will be disrupted when they pass away even if they have the means to meet their children's long-term living expenses. In early 2016 the government announced that it was exploring the feasibility of setting up a trust to provide affordable financial services to people with special needs: pooled arrangements of this kind already exist in Singapore and the US. Partnering with a parents' concern group, in 2016 Lusina Ho and Rebecca Lee of the Faculty of Law organized a large-scale survey of the needs of parents of people with intellectual disabilities for such a scheme and their views on how it should be structured. The responses from over 2,500 parents indicated strong demand for a special needs trust, with a preference for the government as trustee, to be activated when the parents pass away, which would manage funds from parents securely and at low cost, help devise care plans, and monitor the care received by their children. The survey, along with research by Ho and Lee into the mechanisms for such a scheme, convinced the government to take action: in December 2018 it established the Special Needs Trust Office, with the Director of Social Welfare Incorporated as trustee and with an allocation of $50 million to get the scheme up and running.[90]

Animal Welfare

In recent years Australia, New Zealand, Singapore, Taiwan, the US, and countries in Europe have enacted laws requiring that animals in captivity are provided with positive experiences – such as companionship, play, and exploration – before their welfare can be said to be acceptable. Lawyers in the US have even filed habeas corpus suits demanding the right to bodily liberty for individual animals. Hong Kong lags far behind any of these developments, despite changes in public sentiment. Its main animal protection law, the Prevention of Cruelty to Animals Ordinance 1935, modelled on a now obsolete English act

---

89. Katherine Lynch, interview with the author, 22 November 2018.

90. Rebecca Lee and Lusina Ho and the Concern Group of Guardianship System and Financial Affairs, *Ascertaining the Need for Special Needs Trusts in Hong Kong* (January 2017); Lusina Ho and Rebecca Lee, 'Introducing the special needs trust to Hong Kong,' *Trusts and Trustees*, Vol. 23 No. 10 (December 2017), 1111–21.

of 1911, relies on vague and antiquated ideas of cruelty, makes no provision for how animals *ought* to be treated, and lacks sufficient enforcement powers. Other laws, for example for the protection of wild animals, the regulation of slaughterhouses, and the control of animal experiments, are fragmented, confusing, and unevenly enforced. These were the findings of a major review of Hong Kong's animal protection laws in 2010 by Amanda Whitfort of the Faculty of Law and Fiona Woodhouse of the Society for the Prevention of Cruelty to Animals. The review made recommendations for comprehensive legislation across the whole range of animal welfare, from the pet trade to the handling of feral animals.[91] It focused political attention on the problem and resulted in a clear commitment by the government in 2018 to reform the laws on animal welfare.[92]

After the 2010 report, Amanda Whitfort turned her attention to Hong Kong's animal and plant protection laws, resulting in a report in 2013 which found that over 500 locally endangered and vulnerable species lacked legal protection, partly because the schedule of protected species in the Wild Animal Protection Ordinance had not been revised since 1996 and did not recognize fish as animals. The report made sixteen key recommendations for reforming this and other ordinances, ranging from updating the list of protected animals to improving mechanisms for dealing with invasive animal and plant species.[93] In a project in 2015 Whitfort investigated the laws against trading in endangered species and concluded that the government and the courts were not doing enough to prevent the illegal flow of ivory. Her work, widely disseminated to policymakers and legislators, helped spur amendments to legislation in 2018 increasing penalties for traffickers. Not long after this, a victim impact statement prepared by Whitfort and staff at Kadoorie Farm and Botanic Garden was used by prosecutors in a case of smuggling of rhinoceros horns, resulting in a sentence of twelve months (reduced to eight on a guilty plea) for the offender – the highest so far in Hong Kong for this crime.[94]

Rectifying Injustice: The Clinical Legal Education Programme

Clinical legal education (CLE) courses are held under the LLB programme as a way of cultivating a pro bono ethos among Hong Kong's future lawyers by participating in real-life cases under the supervision of qualified lawyers. Each year an average of about seventy students attend three CLE courses, taking place in the autumn, spring, and summer semesters. The designers of the programme faced concerns from the Law Society that it would

91. Amanda S. Whitfort and Fiona M. Woodhouse, *Review of Animal Welfare Legislation in Hong Kong* (2010).

92. Chief Executive Carrie Lam, Policy Address 2018, paragraphs 283–4.

93. Amanda S. Whitfort, Andrew Cornish, Rupert Griffiths, and Fiona M. Woodhouse, *A Review of Hong Kong's Wild Animal and Plant Protection Laws* (September 2013).

94. *Sing Tao Daily*, 19 October 2018 (translated into English on the HKU Legal Scholarship Blog).

create a 'third branch' of the profession. At first, the plan was to limit cases to the Small Claims Tribunal, where lawyers are not permitted to appear but where claims, despite their small size, sometimes raise difficult legal points. The Judiciary supported this in principle as a way of helping to manage cases more efficiently. But concerns arose about inequality, if only one party received help. A proposal that the Chinese University of Hong Kong support the opposing parties failed to take root. Another proposal to take only cases in which the other party was the government also failed to make progress when a pilot scheme found that most of these cases – for payment of rent or tax arrears – involved no real dispute. The Faculty therefore revived and developed an old practice, adopted briefly under the PCLL programme in the late 1970s, of participating in the Free Legal Advice Scheme under the Duty Lawyer Service operated by the Law Society. After several years of preparation, the CLE programme was launched in 2010.[95]

At the CLE Centre on campus students assist volunteer lawyers with research and preparation. In some cases, as a result of detailed research and follow-up, the centre helps obtain legal aid for clients where it has previously been denied for lack of merit. In some others it arranges pro bono representation, either by volunteer lawyers or by the centre's director, Eric Cheung (LLB 1986), an experienced solicitor with higher rights of audience in criminal cases. A growing number of cases in recent years have arisen from letters received from prison inmates seeking help to appeal against their convictions or sentences: the centre has become widely known within prison communities and has so far handled 280 such cases. Clinical legal education gives students hands-on experience of real-life cases. They see the differences between studying law and actually practising it, and learn how to explain complex legal principles in everyday language to clients who may be distressed or emotionally unstable. Johannes Chan, who introduced the programme against considerable obstacles, regards the CLE Centre as the achievement he was most proud of as Dean.[96]

The CLE Centre is sometimes a last resort for people who feel they have been unjustly treated by the legal system. It is the only programme of its kind in Hong Kong. The centre has had notable successes in rectifying injustices. For example, in a case in 2013 a man sentenced to eight and a half years' imprisonment for conspiracy to rob was refused legal aid to appeal for lack of merit. After he sought help from the CLE programme, research by students found arguable grounds for appeal. Legal aid was then granted, and Eric Cheung was assigned as his solicitor advocate. The Court of Appeal quashed the conviction when it was shown that the prosecution had failed to disclose telephone records disproving the testimony of a key witness, a participant in the robberies whose sentence had been reduced in return for helping the prosecution. The defendant had already spent thirty-three months in custody.[97]

---

95. Eric Cheung, interview with the author, 15 October 2018; Chan, *Paths of Justice*, 89–96.
96. Johannes Chan, interview with the author, 20 June 2018.
97. *HKSAR v A* [2015] HKCA 443.

Several cases supported by the CLE Centre have gone all the way to the Court of Final Appeal (CFA). In 2015 the court overturned the conviction of a man sentenced to six weeks' imprisonment merely for closing the door of a vehicle not belonging to him, ruling that this did not constitute tampering with a vehicle, a criminal offence under the Road Traffic Ordinance. The injustice was so obvious that the court allowed the appeal, quashed the conviction, and awarded costs. Although the appellant had already served his sentence, it was fortunate, said Joseph Fok, one of the Permanent Judges of the CFA, that with the pro bono assistance of the CLE programme his case had been pursued so far.[98] In another case, in 2016, the CFA reinstated a District Court decision, reversed by the Court of Appeal, awarding damages against an insurance company for failing to report to the Insurance Agents Registration Board the termination of an employee; without this he could not work as an agent for another company. Research by CLE students had shown errors in the Court of Appeal's judgment. Eric Cheung sought advice from tort law experts in the Faculty and persuaded the Legal Aid Department to fund an appeal to the CFA. Audrey Eu SC then took over the case, but CLE students continued to give assistance up to the hearing in the CFA.[99]

In a third case, decided in 2018, a former prisoner had started a niche business arranging visits to prisoners on remand at Lai Chi Kok Reception Centre pending trial. Under prison rules remand prisoners have certain privileges, such as having food, books, and magazines brought in by friends or relatives. For inmates whose relatives or friends were unable to visit, the entrepreneur offered 'representative visiting services' for a fee. He recruited part-time staff to take in items to prisoners on behalf of their friends and relatives, and to convey messages to and fro. The staff wore uniforms and the business was openly conducted. The authorities only took action after the business collapsed. Along with various others the entrepreneur was convicted by a magistrate of conspiring to defraud prison officers by falsely representing that they were friends. The Court of Appeal dismissed their appeals. The case went to the CFA, which found that the lower courts had applied too narrow a definition of 'friend' and held that the entrepreneur's services were entirely within the purposes for which visits to remand prisoners are permitted. In quashing the convictions, the court expressed surprise that such a 'heavy-handed' conspiracy charge had been used to prosecute the appellants. Unusually, Eric Cheung and his CLE students had handled this case from its beginnings in the magistrate's court right up to the CFA, where Cheung acted as solicitor advocate for one of the two appellants, while Johannes Chan was counsel for the other.[100]

98. *HKSAR v. Law Tat Ying* [2015] HKCFA 71.

99. *Gill Gurbux Singh v Dah Sing Insurance Services Ltd* [2016] HKCFA 22; *Faculty of Law Newsletter*, January 2017.

100. *HKSAR v Wan Thomas and Guan Qiaoyong* [2018] HKCFA 15. For other cases assisted by the CLE programme see Chan, *Paths of Justice*, 93–5.

Information Technology and the Law

Information technology has revolutionized research in all disciplines by enabling large amounts of data to be stored and analysed and by disseminating scholarship through the Internet and other channels. Lawyers and legal scholars now rely on extensive databases of cases, legislation, and commentaries, spanning many jurisdictions. Scholarly journals are now increasingly web-based. Government departments and agencies, the Judiciary, professional bodies, research institutes, NGOs and other organizations maintain dedicated websites with a wealth of current and archived information. In addition to its own website, the Faculty of Law maintains websites for each of its research centres, as well as a comprehensive HKU Legal Scholarship Blog, started in 2014 by Simon Young, the Associate Dean (Research). The blog contains news about research, conferences, and other events, and about Faculty members' participation in public affairs. Special websites play a key role in knowledge exchange initiatives. Some, notably those for the Rule of Law Education Project and Design Democracy Hong Kong – are integral to their effectiveness in engaging the wider public with the Faculty's research. Others maintain large and expanding databases of primary documents and research for the benefit of scholars and the general public: among these are the extensive Human Rights Portal, which covers human rights knowledge for the Asia region, and an online database of documents about the drafting of Hong Kong's Basic Law.

Two of the most widely used websites are those of the Hong Kong Legal Information Institute (HKLII) and the Community Legal Information Centre (CLIC). Both are projects of the Law and Technology Centre at HKU, a joint venture by the Faculty of Law and HKU. The HKLII, launched in 2001, is a massive, ever-expanding online compendium of Hong Kong judgments, laws, regulations, treaties, constitutional instruments, and other resources, spread across thirty-seven databases in English and Chinese. Part of the Free Access to Law movement, and linked to similar websites in other jurisdictions, the HKLII website was developed with financial support from the Department of Justice and with the help of Graham Greenleaf, a pioneer in electronic access to legal information in Australia and a distinguished visiting professor at the Faculty 2001–2002.[101] The project has been managed in recent years by Anne Cheung (LLB 1991) of the Faculty of Law and the Law Librarian, Irene Shieh, who are assisted by a small team of information technology experts. Regularly updated, and recently made available through a mobile telephone app, the HKLII is freely accessible to the general public. It has received an average of over 1 million visits a year since 2011.

---

101. For its early development see Graham Greenleaf, Philip Chung, Andrew Mowbray, Ka Po Chow, & K.H. Pun, 'The Hong Kong Legal Information Institute (HKLII): Its Role in Free Access to Global Law via the Internet', 32 *HKLJ* (2002), 401–27.

Whereas the HKLII is perhaps of greatest use to practitioners and researchers, its companion website, CLIC, is aimed at explaining Hong Kong with an emphasis on law to the general public. CLIC, developed with the support of the Department of Justice, provides legal information on a wide range of topics in Chinese (traditional and simplified) and English through an attractively designed website. It does not offer legal advice but sets out the main elements of law and procedure in clear and jargon-free language, with an emphasis on rights, obligations and liabilities, and routes to redress. 'Legal issues are everywhere, they are part of daily life,' says Anne Cheung, who manages the project with Felix Chan and Eric Cheung, adding that CLIC serves a dual purpose 'raising awareness and at the same time responding to people's needs. When we answer questions from the public, people are most eager to find out what legal consequences they may face.'[102] New topics and resources are frequently added: among the most recent additions are a section on competition law and a DIY template residential tenancy agreement e-package, produced by Dora Chan (LLB 1988), an expert on landlord and tenant law. The tenancy agreement e-package has proved to be one of the most popular topics; the other top topics are probate, police and crime, common traffic offences, and landlord and tenant. CLIC has also launched Youth, Senior, and Family CLIC websites focusing on legal issues of special interest to these groups. CLIC's websites have also been made available on mobile telephone apps. The main CLIC website has received an average of over 2 million visitors a year since 2012.[103]

In separate projects, Anne Cheung has also explored other aspects of information technology and the law, including cyberbullying, the use of artificial intelligence for legal research, and, with Chen Yongxi (PhD 2013) of the Faculty of Law, the implications of China's social credit system for personal data privacy.[104] Her colleague in the Faculty, Felix Chan, has worked with Chan Wai-sum, an expert in actuarial science at the Chinese University of Hong Kong, on an interdisciplinary project to produce a set of actuarial tables for the assessment of monetary damages in personal injury cases. These draw on practices in the UK and other jurisdictions but are tailored to the circumstances of Hong Kong, where, for example, life expectancies are higher – in fact the highest in the world. Drawing on life tables and population projections published by the Census and Statistics Department, the 'Chan Tables' are routinely referred to by the courts, where they have greatly increased the efficiency of the tort system and have helped to achieve fairness; they have also allowed parties to save time and cost through compromise. The two Chans have now extended their research to other jurisdictions, including Singapore and Mainland

---

102. Anne Cheung, quoted in Faculty of Law, HKU, *Knowledge Exchange and Impact* (2016), 17.

103. Anne Cheung, interview with the author, 6 October 2018.

104. Yongxi Chen and Anne S.Y. Cheung, 'The Transparent Self under Big Data Profiling: Privacy and Chinese Legislation on the Social Credit System,' *Journal of Comparative Law*, Vol. 12, Issue 2 (2017), 356–78; Anne Cheung, interview with the author, 6 October 2018.

China, where, they argue, there are signs of convergence in this area between common law and civil law systems. Their work on under-compensation in the UK and Hong Kong has drawn international attention.

Financial Regulation and the Asian Institute of International Financial Law

In the late 1990s the Faculty recognized a need for improving its expertise in financial law. Commercial law, including banking and securities law, had long been one of the Faculty's strengths, and over the years several Faculty members – for example, Ted Tyler, Judith Sihombing, Betty Ho, Ian Tokley, Philip Smart, Charles Booth, Say Goo – had published works on the subject. Financial law reform in Hong Kong tends to be driven by crisis: the Banking Ordinance (1986) followed bank failures in the early 1980s, the Securities and Futures Ordinance (1989) addressed shortcomings exposed by the 'Black Monday' stock market crash of 1987. After the Asian financial crisis 1997–1998, policymakers, regulators, and academics saw the need for better regulation of financial markets and for more co-ordinated study of financial issues as markets became more interdependent. At this time, one of the world's leading experts on financial law, Joseph J. Norton, was the Faculty's Chief Examiner (1995–1998). In 1998 he took on a two-year term as Distinguished Visiting Professor. Norton worked with Charles Booth, Say Goo, Douglas Arner, and the Dean, Albert Chen, to strengthen the Faculty's research and teaching in this field, reinvigorate links with the financial sector, and capitalize on Hong Kong's role as a financial centre. The immediate results were the creation of the Asian Institute of International Financial Law (AIIFL) and the launch of the LLM in Corporate and Financial Law in 1999. Another specialized LLM, in Compliance and Regulation, was launched in 2016, attracting a large enrolment. Corporate and Financial Law has become the single most popular specialization under the four-year LLB. The Faculty now has one of the widest selection of courses on financial law in the world.

Over the last twenty years the AIIFL has developed into the leading research centre of its kind in the Asia-Pacific region, drawing on a large body of expertise within Hong Kong's own legal and financial community and maintaining a worldwide network of advisors and fellows. The AIIFL has become the Faculty's umbrella institute for a wide range of projects relating to finance and economics, fostering research by Faculty members on cross-border insolvency (Charles Booth, Emily Lee, Anselmo Reyes, and Maisie Ooi), insurance law (Garry Meggitt), China's Belt and Road Initiative (Say Goo), taxation (Richard Cullen), debt market development (Paul Lejot), international copyright (Yahong Li), financial law in Mainland China (Yu Guanghua), real estate law and finance (Malcolm Merry), corporate governance (Nigel Davis), company law reform in Mainland China (Zhang Xianchu), and many other topics.

The AIIFL's largest research project has drawn on cross-disciplinary expertise and collaboration with other universities. 'Enhancing Hong Kong's Future as a Leading International Financial Centre' (2012–2017) was led by Douglas Arner, the Kerry Holdings Professor in Law at HKU. Nine other principal investigators took part in the project, including Say Goo of the Faculty of Law and other experts in law, economics, public administration, and geography from HKU, the Chinese and Polytechnic Universities of Hong Kong, and Oxford University. In 2018, for the third year running, the Global Financial Centres Index ranked Hong Kong as the third-largest financial centre in the world, behind New York and London, with the gap between Hong Kong and London fast closing.[105] The financial services sector produces 18 per cent of Hong Kong's GDP and employs a quarter of a million people.[106] The Basic Law guarantees the free convertibility of the Hong Kong dollar and the free flow of capital within, into, and out of the Hong Kong SAR. It requires the SAR government to provide 'an appropriate economic and legal environment for the maintenance of the status of Hong Kong as an international financial centre.'[107] The rule of law, freedom of information, and a concentration of expertise have enabled Hong Kong to continue to develop its role as a global financial centre. Recently, intensified controls on financial and information flows on the Mainland have increased Hong Kong's attractions as a financial centre for the whole of China: Mainland-linked companies now represent 67 per cent of capitalization of Hong Kong's stock exchange and account for 79 per cent of its turnover.

In the light of these developments, and drawing on lessons from the global financial crisis of 2008, the research by Arner's team sought to identify key elements of the economic, legal, and institutional environment that support development of international financial centres, with a particular focus on Hong Kong, its role in China's continuing financial reform and its participation in international financial regulatory processes. The project explored Hong Kong's weaknesses as well as its strengths and aims at disseminating its recommendations widely to better inform policymaking. It helped the AIIFL to develop a permanent forum for international experts to discuss issues related to Hong Kong and its role in the Chinese and global financial systems. To this end, the project has hosted five international conferences and over thirty seminars. It has produced several books, dozens of articles and working papers, some of which have been cited in the *Financial Times* and *The New York Times* and have been influential in the work of the Hong Kong Financial Services Development Council, of which Arner is a member.

A key area of research is financial technology – or fintech – covering everything from stored value cards and automated banking services to global payment systems and

---

105. Long Finance, *The Global Financial Centres Index 24* (September 2018). The index draws on both quantitative measures and assessments by respondents.

106. 2016 figures: Census and Statistics Department, Hong Kong SAR, *Hong Kong Monthly Digest of Statistics, April 2018: Feature Article: The Financial Services Sector in Hong Kong.*

107. Basic Law, Articles 109 & 112.

data-driven investment flows relying on artificial intelligence. Fintech promotes diversity and efficiency in financial services. It has flourished in large developing countries, including China and India, where mobile-phone payment systems now account for a large proportion of transactions. Fintech also presents challenges to regulators, who have traditionally been slow in reacting to rapid technological change. It has entered a new era since the 2008 global financial crisis, which brought tighter regulation of the traditional banks held responsible for it, and, combined with technological advances, encouraged innovations by non-bank financial service providers. Increasingly, regulators, including the Hong Kong Monetary Authority, have focused on the benefits and risks of fintech with the aim of supporting its healthy development while minimizing risks to data security and financial stability. The AIIFL has become a pioneer in research into fintech, hosting conferences and seminars and regular 'FinTech Days'. A seminal article in 2015 by Douglas Arner, his PhD student Janos Barberis, and Ross Buckley of the University of New South Wales, created a framework for understanding fintech and has been widely cited around the world.[108] Barberis went on to found SuperCharger, an initiative to train individuals and help businesses in developing fintech. In 2015 the Faculty launched its first LLM course in fintech, and in 2018 it launched Asia's first online course on the subject.

Members of the AIIFL have also contributed to one of Hong Kong's most important law reform projects of recent years, the new Companies Ordinance 2011, a complete rewrite of an ordinance last substantially reviewed in 1984. Douglas Arner and Say Goo took part in advisory groups for the rewrite and Maisie Ooi (then at the National University of Singapore; from 2010 at HKU) was appointed a consultant to the government on key provisions. Research by the AIIFL into competition and antitrust law has played a key role in the introduction of a competition law in Hong Kong. Three Faculty members – Thomas Cheng, Angela Zhang, and Kelvin Kwok (Bachelor of Business Administration (Law) and LLB 2008) – specialize in the subject and teach courses on it. Cheng (a former member of the Consumer Council) and Kwok (a practising barrister) were closely involved in drafting the Competition Ordinance, which came into force in 2015. A Competition Commission and a Competition Tribunal have been established to enforce the ordinance and promote research and public understanding of the value of competition. The first Chairperson of the commission, Anna Wu (LLB 1974), is a former Chairperson of the Equal Opportunities Commission and was a member of the Executive Council 2009–2017. The commission's investigations have so far led to three cases before the Competition Tribunal: the first two of these, decided in May 2019, have resulted in findings of bid rigging, market sharing and price fixing.

---

108. Douglas Arner, Janos Barberis & Ross Buckley, 'The Evolution of Fintech: A New Post-Crisis Paradigm?' [2015] HKU Faculty of Law Research Paper No. 2015/047 (online).

Reforming Law Reform

The new Companies Ordinance and the Competition Ordinance were enacted after many years of research and consultation. Other important enactments in recent years have included a Race Discrimination Ordinance (2008), a Minimum Wage Ordinance (2010), a new Arbitration Ordinance (2010), a Mediation Ordinance (2012), and an Apology Ordinance (2017), the first of its kind in the Asia-Pacific region, aimed at encouraging amicable settlement of disputes. However, much new legislation and the reform of old legislation has been impeded by lack of will within the government, disagreement among stakeholders, dysfunction between the executive and the legislature, and unproductive confrontation within the Legislative Council, where the continuing presence of functional constituency seats also serves to protect vested interests. As a result, legislation tends to be piecemeal. The enactment of substantial new ordinances has been reduced to a trickle. Many older ordinances – on matters ranging from data privacy to mental health and employment – are in critical need of revision. New bills on subjects such as corporate rescue or copyright have been delayed at the drafting stage or rejected in council, leaving Hong Kong far behind many other jurisdictions. A Land Titles Ordinance, enacted in 2004 to replace Hong Kong's onerous system of deeds registration, remains unimplemented because stakeholders cannot reach consensus on various issues.

The slow pace of law reform was the topic of a conference at the CCPL held in September 2011 and resulting in the publication in 2014 of an influential book, *Reforming Law Reform: Perspectives from Hong Kong and Beyond*, edited by Michael Tilbury, Simon Young and Ludwig Ng (LLB 1986).[109] The central focus of the book was the slow pace with which the government responded to recommendations from Hong Kong's Law Reform Commission, in contrast to the speed with which the commission's recommendations were adopted in law in the decade or so after its creation in 1980. The commission is – or should be – an important driver of law reform. By tradition the deans of the law schools are appointed to the commission, and other Faculty members have occasionally been members: Eric Cheung was a member in 1994–2000 while still in his twenties, the youngest ever. Other Faculty members have also sat on the commission and its specialist committees. The 2011 conference examined other bodies pursuing law reform, the practice in other jurisdictions, and the impact of the courts. The 2011 conference called for a better-resourced commission, closer cooperation with the law schools, and guidelines on how the government should handle its reports. These calls were answered in part by commitments by the then Secretary for Justice, Wong Yan Lung SC, to introduce guidelines for bureaux to respond substantively to recommendations within a time frame and to report annually on implementation to the Legislative Panel on Administration of Justice and Legal Services.

---

109. Michael Tilbury, Simon N.M. Young, and Ludwig Ng (Eds.), *Reforming Law Reform: Perspectives from Hong Kong and Beyond* (Hong Kong: Hong Kong University Press, 2014).

In the commission's five completed reports since 2012, the new guidelines have resulted in one commitment to legislate (on double jeopardy) and explanations, some quite detailed, of the work in progress to consider the implications of the reports and map out a way forward.[110] The recent disqualifications of members of the Legislative Council for failing to take their oaths properly, combined with a poor showing by pan-democrats in the subsequent by-elections, have given an effective majority in the Council to the pro-establishment parties. In the interval between the disqualifications and the by-elections, the Council amended its rules of procedure to curb the filibustering and other time-wasting tactics – used by both sides of the political divide – that had so diminished the Council's reputation in the eyes of the public. The measures came at a time of pessimism about the prospects for democracy and good governance in Hong Kong. Far from making the process of governance more effective, these measures, along with grave errors of judgment by the SAR government, have shifted political confrontation back onto the streets.

In early 2019 the Hong Kong SAR Government introduced a bill to enable it to handle extradition requests from jurisdictions with which Hong Kong has no extradition agreement, including Taiwan and Mainland China. The possibility that people could be sent for trial on the Mainland for offences against Mainland law raised fears of a breach of the 'judicial firewall' that separates the Hong Kong and Mainland legal systems. Proposals to reduce the number of offences to which extraditions would apply and to add other safeguards failed to allay these fears. An attempt to enact the bill urgently, purportedly to deal with a murder committed in Taiwan by a man from Hong Kong,[111] triggered the largest street demonstrations ever seen in Hong Kong: participants in a peaceful procession on Sunday 16 June 2019 were estimated by organizers to have numbered nearly 2 million.[112] Two days before that procession the Chief Executive, Carrie Lam, announced a 'suspension' of the legislative process for the bill, and on 18 June she apologized for her government's handling of the bill. This failed to alleviate the widespread discontent. Further demonstrations took place over the summer in various parts of the city. Episodes of violence included clashes between police and protestors, the storming of the Legislative Council building by protestors on 1 July, and a horrific incident at Yuen Long MTR Station on the night of 21 July when mobs of men in white shirts, with metal bars and rattan sticks,

---

110. Legislative Council Panel on Administration of Justice and Legal Services: Implementation of the Recommendations made by the Law Reform Commission (2018), Law Reform Commission website.

111. The man was accused of murdering his girlfriend while on holiday in Taiwan in 2018. After his return to Hong Kong he was convicted of money-laundering offences, triable in Hong Kong, and sentenced to 29 months' imprisonment. The government argued that his imminent release, possibly as early as October 2019 with remission for good behaviour, made the bill urgent. However, Taiwan officials said in May 2019 that they would not seek the man's extradition under the proposed bill.

112. The police estimate, which refers to the number of people who joined at the peak of the demonstration rather than total numbers, was 338,000 participants.

indiscriminately attacked people, some of whom were returning from a demonstration on Hong Kong Island, others from work or social events: 45 people were injured; police did not arrive in force until 35 minutes after the attack began. Protestors have been calling for a complete withdrawal of the extradition bill and an independent commission of inquiry into the police handling of the protests – demands echoed by several prominent figures. Many protestors have also called for the resignation of Carrie Lam and the implementation of universal suffrage. The crisis – the worst since the establishment of the Hong Kong SAR – continues as this book goes to press.

Golden Jubilee: The Faculty at Fifty

On 25 June 2018 the Faculty of Law launched its Golden Jubilee celebrations with a special ceremony presided over by the Chief Justice, Geoffrey Ma. The date has no special significance in the Faculty's history, but it coincided with the fifth Annual Conference of the International Society of Public Law (ICON-S 2018), the largest international event so far hosted by the Faculty. Events to mark the Golden Jubilee include a series of distinguished lectures, the creation of the Warren Chan Professorship in Human Rights and Responsibilities, and the hosting of the Asian Philosophy of Law Conference. Among the celebrations are a concert by the HKU Law Alumni Choir, an RTHK documentary series on the Faculty's contributions to Hong Kong, the launch of an online video archive of conferences and lectures, walking tours exploring sites connected with the evolution of Hong Kong's legal system, and the publication of this history of the Faculty. The celebrations will culminate in a grand gala dinner in November 2019. The Jubilee looks to the future as well as to the past: its theme is 'Law, Justice and Humanity: 50 Years and Beyond.'

The academic year 2018–2019 also sees a number of other events not directly connected with the Jubilee but illustrative of the breadth of the Faculty's activities. Among these, a new LLM programme will be launched in 2019: the Master of Laws in Medical Ethics and Law, developed through the Faculty's Centre for Medical Ethics and Law by Terry Kaan and Daisy Cheung. In April 2018 the Faculty represented Hong Kong in the International Rounds of the annual Jessup Moot. The team came 11th out of 121 in the preliminary rounds, and one of its members, Natalie So, was ranked the first out of the Top 100 Oralists. In October 2018 Andrew Cheung (LLB 1983) became the second graduate of the Faculty to be appointed to the Court of Final Appeal, Hong Kong's highest court. In April 2019 two other judges of the Court of Final Appeal with long connections with the Faculty were each awarded an honorary Doctor of Laws by HKU in recognition of their distinguished public service: the Chief Justice, Geoffrey Ma, who had served as an honorary lecturer in the Faculty since 1987, and Robert Ribeiro, one of the earliest teachers in the Department of Law 1972–1980.

A more sombre note was struck in February 2019 when the Faculty's longest-serving teacher, Michael Wilkinson, passed away after a long illness, during which he had valiantly continued to teach: it was, he said, his teaching and his students that kept him strong. A much-loved teacher with a long record of service to the law in Hong Kong, Wilkinson taught several generations of law students in conveyancing, civil procedure, professional ethics, and advocacy; in fact, the majority of lawyers now in practice in Hong Kong were taught by him at one time or another.

One of the challenges in the Faculty's fiftieth anniversary year is the selection of a new dean to replace Michael Hor, who steps down at the end of his five-year term on 30 June 2019; he will stay on in the Faculty to teach criminal and public law. The recruitment of a new dean involves a lengthy global search by a university-appointed selection committee and consultation within the Faculty. While this is in progress, Fu Hualing serves as Interim Dean. The challenge is to find someone able to build on the achievements of previous deans and their colleagues, to lead the Faculty in politically complex times, and to manage a large and diverse institution. The Faculty of Law now has over eighty full-time academic staff who between them have qualifications from a dozen jurisdictions in five continents. More than 2,000 students are currently enrolled in the Faculty, 565 in undergraduate programmes, the remainder in postgraduate programmes, including the PCLL, LLM, MCL, JD, SJD, and PhD. When they graduate in the course of the next few years they will join over 6,000 men and women with LLBs or related degrees, over 9,500 with PCLLs, and over 4,000 with postgraduate law degrees from HKU. 'Whoever comes to lead the Faculty would do well to realize just how good it is,' observes Michael Hor.[113]

At the Faculty's Graduation Ceremony on 30 November 2018 Andrew Li, the first Chief Justice of the Hong Kong SAR (1997–2010), now an honorary professor and teacher at the Faculty, remarked on the rapid political, social, and technological changes over the past fifty years. He observed that those graduating would reach the prime of their working lives in the middle of the present century.[114] Just as an earlier generation of Hong Kong lawyers were called on to help with the transition to 1997, it will fall on them to address the challenges of the next great milestone in Hong Kong's history: the conclusion in 2047 of the fifty-year period in which the PRC's policies for Hong Kong and its previous lifestyle and capitalist system 'shall remain unchanged.'[115] It is too early to predict what changes may flow from this milestone, or from the many other challenges, political, technological and environmental, which the world now faces. What is certain, however, is that the staff and graduates of the Faculty of Law will continue to contribute to safeguarding and advancing the rule of law, which is so cherished in Hong Kong.

---

113. Michael Hor, interview with the author, 2 November 2018.
114. *Ming Pao*, 1 December 2018.
115. Joint Declaration, Article 3(12) & Annex 1(I); Basic Law, Article 5.

Afterword

I am honoured to be asked to write this afterword. What a journey it has been for legal education in Hong Kong and what a difference it has made to Hong Kong and our individual lives.

If the Department of Law had not started in 1969, it would not have been possible for me to study law in Hong Kong and become a practising lawyer thereafter. I did not start with any interest to study law. Many of my friends know that my dream career was to be an archaeologist, a town and country planner, a reporter, or even to have a job with the United Nations (UN). It was anything but law. In the event, I learned to like law and it has become a lifetime passion.

I am so glad that today the Bachelor of Laws (LLB) is a four-year course with a general liberal foundation and the Postgraduate Certificate in Laws (PCLL) has been dramatically transformed in the last fifteen years. The Faculty of Law now provides a significant range of core and specialist studies. It has also moved into emerging issues, like financial technology (fintech), medicine and ethics, as well as law and technology.

I went through the earlier three-year degree course 'zombie-like' because I did not see how law was connected to the rest of society. All the pursuits that I had found interesting had been outside the Department of Law then and my legal practice, but those pursuits have ultimately taken me back to law. Today I actually find the academic environment at the Faculty of Law appealing because of the diversity and depth of knowledge it provides, as well as the freedom to push the boundaries and explore future issues.

The law prescribes how people should live and behave. Having to live within its confines can be suffocating at times. However, we in the legal community play an important role in shaping the law and positively influencing outcomes, which can be liberating. Legal decisions can change individual lives. Academic research, advocacy, and reform can help the law catch up with changes in society. And on the rare occasions that we can participate in the process of lawmaking, we can help to change public policy. And if we ever get hung up with the dryness of law, not knowing what to do with it or hating it, we have the privilege of debating anything until kingdom come because that is part of our God-given domain and talent. We can open up the whole field of discussion from ethics and values to the sheer drudgery of technicalities. Either way we can debate it to death.

Building up legal education in Hong Kong to what it is today has been exhilarating, turbulent, and challenging against a forever-changing landscape. At the University of Hong Kong (HKU) what began as the Department of Law evolved into the School of Law before becoming today's Faculty of Law. Those involved in its various phases are either its products or its progenitors, and occasionally both.

'One country, two systems' is a visionary and pragmatic policy but by definition contradictory. Hong Kong is the only Chinese city where common law is practised. During the Sino-British negotiations over the future of Hong Kong, I raised with the British side the possibility of the establishment of a constitutional court for determination of conflicts between the Mainland socialist and the Hong Kong capitalist systems. This was flatly turned down by the British negotiating team. I recognized that the constitutional arrangements for Hong Kong were not based on federalism and, with the Standing Committee of the National People's Congress having the ultimate right of interpretation over the Basic Law, much would depend on the wisdom of those developing the constitutional interphase – and there were no precedents to go by.

I was born a British subject in colonial Hong Kong and I became a Chinese citizen under the Basic Law when China resumed the exercise of sovereignty over Hong Kong in 1997. I stopped breathing for a split second the moment I heard the British conceding sovereignty to China. Like many in my generation, I was born in Hong Kong after my parents had fled here as refugees. Could anything be more traumatic? Now we were about to start on a different journey, into a new constitutional order and through an identity change.

Despite the uncertainties and the challenges faced by us both as a community and individually in the run-up to 1997, it was also a time when Hong Kong was at its most engaging, collaborative, and participatory; for better or for worse, we had to put in the effort to make things work.

Many of us studied the future constitutional framework; we pushed for the rule of law, an independent judiciary, protection of human rights, a government with a high degree of autonomy, a free market, a separate customs area, no exchange controls, protection of private property rights, and numerous other issues.

Many also actively engaged the Beijing authorities on these issues. Large numbers of delegations were invited to visit Beijing during the 1980s. I was part of a Law Society delegation and separately led a delegation of the Hong Kong Observers, Hong Kong's first political pressure group, to Beijing to give views on questions that we considered to be of significance to our future.

If anything, these events sharpened our legal sense as to what the law should be and what it could do. And these events touched every single individual, not just some and not others. It was everybody.

As a core member of the Hong Kong Observers, I was subject to monitoring and surveillance by the Special Branch of the Hong Kong Police, although I was not aware of this until years later. The Hong Kong government feared the calls for greater participation in the governance of Hong Kong and for faster localization of the civil service. These challenged the status quo and, in the government's mind, verged on subversion.

Internationally, the status of Hong Kong as a British colony was challenged in the 1970s, shortly after the People's Republic of China entered the UN. One of the first things the new Chinese delegation did was to demand the removal of Hong Kong from the UN decolonization agenda on the ground that Hong Kong was not a British colony but a part of China. This was followed by Britain's renaming of Hong Kong's Colonial Secretary as Chief Secretary and the reform of the British Nationality Act, which, when it came into effect, downgraded the status of Hong Kong British subjects. The Hong Kong colonial government during this period perceived itself as being under siege, externally and domestically.

Other activists were similarly subject to monitoring and surveillance, although they, like me, were not aware of this until years later. We were all very conscious of the need for social justice, liberty, and rights.

The establishment of the Department of Law in 1969 was truly a watershed in Hong Kong's history: it helped to foster a sense of Hong Kong identity as well as empowerment among its graduates. Beginning in the early 1970s, Hong Kong began to produce its own lawyers, many of whom were highly sensitive to political and social issues, and together we began to build the legal infrastructure necessary for Hong Kong's future development. Where would we be today if this development had not taken place then?

Christopher Munn provides a brick-by-brick and blow-by-blow account of how the Faculty of Law was built, and the immense courage and persistence of the founders, their successors, and supporters in establishing legal education at HKU. The history of legal education is a fascinating social history of Hong Kong and this account will touch everyone who shares a common past through legal education at HKU.

Against the background of the immense changes that Hong Kong has faced throughout its history, it is little wonder that HKU Law's faculty, students and alumni became active participants in building up the legal infrastructure from practically virgin territory, in strengthening legal institutions and the administration of justice, and in building up jurisprudence in every facet of our lives. The faculty, students and alumni of HKU Law have contributed to many cases that have made a difference in individual lives, and to systemic reforms and changes in public policy essential to Hong Kong's development. Awareness of the law and access to justice have continuously been promoted. Bilingualism, legal clinics, and the use of information technology are all crucial tools being developed.

I believe strongly that law drives change and the study of law should not be thought of as slogging through dull rule books gathering dust on a shelf. Law is a living code and is meant to be used to change lives. Law is also an empowerment tool. When our individual rights are violated, we seek the law's protection and nothing can be more powerful than to be able to say, 'I have been wronged and you have broken the law.'

In conclusion, I wish to express deep-seated gratitude to Dafydd Evans for his vision of the future of the Department of Law and his conviction that we would succeed. The vibrancy of our legal community today owes much to him. I also wish to voice my appreciation to John Rear, who on one occasion did me the honour of telling me that I had asked a question from a perspective that he had not considered. It is so important for lecturers to encourage students to think for themselves, and in my case he succeeded in keeping my legal curiosity alive. Finally, I wish to thank my former classmates, many of whom have become friends for life.

Anna H.Y. Wu (LLB 1974)

Acknowledgements

My first debt of gratitude goes to the Faculty of Law at the University of Hong Kong for commissioning me to write this book and for giving me the time and encouragement to complete it on schedule for its fiftieth anniversary. The Dean, Michael Hor, his two predecessors, Johannes Chan and Albert Chen, and the late Michael Wilkinson have generously devoted many hours of their time to guiding me through the intricacies of the Faculty's history, introducing me to other staff and alumni, and saving me from many errors and misunderstandings: needless to say, any mistakes that remain are my own responsibility. The Faculty's administrative staff – in particular Vivian Wong, Rachel Li, Gloria Wong, Jessica Cheng, Eddie Leung, Alan Tsang, Raymond Lam, Calvin Cheung and Hing Mak – have been unstinting in sharing information, checking facts, and finding illustrations. It has been a pleasure to work with such friendly and enthusiastic people.

The staff at the Hong Kong Public Records Office and the HKU Libraries Special Collections have, as always, been patient and helpful in locating materials. This project has also taken me for the first time to the HKU Archives, a model of professional records management: I am grateful to Stacey Belcher-Lee, the University Archivist, and to Anna McCormick, Garfield Lam and Hemans Chan for all of their advice and assistance.

Many others have helped with this project by taking part in interviews and informal discussions, providing information, commenting on the manuscript, and offering advice and encouragement. These are, in alphabetical order, Shahla Ali, Douglas Arner, John Budge, John Carroll, Cora Chan, Patrick Chan, the late Chan Sui-jeung, Cecilia Chen, Anne Cheung, Cheung Chan-fai, Daisy Cheung, Eric Cheung, Cheung Ting, Patricia Chiu, Wilson Chow, William Clarke, Alison Conner, Peter Cunich, Stephen Davies, Vaudine England, Fu Hualing, Rick Glofcheski, Gallant Ho, May Holdsworth, Victor Joffe, Puja Kapai, Douglas Kerr, Humphrey Ko, Kwan Man-kwong, Kevin Lau Chun-to, Tony Lau Hon-yiu, Alice Lee, Emily Lee, Andrew Li, Lee Guan Ling, Elsie Leung Oi-see, Monnie Leung, Henry Litton, Katherine Lynch, Robin McLeish, Patrick Munn, Roda Mushkat, Michael Ng, Roderick O'Brien, Carole Petersen, Veronica Pearson, John Rear, Peter Rhodes, Kim Salkeld, Judith Sihombing, Elizabeth Sinn, Benny Tai, Agnes Tam Nga-yin,

Gavin Ure, Scott Veitch, Marco Wan, Peter Wesley-Smith, Woo Po-shing, Anna Wu, Nancy Yang Xiaonan, Geoffrey Yeung, Simon Young, Zhao Yun and Zhang Xianchu.

The staff at Hong Kong University Press have worked hard to ensure this book comes out in time for the Faculty's anniversary celebrations in late 2019. I am particularly grateful to Malcolm Litchfield, Susie Han and Clara Ho for their practical handling of this project, to the two anonymous external readers for their incisive suggestions, to Jason Beerman for his painstaking editing of the text, and to Jennifer Flint for designing such an elegant and attractive book.

Christopher Munn
Hong Kong
August 2019

Appendix 1

Brief Chronology

1964 The Department of Extra-Mural Studies begins a five-year pilot scheme of part-time evening courses for the external Bachelor of Laws (LLB) degree of the University of London. Among the teachers are Dafydd Evans and John Rear.

1965 External advisors Zelman Cowen, Clifford Pannam (Melbourne) and A.G. Guest (Oxford) submit their report to the Vice-Chancellor recommending the establishment of a law school at the University of Hong Kong (HKU).

1966 A working party appointed by the Vice-Chancellor of HKU and the Chief Justice recommends the establishment of a department of law at HKU.

1967 The Faculty of Social Sciences is established, with Dafydd Evans as first Dean.

1968 The University Grants Committee endorses in principle the establishment of a Department of Law at HKU which would teach courses leading to an LLB degree and to a further postgraduate professional examination for those intending to practise law.

1969 A second working party appointed by the Vice-Chancellor of HKU and the Chief Justice makes recommendations on the syllabus and resources for the LLB degree and on the further post-graduate education needed for intending legal practitioners to qualify entirely in Hong Kong. It also recommends the establishment of a statutory Advisory Committee on Legal Education. The Department of Law is established within the Faculty of Social Sciences, offering a three-year full-time undergraduate programme leading to the honours degree of LLB. The department, located initially on 154–158 Caine Road, has three staff: Dafydd Evans (Head), John Rear, and Bernard Downey. Its first intake consists of forty students.

1971 Launch of the *Hong Kong Law Journal*, with Henry Litton QC as its first editor-in-chief and John Rear as its first editor.

1972 The first LLB graduates enter the new Postgraduate Certificate of Laws (PCLL) programme.

1972 Launch of the HKU Law Association's journal *Justitia*.

1973 The Department of Law moves to the new Knowles Building on the main HKU campus.

1978 The Department becomes an autonomous School of Law, with Dafydd Evans as Dean.

1984 The School becomes the Faculty of Law, with Dafydd Evans as first Dean. The Faculty consists of two departments: the Department of Law, headed by Robert Allcock, and the Department of Professional Legal Education, headed by Peter Willoughby. The number of academic staff now exceeds thirty. The LLB intake for this year is over a hundred.

1986 Launch of the Master of Laws (LLM) degree.

1988 The Faculty moves to the K.K. Leung Building.

1995 The Centre for Comparative and Public Law (CCPL) is established.

1996 Launch of the Faculty website.

1997 Launch of the Master of Common Law (MCL) and Postgraduate Diploma in Common Law, and of the LLM in Chinese Commercial Law (later the LLM in Chinese Law).

1998 Launch of the Doctor of Legal Science (SJD) degree.

1999 The Asian Institute of International Financial Law (AIIFL) is established.
      Launch of the LLM in Corporate and Financial Law.

Launch of the first LLB mixed degree programmes – Bachelor of Business Adminstration (Law) and Bachelor of Social Sciences (Government and Law).

Launch of the LLM in Human Rights.

2001 Completion of the *Report on Legal Education and Training in Hong Kong* ('the Redmond-Roper Report').

Launch of the LLM in Information Technology Law (now Information Technology and Intellectual Property Law).

2002 Introduction of the Law Mentorship Programme.

2004 Introduction of the four-year LLB programme.

Establishment of the China Technology and Law Centre (now the Law and Technology Centre).

2005 Launch of Community Legal Information Centre (CLIC) website.

The Standing Committee on Legal Education and Training (SCLET) is established in place of the Advisory Committee on Legal Education (ACLE).

2007 Launch of the LLM in Arbitration and Dispute Resolution.

2008 Launch of the LLB-Juris Doctor (JD) programme with the University of British Columbia.

Launch of the double master's degree with the University of Zurich.

2009 Launch of the double undergraduate degree arrangement with King's College London.

Launch of the JD Programme.

Establishment of the Centre for Chinese Law.

2010 Launch of the Clinical Legal Education Programme.

JD-LLM double degree agreement concluded with the University of Pennsylvania Law School.

Launch of a double master's degree in law with Peking University.

2011 Launch of the double degree in Law and Literary Studies (Bachelor of Arts (Literary Studies & LLB)).

2012 The Faculty of Law moves into the Cheng Yu Tung Tower on the new Centennial Campus of HKU.

General introduction of four-year undergraduate programmes at HKU.

Establishment of the Centre for Medical Ethics and Law.

2014 Launch of the Faculty's Legal Scholarship Blog.

2018 Final report on the Comprehensive Review of Legal Education by consultants commissioned by SCLET, recommending, among other things, improvements in access and quality assurance for the PCLL.

2019 The Faculty of Law celebrates its fiftieth anniversary.

Launch of the LLM in Medical Ethics and Law.

Appendix 2

Succession Lists

Deans

1969–1987	Professor Dafydd Evans OBE (Head of Department 1969–1978; Dean of the School 1978–1984; Dean of the Faculty 1984–1987)
1987–1993	Mr Peter Rhodes
1993–1996	Professor Peter Wesley-Smith
1996–2002	Professor Albert H. Y. Chen SBS, JP
2002–2014	Professor Johannes M. M. Chan SC (Honorary)
2014–2019	Professor Michael Hor

Faculty Board Chairs

Up to 2005, the elected Dean chaired the Faculty Board. Since the introduction of an appointed deanship in 2005 the Board has elected its own Chair.

2006–2015	Professor Michael Wilkinson
2015–	Professor Albert H. Y. Chen SBS, JP

Sub-Deans and (from 1992) Associate Deans

1987–1990	Professor Peter Wesley Smith
1990–1991	Professor Michael Wilkinson
1990–1993	Professor Yash Ghai
1992–1993	Dr Gary Heilbronn
1994–2002	Professor Andrew Halkyard
1994–1999	Professor Jill Cottrell
1996–1999	Mr Charles Booth
1999–2002	Ms Katherine Lynch
1999–2008	Mr Benny Tai
2002–2005	Dr Richard Wu
2002–2014	Professor Zhang Xianchu
2005–2008	Professor Christopher Sherrin
2008–2014	Dr Felix Chan
2008–2011	Professor Chin Leng Lim
2011–2019	Ms Alice Lee
2013–2014	Ms Jolene Lin
2014–2017	Dr Marco Wan
2014–2019	Professor Fu Hualing
2014–2019	Professor Simon Young
2017–2019	Dr Shahla Ali

Heads of Department

Department of Law

1969–1978	Professor Dafydd Evans OBE
1984–1986	Mr Robert Allcock SBS
1986–1993	Professor Raymond Wacks
1993–1996	Professor Albert H. Y. Chen SBS, JP
1996–1999	Professor Rick Glofcheski
1999–2003	Professor Johannes M. M. Chan SC (Honorary)
2003–2005	Professor Roda Mushkat
2005–2008	Mr Michael Jackson
2008–2011	Professor Fu Hualing
2011–2014	Professor Douglas Arner
2014–2016	Professor Lusina Ho
2016–	Professor Zhao Yun

Department of Professional Legal Education

1978–1986	Professor Peter Willoughby OBE
1986–1991	Professor Edward Tyler
1991–1993	Professor Michael Wilkinson
1993–1997	Professor Christopher Sherrin
1997–2005	Professor Michael Wilkinson
2005–2011	Mr Wilson W. S. Chow
2011–2014	Mr Malcolm Merry
2014–	Mr Wilson W. S. Chow

Faculty Secretaries

1981–1985	Mrs Renee Tsang
1985–1990	Mr Colin Smyth
1992–1997	Mr Cathay Chan
1992–1997	Mr J. W. Cruddas
1997–	Ms Vivian Wong

Law Librarians

1969–1975	Mr Malcolm Quinn
1975–1991	Mrs Felicity Shaw
1991–1992	Ms Margaret Whitstock (acting)
1992–1996	Ms Elizabeth Nash
1996	Mr Daniel Wong
1997–2001	Mrs Sng Chan Yok Fong
2001–	Ms Irene Shieh

Appendix 3

Research and Teaching Awards for Members of the Faculty of Law

Distinguished Research Achievement Award
Yash Ghai (2000–2001)

Outstanding Young Researcher Award
Xue Hong (2004–2005)
Lusina Ho (2005–2006)
Douglas Arner (2006–2007)
Anne Cheung (2007–2008)
Simon Young (2008–2009)
Rebecca Lee (2009–2010)
Zhao Yun (2011–2012)
Thomas Cheng (2012–2013)
Shahla Ali (2013–2014)
Yap Po Jen (2015–2016)
Cora Chan (2017–2018)
Gu Weixia (2017–2018)

Research Output Prize
Fu Hualing (2005–2006)
Janice Brabyn (2006–2007)
Thomas Cheng (2007–2008)
James Fry (2008–2009)
Oliver Jones (2009–2010)
Rick Glofcheski (2010–2011)
Shahla Ali (2011–2012)
Cora Chan (2012–2013)
Shahla Ali (2013–2014)
Michael Ng (2014–2015)
Po Jen Yap (2015–2016)
Marco Wan (2016–2017)
Qiao Shitong (2017–2018)

University Teaching Fellowships
Benny Tai (1996–1997)
Alice Lee (1998–1999)
Lusina Ho (1999–2000)
Rick Glofcheski (2003–2004)
Katherine Lynch (2003–2004)

Outstanding Teaching Awards
Rick Glofcheski (2007–2008)

Alice Lee (2011–2012)
Katherine Lynch (2014–2015)
Marco Wan (2014–2015)
Shahla Ali (2016–2017)

University Distinguished Teaching Awards
Rick Glofcheski (2008–2009)
Rick Glofcheski (2014–2015)

Early Career Teaching Awards
Kelvin Kwok (2016–2017)

Bibliography of Main Works Consulted

Indicates sources freely accessible online, in whole or in part.

1. Archival and other unpublished sources

Smith, Carl T., 'The Firm of Wilkinson and Grist, Solicitors' (unpublished manuscript, kindly provided by John Budge of Wilkinson & Grist).

Hong Kong Executive Council: Minutes and Papers.

University of Hong Kong (HKU) Archives.

Public Records Office, Hong Kong: Miscellaneous files.

The National Archives, Great Britain, Colonial Office: Original Correspondence: Hong Kong, 1841–1951, Series 129 (CO 129) (Selected files).

The National Archives, Great Britain, Colonial Office and Commonwealth Office: Far Eastern Department and Successors, 1941–1967 (CO 1030) (Selected files).

The National Archives, Great Britain, Commonwealth Office & Foreign and Commonwealth Office: Hong Kong Departments: Registered Files, Hong Kong, 1967–1983 (FCO 40) (Selected files).

2. Newspapers, journals, and other serials

Appointments Service, HKU, *Graduate Employment Surveys,* 1985–1994.

Bill of Rights Bulletin.

*Centre for Comparative and Public Law, Faculty of Law, HKU, *Annual Reports.*

*Faculty of Law, HKU, *Newsletter,* 1999–.

Faculty of Law, HKU, *Prospectuses.*

Hong Kong Bar Association, *Annual Reports and Statements.*

Hong Kong Government Gazette.

Hong Kong Hansard.

Hong Kong Law Journal.

Hong Kong Law Reports.

Hong Kong Law Society Gazette.

Hong Kong Lawyer.

Hong Kong Public Law Reports.

Hong Kong Student Law Review, 1994–2006.

Journal of Professional Legal Education.

Justitia.

Law Lectures for Practitioners.

Law Media.

Law Society of Hong Kong Gazette.

Ming Pao.

New Gazette.

Office of Student Affairs, HKU, *Profiles of New Students,* (annual) 1985–2000.

*Research Grants Council, Hong Kong, *Annual Reports.*

*Standing Committee on Legal Education and Training, *Annual Reports.*

South China Morning Post.

Undergrad Magazine.

University of Hong Kong Bulletin.

HKU, *Calendar.*

University of Hong Kong Gazette.

HKU, *Vice-Chancellor's Reports,* 1962–1963 to 1990–1991.

*University Grants Committee/University and Polytechnic Grants Committee, Hong Kong, *Annual, Biennial and Triennial Reports,* 1965–.

3. Websites

*British and Irish Legal Information Institute (BAILII): covering Privy Council decisions on Hong Kong.

*Faculty of Law, HKU.

*HKU Legal Scholarship Blog.

*Hong Kong Bar Association.

*Hong Kong Judiciary.

*Hong Kong Legal Information Institute
   (HKLII): covering judgments, legislation,
   and other documents.
*Hong Kong Public Libraries Multimedia
   Information System (MMIS): containing
   digitized versions of various Hong Kong
   newspapers.
*Hong Kong University Libraries Digital
   Initiatives (HKUL): covering the Hong
   Kong Government Gazette, Blue Book,
   Sessional Papers and Administrative
   Reports up to World War II, Historical
   Laws of Hong Kong, Hong Kong War
   Crimes Trials Collection, and other
   materials.
*HKU Public Opinion Programme (POP).
*HKU Scholars Hub: containing theses and
   various scholarly publications.
*Law Reform Commission of Hong Kong:
   containing all the commission's reports,
   consultation papers, and other materials.
*Law Society of Hong Kong.
*Legislative Council of Hong Kong: including
   Hong Kong Hansard and papers and
   minutes of Legislative Council Panels and
   Committees.
*University Grants Committee, Hong Kong.

(URLs are not given here, since they change over
time: the websites can be easily accessed using the
titles above through standard search engines.)

4. Interviews by the author
Arner, Douglas, 7 December 2018.
Chan Man-mun, Johannes, 20 June 2018.
Chan Sau Wai, Cora, 26 November 2018.
Chan Siu-oi, Patrick, 1 June 2016.
Chen Hung-yee, Albert, 13 March & 8 August
   2018.
Chen Sheau-ling, Cecilia, 15 August 2018.
Cheung, Anne S. Y., 5 October 2018.
Cheung Tat Ming, Eric, 15 October 2018.
Cheung Tin Muk, Daisy, 18 October 2018.
Cheung Ting, 22 September 2018.

Chow Wai Shun, Wilson, 28 September 2018.
Clarke, William S., 4 January 2018.
Conner, Alison, 17 July 2017.
Fu Hualing, 8 November 2018.
Glofcheski, Rick, 8 October 2018.
Ho Yiu Tai, Gallant, 29 November 2017.
Hor, Michael, 2 November 2018.
Kwan Man Kwong, 18 October 2017.
Lau Chun-to, Kevin, 1 March 2018.
Lau Hon Yiu, Tony, 16 August 2018.
Lee, Emily, 3 October 2018.
Lee Suet Ching, Alice, 14 April 2018.
Leung, Monnie, 13 September 2017.
Leung Oi-see, Elsie, 14 November 2017.
Lynch, Katherine, 22 November 2018 (by email).
Mushkat, Roda, 5 September 2017.
Ng, Michael H. K., 26 November 2018.
O'Brien, Roderick, 4 July 2018.
Petersen, Carole J., 7 December 2017.
Rear, John, 2 December 2017 (by email).
Rhodes, Peter, 22 February 2018.
Sihombing, Judith, 11 November 2017.
Tai Yiu Ting, Benny, 12 October 2018.
Tam Nga-yin, Agnes, 7 September 2018 (by
   email).
Veitch, Scott, 26 October 2018.
Wan, Marco, 30 November 2018.
Wesley-Smith, Peter, 24 & 27 October 2017.
Yang Xiaonan, 19 September 2017.
Yeung Ka Wai, Geoffrey, 29 September 2018.
Young, Simon N. M., 23 November 2018.
Zhang Xianchu, 5 October 2018.

5. Published books, reports, and articles

Ali, Shahla F., *Court Mediation Reform: Efficiency, Confidence and Perceptions of Justice* (Cheltenham: Edward Elgar Publishing Ltd, 2018).

*The Basic Law of the Hong Kong Special Administrative Region of the People's Republic of China.

Bingham, T. H., *The Rule of Law* (London: Allen Lane, 2010).

Bokhary, Kemal, *Recollections* (Hong Kong: Sweet & Maxwell, 2013).

Byrnes, Andrew, and George E. Edwards (Eds.), *Hong Kong's Bill of Rights: the First Year* (Hong Kong: Faculty of Law, HKU, 1993).

Byrnes, Andrew, and George E. Edwards (Eds.), *Hong Kong's Bill of Rights: Two Years On.* (Hong Kong: Faculty of Law, HKU, 1994).

Chan, Cora, 'Deference, Expertise and Information-Gathering Powers,' *Legal Studies*, Vol. 33 No. 4 (2013), 598–620.

Chan, Cora, 'Legalizing Politics: An Evaluation of Hong Kong's Recent Attempt at Democratization,' *Election Law Journal*, Vol. 16 No. 2 (2017), 296–305.

Chan, Cora, 'Proportionality and Invariable Baseline Intensity of Review' (2013) 33(1) *Legal Studies*, 1–21.

Chan, Johannes, 'A storm of unprecedented ferocity: The shrinking space of the right to political participation, peaceful demonstration, and judicial independence in Hong Kong,' *I-CON* (2018), Vol. 16 No. 2, 373–88.

Chan, Johannes, 'Administrative Law, Politics and Governance: The Hong Kong Experience' in Tom Ginsburg and Albert Chen (Eds.), *Administrative Law and Governance in Asia: Comparative Perspectives* (London & New York: Routledge, 2008).

Chan, Johannes, *Paths of Justice* (Hong Kong: Hong Kong University Press, 2018).

Chan, Johannes, & C. L. Lim, *Law of the Hong Kong Constitution* (Hong Kong: Sweet & Maxwell Hong Kong, 2011).

Chan, Johannes, Fu Hualing, and Yash P. Ghai, *Hong Kong's Constitutional Debate: Conflict Over Interpretation* (Hong Kong: Hong Kong University Press, 2000).

Chan, Johannes, & Yash Ghai (Eds.), *The Hong Kong Bill of Rights: A Comparative Approach* (Hong Kong: Butterworths Asia, 1993).

Chan Lau Kit-chin, & Peter Cunich (Eds.), *An Impossible Dream: Hong Kong University from Foundation to Re-establishment, 1910–1950* (Hong Kong: Oxford University Press, 2002).

Chan, Ming K., 'The Legacy of the British Administration of Hong Kong: A View from Hong Kong', *China Quarterly* (1997), 567–82.

Choa, G. H., *The Life and Times of Sir Kai Ho Kai: A Prominent Figure in Nineteenth-Century Hong Kong* (Hong Kong: Chinese University Press, 2000).

Chen, Albert H. Y., 'Constitutional Adjudication in Post-1997 Hong Kong', 15 *Pacific Rim Law and Policy Journal* (2006).

Chen, Albert H. Y., '1997: The Language of the Law in Hong Kong.' 15 *Hong Kong Law Journal* (1985), 19–47.

Chen, Albert H. Y., 'The Law and Politics of the Struggle for Universal Suffrage in Hong Kong, 2013–15,' 3 *Asian Journal of Law and Society* (2016), 189–207.

Chen Yongxi, and Anne S. Y. Cheung, 'The Transparent Self under Big Data Profiling: Privacy and Chinese Legislation on the Social Credit System,' *Journal of Comparative Law,* Vol. 12, Issue 2 (2017), 356–78.

Cheung, Gary Ka-wai, *Hong Kong's Watershed: The 1967 Riots* (Hong Kong: Hong Kong University Press, 2009).

Chinese Law and Custom in Hong Kong: Report of a Committee appointed by the Governor in October, 1948. ('The Strickland Report') (Hong Kong: Government Printer, 1953).

Chiu, Lawrence M. W., and Peter Cunich. *HKU SPACE and Its Alumni: The First Fifty Years* (Hong Kong: Hong Kong University Press, 2008).

Chiu, Vermier, *Comparative Study of the Free Press in England and the Control of Publications in Hong Kong.* Hong Kong: Newspaper Society of Hong Kong, 1963.

Clark, Douglas, *Gunboat Justice: British and American Law Courts in China and Japan (1842–1943)* (Hong Kong: Earnshaw Books, 2015).

Collett, Nigel, *A Death in Hong Kong: The MacLennan Case of 1980 and the Suppression of a Scandal* (Hong Kong: City University of Hong Kong Press, 2018).

Conner, Alison W., 'Training China's Early Modern Lawyers: Soochow University Law School,' 8 *Journal of Chinese Law* (1994), 1–46.

Cottrell, Jill, *Legal Research: A Guide for Hong Kong Students* (Hong Kong: Hong Kong University Press, 1997).

Cottrell, Jill, and Yash P. Ghai, 'The Legal Profession and Transfer of Sovereignty: Hong Kong' in Rob McQueen and W. Wesley Pue (Eds.), *Misplaced Traditions: British Lawyers, Colonial Peoples* (Leichhardt: Federation Press, 1999).

Cunich, Peter, *A History of the University of Hong Kong,* Vol. I. (Hong Kong: Hong Kong University Press, 2012).

Duman, Daniel, *The English and Colonial Bars in the Nineteenth Century* (London: Croom Helm, 1983).

Edwards, George, and Johannes Chan (Eds.), *Hong Kong's Bill of Rights: Two Years Before 1997* (Hong Kong: Centre for Comparative and Public Law, Faculty of Law, HKU, 1995).

*Emerton, Robyn, and Carole J. Petersen, *Migrant Nightclub/Escort Workers: An Analysis of Possible Human Rights Abuses* (Centre for Comparative and Public Law, HKU, April 2003).

Endacott, G. B., *A Biographical Sketch-Book of Early Hong Kong* (Hong Kong: Hong Kong University Press, 2005).

England, Joe, and John Rear, *Industrial Relations and Law in Hong Kong* (Hong Kong: Oxford University Press, 1981).

Evans, D. M. Emrys, *Legal Education in Hong Kong: Reports of the 1966 and 1969 Working Parties on Legal Education* (Hong Kong: Hong Kong University Press, 1974).

Faculty of Law, HKU, *Knowledge Exchange and Impact* (Hong Kong: Faculty of Law, HKU, 2016).

Faculty of Law, HKU, *Thirty Years: The HKU Law School 1969–1999* (Hong Kong: Faculty of Law, HKU, 1999).

Faculty of Law, HKU, *Building for Tomorrow on Yesterday's Strengths* (Hong Kong: HKU Law Alumni Association, 2004).

Faculty of Law, HKU, *Res Ipsa Loquitur: The Fact Speaks for Itself* (Hong Kong: Faculty of Law, HKU, 2012).

Faculty of Social Sciences, HKU, *Handbook for Undergraduate Applicants,* 1971 & 1972.

First & Second Reports of the Commission of Inquiry under Sir Alastair Blair-Kerr (Hong Kong: Government Printer, 1973).

Fu Hualing, Carole J. Petersen, and Simon N.M. Young (Eds.), *National Security and Fundamental Freedoms: Hong Kong's Article 23 Under Scrutiny* (Hong Kong: Hong Kong University Press, 2005).

Ghai, Yash P., *Hong Kong's New Constitutional Order: The Resumption of Chinese Sovereignty and the Basic Law* (Hong Kong: Hong Kong University Press, 1997, second edition 1999).

GML Consulting Limited, *Study on the Manpower Needs of the Legal Services Sector of Hong Kong, Final Report* (April 2001).

Goodstadt, Leo F., *A City Mismanaged: Hong Kong's Struggle for Survival* (Hong Kong: Hong Kong University Press, 2018).

Gower, L.C.B., 'English Legal Training: A Critical Survey' 13 *Modern Law Review* (1950), 137–205.

Greenwood, Walter, 'John Joseph Francis, Citizen of Hong Kong, A Biographical Note.' *Journal of the Hong Kong Branch of the Royal Asiatic Society* 26 (1986): 17–45.

Griffiths, John, *Reminiscences and Observations of a Hong Kong Chai Lo* (Bishop Auckland: The Pentland Press Ltd, 1997).

Haydon, Edwin, 'The Choice of Chinese Customary Law in Hong Kong.' 11 *International and Comparative Law Quarterly* (1962), 231–50.

何俊仁，謙卑的奮鬥 (香港：香港大學出版社，2010). [Albert Ho Chun-yan, *My Humble Struggle* (Hong Kong: Hong Kong University Press, 2010)].

Heilbronn, Gary (Ed.), *Essays on Aviation and Travel Law in Hong Kong* (Hong Kong: Hong Kong University Press, 1990).

Ho, Lusina, and Rebecca Lee, 'Introducing the special needs trust to Hong Kong,' *Trusts and Trustees,* Vol. 23 No. 10 (December 2017), 1111–21.

Holdsworth, May, and Christopher Munn, *Dictionary of Hong Kong Biography.* Hong Kong: Hong Kong University Press, 2011.

Hong Hing-cheung, 'A phenomenographic investigation of student experiences of learning in the context of the Law Faculty at the University of Hong Kong' (HKU PhD thesis, 1997).

Hong Kong Bar Association, *Fighting Crime: Comments on the Fight Violent Crime Campaign Compiled by The Special Committee on Crime and Punishment of the Hong Kong Bar Association* (1973).

Hong Kong Bar Association, *Hong Kong Bar Association 50th Anniversary* (Hong Kong: Sweet & Maxwell, 2000).

Hong Kong Bar Association, *The Future of the Legal Profession* (1994).

Hong Kong Law Reform Committee, *Reports* (Hong Kong: Government Printer, 1957 (2), 1959, 1963 & 1964).

Hong Kong: A Case to Answer (Hong Kong: Hong Kong Research Project, c. 1974).

Hopkins, Keith (Ed.), *Hong Kong: The Industrial Colony: A Political, Social and Economic Survey* (Hong Kong: Oxford University Press, 1971).

*Joint Declaration of the Government of the United Kingdom and the Government of the People's Republic of China on the Question of Hong Kong (1984).

Jones, Carol A.G., *Lost in China? Law, Culture and Identity in Post-1997 Hong Kong* (Cambridge: Cambridge University Press, 2015).

Jones, Carol A.G., 'Politics Postponed: Law as a substitute for politics in Hong Kong and China' in Kanishka Jayasuriya (Ed.), *Law, Capitalism and Power in Asia: The rule of law and legal institutions* (London: Routledge, 1999).

Jones, Oliver, 'Noxious Antiquity? Life in Hong Kong without the Application of English Law Ordinance,' 39 *Hong Kong Law Journal* (2009), 793–834.

*Kapai, Puja, *Status of Ethnic Minorities in Hong Kong 1997–2014* (Centre for Comparative and Public Law, HKU, 2015).

Keeton, George Williams, *The Development of Extraterritoriality in China* (London: Longmans, 1928).

Keeton, George Williams, *The Elementary Principles of Jurisprudence* (London: A & C Black, 1930).

Kent, Ann, *China, The United Nations, and Human Rights: The Limits of Compliance* (Philadelphia: University of Pennsylvania Press, 1999).

Kirk, Harry, *Portrait of a Profession: A History of the Solicitor's Profession, 1100 to the Present Day* (London: Oyez Publishing, 1976).

Kowloon Disturbances 1966: Report of Commission of Inquiry (Hong Kong: Government Printer, 1967).

Law Society of Hong Kong, *Celebrating a Centenary: The Law Society of Hong Kong 1907–2007* (Hong Kong: The Law Society, 2007).

Law Society of Hong Kong, *The Future of the Legal Profession* (Hong Kong: The Law Society, 1993).

Law Society Legal Advice & Assistance Scheme: Report of the Management and Administration Committee (1979).

Law Teachers Association of Hong Kong, *Directory of Law Teachers* (Hong Kong, 1989).

*Lee, Rebecca, Lusina Ho, and the Concern Group of Guardianship System and Financial Affairs, *Ascertaining the Need for Special Needs Trusts in Hong Kong* (January 2017).

*Legal Aid Services Council, Hong Kong, *Legal Aid in Hong Kong* (Hong Kong: Legal Aid Services Council, 2006).

Lethbridge, Henry J., *Hard Graft in Hong Kong: Scandal, Corruption, the ICAC* (Hong Kong: Oxford University Press, 1985).

Litton, Henry, *Is the Hong Kong Judiciary Sleepwalking to 2047? Have Abstract Principles Smothered an Effective Legal System?* (Hong Kong: Sherriff Books, 2019).

Lo Hin-shing, *Reminiscences and Observations* (Hong Kong: Cosmos Printing Press Ltd, 1975).

Logan, D.W., and A. Rowe-Evans, *Report on the Academic Governance of the University of Hong Kong* (Hong Kong: HKU, 1974).

M.K.: Born 21st July 1893, Died 7th March 1959 (Hong Kong, ?1959).

馬沅編，香港法例彙編 (香港：華僑日報，1936 & 1953) [Ma Yuan, *Compendium of Hong Kong Laws* (Hong Kong: Wah Kiu Yat Po, 1936 & 1953)].

Matthews, Clifford, & Oswald Cheung (Eds.), *Dispersal and Renewal: Hong Kong University During the War Years* (Hong Kong: Hong Kong University Press, 1998).

McCoy, Mildred, and Erik Kvan, *Attitudes Towards Punishment: A Repertory Grid Study of Young Offenders in Hong Kong* (Hong Kong: Centre of Asian Studies, HKU, 1979).

Mellor, Bernard, *The University of Hong Kong: An Informal History* (Hong Kong: Hong Kong University Press, 1980).

*Newby, Howard, *Governance in UGC-funded Higher Education Institutions in Hong Kong: Report of the University Grants Committee* (Hong Kong: University Grants Committee, 2015).

Munn, Christopher, *Anglo-China: Chinese People and British Rule in Hong Kong, 1841–1880* (Richmond: Curzon, 2001. Repr. Hong Kong: Hong Kong University Press, 2009).

Munn, Christopher, 'Margins of Justice in Colonial Hong Kong: Extrajudicial Power, Solicitors' Clerks, and the Case of Li Hong Mi, 1917–1920,' *Law and Humanities* 11, no. 1, (2017): 102–20.

Norton-Kyshe, James William, *The History of the Laws and Courts of Hong Kong from the Earliest Period to 1898* (Hong Kong: Noronha & Co., 1898. Repr. Hong Kong: Vetch and Lee, 1971).

Ng, Jason Y., *Umbrellas in Bloom: Hong Kong's Occupy Movement Uncovered* (Hong Kong: Blacksmith Books, 2016).

Ng Kwai-hang, *The Common Law in Two Voices: Language, Law and the Postcolonial Dilemma in Hong Kong* (Stanford: Stanford University Press, 2009).

Ng, Michael H. K., and John D. Wong (Eds.), *Civil Unrest and Governance in Hong Kong: Law and Order from Historical and Cultural Perspectives* (Abingdon: Routledge, 2017).

Oblas, Peter, 'Britain's First Traitor of the Pacific War: Employment and Obsession,' *New Zealand Journal of Asian Studies* 7, No. 2 (December 2005): 109–33.

O'Hara, Randolph, 'The Library of the University of Hong Kong, 1911–1973: A Brief History', Thesis submitted for Fellowship of the Library Association. Ann Arbor, Michigan: University Microfilms International, 1984.

*Oxfam Hong Kong, *Hong Kong Inequality Report* (Hong Kong: Oxfam, 2018).

Pepper, Suzanne, *Keeping Democracy at Bay: Hong Kong and the Challenge of Chinese Political Reform* (Lanham: Rowman & Littlefield, 2008).

Petersen, Carole M., and Alvin Y. H. Cheung, 'Academic Freedom and Critical Speech in Hong Kong: China's Response to Occupy Central and the Future of "One Country, Two Systems"', *North Carolina Journal of International Law and Commercial Regulation*, Vol. 42, No. 3 (2016), 1–64.

*Petersen, Carole M., Janice Fong, and Gabrielle Rush, *Enforcing Equal Opportunities: Investigation and Conciliation of Discrimination Complaints in Hong Kong* (Centre for Comparative and Public Law, HKU, July 2003).

Petersen, Carole M., 'Equality as a Human Right: The Development of Anti-Discrimination Law in Hong Kong', 34 *Columbia Journal of Transnational Law* (1996), 335–88.

Petersen, Carole M., and Jan Currie, 'Higher Education Restructuring and Academic Freedom in Hong Kong' *Policy Futures in Education*, Vol. 6 No. 5 (2008), 589–600.

Pomerantz-Zhang, Linda, *Wu Tingfang (1842–1922): Reform and Modernization in Modern Chinese History* (Hong Kong: Hong Kong University Press, 1992).

Redmond, Paul and Christopher Roper, *Legal Education and Training in Hong Kong: Preliminary Review, Consultation Paper* (September 2000).

Redmond, Paul and Christopher Roper, *Legal Education and Training in Hong Kong: Preliminary Review: Report of the Consultants* (August 2001).

Report of the Committee on Higher Education in Hong Kong, 1952 (Hong Kong: Government Printer, 1952).

Report of the Committee on Legal Education (the 'Ormrod Report') (UK), presented to Parliament in March 1971.

Report of the University (1937) Committee (Hong Kong: Noronha & Co., 1937).

Report to the Council of The University of Hong Kong by the Independent Investigation Panel (2000).

Rhind, J. J., *Proposals for a Statistical Study of Corporal Punishment in Hong Kong; A Draft Research Proposal* (Hong Kong: Centre of Asian Studies, HKU, c.1973).

Rigby, Ivo, 'Some Observations in Retrospect,' 1 *Commonwealth Judicial Journal*, No. 4 (December 1974), 16–19.

Roebuck, Derek, 'The Chinese Digest of the Common Law,' *Institute of Advanced Legal Studies Bulletin*, Issue 6, Autumn Term 1990–1991, 17–21.

Rwezaura, B., 'Constraining Factors to the Adoption of Kiswahili as a Language of the Law in Tanzania,' 37 *Journal of African Law* (1993).

Simpson, R. F., *Graduate Employment in Hong Kong and the Problems of University Expansion* (Hong Kong: HKU, 1959).

*Standing Committee on Legal Education and Training, *Comprehensive Review of Legal Education and Training in Hong Kong: Final Report of the Consultants* (2018).

Stone, William, & John Rear, *A Study of Sentencing Levels and Sentencing Policies, Current and Past, in the Courts in Hong Kong : A Draft Research Proposal* (Hong Kong: Centre of Asian Studies, HKU, c.1972).

*Sutherland, Stewart R., *Higher Education in Hong Kong: Report of the University Grants Committee* (2002).

Sweeting, Anthony, *Education in Hong Kong Pre-1841 to 1941: Fact and Opinion: Materials for a History of Education in Hong Kong* (Hong Kong: Hong Kong University Press, 1990).

Tai, Benny, 'Chapter 1 of Hong Kong's New Constitution' in Ming K. Chan & Alvin Y. So (Eds.), *Crisis and Transformation in China's Hong Kong* (Hong Kong: Hong Kong University Press, 2002).

Tan, Carol G. S., *British Rule in China: Law and Justice in Weihaiwei 1898–1930* (London: Wildy, Simmonds and Hill, 2008).

Tarrant, William, *Hongkong. Part 1, 1839 to 1844* (Canton: Friend of China, 1861).

Third Report of the Chinese Language Committee: Court Proceedings and the Language of the Law, June 1971 (Hong Kong: Government Printer, 1971).

Tilbury, Michael, Simon N. M. Young, and Ludwig Ng (Eds.), *Reforming Law Reform: Perspectives from Hong Kong and Beyond* (Hong Kong: Hong Kong University Press, 2014).

Tindall, Robert E., 'The Graduate School of Law, Soochow University, Republic of China,' 7 *International Lawyer* (1973), 711–15.

Tsang, Steve Yui-sang, *A Modern History of Hong Kong* (Hong Kong: Hong Kong University Press, 2004).

Tsang, Steve Yui-sang (Ed.), *Government and Politics* (Hong Kong: Hong Kong University Press, 1995).

Turner, John A., *Kwang Tung, or Five Years in South China* (London, S. W. Partridge & Co. 1894).

Twining, William, *Blackstone's Tower: The English Law School* (Hamlyn Lectures, London: Stevens & Sons, 1994).

University Grants Committee, Hong Kong, *Higher Education in Hong Kong – A Report by The University Grants Committee* (October 1996).

University of Hong Kong, *Committee on the Development of the University, Report of 4 March 1939* (Hong Kong: HKU, 1939).

*University of Hong Kong, *Fit for Purpose: A review of governance and management structures at The University of Hong Kong* (February 2003).

*University of Hong Kong, *Report of the Review Panel on University Governance* (February 2017).

Wacks, Raymond (Ed.), *Civil Liberties in Hong Kong* (Hong Kong: Oxford University Press, 1988).

Wacks, Raymond (Ed.), *Hong Kong, China and 1997: Essays in Legal Theory* (Hong Kong: Hong Kong University Press, 1993).

Wacks, Raymond (Ed.), *The New Legal Order in Hong Kong* (Hong Kong: Hong Kong University Press, 1999).

Wacks, Raymond (Ed.), *The Future of Legal Education and the Legal Profession in Hong Kong: Papers Presented at a Conference Held by the Faculty of Law, University of Hong Kong to Commemorate Twenty Years of Law Teaching, Hong Kong, 15 and 16 December 1989* (Hong Kong: Faculty of Law, HKU, 1989).

Wacks, Raymond (Ed.), *The Future of the Law in Hong Kong* (Hong Kong: Oxford University Press, 1989).

Wacks, Raymond (Ed.), *The Right to Representation: Problems and Prospects* (Hong Kong: Faculty of Law, HKU, 1994).

Wacks, Raymond and Andrew Byrnes (Eds.), *Human Rights in Hong Kong* (Hong Kong: Oxford University Press, 1992).

Wan, Marco, 'The artwork of Hong Kong's Occupy Central Movement,' in Michael H. K. Ng and John D. Wong, *Civil Unrest and Governance in Hong Kong: Law and Order from Historical and Cultural Perspectives* (Abingdon: Routledge, 2017).

*Whitfort, Amanda S., Andrew Cornish, Rupert Griffiths, and Fiona M. Woodhouse, *A Review of Hong Kong's Wild Animal and Plant Protection Laws* (September 2013).

*Whitfort, Amanda S., and Fiona M. Woodhouse, *Review of Animal Welfare Legislation in Hong Kong* (2010).

Wilkinson, Michael, Eric T. M. Cheung, and Gary Meggitt, *Civil Procedure in Hong Kong Sixth Edition* (Hong Kong: LexisNexis, 2017).

Wesley-Smith, Peter, 'Anti-Chinese Legislation in Hong Kong' in Ming K. Chan (Ed.), *Precarious Balance: Hong Kong Between China and Britain, 1842–1992* (Armonk, New York: M. E. Sharpe, 1994).

Wesley-Smith, Peter, *Legal Literature in Hong Kong* (Hong Kong: Centre of Asian Studies, HKU, 1979).

Wesley-Smith, Peter, *The Sources of Hong Kong Law* (Hong Kong: Hong Kong University Press, 1994).

Yang Ti Liang, *An Introduction to Our Family* (Hong Kong: Ye Olde Printerie, 1979).

Yap, Po Jen, '10 Years of the Basic Law: the Rise, Retreat and Resurgence of Judicial Power in Hong Kong,' 36 *Common Law World Review* (2007), 166–91.

Yap, Po Jen, *Courts and Democracies in Asia* (Cambridge: Cambridge University Press, 2017).

Yep, Ray, 'The crusade against corruption in Hong Kong in the 1970s: Governor MacLehose as a zealous reformer or reluctant hero,' *China Information* 27(2), 197–221.

Yep, Ray & Tai-lok Lui, 'Revisiting the golden era of MacLehose and the dynamics of social reforms,' *China Information* 24(3), 249–72.

Yeung, Albert T., Thomas Ng, L. George Than, & Peter K. Lee, 'HKU's double professional civil engineering and law programme,' *Proceedings of Institution of Civil Engineers: Management, Procurement and Law*, Vol, 163 No. 2 (2010), 77–85.

Young, Simon N. M., and Richard Cullen, *Electing Hong Kong's Chief Executive* (Hong Kong: Hong Kong University Press, 2010).

Young, Simon N. M., and Yash P. Ghai, *Hong Kong's Court of Final Appeal: The Development of the Law in China's Hong Kong* (Cambridge: Cambridge University Press, 2014).

Yu, Patrick Shuk-siu, A Seventh Child and the Law (Hong Kong: Hong Kong University Press, 1998).

Yung Wing, *My Life in China and America* (New York: Henry Holt, 1909).

Index

References to photographic plates are in **bold**.

ACLE. *See* Advisory Committee on Legal Education

Addison, Frank, 112

administrative staff, 247–48

Advisory Committee on Legal Education, 107, 155, 211, 221; establishment of, 75; and the Postgraduate Certificate in Laws, 154; and the legal profession, 75–76, 92, 146. *See also* Redmond-Roper Report; Standing Committee on Legal Education and Training

Aitken, Lee, 225, 232

Allcock, Bob, 88, 90, 112, 127, 214, **plate 12**

alumni. *See* graduates; Law Alumni Association

Anderson, Donald, 24

Arner, Douglas, 243, 284–86

articled clerks, 7–10, 38, 38n33, 46, 55n103; Articled Clerks' Association, 38–39, 83. *See also* trainee solicitors

Asian Institute of International Financial Law, 236, 275, 284–86; East Asian International Economic Law and Policy Programme, 235–36; 'Enhancing Hong Kong's Future as a Leading International Financial Centre' research project, 285; establishment of, 134, 166; and financial technology, 285–86. *See also* legal research and knowledge exchange

Aslam, Farzana, 232

Au, Astina, **plate 31**

Au, Eric, 142, 183, 245

awareness raising about legal issues, 175–80; about the Bill of Rights, 189–90, 190–91; about democratic reform, 178–79. *See also* legal research and knowledge exchange

Bachelor of Laws, 63–64; admissions, 78, 93, 145n50, 159, 159n105; approval of degree regulations, 60; curriculum and courses, 64–65, 95–97, 146–47, 225–26, 228–29; enrolment and intake, 91–92, 132; examinations and honours, 65–66, 162, 162n117; four-year Bachelor of Laws implemented, 225–30; four-year Bachelor of Laws proposals, 52, 95, 143–46, 220–22; funding and access to education, 218, 218n25; graduates and career choices, 160, 239–41; impact of university-wide four-year undergraduate degrees, 228–29; initial cohort, 62; initial uncertainties, 61–62; localization of the curriculum, 66–68; overseas

advisors and 1965 and 1967 reports, 51–53, 55; pedagogical approach, 229–30; reform and the Miller and Wesley-Smith Reports, 144–47, 225; students and student life, 78–86, 158–63. *See also* Department of Extra-Mural Studies; First Working Party (on Legal Education); graduates; Postgraduate Certificate in Laws; students; Redmond-Roper Report

Baillie, Brian, 165

Bar Association. *See* Hong Kong Bar Association

Barberis, Janos, 286

Bar of England and Wales; admission to, 6, 7, 93

Barker, Denis, 113, 113n33, 209n148

barristers; barriers to practise for University of Hong Kong graduates, 105; classification, 3n3; conflicts with solicitors, 208–209; eligibility in Hong Kong for overseas lawyers, 108; and the growth of Hong Kong's legal profession, 205–206; reciprocal training and qualification in Hong Kong and England, 54, 70, 94–95, 106; training and qualification, 12–15, 15n49, 55n103, 69. *See also* Bar of England and Wales; Hong Kong Bar Association; Postgraduate Certificate in Laws; solicitors

Basic Law of the Hong Kong Special Administrative Region, 129, 133–34, 163, 172, 256; and academic freedom, 256; and the Bill of Rights, 182–83; and capitalism and finance, 196, 285; consultative process, 197; and the Court of Final Appeal, 198–99, 201; and democratic reform, 179, 198, 253, 262–65, 262n38, 263n42; Drafting Committee, 185, 197; Faculty of Law courses and publications about, 147, 150, 174; impact on legal education, 133; and the International Covenant on Civil and Political Rights, 185, 196; interpretations by the Standing Committee of the National People's Congress, 198, 201–202, 260, 271; and national security legislation (Article 23), 260, 261, 271; and political friction, 260; and right of abode, 201–2; and the rule of law, 179. *See also* Court of Final Appeal; 'one country, two systems'; Hong Kong Bill of Rights Ordinance; rule of law, Sino-British Joint Declaration

Baty, Thomas, 18, 18n64, 22